P9-DWT-042

IN COUNTRY

Other Books by John Prados

Normandy Crucible: The Decisive Battle that Shaped World War II in Europe
How the Cold War Ended: Debating and Doing History
William Colby and the CIA: The Secret Wars of a Controversial Spymaster
Vietnam: The History of an Unwinnable War, 1945–1975
Safe for Democracy: The Secret Wars of the CIA
Hoodwinked: The Documents That Reveal How Bush Sold Us a War
Inside the Pentagon Papers (written and edited with Margaret Pratt Porter)
The White House Tapes: Eavesdropping on the President (written and edited)
Lost Crusader: The Secret Wars of CIA Director William Colby
Operation Vulture
America Confronts Terrorism (written and edited)
The Blood Road: The Ho Chi Minh Trail and the Vietnam War
*President's Secret Wars: CIA and Pentagon Covert Operations from
    World War II Through the Persian Gulf*
*Combined Fleet Decoded: The Secret History of U.S. Intelligence and the
    Japanese Navy in World War II*
The Hidden History of the Vietnam War
Valley of Decision: The Siege of Khe Sanh (with Ray W. Stubbe)
*Keepers of the Keys: A History of the National Security Council from
    Truman to Bush*
Pentagon Games
The Soviet Estimate: U.S. Intelligence and Soviet Strategic Forces
The Sky Would Fall: The Secret U.S. Bombing Mission to Vietnam, 1954

IN COUNTRY
Remembering the Vietnam War

Edited by John Prados

IVAN R. DEE

Lanham • Boulder • New York • Toronto • Plymouth, UK

Ivan R. Dee, Publisher
An imprint of The Rowman & Littlefield Publishing Group, Inc.
4501 Forbes Boulevard, Suite 200, Lanham, Maryland 20706
httpp://www.rowmanlittlefield.com

Estover Road, Plymouth PL6 7PY, United Kingdom

Distributed by National Book Network

British Library Cataloguing in Publication Information Available

Library of Congress Cataloging-in-Publication Data

In country : remembering the Vietnam War / edited by John Prados.
    p. cm.
  Includes index.
  ISBN 978-1-56663-868-5 (cloth : alk. paper)
  1. Vietnam War, 1961-1975—Personal narratives, American. 2. Vietnam War, 1961–
1975—Campaigns. 3. United States—Armed Forces—Biography. 4. Vietnam War,
1961–1975—Biography. I. Prados, John. II. Title: Remembering the Vietnam War.
  DS558.I74 2011
  959.704'33730922—dc23

                                                                      2011035340

⊗™ The paper used in this publication meets the minimum requirements of American
National Standard for Information Sciences—Permanence of Paper for Printed Library
Materials, ANSI/NISO Z39.48-1992.

Printed in the United States of America

To

Ray W. Stubbe, chaplain

who ministered to his flock before, during, and after the battle

Men must know that in this theatre of man's life it is reserved only for God and angels to be lookers on.

—Francis Bacon

Contents

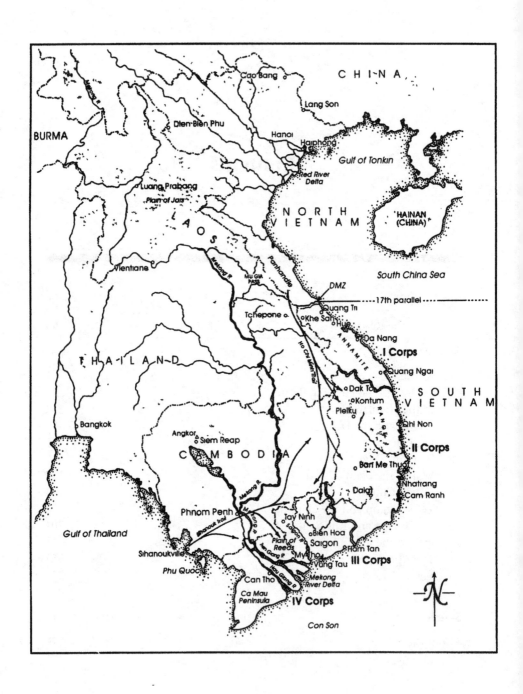

Introduction

THIS BOOK BEGAN WITH A TELEPHONE CALL. One of my editors, the very distinguished Ivan Dee, had been reading in another of my works, *Vietnam: The History of an Unwinnable War,* and that got him to thinking the Vietnam story might be told directly by participant voices. Not the story of decisions—of presidents and prime ministers, of politicians and generals, of hawks and doves. This is the reality of Vietnam through the eyes of men and women in the thick of that surreal experience—amid flying bullets, wading through the muck, hacking up the jungled peaks, stuck in the paddy, treating the horribly wounded soldiers delivered by the choppers or the civilians who staggered in off the street. Ivan and I went back and forth on the idea of an anthology for some weeks, refining that concept, defining a more concrete approach. I was probably the one who needed more convincing. Ivan deserves additional credit for his perseverance in doing that. *In Country* is the result.

Many possible directions could have been taken here. From the beginning the idea was to rely on previously published material, primarily soldiers' memoirs. This excluded documents, which was unfortunate, since a number of fine battle histories, a great deal of pertinent information, and much of our first-person knowledge of the adversary in the war resides in those sources. On the other hand, documentary presentations typically lack the punch of personal narrative. Even within that genre, however, choices were necessary. Excluded here, for the most part, are the memoirs of top players. The rarified deliberations of the senior leadership and the high command led, by inexorable reduction, to terrified soldiers in the paddy and on the mountains trying to carry out those decisions. *In Country* is the ground truth—the reality of strategies playing out, not being made. The voices are those of people facing agonizing necessity, often choices to be made in a split second.

The literature on the Vietnam conflict is vast. Novels on the war are more numerous than factual accounts, yet there are probably enough of the latter to fill two or three C-130 pallet loads. Recently another author consulted me in his attempt simply to derive a number for the books on the subject. He was estimating between three and five thousand. I have no idea of the true number, but that figure is undoubtedly in the ballpark and may be an undercount. Clearly some important judgments had to be made in selection. There are many voices in *In Country*, but nowhere near so many as constitute the whole. Since 2,900,000 Americans served in Vietnam, the literature, huge though it may be, reflects only fragments of the experience. Add the realities of war for between thirty and forty million Vietnamese, Laotians, and Cambodians; several hundred thousand communist Chinese; and upward of a hundred thousand South Koreans, Australians, Thais, Filipinos, Canadians, New Zealanders, and Soviets—plus a sprinkling of nationalist Chinese and North Koreans—and the magnitude of the epic becomes quite evident. No single book can do justice, but *In Country* presents a representative cross-section of the voices of participants across Vietnam and over the span of the American war.

Vietnam recollections—and here I include memoirs, oral histories, and biographies, plus a certain segment of histories constructed primarily from interviews—have evolved significantly over time. In some respects the evolution parallels the quest in Vietnam fiction for the "authentic" novel on the war. While the conflict was still in progress, books aimed to reveal what the war was really like. In the immediate aftermath veterans began writing cathartic and heartfelt depictions of their experience or their units. Certain units, for example the First Cavalry Division or the Fifth Special Forces, have been better represented than others. For certain services—the U.S. Marines being the object case—the same is true. Perhaps this was romanticism, maybe passion. At some point, probably in the 1980s, a stream of works began that sought to memorialize comrades and comradeship in the war. Sheer fashion has played a role as well, as in the late 1980s and the 1990s, when accounts of long-range scout forces and missions proliferated. More recently the veterans of sniper teams have come to their day in the bookstalls. Some recent accounts—commendably—have begun to search out information on the other sides of battles and campaigns. Secrecy concerns over certain operations long dissuaded veterans of certain special units from writing their recollections. The past decade has featured a spate of accounts from vets of the commando and special mission forces. In contrast, veterans of the Vietnam air campaigns have written relatively little, and sailors almost nothing—save for the Navy's

SEALs, who functioned in the war as special mission troops. Winnowing this literature required a series of criteria.

When two Vietnam veterans meet, their first question of each other is, what unit were you with? The second and third questions are where and when. I tried to incorporate excerpts that touched on major events of the war while covering each geographical region of South Vietnam and as many different units as possible in a text of this length. This was especially difficult for some periods. For example, there are virtually no memoirs for the early advisory era (1961–1963) and only a small number for the late stages of the war (1969–1972). A number of journalists cover both portions of the conflict, and there are histories that could have been excerpted, but I have sought to emphasize the vets' viewpoint and have therefore excluded them. Thus, for example, there is no extract from Neil Sheehan's *A Bright Shining Lie* to profile the 1963 battle for Ap Bac. It is also odd that memory shrivels so for the last period of the war, and I have therefore made a special effort to cover it.

Readers may encounter voices they wish to explore at full length. That posed a different problem because of the nature of the Vietnam memoir literature, much of which went straight to paperback and in due course went out of print. Access is important. I therefore tried to select as many excerpts as possible from either more recent works or ones of such stature that they remain in print. That meant abandoning many possible choices from older narratives that are simply not available. Some are quite fine accounts, as a deep reader in this literature will know, and leaving them out was positively painful. I apologize here to those vet memoirists who should have been in here but are not.

Another criterion followed *In Country*'s basic aim of telling the Vietnam story in concrete terms. Excerpts had to be explicit enough in terms of time and place that I could situate them for the reader or establish the locale explicitly though my own research. A portion of the literature is composed of works that are all action and atmosphere and lack the kinds of detail that can be used to place events. These have been put aside, as have most in which details and conversations are clearly made up. There is plenty of action in *In Country*—and a good deal of reflection also—but it is factual, solid, and specific.

Not that *In Country* ignores atmosphere. It has also been an aim to recapture the smell and taste of Vietnam and the feelings of the vets confronting the land and the adversary. An eye to those elements figured in the excerpting. Two chapters focus specifically on aspects of the GI experience, but many other selections touch on these themes. The viewpoints featured include those of soldiers, Marines, airmen, and CIA officers; American, South Vietnamese, and North Vietnamese participants; men and women; military and civilians.

In keeping with the aim of presenting the ground's-eye view, the selections are overwhelmingly from military veterans. However, in order to present certain aspects of the Vietnam experience, it was quite necessary to incorporate a few civilian perspectives. The reasons why will be apparent from the entries themselves. Again, I have avoided calling upon the journalists, which, though they participated in a different way, would have distracted from the aim of focusing on the grunts'-eye view.

No political criteria were employed in selecting material for this anthology. Some veterans excerpted here came to oppose the Vietnam War; the overwhelming majority of the entries are from those who supported U.S. participation. But all the vets are valued commentators. Presenting their experiences is the central aim of *In Country*. If there is a message or picture that emerges here, it is one built from the ordeals and adventures of men and women thrown into the maelstrom of this war.

A very small number of entries are drawn from the work of historians. This was necessary to cover certain events of critical importance—such as the final South Vietnamese victory in the Imperial City of Hue during Tet, 1968—for which personal narratives are simply not available. For the air war also, selections from historians have completed the story. In most cases these historians were vets simply presenting their experiences on a larger canvas or writing about parts of the war in which they did not personally participate. Some excerpts are from the official historians of the military services, including, in one instance, the South Vietnamese army. Utilizing histories, including oral histories, was important to covering the South and North Vietnamese sides, for reasons I will discuss in a moment. In a handful of cases I did, ultimately, bring in a few documents. These were Medal of Honor citations, which furnished thumbnail sketches of certain combat actions, and, in one instance, a State Department reporting cable that tells of the Americans caught inside the U.S. embassy at Saigon during the Tet attack.

It was a goal of *In Country* to craft an anthology that includes Vietnamese perspectives, both South and North. For contrasting reasons, presenting each posed difficulties. For the South Vietnamese, while there is a fairly ample Vietnamese-language literature among the *viet kieu* diaspora, there are only a handful of works in English, and I did not enjoy the luxury or time for producing translations. Some works that do appear in English are political memoirs. The combat narratives that exist mostly function as memorials for certain units (the ARVN armor corps, for example) or persons, or focus on high points of the history (the 1972 battle of An Loc or the 1975 collapse of South Vietnam are dominant cases). The works of former South Vietnamese generals Lam Quang Thi and Tran Van Nhut are exceptions, and they have been used here. Vietnamese commentaries have been culled from other works where I could find them.

The North Vietnamese side poses different difficulties. There is a good-sized body of Vietnam People's Army official histories that have been collected and translated by U.S. military history offices. In addition, Vietnamese publishers, led by government presses, continue to publish a broad array of histories and memoirs. In both cases copyright issues threatened inordinate delay in completing this anthology, and there are also questions of unapproved translations (with the military holdings) and poor ones (with the Vietnamese literature). I have therefore relied upon a handful of oral histories and on Vietnamese accounts drawn from works by American writers.

Now a few words about the organization of this book. For every entry, so far as possible, *In Country* takes note of the time the commentators had so far spent in the war theater, their location in South Vietnam, the moment of the specific incident remarked upon, and the unit to which the person belonged. This affects the depth and breadth of narrators' observations. The book opens with one chapter that is a bare-bones account of major features of the war. This helps put the personal accounts into a broader context. Thereafter—except where following some specific action from a variety of perspectives—I have often inserted text that introduces the commentator and outlines the significance of her or his observations.

Throughout the project there was a tension between adopting a strictly chronological presentation or one centered on geographical regions. I have adopted a mixed approach. The first of the personal narrative chapters focuses on a single key U.S. battle—the first big American engagement of the war—the late 1965 combat in the Ia Drang Valley. This is the only action treated at this level of detail, although there are others (Tet, Hue, Khe Sanh, the Easter Offensive) that have been prominently featured as well.

In keeping with the vets' concerns regarding time and place, most of *In Country* has been arranged along regional lines, with chapters corresponding to broad regions of South Vietnam. These loosely follow the Saigon government's own separation of the land into four "corps tactical zones." The "Eye Corps" chapter excerpts personal narratives of individuals who served in the northernmost part of South Vietnam, which Saigon called I Corps or Military Region One. It was more suitable to use the South Vietnamese nomenclature since the war was about Vietnam, not the U.S. military, and because at different times at least four American headquarters controlled Marine and GI activities here (III Marine Expeditionary Force, III Marine Amphibious Force, MACV Forward, and XXIV Corps). What Saigon called II Corps really included two separate regions that involved different styles of warfare, the Central Highlands and a coastal and plains area below the mountains. Each receives its own chapter here. The region from the sea through Saigon to the Cambodian border, and down into the Mekong Delta, the South Vietnamese separated into III and IV Corps, plus a capital military region. Few American forces were actually assigned to the Mekong, and the bulk of U.S. activity centered to the north and east of Saigon, so these personal narratives have been grouped into a single chapter. Within the chapters the excerpts are placed in chronological order, except where similar tactics or activities are being examined.

There are a number of chapters that cover activities throughout the land. Two concern experiences that were common to Americans everywhere: general aspects of operating in South Vietnam and "life on the line," the characteristics that put the war outside the traditional framework of the American military experience. Another of these chapters focuses on the personal narratives of soldiers who worked behind enemy lines, in "Indian Country." As the war passes the 1968 Tet fighting, the book shifts into a chronological mode that features personal narratives from throughout South Vietnam, though the regional chapters contain recollections from the later period that serve to illustrate the continuity of experience.

A Note to the Reader

IN THE PERSONAL NARRATIVES that make up the bulk of this book, the identifications of individuals, their unit assignments, locations, and the dates—the headings—are given in bold. The editor's introductions to the material are presented in italics. The substance of the excerpts appears in plain text. Within the excerpts themselves, italics are inserted by the editor within brackets to replace jargon, explain abbreviations or arcane references, connect material, and summarize intervening material when an entry needs to be condensed. Italics that are not encased in brackets represent emphasis by the original authors. Ellipses (. . .) are used in condensing the excerpts. Text in parentheses is the narrator's own words.

I have adopted certain conventions in this presentation. Anyplace where times of day appear in the military (and European) twenty-four-hour style, they have been converted into a.m. and p.m. hours. Where the narrators abbreviate military ranks (except in Medal of Honor citations), these ranks have been spelled out (thus "Lieutenant Colonel" for "Lt. Col." or "LTC"). To preserve narrators' voices, on the other hand, I have *not* made any attempt to insert commonality in the spelling of certain names or terms. Thus words like "Vietnam" and "Viet Nam," or "hootch" and "hooch" (a hut or living place), appear as the various authors rendered them.

A significant difference in transliteration between authors and editor exists in naming the adversary. Vietnam memoirs and texts commonly refer to the enemy as "Viet Cong," for the guerrilla foe, and "NVA" or "PAVN" for the North Vietnamese regular army. "Viet Cong" was, in fact, a pejorative term invented by the Saigon government, and I do not use it in any of the editorial commentaries. The actual insurgent organization was the National Front for the Liberation of South Vietnam (NFLSV), commonly simplified as NLF, and its military was known as the People's Liberation Armed Forces (PLAF). The latter name is rather awkward. While I use it in full in one or two places, I have usually referred to "NLF" or "Liberation Front" in the commentaries. Similarly, the name for the North Vietnamese forces was the Vietnam People's Army (VPA). Both "NVA" and "PAVN" were American wartime inventions. The editorial commentaries refer to the "People's Army" or "VPA." In the excerpts, I leave untouched the widely used "NVA," but occasionally insert "North Vietnamese forces" or "People's Army" in the texts, especially in substituting for "PAVN," which appears less frequently and is confusing in a situation in which "NVA" refers to the same forces and was the lingua franca of GIs in Vietnam.

Acronyms

AAA	anti-aircraft artillery
ACAV	armored cavalry assault vehicle
ALO	air liaison officer
AO	area of operations
ARA	aerial rocket artillery
ARVN	Army of the Republic of Vietnam
ASA	Army Security Agency
BDQ	Biet Dong Quan (ARVN Rangers)
BEQ	bachelor enlisted quarters
BFO	a type of built-in antenna
BLT	battalion landing team
BOQ	bachelor officers' quarters
C&C	command and control
CAC	combined action company
CAP	combined action platoon
CBU	cluster bomb unit
CCC	Command and Control Center (SOG subunit)
CCN	Command and Control North (SOG subunit)
CDEC	Combined Document Exploitation Center
CIA	Central Intelligence Agency
CIB	Combat Infantryman Badge
CIC	combat information center
CID	Criminal Investigation Division
CIDG	Civilian Irregular Defense Group
click	kilometer (also klick, klic)

CO	commanding officer
COSVN	Central Office for South Vietnam
CP	Command Post
Cpl	corporal
CS	tear gas
CSF	Camp Strike Force
CTF	Coastal Task Force
CTZ	corps tactical zone
DEROS	date eligible to return from overseas
DF	direction finding
DMZ	demilitarized zone
DRV	Democratic Republic of Vietnam
FAC	Forward Air Controller
FM	frequency modulation (radio)
FNG	fucking new guy
FO	forward observer
FOB	forward operating base
FRAC	First Region Assistance Command
FSB	fire support base
FSCC	fire support control center
FULRO	Front unifié pour la liberation des races oprimées (montagnard political front)
GI	government issue (colloquial for a U.S. Army soldier)
HFDF	high frequency direction finding
IP	initial point
IV	intravenous (medical term)
JTAD	joint technical advisory detachment
KKK	Ku Klux Klan
KP	kitchen police (cooks' helper)
LAW	light antitank weapon
LBJ	Lyndon Baines Johnson
LDNN	Vietnamese Navy SEALs
LDS	Latter-day Saints (Mormons)
LLDB	Luc Luong Dac Biet (ARVN special forces)
LRP	long-range penetration
LRRP	long-range reconnaissance patrol
LST	landing ship tank
Lt.Col.	lieutenant colonel
MACV	Military Assistance Command Vietnam
MP	military police
MPC	military payment certificate
MR	military region
MSF	Mobile Strike Force (Mike Force)
NCO	noncommissioned officer
NIC	new in country (U.S. Marine jargon for FNG)

NIS	Naval Investigative Service
NLF	National Liberation Front
NLO	naval liaison officer
NVA	North Vietnamese Army
PAVN	People's Army of Vietnam
PBR	patrol boat, river
PF	Popular Forces
PLAF	People's Liberation Armed Forces
POL	petroleum, oil, lubricants
POW	prisoner of war
PRC	field radio designator
PRU	Provincial Reconnaissance Unit
PX	post exchange
PZ	pickup zone
R&R	rest and relaxation
REMF	rear-echelon motherfucker
RF	Regional Forces
RIO	radio intercept officer
RPG	rocket-propelled grenade
rpm	revolutions per minute
RT	reconnaissance team
RTO	radio telephone operator
S-2	battalion staff intelligence officer
S-3	battalion operations staff officer
SAC	Strategic Air Command
SAM	surface-to-air missile
SAR	search-and-rescue
SEAL	sea, air, and land (U.S. Navy Special Forces)
SigInt	signals intelligence
SOG	Studies and Observation Group
TACAN	tactical air navigation
TAOR	tactical area of responsibility
UHF	ultrahigh frequency (radio)
USAF	United States Air Force
USAR	United States Army
USARV	United States Army Vietnam
USMC	United States Marine Corps
USN	United States Navy
VC	Viet Cong
VIP	very important person
VNAF	South Vietnamese Air Force
VNMC	South Vietnamese Marine Corps
VPA	Vietnam People's Army
WO	warrant officer
XO	executive officer

1

A Brief Overview

UNTIL WORLD WAR II, the nations of Vietnam, Laos, and Cambodia all formed part of the colony of French Indochina. Beginning in 1940, Japan, as it pursued a war in China and prepared to attack the Western powers in Asia and the Pacific, put increasing pressure upon France for concessions to aid the Japanese imperial enterprise. These led to a Japanese military occupation of French Indochina in 1941, but one that left the colonial administration in place. The French strove to preserve their authority in the face of the Japanese occupation. The Japanese encouraged Vietnamese nationalism as a counterweight. They worried—correctly—that as the war turned against Japan, the French in Indochina would secretly begin cooperating with the Allies, who by 1944 were coming closer to being able to wage a military campaign in Southeast Asia. In March 1945, to remove the threat of the French, the Japanese mounted a coup de force in Indochina and overthrew the French colonials.

Communism was one variety of Vietnamese nationalism. It was not quite as old as certain of the other nationalist groups, but in 1945 the Vietnamese communists had over two decades of experience and were far better organized than their competitors. The Vietnam People's Army had been created in December 1944. The Japanese overthrow of the French represented an opportunity to the communists, one they seized with alacrity. The communists also saw a chance to collaborate with the Allies, a collaboration which became a means of increasing their legitimacy and acquiring a certain number of weapons. They worked with the American intelligence organization known as the Office of Strategic Services (OSS), initially to help rescue Allied air crews shot down over Indochina. The OSS actually sent a training team into northern Vietnam and indeed provided some weapons to the communists.

Japan's March 1945 power play in Indochina, followed by its August surrender to the Allies, created a vacuum that the communists moved immediately to fill. On March 11 the Vietnamese emperor, Bao Dai, until then a French-backed puppet, declared independence. Organizing a united front with nationalists, the communists created a national government and induced Emperor Bao Dai to abdicate in favor of their government. That "August Revolution" became the basis for a new Vietnamese nation–state, centered in Hanoi and dominated by the communists. Such nationalist figures as Bao Dai and Nguyen Van Thieu initially cooperated with the Democratic Republic of Vietnam (DRV), as the communist government styled itself. From a legal standpoint there was a direct progression from the Vietnamese imperial state of the French colony to the DRV. In fact, the French government in Paris negotiated diplomatic agreements with the DRV, recognizing it as the Vietnamese state. Indeed between August 1945 and September 1947, no national government existed in Vietnam except the DRV.

The origins of the "French war" in Vietnam need to be seen in this context. That conflict began as a French effort to return to Indochina. Because of the March 1945 Japanese coup, there was no official French presence in any of the countries of the former colony. Due to Allied arrangements for implementing the Japanese surrender, Chinese nationalist troops were to occupy northern Indochina, and British ones, the south. This was important because in the north the DRV accommodated the Chinese and solidified its control, while in the south the British acquiesced in—and shielded—the arrival of French troops. In the south, meanwhile, the Vietnamese communists were less well-organized and faced stronger opposition from both other communist groups (Trotskyists) and other nationalist organizations. The communist national front, soon known as the Viet Minh, proved unable to mobilize sufficient resistance to prevent the French from moving out of their landing points at Saigon and Vung Tau to occupy southern Vietnam. The French also quickly reestablished themselves in Cambodia and Laos. But to reenter the north, the French had no alternative except to deal with the Viet Minh.

From an early date the French military commander in Indochina recognized that the broad alternatives were only to negotiate with the Viet Minh or fight them. He sent a report to Paris predicting that war would require half a million troops, a number the French could not hope to raise. French representatives therefore bargained with the DRV, succeeding in returning to the north peacefully. Subsequent talks to define postcolonial relations between Paris and Vietnam, however, were stymied by certain French officials committed to restoring colonial Indochina. Shooting incidents and insincere diplomacy led to a final break. In December 1946 Viet Minh troops attacked the French at many places in northern Vietnam, the start of the French war. From the beginning the Viet Minh emphasized the goal of uniting Vietnam as a single, sovereign nation–state—a nationalist appeal—and muted their communist ideology.

As in the later American war, the French benefited from technology, massive firepower, an air force, and a navy, and they had better-trained and better-armed troops. For a long time they won every pitched battle, including the first big contest in a siege of Hanoi. The French pushed out from there and within a year had gained control over most of northern Vietnam—Tonkin as it was known. The Viet Minh were driven underground in the populated areas and their regular troops were driven back into the Tonkinese mountains. But the French—as predicted—lacked the troops to occupy the land and defeat the Vietnam People's Army in its base areas.

It was only once they reached this impasse, in late 1947, that Paris attempted to create a competitor to the DRV, a government initially limited to the Saigon area and the Mekong Delta, the region known as Cochinchina. This was extended to all of Vietnam in June 1948 in the political initiative known as the Bao Dai Solution. But while the French accorded theoretical independence to this government—a status equivalent to a British commonwealth country—they dragged their feet on according it real authority. In fact, the Franco-Vietnamese treaty that recognized Vietnam as a sovereign nation was not signed until June 1954. That treaty was never ratified by France. From an international legal perspective, the Democratic Republic of Vietnam remained the juridical successor to the Vietnamese state of French colonial days.

The French war proceeded along lines eerily familiar to Americans a decade later. The Viet Minh were long unable to secure a major victory, but they steadily built and improved their forces and kept up the pressure with pinprick attacks. Sometimes they won. The French, unable to bring the Viet Minh main forces to battle, increasingly turned to pacification. Winning hearts and minds was difficult with a Vietnamese people aware of the illusory nature of the French-backed state versus the clear Viet Minh goal. In the villages Viet Minh networks deepened their roots until, in Tonkin and central Vietnam at least, even those areas occupied by French troops were actually disputed by Viet Minh guerrillas. The cost of the war weighed heavily on France, and political opposition to it gradually grew. In a move that again prefigured the American experience (in this case, the decision to shift to an all-volunteer army), in 1951 the French decided that draftees would no longer be sent to Indochina.

Striving to reduce the cost of the war, France worked to convince the United States that the Indochina war really formed part of the global struggle against communism. With the fall of Nationalist China as a catalyst, Paris proved successful. The onset of the Korean War solidified the American commitment beginning in May 1950, and that commitment expanded until by the time of the Eisenhower administration the United States was paying 80 percent of the cost of Indochina and supplying the French and the nascent Vietnamese army with the bulk of their equipment. A U.S. military attaché office was added to the American legation in Saigon and became the foundation of the later advisory mission.

This escalation was not one-sided. Although the Viet Minh and the Vietnam People's Army had grown stronger, this process accelerated once Chinese communists reached the Vietnamese border at the end of 1949. From early 1950 the Chinese supplied armaments to the Viet Minh, and they soon sent their own military advisory mission to assist the Viet Minh high command. The Chinese communists built training camps in their provinces bordering on Tonkin, and major units of the Vietnam People's Army were drilled and rearmed there. The Viet Minh forces returned to Tonkin in the fall of 1950, inflicting a significant defeat on the French army for the first time, taking the line of garrisons with which the French had blocked the Chinese border. From that moment the French war intensified.

Between 1951 and 1954 a succession of major battles took place. The French built up with their American aid, the Viet Minh with Chinese, and then Soviet, help. A new French commander in chief instilled fresh spirit in his forces and galvanized the expansion of the Vietnamese National Army—which would one day become the Army of the Republic of Vietnam (ARVN). They still won the big battles, but with French forces increasingly embattled, the Viet Minh deepened their hold on the villages. After 1952, when the Viet Minh and their Chinese advisors hit upon a strategy of attacking into the Annamite Mountains and toward Laos, the French lost control of key portions of Tonkin. Another new French commander in late 1953 sought to block the way into Laos by occupying a place called Dien Bien Phu, and he elected to accept battle there as a means of inflicting losses on the Viet Minh main force. However, the French lacked the air power and resources for extended combat at Dien Bien Phu, which was far from their bases, and when the Viet Minh laid siege to it, the French were trapped into a battle they eventually lost. Defeat at Dien Bien Phu ended their war.

France extracted itself from the conflict by means of the international agreements reached at Geneva in 1954. These agreements created two "regroupment zones" in Vietnam that were to be reunified on the basis of a nationwide referendum. French and Bao Dai troops would withdraw from the north, along with any civilians who wished to leave with them. Viet Minh forces would regroup from the south. The northern zone became known as North Vietnam—and was still the DRV. South Vietnam was the area in which the Bao Dai government held sway, and the emperor appointed a nationalist named Ngo Dinh Diem as prime minister. Diem rejected the provisions of the Geneva Accords, including the reunification referendum, creating a new basis for conflict. The United States supported Diem and conspired with him to push the French out of South Vietnam, a process completed in 1956. From that time the United States was the dominant ally of South Vietnam and its benefactor.

Dissatisfied with his powers as an official under Bao Dai, Ngo Dinh Diem first maneuvered to neutralize groups that supported the imperial state, then declared a republic with himself as president, a move sanctioned by a rigged election. Diem consolidated power but behaved in such an autocratic fashion that he alienated various South Vietnamese elites. The result was a new coup attempt in 1960—Diem had eluded previous attempts in 1954–1955—which he again defeated. In 1962 disaffected Vietnamese air force pilots attempted to trigger a coup by bombing the presidential palace. In each of these events, the United States sided with Diem and helped him defeat his opponents. Meanwhile Diem used his reconstituted military—the Army of the Republic of Vietnam (ARVN)—to move against the political-religious sect groups that had opposed him and root out remnants of the Viet Minh apparatus in South Vietnam. In this he was nearly successful.

Eventually, sorely tried elements of the Viet Minh rekindled the guerrilla war they had fought before. The DRV decided to support—and take control of—these efforts in May 1959, creating a supply line by land and by sea to succor the South. The land portion of this would become known as the Ho Chi Minh Trail. The guerrillas started with local actions that challenged Saigon's control of the countryside, murdering Diem government officials. Soon they began making armed attacks against the recently constituted ARVN. In December 1960 the communists reprised the initiative of the August Revolution, creating a new nationalist-communist front called the National Front for the Liberation of South Vietnam, better known as the National Liberation Front, or NLF.

Meanwhile, in neighboring Laos, where the DRV and Vietnamese Workers' (communist) Party had close relations with the Laotian communist Neo Lao Hak Xat (Pathet Lao) front, civil war broke out after the failure of attempts to form a neutralist government. Once Hanoi began sending troops and supplies down the Ho Chi Minh Trail, Laos acquired even greater importance because the North Vietnamese located their main route there. As it did in South Vietnam, the United States sent military aid to Laos. Washington also played a key role in prodding the Laotian royalist government to spurn accommodation with the Pathet Lao. The first American Green Berets sent to Southeast Asia went to Laos, not Vietnam. In the summer of 1959 Special Forces began to train Laotian army troops. When the CIA started creating paramilitary units in both northern and southern Laos, Green Berets helped with the southern initiative.

When President Dwight D. Eisenhower handed over to John F. Kennedy, there was an active military aid program in Laos and a larger one in South Vietnam, backed by 685 U.S. military advisors. Eisenhower actually warned Kennedy that the greater risk was in Laos, but the new president recognized the difficulties of attempting a military campaign in that landlocked country, and he resisted repeated proposals for open U.S. intervention, instead backing a renewed Geneva Accord (reached in 1962) to ensure Laotian neutrality. Meanwhile, in the spring of 1961, several months after President Kennedy assumed office, North Vietnamese regulars entered Laos to secure their supply line to the South. The Royal Laotian Army was never strong enough to threaten the Ho Chi Minh Trail. For a decade Hanoi's supply route would be challenged only by American-led reconnaissance teams operating in Indian Country or by bombing. The Laotian war stopped for a time after the 1962 Geneva Accord, but it resumed in the spring of 1963 and thereafter proceeded in tandem with the conflict in Vietnam.

Within South Vietnam the Diem government, despite a huge preponderance, failed to suppress the National Liberation Front (NLF) or its guerrillas. The insurgency expanded and the NLF gained strength. Despite successive U.S. military aid increases, each designed to support the buildup of ARVN regulars, rangers, or militia, the balance between South Vietnamese and NLF forces would never again be so favorable as at the very dawn of the war. In the meantime the level of American commitment grew. By the end of Kennedy's first year, the Military Assistance Advisory Group (MAAG) had more than tripled, to 3,200 personnel of all services. The MAAG tripled again over the next six months as President Kennedy added combat support units, primarily helicopter companies to carry ARVN soldiers to battle. Outgrowing its advisory group function, the new Military Assistance Command Vietnam (MACV) was created to control all U.S. operations in country. By the end of 1962 the United States had a covert air bombardment unit, "Farm Gate"; Special Forces creating a montagnard paramilitary force under CIA aegis; the helicopter units; and advisory detachments down to very low levels of ARVN, all of which required 11,300 American military personnel. The number of Americans reached 15,400 in June 1963. Despite controversy among historians regarding whether President Kennedy intended to withdraw from Vietnam, and the actual October 1963 order for a thousand-man reduction, by the end of that year U.S. personnel had reached 16,300—an increase of nearly a thousand.

During that last six-month period a series of fateful events occurred. One was the overthrow and assassination of Ngo Dinh Diem by a junta of ARVN generals with secret U.S. backing. Many contend that complicity in the Diem coup irrevocably trapped the United States into the war. Only a few weeks later President Kennedy himself was murdered by an assassin in Dallas, Texas. Lyndon Baines Johnson (LBJ) succeeded to the presidency. It was under President Johnson that the Vietnam War reached its apogee for the United States, at least as measured by numbers of troops in combat. Simultaneously with the sudden presidential transition in late November 1963, the decision was made that deepened the U.S. combat role—an agreement to conduct a campaign of "graduated military pressures" against the DRV. The military knew this program as OPlan 34A. President Johnson approved the final version on January 5, 1964. The first missions took place within the month.

These "34A" operations led to a turning point for American involvement. The best-developed portion of 34A was for maritime operations that used fast patrol boats to raid installations along the DRV coast. The Swift boats were procured and maintained by U.S. sailors at a secret base in Da Nang. Their target plans prepared by the CIA, the boats had crews of raiders advised by Marines of the Force Reconnaissance special warfare outfit. In any case, some of these raids were under way on August 2, 1964, when the U.S. destroyer *Maddox*, nearby, conducted an electronic intercept mission against the DRV. North Vietnam responded to the 34A raid by sending torpedo boats to attack the *Maddox*. President Johnson answered by reinforcing the destroyer with a second ship and ordering continuation of its "DeSoto Patrol." Confused interpretation of radio intercepts, ambiguous radar and sonar readings, and fanciful sightings by the watch led U.S. sailors to think there had been a second North Vietnamese attack on the night of August 3–4—an incident since determined to have been fictitious. But LBJ now ordered retaliatory bombing of the DRV and sought congressional authorization, the Gulf of Tonkin Resolution, which he subsequently used to justify the American war in Vietnam.

Over the last part of 1964 both sides made fateful decisions to escalate the conflict. The NLF began a series of attacks that became known as "spectaculars" due to their daring and impact, among them shelling of the U.S. airbase at Bien Hoa, and, on Christmas Eve, the destruction by car bomb of the Brinks bachelor officers' quarters in Saigon. This campaign continued into 1965 with strikes at the air bases at Pleiku and Qui Nhon and the car bombing of the U.S. embassy itself. Hanoi, meanwhile, made the decision to send regular troops to South Vietnam and dispatched its first major formation, the Vietnam People's Army 325th Division, which arrived in the Central Highlands in February–March 1965. In South Vietnam a succession of military coups seemed to underline the ineffectiveness of the Saigon government. In

Washington, the Joint Chiefs of Staff prepared a target list for bombing North Vietnam. President Johnson's decisions included approval of resumption of 34A operations—suspended with the Tonkin Gulf incident—and DeSoto patrols; the initial deployment of U.S. Air Force combat aircraft; the dispatch of a Hawk surface-to-air missile battalion to protect them; the subsequent addition of Marines to defend "enclaves" around the bases; and the deployment of the 173rd Airborne Brigade to serve as a general reserve, responding to emergencies throughout the land.

President Johnson's decisions formed only part of a more extensive sequence that finally ignited the American war. From Saigon, MACV commander General William C. Westmoreland had already requested major commitments of ground troops. Though rejected late in 1964, Westmoreland's proposals gained LBJ's incremental approval in bits and pieces, preserving MACV hopes. An interagency group asked Westmoreland to prepare a more comprehensive program, which he did, calling for thirty-four and then forty-four combat battalions to fight in South Vietnam. The 173rd Brigade deployment, and the dispatch of Marines to Da Nang and Chu Lai, represented the leading edge of that initiative. When NLF local forces attacked Pleiku Air Base in February 1965, LBJ ordered more retaliatory bombing of North Vietnam, and by that spring "tit-for-tat" raids had morphed into a regular air campaign, Operation Rolling Thunder.

In July, searching for a more comprehensive approach, President Johnson considered General Westmoreland's large-scale reinforcement and approved it. The deployment of the First Cavalry Division (Airmobile), along with the Third Marine Division, followed by the First Infantry Division and the First Brigade/101st Airborne Division, was the first wave of the new MACV force. Although some war critics deplore the slow U.S. deployment to Vietnam, the fact is that in the twelve months ending in December 1965 the American force level in country increased from twenty-three thousand to 183,000 personnel. Another twenty-two thousand troops arrived from allied nations. Of the combat troops introduced in 1965, eighty-nine thousand were soldiers and thirty-seven thousand were Marines. President Johnson secured contributions from South Korea, Thailand, Australia, New Zealand, and the Philippines. At the end of 1965 the total "Free World Forces" in South Vietnam stood at 205,000 men. A very small port, airfield, and road infrastructure limited the physical capacity for force expansion until new facilities were built, making the 180,000 surge over 1965 a very solid performance. The buildup of American and allied forces continued through 1966 and accelerated to twenty thousand to thirty thousand monthly through the last half of the year. American forces would eventually peak at 542,000 troops in January 1969 and the allied presence peaked at seventy-two thousand men later that year. As conceptualized by U.S. Army official historians, the 1965–1966 troop surge corresponds to a period of stemming the enemy tide, and in 1966–1967 the allies assumed the offensive.

The Cav, as the troopers of the First Cavalry Division (Airmobile) styled themselves, arrived in South Vietnam by ship, landed at Qui Nhon, and moved to a home base at An Khe in the Central Highlands. From there the Cav were sent to Pleiku and into the first major battle of the American war, that of the Ia Drang Valley (chapter 2) in late 1965, officially known as Operation Silver Bayonet. A corresponding endeavor in the Marine Corps's zone, which the South Vietnamese knew as I Corps and the Marines as the III Marine Amphibious Force (III MAF), was Operation Starlite. As American troops multiplied the missions, code names followed one another closely, even overlapped, in a blizzard of activity.

Fighting the Americans at the Ia Drang convinced the North Vietnamese that they could confront U.S. firepower successfully. Hanoi carried out a troop buildup that matched the American one, using the Ho Chi Minh Trail to move individual replacements and reinforcements, alongside full, con-stituted combat units. In July 1965 there were four Vietnam People's Army (VPA) regiments in South Vietnam. The VPA added seven more that year, and sent fifteen additional regiments south in 1966. From then until the last part of 1967 People's Army infiltration consisted mainly of individuals plus small specialist units. Unlike the Americans, who by then had their powerful combat divisions ensconced in large base camps throughout South Vietnam, and could simply fly new troops into Vietnam to integrate into the existing units, the VPA pretty much moved by foot—hundreds of miles from the DRV to the South. Physical hardening at training camps preceded an arduous trek down the Trail. Even by 1967 trucks, still limited in numbers, were reserved mostly for supply movements.

In Saigon, MACV and ARVN commanders incessantly issued press re-leases and had daily briefings where spokesmen told reporters of the troops' exploits. Claims as to the number of NLF and VPA troops killed were a staple here, and commanders instilled in subordinates the necessity of achieving a high "body count" of the enemy. Through 1966–1967 Americans initiated 2,784 operations of battalion size or larger, ARVN troops conducted 7,816 such operations, and there were 377 large missions by combined forces. During this interval the allied forces claimed to have killed nearly 144,000 of the enemy. Over this same period the number of People's Army regu-lars estimated to be in South Vietnam tripled, casting some doubts on the body count. Intelligence reckoned the total force fighting Saigon at between 240,000 and 270,000—a numerical assessment that hardly varied despite the claimed losses. Indeed the CIA had evidence suggesting a much larger enemy force with a strength of four hundred thousand or more, and MACV intelligence worked hard in 1967 to challenge that data and ensure an overall estimate that came in at the lower figure.

The big military operations of 1967—Cedar Falls and Junction City above Saigon, Wheeler/Wallowa in I Corps, Pershing in the coastal area of II Corps, and MacArthur around Pleiku—the locus of the bitter fight for Hill 875 (chapter 3)—did not blunt Hanoi's aims. It was in mid-1967 that North Vietnam decided to proceed with the massive Tet Offensive. The Pleiku battle just mentioned formed part of the deceptions laid on to protect the secret of Tet. Over the final months of 1967 and January 1968 the VPA sent ten more regiments to South Vietnam—three full divisions—to complete its Tet preparations.

The impact of the Tet Offensive is still debated. The NLF and VPA certainly lost tremendous numbers of fighters. Projections vary between sixty-eight thousand and eighty-four thousand soldiers. From that perspective Tet was an allied military victory, and South Vietnam certainly regarded it as such. The verdict in Washington was more uncertain. The degree of military success depended directly on the true size of the adversary force. If the enemy had many more troops than MACV believed, success was diminished. In addition, Tet produced a major political setback in the United States, where the Johnson administration crafted an information campaign designed to convince Americans that victory could be foreseen—the "light at the end of the tunnel"—but then the enemy had attacked all over South Vietnam. Hanoi took comfort in that the major losses were incurred by the NLF, not the People's Army. Except for the fighting around Khe Sanh, at Hue, and in certain other places, the VPA had stayed in the background and remained largely intact. The People's Army sustained much greater damage in a second wave of the offensive unleashed in May and tailing off in the summer of 1968.

By then General Westmoreland had gone, his place at the head of MACV taken by General Creighton W. Abrams. The new commander changed U.S. tactics, emphasizing small unit operations and pacification while conducting "logistics offensives" to limit Hanoi's ability to operate in the field. The People's Army indeed withdrew into base areas, most prominently in Cambodia and Laos, but within South Vietnam also. The losses of Tet were reflected in the fact that increasing numbers of VPA soldiers were incorporated into NLF units, indicating that the guerrilla force was both weakened and finding it more difficult to recruit South Vietnamese. There were more defections from the enemy side. The Ho Chi Minh Trail was burdened to support the forces in the South. Abrams's strategy made 1969 the hardest year for the People's Army and Liberation Front. Hanoi decided to shift from guerrilla to conventional warfare.

It proved impossible for the allies to capitalize on their success. The most important reason was that the political trauma of Tet had made United States withdrawal inevitable. Inflation, the collapse of the dollar, and American economic problems—partly caused by the war—ensured the pullback and even accelerated it. The United States simply could not prosecute the war at the same level. General Abrams confronted this reality only two months into Richard Nixon's presidency, when Secretary of Defense Melvin Laird visited South Vietnam and insisted on the necessity of withdrawal. The resulting plan emphasized bringing ARVN to the fore and was called Vietnamization. Abrams tried to obtain favorable military results despite troop reductions that gradually removed the U.S. combat capability, except that of air and naval forces. When President Johnson terminated Rolling Thunder in November 1968, the weight of air bombardment was turned directly against the Ho Chi Minh Trail and further complicated Hanoi's efforts to supply its forces in the South.

The American withdrawal continued over four years. During that time GIs carried out the same kinds of operations as before. The patrolling, emplacement and defense of firebases, and scout missions into Indian Country all proceeded. For example, in 1969, at 1,201, battalion-size or larger operations outnumbered those out during the year of Tet. There was concern in early 1969 that the North Vietnamese might repeat their Tet Offensive, but in the event the adversary made only limited ground attacks and mostly bombarded South Vietnamese targets with rockets and mortars. In fact, the North Vietnamese modified their tactics too, converting to a new mode of small strikes by sapper units combined with "attacks by fire"—rockets and mortars. Many of the major battles of 1969 took place in the Central Highlands and involved the montagnard camps. The North Vietnamese main forces focused on rebuilding and stockpiling supplies for new offensives.

The Nixon administration feared those potential offensives, starting with 1969 Tet. Washington repeatedly ordered measures to hit the enemy in their base areas, starting with the secret bombing of Cambodia with B-52 bombers, which began soon after the abortive Tet. In April 1970 came a major U.S.–South Vietnamese invasion of Cambodia. The growing unpopularity of the Vietnam War in the United States became explicit when the Cambodian incursion led to passage of legislation prohibiting the use of American troops in Cambodia or Laos. When an offensive against the Ho Chi Minh Trail in Laos was conducted in February 1971, no American troops entered that country, and the U.S. advisors with ARVN units stayed behind, inside South Vietnam. Operations like those into Cambodia and Laos conformed to General Abrams's concept of logistics offensives. In any case, as U.S. troop numbers diminished, it became physically impossible to carry out such large attacks. The Cambodian offensive took place at the last moment when massing the considerable force involved remained possible. The last big American operation occurred in the A Shau Valley in the spring and summer of 1970.

More and more the focus turned to Saigon and its military. Making a virtue of necessity, the Nixon administration touted Vietnamization and pumped equipment and military aid into South Vietnam. The South Vietnamese navy grew to include large numbers of (mostly small) vessels, and the air force became one of the biggest in the world and received jet fighter-bombers for the first time. The ARVN created its first armored brigades, equipped with newer, more powerful tanks; added increased amounts of artillery; expanded its Ranger corps by absorbing the montagnard units created by U.S. Special Forces; and formed a new infantry division.

South Vietnamese elite units fought well, and ARVN line forces performed adequately where they received the kinds of massive firepower support that had sustained American forces. During the Cambodian invasion the ARVN made significant contributions. In the Central Highlands over 1969–1970 South Vietnamese military weaknesses were more evident. These came to the fore in the 1971 Laotian invasion, where even the best South Vietnamese troops were fought to a standstill and driven back. At the same time, other ARVN troops in Cambodia were also subjected to heavy military pressures. As it turned out, Saigon had a year to rectify its deficiencies before its forces were put to the test in the biggest campaign to date.

The 1972 Easter Offensive, which began on March 30 and raged through the summer and into the fall, featured major North Vietnamese attacks in several war theaters. Below the demilitarized zone (DMZ), the Vietnam People's Army smashed ARVN defenses and for a time threatened to capture the old Imperial City of Hue. In the Central Highlands, VPA forces threatened Kontum and Pleiku. In the Saigon region, North Vietnamese and NLF troops came out of Cambodia and laid siege to An Loc. Backed by massive American airpower and naval gunfire support, the ARVN resisted successfully. At An Loc, where they beat off repeated assaults, the Vietnamese believed they had won a major victory. In I Corps the Saigon forces rallied and began a counterattack that brought them to the gates of Quang Tri City, which the North Vietnamese had taken early in the campaign. They recaptured the city on September 15. But despite the efforts of the very best South Vietnamese troops plus plentiful U.S. and Vietnamese air force support, including many Arc Light B-52 strikes, the Quang Tri fight had required four months. There was no question afterward—either at the DMZ or around An Loc—of driving the enemy back where they came from. The 1972 campaign ended with Hanoi and the Liberation Front possessing a solid foothold inside South Vietnam.

In the meantime negotiations for a cease-fire progressed in Paris. These peace talks, conducted in secret by American national security advisor Henry Kissinger, reached an advanced stage in the summer of 1972. For whatever reason, Richard Nixon, the American president, had kept the details from South Vietnamese leader Nguyen Van Thieu. In August, Nixon sent Kissinger to Saigon to brief Thieu on the developing arrangement. Thieu objected to much of the prospective agreement, most vociferously to provisions that might have been interpreted as creating a coalition government in South Vietnam. The American negotiator, meeting with Hanoi's delegates, considered by October that he had reached an acceptable accommodation, and at a certain point both Washington and Hanoi announced an imminent cease-fire. But Thieu again rejected the agreement. In fresh meetings with Kissinger the North Vietnamese made some concessions. President Thieu's emissary was told in Washington that the United States would settle whether or not Saigon did so and that carrying on the war was no longer possible. The North Vietnamese walked out of a further meeting in early December in which Kissinger demanded additional concessions. In response the Nixon administration initiated the "Christmas Bombing," a massive air campaign featuring B-52s sent to hit Hanoi itself. This marked America's last Vietnam battle, which the North Vietnamese proclaimed a "Dien Bien Phu of the air" as a result of the losses inflicted on U.S. air forces.

The bombing aimed as much at reassuring Saigon that the United States stood ready to intervene once more as it did at convincing Hanoi to return to the bargaining table. After a final negotiating session the cease-fire was signed at Paris on January 27, 1973. By March the last U.S. forces were out of Vietnam and American prisoners held by Hanoi had been returned. The Nixon administration created a large consortium under the Saigon embassy's Defense Attaché Office to provide technical assistance, maintenance, and advice. During the final days leading up to the Paris agreement the United States also pumped huge amounts of equipment—even broken equipment—into South Vietnam on the theory that it could later be replaced by serviceable items on a one-for-one basis as permitted by the accord. And American military aid continued to flow.

President Nguyen Van Thieu remained intransigent with respect to the joint commissions established by the agreement—one bringing together the United States, South Vietnam, North Vietnam, and the Liberation Front; the other directly associating South Vietnam and the NLF. Both Saigon and the NLF initiated "land-grabbing" operations and a "war of the flags" to lay claim to the largest possible territory. The war continued, now with the United States playing a less direct role. Nixon administration concerns turned in other directions, especially the Middle East, where the October War later in 1973 threatened some of its primary foreign policy interests. That conflict led to an Arab oil embargo and a global rise in energy costs that affected South Vietnam because it greatly increased the cost of operating Saigon forces. American military aid was reduced after 1973, sharpening Thieu's problems. Hanoi intensified its own preparations for military action in the South.

Over 1973 and 1974 a succession of battles gradually weakened South Vietnamese forces. By early 1975 Saigon was facing the prospect of extended war under adverse conditions. But President Thieu could not make up his mind for a strategic retreat. In January the North Vietnamese began probing ARVN forces in the foothills of the Central Highlands. The ARVN collapsed and Hanoi saw an opportunity for a go-for-broke offensive, initiating a new round of attacks. In mid-March Thieu ordered withdrawal from the Central Highlands, but this maneuver swiftly turned into a rout. South Vietnamese troops panicked and successively lost the Highlands, I Corps, and the central coast, and were finally driven back to the very outskirts of Saigon. United States naval and air forces helped evacuate Vietnamese to the Saigon area. A heroic ARVN stand at Xuan Loc delayed the People's Army advance, but other South Vietnamese defenses continued to crumble. The U.S. evacuation finally focused upon getting Vietnamese out altogether. Nguyen Van Thieu resigned on April 21 and left South Vietnam. North Vietnamese troops fought at Tan Son Nhut and directly for the city of Saigon. A final, desperate helicopter evacuation succeeded in getting seven thousand more people to ships offshore. North Vietnamese tanks broke into Thieu's former presidential palace. Saigon fell on April 29, 1975, ending the Vietnam War.

2

Ia Drang: The First Big Battle

THE RELIEF OF DUC CO

Captain H. Norman Schwarzkopf
advisor to the Vietnamese Airborne Brigade
Duc Co, August 1965

North Vietnamese regulars moved into the Central Highlands in the late winter and spring of 1965 and initiated a series of powerful attacks, first overrunning the Special Forces camp at Dak Sut. A border surveillance camp at Duc Co was besieged from late June. A month later a task force of ARVN paratroops received orders to drive the enemy away from here. Captain Schwarzkopf, the U.S. senior advisor to the paratroopers, received an impressive operation order "written in letter-perfect U.S. Army style" by Vietnamese officers, then discovered that no arrangements had been made for the promised air support, no artillery was available, and the planned LZ (landing zone) actually did not exist. Requests for a delay brought harsh threats from the South Vietnamese general commanding II Corps. The action was finally conducted by using Duc Co's own airstrip as the LZ.

The LZ was hot. Now my mouth was *really* dry. As we flew in I could see a sunbaked red clay airstrip surrounded by jungle on three sides, with the camp in a clearing to the south.

Mortar rounds started falling around us as we landed, but no one was hit as we ran up a small incline and into the camp. Duc Co itself was not much to look at—a triangular barbed-wire enclosure smaller than a football field. It had obviously taken a pounding. I could see craters and caved-in bunkers

everywhere. An American second lieutenant was waiting for me. He introduced himself as the camp advisor—I don't think I'd ever seen a happier man.
For weeks he'd been out here with fifty South Vietnamese, constantly getting
reports that they were about to be overrun; we represented his salvation.

The next day we moved out of the gate on the north side of the camp and
began our two-day sweep. The plan was still to work our way west to the
Cambodian border, then turn south, and finally circle back to the west side
of the camp. . . .

We were within a few miles of the Cambodian border when I heard firing
up front. I radioed the lieutenant [*Chuck Gorder*] and said, "Gorder, what's
going on?"

"Sir, it's VC."

"Gorder, I *know* it's VC. How many VC are there? What's their disposition?"

"Sir, all I know is there's a whole hell of a lot of them! We're getting fire
from all sides and we're taking casualties."

[*Major Schwarzkopf caught up to his lead unit. The ARVN drove off the enemy
with help from helicopter gunships. The Vietnamese paratroops wanted to send
out their dead bodies aboard the choppers, but the American pilot refused.
Schwarzkopf had to threaten him with a pistol to get aircrew to comply. The
ARVN managed to return to Duc Co, where they were caught in the siege too.
The adversaries were now reckoned at two full People's Army regiments, not the
two Liberation Front regional battalions that were estimated.*]

Each night we went to bed with the conviction that the camp would be
overrun and we would be killed. I learned to sleep with one ear cocked, because I knew that at some point every night there would be a mortar barrage.
The thunk of the rounds dropping into the mortar tubes was audible hundreds of yards away, and when I heard that sound I had maybe eight seconds
to make it to a foxhole. Many nights I'd find myself sprinting . . . without
quite knowing why. . . .

As the days went by, conditions in the camp became grim. Early on,
the mortars destroyed the water tank. Although there was a watering hole
outside camp, the enemy knew about it; so when we needed water we had
to send a platoon to fight its way down and back. Food ran low, but when
the airborne tried dropping fresh supplies, the planes stayed so high that
the wind blew the parachutes outside the perimeter. We asked them to stop
because all they were doing was feeding the enemy. We were soon down to
rice and salt. [*After about ten days Duc Co was finally relieved by a task force
of South Vietnamese Marines.*]

INITIATION

Lieutenant Colonel Kenneth D. Mertel
First Battalion, Eighth Cavalry, First Cavalry Division
near An Khe, September 1965
Colonel Mertel's battalion came to South Vietnam aboard ship with the rest of Major General Harry O. Kinnard's First Cavalry Division (Airmobile), the "Cav." General Westmoreland sent the Cav into the Central Highlands to coun-ter North Vietnamese attacks against the Special Forces camps. Mertel's unit initially deployed to a base at An Khe on the rim of the Highlands and carried out preliminary operations nearby. Here he recounts the first air assault.

The birds were on final approach to the LZ, a few seconds out. As the gun ships completed their final pass, the door gunners on the flank transports picked up fire with their M-60 machine guns, providing continuous firepower until the actual landing of the troops. The birds were on the ground now, landing eight at a time. The infantry from C Company made their first assault as they sprinted from the birds to the distant tree line, immediately taking over the suppressive fire of the . . . helicopter.

The purpose of continuous fire from the minute the close air support began until the landing of the riflemen was to keep enemy heads down, return fire, and prevent reinforcement or movement or any final preparations of the enemy. . . .

The first two platoons were on the ground. There was some shooting—the report from C Company was minimum enemy contact. . . . The platoons fanned out rapidly to seize and secure the LZ. The birds returned to "Mus-tang" to pick up the remaining rifle platoon and elements of the weapons platoon. They would return in a few minutes, this time escorted by both the Airborne Rocket Artillery [ARA], not firing but prepared to, and by the gun-ships, which would provide protection to the landing aircraft. There would be no firing this time immediately around the LZ by the ARAs, gunships, or transport door gunners, since the LZ was now in friendly hands. All fire in the immediate vicinity . . . would be coordinated by Captain Smith, the company commander on the ground. If he needed help, he would call through his artil-lery FO to obtain the necessary tube artillery or ARA.

The battle was progressing well—with some sniper fire. The primary enemy were the hundreds of punji-sticks scattered throughout the LZ, all around it.

The Montagnards were adept at making punji-sticks. Originally this device was used for building fences or to kill animals for food. These traps were easily adapted for use against human beings. The VC learned in the highlands that they could create considerable damage to helicopter-borne forces by placing thousands of inexpensive punji-sticks around likely landing zones.

Within a few minutes half a dozen men from C Company were wounded, having run into punji-sticks; stepped on, the sticks impaled a foot, piercing through the sole or leather of the shoe into the foot. The particularly vulnerable zone was the leg from knee to ankle.

Punji-sticks were serious. They created a puncture-type wound. In addition, Montagnards and VC put poison or filth on the tips of the sticks to infect the wound. The Division experienced difficulty the first month handling the punji-stick wounds, as they had not learned exactly how to care for them.

Major Charlie A. Beckwith
Special Forces Detachment B-52, Project Delta
Plei Me, October 22, 1965

Tensions continued for months as the Vietnam People's Army (VPA) flexed its muscles. On October 19 the VPA Thirty-Second and Thirty-Third regiments attacked the Special Forces camp at Plei Me, southeast of Duc Co. Commanders again dispatched emergency reinforcements. This time the force included Major Beckwith's Project Delta, an experimental scout unit, along with two companies of the ARVN Ninety-First Airborne Ranger Battalion. Beckwith had some familiarity with the terrain because Delta had run missions out of Duc Co after its relief. Now Beckwith would be caught in the siege himself, once his troops hacked their way into the threatened camp.

The first thing I noticed on going through the gate was the Montagnard tribesmen who had been killed while defending the camp; they were still lying in the wire. I mean everywhere. Dead people. Oh shit, I thought, there's going to be a lack of discipline here. If they can't pick up that kind of thing then, man, there's some problems in here. I was right . . . the smell was terrible.

The Special Forces captain in charge . . . was Harold Moore. I let him know quickly that I was the new mayor of Plei Me. Shaped like an equilateral triangle, the camp was in a slight bowl and was surrounded by barbed wire. There was a trench system that ran throughout the inside. . . . About ten wooden buildings with corrugated metal roofs made up the interior. The outside . . . was usually occupied by the Montagnard soldiers' families. Needless to say, under siege the families were now all inside. The camp was crowded and it was dirty. A thick red dust covered everything. It was in turmoil. The Vietnamese camp commander, Captain Moore's counterpart, stayed in his deep bunker. I never saw him once the whole time I was there. Outside the barbed wire there were a hell of a lot of Communists.

I called Pleiku [*II Corps headquarters*] and explained to them that we should fortify the camp first, to make sure we could hold it, and then find out how many of the enemy we were facing. We shouldn't do anything until we knew for sure. [*Special Forces group commander Colonel*] Bill McKean did not agree with me. He said, "I want you to get outside the camp, rummage around, clear the enemy out of there. Then, obviously, if you do that you can hold the camp."

I said, "Sir, that's not a good idea."

He said, "Well, Major, I am ordering you."

In the afternoon we mounted up both [*ARVN*] Ranger companies. Captain Thomas Pusser, a West Pointer I thought a lot of, was the advisor to the Vietnamese Rangers . . . [*we*] discussed the two Vietnamese companies. The leadership of one of them was stronger than the other. I suggested to Tom he go with the stronger unit. He felt because he could kick ass . . . he should go with the weaker one. I finally agreed with him. . . . I shouldn't have let him do that.

The plan was to begin to clear the northern slope area from which most of the heaviest fire was coming. The [*North Vietnamese*] waited for both companies to get outside the gate. Then they came out of their holes and hit us with everything they had. About fourteen men were killed, including Tom Pusser. Many more were wounded. I felt fortunate to get any of those Rangers back inside the camp.

[*The defenders made no more sallies until an ARVN relief force from Pleiku arrived at Plei Me with a company of Nung strikers from Duc Co. Clearing operations began on October 26, and pursuit commenced with the arrival of the Cav's Second Battalion, Eighth Cavalry. Ordered back in to help the Cav, the ARVN Ranger leader rejected the mission. All-American Project Delta teams returned by themselves. Beckwith argued with Cav bosses over control of aircraft and helicopters. General Kinnard's top people decided Delta was a problem. Beckwith finally took his teams home to their Nha Trang base. Not long afterward the Cav would have appreciated having them along.*]

COMMAND AND CONTROL

Lieutenant Colonel Kenneth D. Mertel
First Battalion, Eighth Cavalry, First Cavalry Division (Airmobile)
near An Khe, September 1965
This selection appears outside of chronological order because it describes the system of using helicopters to control battles on the ground, important at Ia Drang but vital throughout the Vietnam War.
My airmobile command party generally consisted of the pilot and copilot, sitting in front; myself on the left side of the rear seat; Artillery Liaison Officer on the outside right seat for good observation; Battalion S-3 [*operations staff*

officer] next to me; and probably the Air Force Liaison Officer (ALO) between the S-3 and the Artillery Liaison Officer. . . .

I monitored the Battalion Command Network on one FM radio. The Artillery Liaison Officer used one on the Fire Control Network of the direct-support artillery battalion. The Air Force Liaison Officer monitored the net with which he communicated to the Airborne Forward Air Controller (FAC), actually directing air strikes. The fourth set was used by the S-3 either to monitor the Brigade Commander's Net, or, during an air assault, to monitor the lift frequency of the assault helicopter company or battalion.

When the fourth net was used on the assault helicopter lift frequency during an air assault, one of my radio operators sat in the right rear compartment serving as [*a*] door gunner . . . monitoring the Brigade Commander's Net on his PRC-25 backpack radio. When a call was received from the Brigade Commander or from Brigade, he called me on the intercom. I either used his radio to talk, or switched one of the four FM sets momentarily. . . . In addition often I carried my second radio operator, sitting in one of the rear compartments, when I planned to go on the ground. On the ground it was essential [*to*] have two radios in operation, one for Battalion . . . one for Brigade. This was the usual . . . the airmobile command control party.

Each member . . . was connected by the intercom so that I could talk to all of them or to any one individually at will. The pilots could talk to me, and I to them. Still left available were the aircraft radios, one FM radio and one UHF, which could be operated by conversing through the pilots. The UHF radio was valuable to the Air Force Liaison Officer if he wished to talk directly to the [*FAC*]. He did this by simply using the pilot's headset, or better yet, by passing the plug back and connecting his own headset. When employing this system, it was necessary for the pilot to press the transmit button whenever the ALO wished to transmit.

Frequently, if I was making a reconnaissance and not actually overseeing a battle . . . I flew as one of the pilots. I flew generally from the left side in the copilot position because habitually our SOP provided for me being on the left; thus my pilots always knew which way to fly in order to give me the best view of the action.

ACTION AT IA DRANG

Lieutenant Colonel Harold G. Moore
First Battalion, Seventh Cavalry, First Cavalry Division (Airmobile)
Ia Drang, November 14–17, 1965
Colonel Moore (no relation to Green Beret Captain Harold Moore) and his battalion first choppered to Plei Me to exploit with an air assault into enemy

territory. This maneuver, into an LZ called X-Ray, ignited the main action. In Army heritage, incidentally, the First Battalion, Seventh Cavalry is the lineal descendant of George Armstrong Custer's unit at the Little Bighorn. The fight at X-Ray would not be as bloody, but it was still a near-run thing. Moore's dramatic book on the battle, plus the movie of the same name, We Were Soldiers Once . . . And Young, *have made this firefight one of the best known of the Vietnam War. Moore gives testament to the heroism of soldiers on both sides.*

At 8:50 a.m., on the west end of the Plei Me strip, I issued orders to the assembled company commanders, liaison officers, pilots, and staff: Assault in to LZ X-Ray to search for and destroy the enemy. Bravo Company lands first, accompanied by my command group, then Alpha, then Charlie, and then Delta companies. Bravo and Alpha will move northwest on my order. Charlie Company will move southwest toward the mountain, likewise on my order. Delta Company will control all mortars. The recon and machinegun platoons will be battalion reserve. Artillery will fire eight minutes each on [*other LZs*] for deception, then a twenty-minute preparatory fire on X-Ray and adjacent areas. Thirty seconds of aerial rocket artillery and thirty seconds of helicopter gunship prep would follow. . . . I set 10:30 a.m. as touchdown time. . . .

Then we got word that because of air movement delays the artillery was not yet in position at LZ Falcon and could not begin the prep fires on the Ia Drang targets before 10:17 a.m. H-Hour slid back . . . and the word was passed down the line. Dillon lifted off in the battalion command helicopter with the fire-support and helicopter-coordination group. Bruce Crandell and I stood beside his helicopter, discussing final details. . . .

We flew over a broad, slightly rolling plain dotted with trees thirty to fifty feet tall, interspersed with a few old Montagnard farm clearings, small winding streams, and dry streambeds. We saw no villages and no people. It was Sunday morning but I did not realize that: over here we paid attention to the date, not the day. In the field in Vietnam all days were the same: hot and wet, or hot and dry, but always dangerous.

Warrant Officer Robert Mason
B Company, 229th Assault Helicopter Battalion, First Cavalry Division (Airmobile)
Landing Zone X-Ray, November 14, 1965
Robert Mason joined the Army because he wanted to fly. He had dreamed of levitation since childhood, so helicopters were the perfect thing. He joined the Cav when it was still an experimental formation called the Eleventh Air Assault Division and deployed with it to South Vietnam, a country he knew nothing about.
"The longest week began on a sun-drenched Sunday morning in a small clearing, designated Landing Zone X-Ray, the Chu Pong foothills. Intelligence had long suspected the Chu Pong massif of harboring a large Communist force

fed from the Cambodian side of the border. X-Ray seemed like a likely spot to find the enemy, and so it was." I read this in *Time*, the week after the Tea Plantation incident.

The results of nearly two weeks of searching and probing by the Cav were hundreds of dead NVA soldiers and a very good idea of where to find the main force of three NVA regiments. On November 14 our battalion lifted the 1st Battalion, 7th Cavalry (Custer's old unit) into LZ X-Ray, where they expected to make contact. Our sister company, the Snakes, made the first as-sault in the morning and received very little opposition. By early afternoon, though, the two companies of the Seventh Cavalry they had lifted in had been surrounded, and suffered heavy casualties. Our company was assigned to sup-port the Snakes, to lift in reinforcements.

We picked up the troopers at the Tea Plantation, eight to each Huey. It was easy to tell where we were going. Although we were still fifteen miles away, the smoke was clearly visible from all the artillery, B-52 bombers, and gunship support concentrated around the LZ to keep the grunts from being overrun. As we cruised over the jungle and fields of elephant grass, I had the feeling this was a movie scene: the gentle rise and fall of the Hueys as we cruised, the per-spective created by looking along the formation of ships to the smoke on the horizon, the quiet. None of the crews talked on the radios. We all listened to the urgent voices in the static as they called in artillery and air strikes on their own positions, then yelled that the rounds were hitting *in* their positions.

LZ X-Ray could accommodate eight Hueys at once, so that was how the ships were grouped in the air. Yellow and White in the first group; Orange and Red in the second. Leese and I were Red Two. As we got closer to X-Ray, the gap between us and the first group got bigger to allow time for them to land, drop off the troopers, and take off.

Five miles away, we dropped to low level. We were flying under the artillery fire going into the LZ.

A mile ahead of us, the first group was going over the approach end of the LZ and disappearing into the smoke. Now the radios came alive with the pilots calling in where the fire was coming from. The gunners on all the ships could hear this. Normally it was helpful, but this time, with friendlies on the ground, they could not fire back. Yellow and White were on the ground too long. The artillery still pounded. The massif behind the LZ was completely obscured by the pall of smoke. We continued our approach. Leese was on the controls. I double- or triple-checked my sliding armor panel on my door side and cursed the army once again for not giving us chest protectors. I put my hands and feet near the controls and stared at the scene.

"Orange One, abort your landing. Fire on the LZ is too heavy," a pathfinder called from X-Ray. Orange flight turned and we followed. There was a whole bunch of yelling on the radios. I heard two ships in the LZ call out that they were hit badly. What a mess. Orange flight led us in a wide orbit two miles away, still low level. Now A1-E's from the air force were laying heavy fire at the front of the LZ along with the artillery and our own gunships. What kept everybody from flying into each other I'll never know. Finally we heard Yellow One call to take off, and we saw each other emerge from the smoke on the left side of the LZ, shy of two ships. They had waited in the heavy fire while the crews of the two downed ships got on the other Hueys. One crew chief stayed, dead. One pilot was wounded.

We continued the orbit for fifteen minutes. I looked back at the grunts who were staring at the scene. They had no idea what was going on, because they had no headsets.

"Orange One, make your approach," the pathfinder called. Apparently a human-wave attack by the NVA on the LZ was stopped. "Orange one, all eight of the ships in your two flights are keyed to pick up wounded." "Keyed" meant that they had groups of wounded positioned to be loaded first.

"Roger. Red One copy?"

"Red One roger."

Orange One rolled out of the orbit and we followed. The A1-E's were gone, but our gunships came back to flank us on the approach. Even with the concentration of friendlies on the ground, the gunships could fire accurately enough with their flex guns and rockets, so the grunts allowed them to. Our own door gunners were not allowed to fire unless they saw an absolutely clear target.

We crossed the forward tree line into the smoke. The two slicks that had been shot down were sitting at the front of the LZ, rotors stopped. That made it a little tight for eight of us to go in, but it was OK. The grunts jumped off even before the skids hit the ground. Almost before our Hueys had settled into the grass, other grunts had dumped wounded men, some on stretchers, into our ships.

Lieutenant Colonel Moore

Our intention with this bold helicopter assault into the clearing at the base of the Chu Pong massif had been to find the enemy, and we had obviously succeeded beyond our wildest expectations. People's Army Lieutenant Colonel Nguyen Huu An, deep in a command bunker no more than a mile and a half away . . . was issuing orders by land-line telephone—remember the commo wire spotted by the H-13 helicopter scouts?—as well as by old, unreliable walkie-talkies, and by foot messenger. His orders to every battalion in the vicinity were simple: Attack!

Shortly after two p.m., with the battle well underway, Colonel An's boss, Brigadier General Chu Huy Man, was safely in his headquarters hard by the

Cambodian border almost ten miles away from the action. My boss, on the other hand, was right over my head. With the battle raging on two sides of the perimeter, Colonel Tim Brown suddenly came up on my radio from his command helicopter, asking if he could land to get a first-hand look at the situation. I waved him off without explanation. There was too much going on to deal with the distraction of a visit by the brigade commander.

THE LOST PLATOON

Captain John Herren
B Company, First Battalion, Seventh Cavalry
Landing Zone X-Ray, November 14, 1965
Among the crises confronting Moore would be that of the "Lost Platoon," a unit of Bravo Company that had advanced ahead of the others, then been cut off and surrounded by People's Army attackers. That afternoon Moore began receiving reinforcements—Lieutenant Colonel Bob Tully's Second Battalion, Fifth Cavalry. GIs tried to rescue the Lost Platoon. Tully's fresher troops were the main force, but Captain Herren of Moore's Bravo Company led the attack. The moment when Herren reached the Lost Platoon proved very poignant.
I was in shock, sort of. I was operating, gee, I don't know, hadn't had any sleep now for two or three days now, pretty much. You could tell [*how exhausted the men were*] in the looks of their faces. I'm sure I looked the same to them. Dark bags under their eyes. They were all covered with clay and red dust. They all just stayed where they were, lying down until we said, "Come on, guys." There were some hugs, and the main thing was to get them up and get all of the dead that we had out there and the wounded and get them, because we didn't know whether or not the North Vietnamese were there in force or not.

Then I moved up and saw the platoon or the small group, and there were sort of three groups in different places. But the majority were in one area, and a North Vietnamese officer was propped against a tree with a grenade in his hand, and he was pretty dead or at least I thought he was dead. But he was sort of twitching, and the guys who were still there said, "Don't touch him. Don't touch him. He's got a grenade in his hand." And we just kicked him over, and he was dead. But they were so convinced, even with [*our*] whole company coming up now, that this one North Vietnamese propped up against the tree next to them—not very far away—they were afraid to shoot him, because they were afraid that grenade was going to go off.

THE SOUTH SIDE

Lieutenant Colonel Moore
November 14–15, 1965
The People's Army 7th Battalion commander, Major Le Tien Hoa, thought he had finally found the open door into Landing Zone X-Ray on the southern side of the perimeter, and he swung his battalion into a broad encircling maneuver around Tony Nadal's left flank toward the south side of the clearing. But thanks to Charlie Company, that open door was closing fast.

Charlie Company's commander, Captain Bob Edwards, raced down the line of newly arrived infantrymen, picking up those who belonged to him and hurrying them into position with the rest of the company on the south and southeast sides of the landing zone. Edwards sited his machine gunners and riflemen along a thinly stretched blocking position that now ran for 120 yards.

No more than five minutes had passed when a huge wave of North Vietnamese, the lead assault units of Major Hoa's 7th Battalion, charged headlong into the thin line of 112 American riflemen. Added to the din of battle in the Alpha and Bravo Company areas was the sudden heavy firing in the woods. . . . Captain Edwards was on the radio to battalion instantly, shouting, "We are in heavy contact. Estimate a hundred seventy-five to two hundred enemy. Damn! These guys are good!"

Private Clinton Poley
C Company, First Battalion, Seventh Cavalry
The next morning when they really hit my company, it was just getting barely daylight. They sent a patrol of our guys to look for infiltrators or something. They were only out there for a few minutes, and one guy came running back and he said, "They're coming. They're coming." And somebody over a foxhole away said, "Who's coming?" You know, like who would you think. We couldn't even see the foxholes. We couldn't even see the rest of our guys. We all opened up firing, and the machine gunner was very much prone, and I was on my knees in a foxhole. I had hooked hundred-round belts of ammunition together for him, and he was firing them pretty fast. So I really didn't get to use my rifle very much. Well, in doing that, that's when I first got wounded in the neck.

Sergeant Robert Jemison Jr.
C Company, First Battalion, Seventh Cavalry
The first time I got hit was right through the stomach. The bullet felt like someone took a log and ran into you and knocked you down. That's how

the force of the bullet was, and after I got hit, I just got up and went back to fight. That's all you could do. You either keep fighting and try to save yourself, or lay there and die or be killed. And I'm not never going to give up, so that's why I'm here today. The battle kept going on and on, and I was bleeding, bleeding, shooting . . . and the last time I got hit was through this arm. I got hit three times. . . . They tore my M-16 up. They just ripped it up. I didn't have nothing but the plastic stock in my hand. One time I thought about, you know, I wouldn't give two cents for my life. Then you start thinking again and you say, "Well, you know, I think I can make it," and that's what I did.

Lieutenant Colonel Harold Moore
November 15, 1965
By 10 a.m. [*the second morning*] the surviving North Vietnamese were withdrawing. Charlie Company had held its ground in a stunning display of personal courage and unit discipline. The brave men . . . had stood and died fighting for each other and held their ground. The senior ranking survivor in those two platoons was Platoon Sergeant Jemison. Asked why the enemy failed to overrun his platoon, Jemison said, "First it was Byrd and Fox on the machine guns on the right. At the end what saved us was Comer's machine gun."

Charlie Company, 1st Battalion, 7th Cavalry had begun this day with five officers and 106 men. By noon it had no officers left and only forty-nine men unhurt. A total of forty-two officers and men had been killed and twenty more wounded in two and a half hours of vicious hand-to-hand fighting. The bodies of hundreds of slain North Vietnamese littered the bloody battleground.

IMPRESSIONS

Lieutenant Colonel David H. Hackworth
operations staff officer, First Brigade, 101st Airborne Division
November 1965
Colonel Hackworth's unit had moved into the Central Highlands ahead of the Cav, and his brigade secured the An Khe base that became the Cav's "Happy Valley." Reassigned as executive officer of a rifle battalion, about this time Hackworth succumbed to gastroenteritis that his unit surgeon proved unable to cure. Hackworth had been sent to the hospital at Nha Trang.
I watched my near-empty officers' ward fill to capacity, with casualties all from the 1st Air Cav and all from a single battle—the battle of the Ia Drang Valley.

The first casualties in were from Lieutenant Colonel Harold "Hal" Moore's 1/7 (Gary Owen) Battalion. The stories they told of their baptism of fire began as echoes of [*Operation*] Gibraltar: inadequate [*helicopter*] lift, landing virtually at the enemy's front door, and being incredibly outnumbered. The first day found Moore's understrength (little more than 50 percent) unit surrounded and caught in a vise of two-plus NVA battalions. The second day was more of the same, except that the two, possibly three North Vietnamese battalions assaulting 1/7 were entirely fresh troops. The enemy made their main attack into Moore's C Company, inflicting heavy casualties and rendering that brave band of men ineffective as a fighting force. But the survivors hung tough and held their ground. Savage hand-to-hand combat was the order of the day as the enemy closed as tight as they could to avoid the Air Cav's superior firepower; close-in employment of artillery severely punished the NVA troops but took its toll in friendly casualties too, the worst case being when a canister of USAF napalm was mistakenly dropped just twenty meters from Moore's CP, scorching many and burning to death one of the troopers dug in there.

Despite these dire stories I heard in my hospital bed, Moore's Ia Drang fight did not smell like a disaster, or a "blundering success". . . . While Moore would later describe his battalion's fight as a "fight-to-live situation," . . . a critical difference . . . was that the commander of the 1/7 was completely in control from the moment his fight began.

ON THE CHOPPERS

Warrant Officer Robert Mason

The number of wounded we were carrying was growing fast. That week Leese and I flew more than a hundred wounded to the hospital tent. Other slicks carried a similar number.

When there was room and time, we carried the dead. They had low priority because they were no longer in a hurry. Sometimes they were thrown on board in body bags, but usually not. Without the bags blood drained on the deck and filled the Huey with a sweet smell, a horribly recognizable smell. It was nothing compared to the smell of men not found for several days. We had never carried so many dead before. We were supposed to be winning now. The NVA were trapped and being pulverized, but the pile of dead beside the hospital tent was growing. Fresh recruits for graves registration arrived faster than they could be processed.

THE FIGHT FOR LZ ALBANY

Lieutenant Colonel Harold Moore
November 15–17, 1965

While the Cav reinforced Moore with the rest of Tully's unit, Colonel Thomas W. Brown maneuvered with his last Third Brigade element, Lieutenant Colonel Robert McDade's Second Battalion, Seventh Cavalry. McDade's troopers advanced overland and reached LZ X-Ray on November 16. McDade's unit then led the march toward a point on the map called Landing Zone Albany. They ran smack into the North Vietnamese Sixty-Sixth Regiment. Despite the horrors of X-Ray, Hal Moore describes this fight as "the most savage one-day battle of the Vietnam War" and records that by November 17 there would be 155 dead plus another 124 Americans wounded.

The North Vietnamese battlefield commander, then Senior Lieutenant Colonel Nguyen Huu An, had watched the Americans leaving the clearing they called X-Ray. He and his principal subordinate, 66th regimental commander Lieutenant Colonel La Ngoc Chau, had one thought uppermost in their minds: General Vo Nguyen Giap's dictum "You must win the first battle." As far as Colonel An was concerned, the fight with the Americans that had begun on November 14, in Landing Zone X-Ray, wasn't over. It was just moving to a new location. . . .

An says, "I think this fight of November seventeenth was the most important of the entire campaign. I gave the order to my battalions: When you meet the Americans divide yourself into many groups and attack the column from all directions and [*cut*] the column into many pieces. Move inside the column, grab them by the belt, and thus avoid casualties from the artillery and air. We had some advantages: We attacked . . . from the sides, and at the moment of the attack, we were waiting for you. This was our reserve battalion and they were just waiting for their turn. The 8th Battalion had not been used in fighting this campaign. They were fresh."

Viewed from the American side, the firefight began at the head of the 2nd Battalion [*2/5*] column and swiftly spread down the right, or east side of the American line of march in a full-fledged roar.

Specialist 4 Dick Ackerman was the right-hand point man in the recon platoon, which was itself at the point of the battalion. Says Ackerman, "We were going to the left in a clearing. We had gone about 100 feet when we heard some shots, then more shots and finally all hell broke loose. The main brunt of the attack was right where we had been standing just a few minutes before. We hit the dirt. I was laying in the middle of a clearing and bullets were kicking dirt in my eyes and breaking off the grass."

Private Jack Smith
C Company, Second Battalion, Seventh Cavalry
November 17, 1965
Smith's company was in McDade's column making for Albany.
The next day we walked to Landing Zone Albany for what we thought was extraction, being lifted out by helicopter. We were out for a Sunday stroll in the woods. We . . . knew there had been this huge battle. We'd seen the bodies. Leaving the landing zone, you walk on bodies a hundred feet outside the dry creek bed and the foxholes. We knew there was a lot of enemy units around and some of us were a little apprehensive about walking in such a casual fashion. But we did, and a number of us remarked about it. "Shouldn't we have guards out?" And, "There are probably bad guys around here. I hope we don't get ambushed. I hope they (meaning our commanding officers) know what they are doing." In retrospect, knowing what I know now, our walk was a big mistake.

A couple of hours maybe to Landing Zone Albany, we were in an area where the brush was denser elephant grass, chest high, waist high, razor grass. In scrub jungle, trees here and there, all around us. Not dense forest but very light forest. You could see the sky. The head of the column broke into the landing zone. A battalion of green troops stumbling around in the jungle the day after the biggest battle of the war against an entire North Vietnamese division, right next to the main infiltration route for them in their territory without any artillery or air cover is just nuts. Without spraying the trees, recon by fire, without having guards on the side. I don't know why we were walking through the jungle. . . . It was clearly a mistake. We were green. It wasn't just the privates who were green. Everybody was green. Our captains were green. Our lieutenants were green. Our battalion commanders were green. The whole division was green. And they showed it. We walked right into a big-time ambush. . . .

I was angry at anybody who had anything to do with that battle. All my friends died there. I was even angry at the state of being human that the weakness of the flesh would succumb to shrapnel and bullets. I said, "How weak and flimsy we are that we all get killed like that." I became very cynical. Not only angry. But I became misanthropic. One day I woke up a few years later and I saw life as it really is. Life is pretty good. . . . People make mistakes. It happens in other wars. There's nothing I can do about it. . . . It struck me that what was remarkable about that experience was not the feebleness of the human beings involved but the magnificent strength that in spite of bullets and shrapnel and things like that, human beings can endure and do endure.

DENOUEMENT AT ALBANY

Lieutenant Larry Gwin
A Company, Second Battalion, Seventh Cavalry
November 17, 1965
Gwin witnessed the final chopper landing at LZ Albany and reflects on the day.
The instructions seemed to echo over the radio net around us. Then the formation came thundering into the LZ—the clearing to the west of us—and the noise and confusion of Hueys making an air assault into a hot LZ took over. They swept in from the south, eight ships at a time, I think, and the woods . . . seemed to spit enemy fire. The Hueys' door gunners were returning it—raking the far tree lines with their M-60s. The noise was horrendous, deafening, unbelievable. I could see Bravo Company troops jumping from the choppers and sprinting through the grass . . . and as they did I could feel this wonderful exhilaration and sense of awe, salvation, and relief. . . . [I]t was the most heroic combat air assault I've ever seen. . . .

All in all, about eighty Bravo Company troopers came in, along with water jugs and crates of extra ammo and grenades that were just dumped into the grass. As the Bravo Company guys closed into our perimeter, we were all up on our feet, cheering and yelling and hooting and waving them on, welcoming them into our position. I saw Sergeant Braden waving a little American flag he had been carrying with him, and thought that was terrific. . . .

Then Major Henry caught my eye and waved me over.

"Okay, Gwin," he said. "I want you to gather up some men pronto and bring in that extra ammo over there."

To my horror, he was pointing across the LZ, to the far side of it, past where the choppers had landed. I could see some ammo crates strewn in the grass, about seventy yards away, beyond the spot where I'd killed those first three [*North Vietnamese*] soldiers during their first rush at us early in the fight.

Oh my God, I thought, You want me to go out there, where the [*enemy*] troops had been massing before the air strikes? You want me to walk across that LZ with some of my people and bring that shit back? You've gotta be out of your fucking mind!

"Yes, sir," I said. . . .

[*Lieutenant Gwin and his GIs moved off to retrieve the crates. All of a sudden there was no fire. The People's Army seemed to have faded away.*] It wasn't long before Bravo Company troops began to venture out from our perimeter to look for survivors. Major Henry was one of the first to lead a party of volunteers back into the jungle and down the long column to see what they could find, and what they found was truly awful. As morning settled in, so did the grim reality of what had happened to the men in the column behind us.

The battalion, roughly four hundred strong when it left X-Ray, had suffered more than seventy percent casualties—155 dead, 124 wounded. Charlie Company was the hardest hit, losing all but 9 of its 110 men. The Delta Company Mortar Platoon was virtually wiped out. And Headquarters Company had been decimated. . . .

We spent the entire day at Albany searching for survivors, rescuing the wounded, and eventually bringing in the dead. A ghastly pall hung over the place. Teams of our men and the people who had come in to help us made the gruesome trek down the column. . . . I suppressed that day for fifteen years, but flashbacks continue to haunt me.

First of all, an unbelievably horrible stench filled the air—a sickening, ghastly putrescence—the same we'd smelled at X-Ray, but worse. Much worse. At Albany it filled your nostrils and permeated your soul. There was no escaping it.

AFTER THE BATTLE

Warrant Officer Robert Mason
The North Vietnamese fought hard to wipe out the 2/7 Cavalry. GIs resisted fiercely. Air Force fighter-bombers gave the Americans the edge they needed. An additional rifle company choppered into the Albany perimeter. The People's Army retreated into the jungle.

By November 26, America had won its first large-scale encounter with the North Vietnamese army. The Cav and the B-52s killed 1,800 Communists. The NVA killed more than 300 GIs. The Ia Drang valley campaign was one of the few battles in which I saw clearings filled with NVA bodies. In all, I might have seen a thousand of their corpses sprawled in the sun, rotting. We left them there.

THE VIETNAM DATA PROBLEM

Lieutenant Colonel Harold Moore
after the battle
Late in the day, November 18, Brigadier General Dick Knowles, whose headquarters were by now besieged by a growing throng of reporters demanding information on exactly what had happened at Landing Zone Albany, convened a news conference at II Corps headquarters. The word that had trickled in . . . was that an American battalion had been butchered in the Ia Drang Valley, and the sharks were gathering. Knowles, who had been aware

of the fighting at Albany since he overflew the battlefield at mid-afternoon the previous day, says, "I did not get timely information. We did not get it sorted out until the next day [the 18th]. That's when we learned the details." Asked if Colonel Brown had reported what he had seen and heard during an early visit to the Albany perimeter the morning of the 18th, Knowles says, "No." It would appear then that Knowles's headquarters got its first real idea of the scope of the tragedy when Associated Press photographer Rick Merron—who had finagled a ride into Albany—returned to Camp Holloway mid-morning of the 18th and staggered into the 1st Cavalry Division press tent, pale and shaken . . . and told his colleagues that the 2nd Battalion, 7th Cavalry had been massacred in an enemy ambush. Division public affairs officers swiftly informed Knowles. . . .

How and why it took more than eighteen hours for the assistant division commander to get the first direct detailed account from the battlefield—and why that information had come, not through command channels, but from a civilian photographer—is a question that lingers. [*The People's Army did not wait to move on to other fights. In April 1975, almost a decade later, it would be troops under Nguyen Huu An—by then a VPA general—who would capture the presidential palace in Saigon, marking the final end to the Vietnam War.*]

3

In the Highlands

TRACKING

Specialist Four David E. McLemore
C Company, Second Battalion, Thirty-Fifth Infantry, Twenty-Fifth Infantry
Division
west of Pleiku, October 28, 1966

More often than not, troops hacked their way through the jungle or slogged across the "boonies" in search of an elusive adversary. The Liberation Front and North Vietnamese were both adept at avoiding contact when they wished, attacking as they wanted. Washington's analyses consistently showed that the enemy controlled the rate of engagement. This example is drawn from the work of S. L. A. Marshall, who wrote several accounts of tactical action while the war was in progress. McLemore's company, incidentally, would be attacked in the night.

It proved to be not a big day for McLemore on the point, or for Second Platoon, which slogged along behind him, or for First Platoon, which had stepped out earlier and was at least 1,000 meters away throughout the march, or for Third Platoon, which moved separately . . . by about the same distance. They did not move by the same trace, nor did any platoon hold to one azimuth. They had been told to zigzag to confuse the enemy, and they followed instructions. Also they had been warned to stay away from trails "as much as possible." But, as things went, much wasn't possible. There were too many trails, all could not be avoided, and, as men grew tired, the temptation to take a trail rather than hack through thick brush became less resistible.

Without incident of any kind, the morning march was simply a sweat, bone-wearying, nervously irritating, and blister-forming. The only open country the men saw were a few rice paddy strips, most of them completely dried out. . . . Not a person was to be seen. Otherwise their route carried them alternately through narrow flats thickly grown with elephant grass, brush, or reeds, and over the sharp ridges, rock-ledged at the base and halfway up the slope, crowned with jungle growth spliced heavily with wait-a-minute thorn vines and creepers.

At [*11:00 a.m.*] they entered upon a well-used enemy base camp. Their early caution was in vain. It had been stripped bare . . . leaving nothing that was worth destroying. But there they rested briefly in the shade. At about [*5:30 p.m.*] Second Platoon came to a hamlet with four hootches. But the day was going fast . . . and so McLemore kept going, not pausing to check the village out. One hour earlier, First Platoon had come that way and had stopped for a look.

In two of the houses there were fires, or there had been, and the coals were still warm. In all four there were jugs of water and the taste was sweet. Each had a supply of rice and eggs, with salt and other pantry stuff. Two had henhouses; the chickens were feeding. The nests were checked by the platoon sergeant. Outside each house was a foxhole. . . .

McLemore led Second Platoon into the rim [*of a knob designated for the company's overnight laager at about 7:00 p.m.*]. Its watering party . . . sped to the creek because the night was now coming with a rush, as it always does in these latitudes. The rest of the platoon fitted into a sector and began looking for the softer spots where digging was possible. [*McLemore had just said he could see nothing when the attack began. The GIs rushed back to the perimeter.*]

MONTAGNARDS AND VIETNAMESE

Staff Sergeant George E. Dooley
Detachment A-226, Fifth Special Forces Group
An Khe, February 1966
Dooley's Special Forces A-Detachment, as operational units were called, briefly stayed with the Fifth Group's headquarters for the Highlands (called Detachment B-22) on its way to Camp Mai Linh, which the Green Berets would work for the next year. What Dooley learned there shows in microcosm the complexities of the Central Highlands. Ed Sprague was the team master sergeant. Both would serve almost continuously in South Vietnam through the end of the war, with intimate connections to the Highland tribes, or "montagnards." Sprague eventually moved to the State Department as a senior pacification official.

"So, where's Mai Linh?" said Ed Sprague.

"It's in Phu Bon province," replied Knight. "Generally it's southeast of Pleiku and due south of An Khe, about fifty miles. It's close to the province capital . . . which is the good news. The bad news is that it's a center of FULRO activity."

Everyone knew what FULRO meant: *Front Unifié Pour la Liberation des Races Oprimées* (Unified Front for the Liberation of Oppressed Peoples) or, succinctly, the montagnard revolutionary organization, which had been fighting both the Viet Cong/North Vietnamese Army and the Republic of Vietnam.

Over the previous two years, there had been numerous examples of FULRO rebellions. . . . Typically, the FULRO leaders would rebel at a Special Forces camp by detaining the SF team and then killing all the Vietnamese, particularly the Vietnamese Special Forces counterpart team. The U.S. A-team would then be released and have to act as the middlemen between the armed FULRO insurgents and an angry Vietnamese government. It wasn't a good way to fight a war against a third party. . . .

We landed at the base camp of the 1st Cavalry Division, which they had begun building in 1965. On our way to the B-team, the supply sergeant . . . explained about the arrival of the 1st Cav in 1965: "An Khe was a sleepy little village of about two hundred people . . . when the Cav arrived. On the first day, the Cav hired 150 people as camp labor, and on the second day they hired 400. By the end of the week they were hiring a thousand people a day from that little village. I wonder where all those laborers came from?" Apparently every local VC guerrilla came out of the woods to work for the Cav.

B-22 sat on the south side of Highway 22 (a misnomer for what was then a two-lane dirt road), overlooking the Song Ba (Ba River). The previous day, one of the Civilian Irregular Defense Group (CIDG) montagnard soldiers was outside the camp, trying to cross the bridge. . . . Two Vietnamese national policemen, commonly called white mice, were guarding the bridge, and one of the policemen demanded that the montagnard surrender his bayonet before he cross[ed] the river. The montagnard gave up his bayonet, returned to his CIDG company atop the hill, and told his company commander what had happened. The company commander ordered his unit to fire on the policemen, which they did, killing both. Since there were no large numbers of Vietnamese in the An Khe area, nothing happened to the CIDG company.

PLEIKU BASE

Private John Ketwig
First Ordnance Battalion, Fourth Infantry Division
Pleiku, September 1967
A mechanic, John Ketwig here provides the simple feel of the U.S. base at Pleiku.
The compound was laid out around a central crossroads. The main road ran east and west. The entrance gate was at the foot of Artillery Hill. Main Street ran from the gate through the crossroads, westward towards the Cambodian border. At the crossroads, having entered the gate, the mess hall and our hootches were in the near right rectangle. In the far right, or northwest,

corner our parts supply men had a hootch area. Some months before, a team of sappers had crept into their area and killed two Americans before being gunned down. The left rectangle nearest to the gate was a field of broken vehicles. Parts were sometimes hard to get, so this "boneyard" of scrapped trucks was maintained for salvage. It was just like a junkyard in The World at first glance, but most of these relics had been sidelined by mines or B-40 rockets, not mechanical breakdowns. Back at the crossroads, looking forward to the left would bring battalion headquarters into view. This was a rust-colored tarpaper building. Behind it loomed the shops. . . . The southernmost third of the compound was unused meadow and swamp, though ringed with guard posts and barbed wire.

It rained every day, starting about nine in the morning and pouring in translucent gray sheets until after midnight. The rain in The Nam was as different from rain in the United States as anything we would encounter in this strange land. The drops were as large as marbles and driven with enough force to sting when they hit you. . . . A few days after I arrived a [*GI*] lost his footing and drowned in a puddle. . . . The drowning changed the atmosphere. We were nestled between Artillery Hill and the Ho Chi Minh Trail in Cambodia. The huge howitzers roared at all hours of the day and night. They should have been a constant reminder that a war was raging just beyond the barbed-wire barriers . . . but, like residents on the flight path to a major airport, we soon grew accustomed to the noise. . . .

Tucking in your mosquito netting was an elaborate nightly ritual. When the lights went out the hootch was taken over by rats. They scampered, squealed, fought, and chewed. They ate crumbs, boots, plastic, books, even soap. They owned the tent. We staked out small territorial claims with the mosquito nets. A solid punch to the filmy gauze would send them squealing into space and convince you these were no field mice. Rats as large as an American house cat were common. . . .

I was far from comfortable, but I grew accustomed to the new way of life. It was a world of exhaustion, heat, mud, mildew, rot, and few pleasures. . . . You couldn't get clean. You couldn't get rested. You grew accustomed to all that; but you never grew accustomed to working on trucks with bloodied seats and holes in their floorboards. You never grew accustomed to the chatter of a nearby machinegun, or long hours on a guard post, peering into the rain and fog, wondering if a tiny form had crawled through the wire and was behind you. . . . Our pleasures were simple. Archie built a barbell from two truck flywheels and an axle shaft. His parents sent jars of wheat germ and he lifted his weights. Fred embroidered. Simmons whittled tiny water buffalos and helicopters. . . . But the ultimate escape was mail. Mail assured you that The World was still turning. Mail was private, and personal, and caring, and concerned, and everything our daily existence was not. A day without a letter from home was only mechanical; your watch ticked and your heart beat and you went through the motions.

MEDICAL HELP

Pat Johnson
Eighteenth Surgical Hospital, Seventy-First Evacuation Hospital
Pleiku, September 1966–March 1968
Pat Johnson was at Qui Nhon as a nurse with the Eighty-Fifth Evacuation Hospital when she learned that a hospital unit would be sent to Pleiku to sup- port the arriving Fourth Infantry Division. She wanted to go because it was in the Highlands—cooler—close to the Cambodian border and seemed even more exotic. Johnson had four months in country when she arrived at Pleiku to find the Eighteenth Surgical working out of tents about a half mile from the airstrip. There was no running water. Later they moved to Quonset huts. A handful of personnel—half a dozen nurses and seven or eight doctors—formed the core. Johnson's twenty-one months were among the longest duty tours of an American nurse.

We had big napalm tanks with holes cut out of them, and that's what we kept the water in. We didn't have enough bandages, we were short of IV fluids, and I remember using outdated penicillin because that's all we had. They said that would be better than nothing.

The hospital commander was a guy by the name of Senac, and the chief nurse was a woman by the name of Mary Berry. . . . They weren't really used to having women there, and they didn't have any provisions for us. We had one shower with a reversible sign on the outside for "Men" or "Women," and it didn't have a top on it. There was a fifty-gallon oil drum. . . . that had an immersion heater down in it. When I worked nights, one of my jobs in the morning was to go up there and turn this gas heater on so there would be warm water for the people in the morning. When we first got there the helicopter pilots discovered that women were taking showers in there, and they would fly over; so they soon put a top on it for us. Our chief nurse was very aware of the fact that because there were so few women we should be very discreet in our activities. She wouldn't let us sunbathe or wear Bermuda shorts on our off-time because she felt (she was really an old-fashioned nurse) that was just too much temptation for the men.

I worked in the emergency room, myself and another nurse. We worked whenever they needed us. We were scheduled for regular shifts, but if it got busy it was not unusual to work fourteen to sixteen hours, have four or five hours off, and then go back and work those long hours again. The casualties, especially in the beginning, would come in big groups; we called them "pushes." When you were really busy, you'd get a whole lot in at once, and then you might not have anything for a couple of days until they organized a sick call. They'd bring in all the malarias and the dengue fevers and other things by ambulance. Most of the other injuries would come in by chopper, dustoff choppers or, many times, other types of choppers too, whatever was available. If there was a battle where they would have some kind of landing zone already established, they would be able to bring casualties very quickly. And you would get people with big wounds who were still alive, chest wounds and that type of thing. If it took a long time to get into an LZ and get the patients to you, then many times those types of casualties would never make it to the hospital.

BLOODY HILL

Captain David H. Milton
A Company, Second Battalion, 503rd Infantry (Parachute), 173rd Airborne Brigade
Hill 1338, June 22, 1967
One of the first American combat units to deploy to South Vietnam, the 173rd Airborne Brigade long served as an independent intervention force, like the Cav, sent to sectors that needed bolstering or for planned offensives. In the summer of 1967 the Pleiku–Dak To area qualified as a threatened position. One big fight took place on Hill 1338 where two companies of the Second Battalion, 503rd Infantry were sent on a sweep. Alpha Company touched off the battle when it encountered People's Army troops early in the morning of June 22. This account is by Edward F. Murphy, an Army veteran.
Milton assigned Lieutenant Judd's 2nd Platoon to the point position. Next came the 3rd Platoon led by Lieutenant Hood. Milton's CP group would follow, and behind them would come Weapons Platoon. Lieutenant Sexton's 1st Platoon was given the task of spreading the CS [*tear gas*] crystals over the LZ and laager site before falling in at the column's rear.

At [*6:25 a.m.*] Lieutenant Judd started off. As the tail end of his platoon disappeared downhill into the jungle, Hood started his platoon forward. The Weapons Platoon members, all eighteen of them, squatted along the trail waiting their turn to move. Lieutenant Sexton's platoon had donned their gas masks and were spreading the tear gas. . . .

Sergeant Nichols had just stood up when the sharp crack of rifle fire broke the morning calm. The firing continued for ten seconds or so, and then died down. It was [*6:58 a.m.*].

Captain Milton radioed Judd. The young lieutenant reported that his point squad had walked smack into ten to fifteen NVA coming toward them on the same trail. The NVA had opened up first, hitting some of Judd's men. He didn't know how many or how badly. Judd had put his remaining men into a defensive perimeter.

Private 1st Class Steer heard someone say that the firing was just 2nd Platoon reconning by fire. "Bullshit," he retorted. "That's AK-47 fire." With that the distinct crack of M16s could be heard. It was 2nd Platoon fighting back.

After getting off the radio with Judd, Milton radioed the battalion [*tactical operations center—TOC*]. He reported the contact to [*Captain*] Ken Smith. Colonel Partain [*the battalion commander*] and his executive officer, [*Major*] H. Glenn Watson, were also present in the TOC. While Partain and Smith plotted coordinates in order to bring in supporting artillery fire, Watson stayed on the radio with Milton.

Major Watson was not overly concerned. Alpha seemed to have the situation under control. He advised Captain Milton to "develop the fight and keep us informed."

Back on Hill 1338 Captain Milton turned to his senior medic, [*Specialist Five*] Richard E. Patterson. "Doc, they need a medic down there," he said.

[*In this classic meeting engagement, Captain Milton's lead platoon recoiled on the following unit, and both set up a perimeter around a clearing, which was subjected to repeated assaults by enemy troops. Doc Patterson had his hands full, as would Eighteenth Surgical at Pleiku. Milton's remaining platoons closed up but so did the enemy—they knew that the closer they got to the Americans the less danger there would be from artillery and air.*]

At the battalion TOC, the reports from Milton were causing increasing concern among the staff. The rapid buildup of enemy fire had finally convinced Partain and Watson that this was no ordinary contact. The faint sound of the firing could already be heard at the TOC. Something big was definitely up.

Colonel Partain grabbed Captain Smith and [*Sergeant Major*] Vincent Rogers and headed for the chopper pad. He wanted to get above the action as soon as the weather permitted and coordinate artillery and upcoming air strikes. Major Watson stayed at the TOC, on the radio.

Back on Hill 1338, the two pinned-down platoons were still holding on. Enemy fire had slackened a bit, giving the paratroopers a little rest. Then, at about [*8:10 a.m.*], Specialist Patterson heard someone up front holler, "Here they come!"

[*Battle was joined in earnest. Gunship helicopters arrived and the paratroopers marked their positions with smoke, which also defined them for the North Vietnamese, who began firing mortars into the U.S. position. The battalion commander ordered in his other available company, but it advanced cautiously,*] *arriving only at mid-afternoon. Captain Milton faced the worst of the fight with only his own GIs. A few grunts went numb with fear or from their wounds. The Americans became so short on ammunition they had to strip magazines from casualties lying in the open. Some of Milton's men became separated. Above the battlefield Partain's command helicopter was hit and forced to return to Pleiku. He commandeered a second chopper and returned, but that was hit too, made for base, and crashed on landing, shaking up everyone and injuring Colonel Partain. He ordered his last rifle company, left behind to guard rear positions, to helicopter into a nearby LZ and break the enemy ring. Those troops did not enter the battle until the next day, when the Second Battalion, 503rd Infantry regrouped at the place where some GIs had been cut off. Lieutenant Phillip Bodine's Second Platoon of Charlie Company led the assembled force up the final slope.]*

Bodine took his platoon forward. A short distance beyond the clump of trees he spotted the mass of bodies. Bodine, ignoring the carnage, moved beyond the site and set up a protective line. Then he radioed to [*company commander*] Captain Leonard to come forward.

A few minutes later Captain Leonard brought the rest of the company down.

No one could comprehend the horrible scene. Dozens upon dozens . . . lay sprawled in death's grotesque grip. A heavy veil of black flies swarmed over the swollen corpses and the thick pools of blood and gore. The smell of death hung so heavily . . . that many of Charlie's paratroopers were unable to control their stomachs. They staggered behind trees to vomit.

[*A number of Captain Milton's GIs had been executed, many of their bodies mutilated. The firefight had almost destroyed Alpha Company, of which just thirty-eight men were left. There had been twenty-three wounded but seventy-six killed. More than half the dead had been dispatched at close range by bullets to the head.*]

MONTAGNARDS

Private John Ketwig
First Ordnance Battalion, Fourth Infantry Division
Pleiku, October 1967
The population of Vietnam consisted of three groups: the haves, the have-nots, and the Montagnards. The Montagnards lived in Stone Age seclusion in the highlands. They had been nomadic until the war. Now they had become our only true allies. Trained by the Green Berets, a Montagnard warrior never ran under fire. He might forsake his M-16 for his crossbow, but he never forsook a friend. He didn't steal, and he didn't beg. He asked nothing, but

offered a sense of family and community found nowhere else in Vietnam. The Montagnards suffered horribly. Despised by the Vietnamese, they had been banished into the mountains, where they had developed a culture not unlike that of the American Indians before Columbus. As European weapons had spelled doom for the North American Indian, helicopter gunships and jet fighter air-support missions signaled the end of the Montagnard civilization. Regardless, they embraced the Americans.

They didn't care much for clothing. As we carried canned ham and soap powder into the village, topless women and men in loincloths gathered. A throng of naked children pressed in around us, knowing we would have candy. No one begged, and no one said, "Fuck you," or "Go home." There were only toothless grins and warm embraces. In the center of the thatched huts the chief accepted our gifts and distributed them to his delighted but orderly followers. He offered us coarse handwoven shirts and rice wine. He would be offended if we did not drink with him.

Drinking Montagnard wine requires a ceremony. It sits, uncovered, in the tropical sun, fermenting in heavy crocks. A slender bamboo is notched and laid across the opening of the jug with a tiny bamboo sliver dangling down into the liquid. The chief adjusts this sliver, to half or three quarters of an inch. You kneel at the jug, and it is filled to overflowing. You drink through a huge bamboo straw, and it is an insult to your hosts if you rise before the liquid falls below the dangling sliver. A quart of this rich brew, the hundred degree sun, and the motion of rising caused many GIs to pass out.

SCRABBLE WITH A MONTAGNARD

Staff Sergeant Alan F. Farrell
A Company, Exploitation Battalion, Command and Control Central, Studies and Observation Group (SOG)
Forward Operating Base Kontum, 1968
A tough fighter, French linguist, and communications specialist with the SOG heavy formations called Hatchet Forces, Alan Farrell naturally gravitated to contact with the montagnard strikers who made up the bulk of his reconnaissance team. They had communicated with French administrators during the Vietnamese colonial period using a pidgin mixture of tribal languages and French called tai boi, *and they developed a similar style in English. Their languages seemed to consist mostly of consonants. Farrell quickly learned to appreciate the 'yards native intelligence and humor, which he commemorated in this poem, its title drawn from a famous phrase in the Gospel of St. John ("and the word became flesh," John 1:14).*

Et Verbum Caro Factum Est

COFFIN. Cee Oh Eff Eff Eye Enn. Ten, times two, that's twenty.

BRRZACHK. Bee Arr Arr Zee Ay Cee Aitch Kay. How much?

Uh, lessee. Three, one, one, ten, one, three, four, five. Tha's, uh . . . twenny-eight.

KNIFE. Kay Enn Eye Eff Eee. Five, six, seven, four's eleven, twelve. And twenny, tha's 32.

GRRATAKX. Gee Arr Arr Ay Tee Ay Kay Ecks. How much?

Hmmm . . . Tha's two, two, one, one one, five, ten. So, uh . . . Twenny-two An' double, tha's forty-four, plus . . . makes seventy-two.

FINISH. Eff Eye Enn Eye Ess Haitch. Twelve. And thirty-two, tha's forty-four.

QORAKHNEKCZ. Kew Oh Arr Ay Kay Haitch Enn Eee Kay Cee Zee. How much?

Well, lessee . . . Ten, thirteen, five, four, um . . . nine is twenny-two and, two, seven, ten, Tha's thirty, and ten makes forty. And that's a triple, soooooo . . . Hundred and twenny plus seventy-two is, uh, hundred ninety-two. Fuck!

Never play Scrabble with a montagnard.

PLEIKU BASE AGAIN

Sergeant Edward Murphy
Fourth Military Intelligence Detachment, Fourth Infantry Division
Pleiku, June 5, 1968
Sergeant Murphy wrote his brother Tom after hearing news of the assassination of Robert F. Kennedy. He was sad about that, but seething about conditions in Vietnam—contractors soaking up war funds, corruption, the ignoring of the people and their culture. Equally interesting, Murphy warns his brother against any idealized vision of GI life at Pleiku, furnishing added perspective on what he had apparently written in an earlier letter. He opens with comments on the situation at nearby Dak To.
No, Dak To is not the place to be. I didn't mean to paint a picture of the Garden of Eden. Although you may hear of Dak To now, it was much worse a while back. We suffered one of our worse losses here [*at Tet*], but there wasn't much said about it. We have expected an attack for a long time, but for some reason it never came off. Pleiku suffered badly during Tet, but right now it is amazingly quiet.

We live in an enormous base camp [*at Pleiku*] and are protected by helicopters 24 hours a day. We hear artillery fire most nights and once in a while see the helicopters shooting their guns at night. I ride back and forth to town to talk to people and make liaison meetings with other agencies, We are always back on the camp before six o'clock. After that the roads are not safe. During the day there are so many soldiers on the road and they are all armed, that any ambush would be suicidal. The fighting is done away from the base camp because there is so much firepower available at a moment's notice. People here live a very relaxed life except when rockets are shot into the camp. This is done seldom, and the aim is poor.

About morale: The morale is very high, as the generals will tell you. The mistake is believing the reasons they give. Americans do have many things to be proud of. Among these is the ability to create a means of survival in an absurd situation. Because the tour is one-year long, you are able to count the days till DEROS. . . .

We have movies five times a week. There is radio and television, when the situation permits. After being out in the field for a while, men will return to base camp and relax for a few days. Everyone knows there are helicopters within minutes of them. There is a hospital on the other side of Pleiku, and the copters pick up the wounded and have them in the operating room within minutes. Everyone knows that the "heroes," the helicopter pilots, will come through the most dangerous combat situations to pick up a wounded man.

What all this means is there is a feeling of being American and taking care of other Americans. The people here see the money being spent and see the uselessness of it. . . . It is a shame to see educated people making the mistakes they are taught to avoid. Remember the *Kulturkampf?* We are doing the same thing here. Remember the Germans in Paris? When everyone was starving, the whores had all they needed. During Tet, when most of the people were starving and clean water was scarce, the GIs were driving up to their girl-friends' houses with trucks [*of*] food and clothes. These girls would flaunt their stuff around town. This was bad in Europe, but think of the Asian mind and the delicate culture of these people. We speak of the black market and the corruption of the people in Saigon. The goods sold on the black market don't come from the Vietnamese, but from the Americans. We buy a coke for 10 cents, sell it for 25 . . . and it is in turn sold for 50 cents. The black marketers have to be supplied, and the GI loves to supply him. The same GI will speak of defending his country and tell war stories when he comes home. . . .

Vietnam is one of our mistakes, and our generation will unfortunately be linked with this mistake, unless we use the means available to rectify this situation. . . .

THE STINK OF WAR

Bruce Weigl, unknown rank
First Cavalry Division (Airmobile)
An Khe, July 1968

Bruce Weigl, a Vietnam vet who became a poet, arrived in country in December 1967, not long before Tet. A communications specialist, Weigl fought alongside the Cav as it struggled to reopen the overland route to Khe Sanh, then besieged by the North Vietnamese. A victim of what was probably amoebic dysentery as a result of the water around Ca Lu, better known as Landing Zone Stud, Weigl was invalidated back to the Cav's home base at An Khe. What he put in a poem from this period recurs in the memories of many veterans. Weigl's Vietnam poetry is searing, and, even two decades after the war, his collection Song of Napalm *was nominated for the Pulitzer Prize.*

Burning Shit at An Khe

Into that pit
   I had to climb down
with a rake and matches; eventually,
   you had to do something
because it just kept piling up
   and it wasn't our country, it wasn't
our air thick with the sick smoke
   so another soldier and I
lifted the shelter off its blocks
   to expose the homemade toilets:
fifty-five gallon drums cut in half
   with crude wooden seats that splintered.
We soaked the piles in fuel oil
   and lit the stuff
and tried to keep the fire burning.
   To take my first turn
I paid some kid
   a CARE package of booze from home.
I'd walked past the burning once
   and gagged the whole heart of myself—
it smelled like the world
   was on fire,
but when my turn came again
   there was no one
so I stuffed cotton up my nose
   and marched up that hill. We poured
and poured until it burned and black

smoke curdled
but the fire went out.
　Heavy artillery
hammered the evening away in the distance,
　Vietnamese laundry women watched
from a safe place, laughing.
　I'd grunted out eight months
of jungle and thought I had a grip on things
　but we flipped the coin and I lost
and climbed down into my fellow soldiers'
　shit and began to sink and didn't stop
until I was deep to my knees. Liftships
　cut the air above me, the hacking
blast of their blades
　ripped the dust in swirls so every time
I tried to light a match
　it died
and it all came down on me, the stink
　and the heat and the worthlessness
until I slipped and climbed
　out of that hole and ran
past the olive-drab
　tents and trucks and clothes and everything
green as far from the shit
　as the fading light allowed.
Only now I can't fly.
　I lay down in it
and fingerprint the words of who I am
　across my chest
until I'm covered and there's only one smell,
　one word.

ACTION IN THE BUSH

Corporal Thomas W. Bennett
B Company, First Battalion, Fourteenth Infantry, Fourth Infantry Division
February 9–11, 1969
Congressional Medal of Honor Citation
For conspicuous gallantry and intrepidity in action at the risk of his life above
and beyond the call of duty, Cpl. Bennett distinguished himself while serving
as a platoon medical aidman with the 2nd Platoon, Company B, during a
reconnaissance-in-force mission. On 9 February the platoon was moving to
assist the 1st Platoon of Company D which had run into a North Vietnamese

ambush when it became heavily engaged by the intense small arms, automatic weapons, mortar and rocket fire from a well-fortified and numerically superior enemy unit. In the initial barrage of fire, 3 of the point members of the platoon fell wounded. Cpl. Bennett, with complete disregard for his safety, ran through the heavy fire to his fallen comrades, administered life-saving first aid under fire and then made repeated trips carrying the wounded men to positions of relative safety from which they could be medically evacuated from the battle position. Cpl. Bennett . . . valiantly exposed himself to the heavy fire in order to retrieve the bodies of several fallen personnel. Throughout the night and following day Cpl. Bennett moved from position to position treating and comforting the several personnel who had suffered shrapnel and gunshot wounds. On 11 February Company B again moved in an assault on the well-fortified enemy positions and became heavily engaged. . . . Five members of the company fell wounded in the initial assault. Cpl. Bennett ran to their aid without regard to the heavy fire. He treated one wounded comrade and began running toward another seriously wounded man. Although the wounded man was located forward of the company position covered by heavy enemy grazing fire and Cpl. Bennett was warned it was impossible to reach the position, he leaped forward. . . . In attempting to save his fellow soldier, he was mortally wounded. Cpl. Bennett's undaunted concern for his comrades above and beyond the call of duty are in keeping with the highest traditions of the military service and reflect great credit upon himself, his unit, and the U.S. Army.

AGONY AT HOSPITAL

Sara McVicker
Seventy-First Evacuation Hospital
Pleiku, March 1969–March 1970
Nurse McVicker was horrified at the wounds suffered by GIs in a battle soon after that for which Corporal Bennett was awarded the Medal of Honor.
I was [*at Fort Dix*] around four months when I got my orders for Vietnam. . . . The guy I was seeing had just come back from Vietnam like six or eight months before—he'd been infantry. I called all over to locate him, and that evening Ken came over to see me. I remember him talking to me, and he took off his CIB and pinned it on my blouse . . . and he said, "You're going to do okay" . . . That meant a lot to me because I knew what a CIB meant to them, you know?. . . .

Flying into Pleiku, I could kind of see out the window, and there was all this incredibly red dirt. It reminded me of Georgia, and of course around the installations, most of the vegetation was gone. So I'm just going, "Oh, yuck," and then we pulled up in front of the hospital and there was all this green grass. They were literally growing grass to keep the dust down. And I remember thinking, "Okay, I can survive a year of this." It was early April 1969, springtime, and it *was* cooler than Long Binh. . . .

I was head nurse on the surgical ward for about five months. We got general surgery patients, neurosurgery, orthopedics, and a real mixture. We supported 4th Division, and one of the times I remember, one of the companies from 1st of the 14th was just getting chewed up, unbelievably chewed up, and we were getting patient after patient after patient. I remember turning around and looking at my ward master and saying, "Is there anybody left out there?" And within the next hour we got the answer. We started getting patients from another company. I was going, "Oh shit, how long is this going to go on?"

Toward the end of my tour, 4th Division pulled east across the mountains to An Khe for their base camp. It was part of the Vietnamization program, getting Americans out of Vietnam, which cut down on our work load some, as far as American patients went, but we filled up with Vietnamese.

I guess the one patient that I really remember out of that period was a young black kid who had a head injury. And we had at that time, unfortunately, a real turkey of a neurosurgeon who did not want to operate on him, and that was not considered acceptable. When I think about it now, it made perfectly good sense; there probably wasn't anything we could do. But I guess the basic philosophy in our hospital was that you always tried, even when it was bad enough where there was not much hope. We were really busy at that time. . . . He'd been there, I don't know, several days . . . when we got all this mail that had been forwarded from his unit. . . . I was going over to this guy's bed to check on him or something, and I said, "I'll just put it in his bedside stand," and I happened to look at the return addresses . . . and all of them were from people at a small black college near my hometown in North Carolina. . . . I guess my thought was, he either dropped out or goofed off and flunked out, got drafted, and here he is in Vietnam . . . and he's going to die. . . . And that really got to me.

TROUBLE AT BEN HET

Captain Robert Evans
A Company, Exploitation Battalion, Command and Control Center, Studies and Observation Group
Ben Het, March 4–10, 1969
In 1969 the Vietnam People's Army closed in on Ben Het camp, northwest of Kontum, to which they laid siege in two rounds, from February through April,

and later from May until July. The campaign bore some similarity to the siege of Con Thien in I Corps two years earlier, with constant enemy shelling, a ground threat despite tremendous suppression efforts, and an attack that seemed less than the sum of its parts, in this case including North Vietnamese PT-76 tanks. Ben Het was the descendent of a firebase created to support the 173rd Airborne Brigade in the 1967 battles around Dak To. It was now known as Fire Support Base Twelve (FSB 12) and had permanently in place a 175-millimeter gun battery, a 105-millimeter howitzer battery plus a 155-milimeter howitzer platoon, and, for the first round of the siege, a platoon of American tanks from B Troop, 1/69 Armor. There was also a Special Forces camp at Ben Het with its own complement of Green Berets (Detachment A-244 under Captain Louis P. Kingsley), Vietnamese Special Forces, montagnard strikers, and an ARVN Ranger battalion, altogether almost 1,200 troops. Two People's Army regiments were in the area, strategic because it dominated the only road from the Laotian border to Dak To and Kontum. Seeking a creative way to stop the People's Army, SOG came up with Operation Spindown, in which a full Hatchet Force company would land behind enemy lines and block the road against them. Before the operation could take place, the VPA tried its own Ben Het attack and failed. The very next morning Captain Evans assaulted with Company A, more than a hundred strikers plus sixteen Americans. They took over a hill overlooking Route 110, as the road was known, and dug in. This account is by John L. Plaster, a Green Beret who served with SOG at this time.

The hill they occupied offered ideal terrain for a roadblock. About 300 yards high, it overlooked Highway 110 on its northern slope. The highway was completely exposed because bomb strikes had wiped the jungle away. Beyond the road lay soft ground where a stream paralleled the highway. There was no way past the choke point: trucks had to run the gauntlet of Hatchet Force guns or not roll at all.

No sooner had the Hatchet Force men finished their bunkers that afternoon than NVA mortars began pounding the hilltop. It had little effect. That night the Americans watched the road with night-vision Starlite scopes. Whenever NVA [*vehicles*] tried to sneak past, the SOG men called in USAF AC-119 and AC-130 gunships on them.

In the dark the NVA climbed the hill to toss grenades and lob RPGs; by dawn they were out of sight, licking their wounds. Daylight also brought a contest between newly arrived antiaircraft guns and SOG choppers that whisked past the hill, kicking out ammo, food and water to the entrenched Hatchet Force. No helicopters were downed.

But that afternoon an F-4 accidentally dropped napalm on the hilltop, killing six Montagnards and badly burning several more. Then NVA mortars wounded the company's only recoilless rifle crew.

On Bright Light [*prisoner rescue*] duty 25 miles away at Dak To, the [*recon-naissance team—RT*] South Carolina [*commander*] announced he was quali-fied with the 90mm recoilless rifle; half an hour later he landed on the hill to take over the crewless antitank weapon.

That night the NVA tried to pin the Hatchet Force with mortars and run a convoy past, but the lead truck was spotted immediately. "In order to get the right trajectory I had to stand on top of one of those bunkers," the RT South Carolina [*leader*] said. "I took aim and blasted that sucker." Caught in the open, the drivers abandoned their vehicles and ran while the SOG men stitched the cabs with M-60 machine guns and blasted them with mortars.

After a few quiet hours, Hatchet Force men watching the road with Starlite scopes spotted NVA creeping forward to salvage the trucks, so they opened fire again, the RT [*leader*] reports. "We fired all three M-60s until the barrels got red and two of the guns finally jammed—we really kicked ass." [*For six days SOG maintained the block, stopping the North Vietnamese supply flow, which piled up and then furnished targets for U.S. air strikes.*]

There were only four U.S. wounded, among them Captain Evans and Staff Sergeant Tom Quinn, plus about twenty Yards. The only deaths were Yards. Their overworked medic, Sergeant Vernon Cantrell, was awarded the Silver Star, as was Captain Evans.

Sergeant First Class John D. Lamerson
Sixth Battalion, Fourteenth Artillery, Fourth Infantry Division
Ben Het Camp, May–July 1969

Ben Het camp was unusual because it functioned as both an artillery fire base (FSB 12) and a Special Forces camp. Sergeant Lamerson was unusual too—an enlisted man serving as intelligence staff officer (S-2) for the Sixth Battalion, Fourteenth Artillery. He had had missions to Ben Het before, but during the siege's second phase he went there full-time as ad hoc artillery coordinator and senior intelligence specialist. He had seven months in country, and this mission delayed his promised R&R in Australia. Massive air support from fighter-bombers and Arc Light B-52s, plus the artillery, prevented the North Vietnamese from actually attacking Ben Het, though Lamerson is convinced that they tried.

My first full day at Ben Het during the June fighting commenced with a trip to the [*Special Forces*] latrine at the Main Hill compound. I had always envied the resourcefulness of the Special Forces troops. Here at Ben Het was this elaborate latrine, fitted out with porcelain sinks and commodes with running water. They even had showers. Well, that was before the enemy shelling. Now, all that remained was a shrapnel-ridden mess of broken sinks and commodes. To make matters worse, some of the ARVN and CIDG still tried to use the facility. By the time I first entered it, it was a stinking cesspool of human waste and urine. Hell, it was bad enough to gag a maggot. I was forced to hold out until the following night after dark. There was no slit trench latrine, so one had to do one's best to dig a hole and cover it. Of course, you knew that the next exploding enemy shell was apt to uncover and scatter the contents of these deposits. . . .

Potable water was in very short supply. However, the monsoons were starting up in northwestern Kontum province. One of the SF team members rotated out and left me his canvas cot. Except for the fact that I would have to fold it up each morning and stow it away for the day, I appreciated the luxury of being able to sleep off the ground.

[*The water point at Ben Het was outside the perimeter, further complicating its defenders' miseries. Men were shot and vehicles lost bringing back water. For Lamerson another danger lay in the fact that the best artillery observation was from a tower the Green Berets had built at one corner of their command post.*]

During those first two days, I spent a lot of time just getting my bearings. . . . I spent time in the tower. I had my artillery binoculars and M-2 compass with me and used them . . . in pinpointing . . . reference points on my map. . . . These were then recorded for my future use. [*A*] convoy was finally able to break through to Ben Het, and my two and one-half ton truck pulling the water trailer (full of 250 gallons of potable water) was with it. [*Sergeant*] Stanley and the survey team also made it in with that convoy. They set to work immediately and by nightfall we had our . . . data to the tower. The convoy people had spent the night, so Stanley and his crew were able to return to Pleiku with them. Aboard my truck was my full supply of maps [*and specialized spotting equipment*]. These were taken up into the tower. The tower would become my second daylight home for awhile. I was now prepared to assume the duties of the camp's only artillery forward observer. . . .

The tower was to become a dangerous place to be, although the ground was very unsafe as well. I found out right off that the driveway between hills was extremely dangerous as well, because the enemy soldiers could come in real close in those two locations. Therefore we avoided travel between compounds as much as possible.

[*As the siege progressed, the allied command brought in a second montagnard company, of strikers from the tribe around Plei Djereng, different from that at Ben Het. This caused its own difficulties.*] Rations provided for the CIDGs were not acceptable to them. They refused to eat rice that was not grown in Vietnam (they knew the difference). These Montagnard tribesmen required fresh meat (water buffalo or pork), and the animals had to be delivered alive so they could be slaughtered in accordance with tribal ritual. Now this may sound strange to westerners, but to the Montagnards, their tribal laws had to be followed to the letter. Fresh pumpkin is an example of food that we had to bring in. Their wounded and dead had to be evacuated back to their tribal homes, too. This posed another problem [*and it accentuated the ethnic and social conflicts between the montagnards and the Vietnamese*]. Special handling of their dead required that the bodies be returned immediately to their tribal village for burial. However, the Vietnamese refused to touch the dead, which complicated matters. Our medical evacuation resources were limited as it was.

VIETNAMESE COOPERATION

First Lieutenant George Dooley
Detachment A-241, Fifth Special Forces Group
Polei Kleng, November 1969
In 1969, after receiving a battlefield commission, George Dooley returned for another tour in the Highlands. After time on a command staff, he took charge of Camp Polei Kleng. The war raged with new intensity, with Liberation Front guerrillas almost entirely replaced by VPA regulars. But some things had not changed, including American difficulties with the ARVN Special Forces, the LLDB (Luc Luong Dac Biet). "The war might be escalating," Dooley recorded, "but we weren't the ones doing the escalating." His problems were annoying and could be dangerous.

The LLDB still tried to sell rides to CIDG dependents on our daily work helicopter, and we had to closely watch. . . . We knew that there was some minor smuggling of cigarettes and other commodities to the A-camps, but we looked at that as a cost of doing business. Then one day the LLDB [*supply*] sergeant offered his U.S. counterpart one thousand dollars if he could get the LLDB a Caribou aircraft to use for a day. The offer was refused, but we began to wonder about the extent of LLDB corruption.

There was an old LLDB warrant officer (or third lieutenant) assigned to the LLDB B-team, whose innocuous title was "finance officer." But *we* were paying the CIDG, so we didn't know what his job really was. Eventually, we found out that he was the LLDB bagman. Every week he'd visit each A-camp and pick up the profits from the LLDB enterprises. . . .

Each camp had an LLDB-sponsored canteen and convenience store (and sometimes a brothel). Under LLDB auspices, a CIDG soldier could get a haircut, buy a beer or cigarettes, purchase the services of a prostitute, or buy additional food (often stolen from CIDG rations in the first place). Of course, if a CIDG member didn't have any cash, credit was available at 5 percent interest, repayable at the end of the month. Then there were the ghost payrollers.

Ghost payrollers were individuals who had quit the CIDG (or who had enlisted twice), but who were still on the payroll. Some camps had as many as an extra one hundred ghosts on the payroll. When payday rolled around, an individual would go through the pay line once for himself and then go around again under somebody else's name with the second pay allowance going to the LLDB. Of course, we tried to stop that with ID cards, fingerprinting, and photographs, but every control method was circumvented. The really bad thing about ghost payrollers was not the loss of money . . . but the loss of available combat power. . . .

Five days before Thanksgiving, [*Special Forces*] sent every camp a frozen turkey for the holiday. Our cook at Polei Kleng was an old Jarai woman who had never seen a frozen turkey before. . . . She put it under a kitchen counter and forgot about it. The day before Thanksgiving, one of the team members went looking for the turkey. The heat had thawed it, and the meat had begun to rot. It was purple and didn't look very appetizing. Our medic, Andy Szeliga, said that it might not be safe to eat.

We called the B-team and asked them to buy another turkey and send it out by helicopter. Just in case that the purple turkey might be okay after all, we baked it Thanksgiving Day morning. Later that morning, a fresh thawed turkey arrived from . . . Pleiku, and we cooked that one too and celebrated Thanksgiving with it that afternoon. Since the questionable turkey didn't look too bad after it was cooked, we give it to the LLDB team. The consensus was that the worst that could happen is that the turkey would poison all the LLDB and that they'd all be replaced. The LLDB didn't get sick so the situation turned out to be win-win all around.

BATTLE AT DAK PEK

Sergeant Leigh Wade
Detachment A-242, Fifth Special Forces Group
Dak Pek Camp, June 1970

The most significant force increase in the South Vietnamese army of 1970 resulted from the absorption of the montagnard CIDG units into the ARVN. This piece of Vietnamization swelled the ARVN by tens of thousands of soldiers in many Ranger battalions. The Vietnamese Special Forces cadres of the CIDGs were promoted and continued commanding the new Ranger units. The significant difference was the disappearance of the Americans, with their close ties to the montagnards and their access to U.S. airpower, fire support, and supplies. The Fifth Special Forces Group went home and was disbanded. Leigh Wade spent his last months at Dak Pek with the montagnard conversion approaching day by day.

Life around camp got really weird those final weeks before the conversion. We'd been issued a new movie projector to replace the one destroyed in April.

The projector was supposedly for the purpose of showing the troops propaganda movies but occasionally we also received fairly recent Hollywood films. One of the movies that came in was my favorite western, *The Wild Bunch.* We showed this one in our team mess hall, and invited the LLDB team to come watch it with us.

As we watched the movie, we all drank beer, and a couple of the LLDB NCOs drank too much. The overwhelming, graphic violence of the movie greatly excited the two men, and as soon as the movie ended, they went outside to have a damn quick draw contest . . . for real! Standing about thirty feet apart, each one went for his .45-caliber M-1911 auto[*matic pistol*]. Each man emptied his gun at the other, but they both missed with all seven shots. After the duel they shook hands, embraced, and were buddies again. As I say, things were definitely strange during those final weeks.

4

Saigon and the Delta

TAKEN PRISONER

Lieutenant James N. Rowe
Special Forces Operational Detachment A-23, Fifth Special Forces Group
Tan Phu, October 1963

Tan Phu was a typical Special Forces camp in the Mekong Delta, where a Green Beret detachment of a dozen worked with a South Vietnamese LLDB team, controlling four companies of Civilian Irregular Defense Group (CIDG) strikers. The whole force amounted to about four hundred men. An isolated outpost, accessible only by helicopter, with National Liberation Front guerrillas dominating the land outside a band of perhaps 1,200 yards in every direction, Tan Phu had been reconstructed after a militia base there was overrun the year before. It had the reputation of being the most frequently embattled Special Forces camp in the Mekong. The archenemy was the Liberation Front's 306th Main Force Battalion, which worked out of the U Minh Forest. Lieutenant Rowe, Lieutenant Tinh (the South Vietnamese camp commander), and most of their troops made a foray to a hamlet roughly five miles to the northwest on October 29. This was the first time they had ever operated in that sector.

I glanced at my watch: [5:57 a.m.]. Ahead, the rifle squads brought their weapons to the on-guard position. A squad leader on the left lifted his arm in a signal to the command group; they were entering the rice paddy. All down the line squad leaders' arms went up. I walked out of the sparse reeds and there, spread out in front of me, was the biggest, widest rice paddy I'd seen in my young life. That paddy seemed at least a mile across, but the distant tree line, marking the canal and the village, was too distinct for that to be true. I could see the thatched walls and roofs of the huts, thin streamers of smoke rising from cooking fires, grayish-white against the dark green of the trees, fences of split bamboo behind some of the huts.

Crack! Bam! Instinctively, I dropped to a crouch. The familiar sound of a round passing nearby, then the report of a weapon was followed by two more. To our left, a sentry had spotted us and fired a warning. The village came to life. Black-clad figures tumbled out of the huts, paused to look out at the advancing troops, then dove back inside. The strikers gave out a terrifying howl, like a pack of wolves, and the line broke into a slogging run toward the village, the strikers stopping only to fire and then rejoin. . . .

The black-suited VC reappeared, carrying weapons and gear. Scattered shots whistled above our heads, but the VC were running. Wait! What the hell? They were going the wrong way. The bastards were going the wrong way! Toward the canals, not the forest!

The VC had elected to retreat toward the more distant sanctuary to the northeast, ignoring the forest and leaving our ambush useless. Tinh was shouting to the company commander, while platoon leaders and squad leaders encouraged the strikers, who at this point really needed no encouragement. The VC were running; it didn't matter to the strikers that they were evading our carefully laid ambush and might escape. All that mattered was that the VC were running and the strikers were the hunters.

Our right flank swept ahead, trying to cut the VC off. The backblast and spray of water to my right front marked a 3.5[-*inch bazooka*] gunner firing a round toward the VC. Seconds later a plume of . . . smoke climbed from behind the trees as the white phosphorous hit.

[*The CIDG took the village and paused to search it. Lieutenant Tinh spoke of setting up an outpost here. When the strikers began to withdraw toward Tan Phu, they not only encountered harassing fire, they realized a guerrilla column was moving to block their retreat, and eventually they ran into a Liberation Front unit deployed to fight. The erstwhile hunters became the prey. Running to escape their pursuers, Lieutenant Rowe became exhausted, hurt his ankle, and fell in a ditch, but pushed on. The CIDG became increasingly disorganized. As ammunition ran short, their discipline broke down. Rowe found himself among a handful of his Green Beret comrades.*]

Rocky stepped ahead of me, taking the lead for our tiny group of Americans. He hadn't gone more than five or ten meters when an automatic weapon fired from our right, and Rocky sagged, then dropped with a low moan. Oh shit, no! Not now! I started toward Rocky's crumpled shape and started to kneel. A muffled *whump* to my front, a spray of stinging hot water, and a huge fist slamming me backward. I sat there, up to my waist in water, the smell of burned black powder in my nostrils, my eyes refusing to focus. Everything was a multicolored haze. Sounds were coming from the end of a long, long tunnel. Everything was so far away. I'm dead. The thought stood out in the gray fog that was my mind. I'm dead.

Slowly the haze began to clear, things roared into focus as I squinted, then slid back into a confusing mess when I relaxed. I'm not dead. This thought was as positive as my first evaluation. I began to think again as my vision became clearer. I could see Rocky now. He hadn't moved. Check yourself out, I ordered mentally. "Yes, sir," I replied.

[*Rowe discovered a grazing thigh wound. He crawled to Rocky, Captain Humbert "Rock" Versace, an intelligence specialist visiting Tan Phu who had come along for the operation. Versace had several wounds. Rowe pulled Rocky out of the way and began bandaging him. At the final turn of the last bandage, a guerrilla fighter burst through the reeds behind them.*]

"*Do tay len!*" came the sharp command.

I tied the bandage and slowly turned my head. There was the muzzle of an American carbine and behind it, the Vietcong. I stood up and two VC pulled my equipment harness from my shoulders, grabbed my arms, and quickly tied them behind me, once at the elbows, once at the wrist.

"God bless you, Nick."

"God bless you too, Rocky."

"*Di!*" They threw me down the path.

[*Taken prisoner, Rowe was shuttled around a succession of hides and NLF camps for sixty-two months. He endured harsh treatment, sicknesses, near starvation, and despair. On Christmas Day 1968, shortly after Lieutenant Rowe saw an order for his transfer to a higher command, which he believed marked him for liquidation, he was found by helicopters from B Troop, Seventh Squadron, First Cavalry, of the First Cavalry Division, who were on the hunt for enemy to take prisoner but found Rowe instead. Rowe would be one of very few American prisoners actually liberated by military action during the war. Rocky Versace was executed by his captors in late 1965—and awarded the Medal of Honor in 2002. Another A-23 Green Beret captured that day is still missing in action.*]

SAIGON DAYS

George W. Allen
Saigon Station, Central Intelligence Agency
South Vietnam, June 1964–June 1966
George Allen was one of America's premier Vietnam experts, tracking this developing conflict, variously for the Army, the Defense Intelligence Agency, and the CIA, since 1954. When the agency opened a small analytical shop right in

Saigon, Allen was a natural for the assignment and knew most of the key players.
He spent two years reporting, crisscrossing the country, and escorting VIPs on
their inspections. It was the very time when President Lyndon Johnson's decision
to commit ground troops transformed the American war into full-scale combat.
Allen's memory of a tragic incident in Saigon is representative of many that oc-
curred during this period.

I . . . had an opportunity to observe . . . the progressive Americanization of
South Vietnam. Aside from the bomb craters and destruction, even more
visible was the spread of American bases and depots. . . . I witnessed the bur-
geoning of huge American bases at Da Nang, Qui Nhon, Nha Trang, Pleiku,
Bien Hoa, My Tho, Long Binh, and Cam Ranh Bay. I observed the spread of
American and Vietnamese "fire bases." I saw elements of the American 25th
Division disembarking from giant jet and turboprop cargo aircraft at Pleiku,
many of them having flown nonstop from their home base in Hawaii; an
entire brigade with the bulk of its equipment was airlifted into Pleiku in just
two weeks. I saw the queuing up of . . . cargo vessels [*at*] Da Nang, Qui Nhon,
and Cap St. Jacques—as many as 35 ships at each location [*waiting*] to tie up
for unloading.

Also evident were the scores of hilltops flattened to accommodate fire
bases, countless acres of land cleared around U.S. bases to provide open
fields of fire . . . and hundreds of miles of defoliated terrain along roads and
waterways to deny cover for potential Viet Cong ambushes. The impact on
the economy of the crater-filled rubber plantations, paddy fields, and stands
of hardwood trees was incalculable. It was rare after the mid-1960s to make
a two-hour flight . . . without witnessing a B-52 flight or one or more tactical air strikes, or a formation of a dozen or more helicopters lifting troops
into combat, or columns of military vehicles moving along roads or across
open fields.

I . . . observed at ground level—as I had at Tarawa during World War
II—the debris of war; the death and mutilation of soldiers and civilians in the
towns and cities; villages being rocketed and bombed because someone there
was thought to have fired at an aircraft passing overhead, the villagers fleeing
into nearby fields, wailing and flailing their arms helplessly. . . .

Vietnam was altogether disheartening and demoralizing for nearly everyone who experienced it. One was never far from the war, even in the heart
of Saigon. Terrorist bombings, mostly targeted at American-occupied facilities, including civilian restaurants, were frequent. When dining out, one
acquired the habit of consciously looking about for suspicious packages or
satchels before ordering a meal. When an explosion was heard, conversation turned to speculating about its approximate location and likely targets

in that area. On many nights we were awakened by the rumble of American medium tanks en route from the docks through the city to the military camps in the countryside. One watched from rooftop vantage points many a spectacular display by American aircraft dropping flares to illuminate areas of enemy activity just beyond the outskirts of Saigon; these were often followed by helicopter gunships and aircraft bombing and strafing. On more than one night, ARVN helicopters circled continuously low over Saigon as troops participated in an attempted coup maneuvered through the streets. One learned to steer clear of throngs of anti-government demonstrators parading through the streets, hastening into the safety of air-conditioned quarters to escape the clouds of tear gas.

Early one dark morning in 1966, while breakfasting before going to MACV to attend a predawn rehearsal of the intelligence staff's briefing for General Westmoreland, I heard a small explosion from the direction of downtown, followed by small arms fire. Shortly thereafter, at MACV headquarters, there was a flurry of activity and excitement generated by reports of an "attack on the Brinks BOQ" by a Viet Cong "armored" vehicle. A firefight was continuing with terrorists. . . . I was forced to make a slight detour en route to the embassy to avoid driving through this action. As I passed the scene two blocks away, I saw tracers from . . . automatic weapons, and several American military jeeps with M-60 machineguns racing to that area. The firefight continued . . . almost an hour before quieting down.

The episode had started with the explosion of a "bicycle bomb," parked by a Viet Cong terrorist across the street from a U.S. military bus stop. When a passing cab driver gunned his engine to get out of the way, his jeep was fired upon by guards at the Brinks Hotel across the street. Guards at another U.S. military billet down the street fired back, believing they were being fired on. . . . Soon there was a continuing fusillade as dozens of armed Americans exchanged fire with one another. Passersby in the early morning rush hour were hit. A large dump truck carrying civilian laborers crashed into a light pole alongside the Brinks, and a dozen or so unarmed women in the back of the truck were killed—this was the enemy "armored" vehicle rumored to have been in the "attack". . . . By the time it was all over, two dozen civilians had been killed, and as many more wounded. No "enemy weapons" were found, no terrorist bodies. The lone terrorist who had parked his bicycle had apparently gotten safely away. . . . [A]t lunchtime . . . driving through traffic still jammed by the incident, I managed to count 147 bullet holes in the front end of the dump truck that was still lodged against the light pole. . . . It had been several hours before anyone [got] close enough . . . to see the bodies of the dozen women laborers who had bled to death.

LOST INNOCENCE

Judith Drake
USO visitor
Saigon and elsewhere, 1965
Oklahoma-born actress Judith Drake played behind Mary Martin in the inter-national production of the musical Hello Dolly, *which was brought to Vietnam to entertain American troops during 1965. The show staged in Saigon and at a number of U.S. airbases. Crews made a documentary film depicting the experi-ence that was released in February 1966. Judith Drake never attained major star-dom, but she pursued a career as a supporting actress on stage and in television. This poem captures Drake's impressions of the war zone at that time.*

Vietnam 1965

A sea of olive green
Covering the floor
Hanging from the rafters
Sitting on the hill outside.

110 degrees radiating from
The roof of the very steel,
Very grey, very hot hangar.

Mildewed costumes that
Never dry
Blue clothed wounded in
Bandages with faces that
Match the color of the hangar.

Steel mesh curtains across
The windows of our bus
Rifled guards outside our
Doors and windows.

Small arms fire in the distant hills
Seems like the 4th of July from our roof.
Fireworks, only for entertainment

Stomach cramps
Vomiting
Weakness
The food and water are not
From Oklahoma.

This market gives forth a
Sickening stench

Unlike Sears.
Women and babies
Babies and women
Five year old hustlers with
Candy bars and shoe polish.
Home is six inches on the curb

THE POST EXCHANGE (PX)

Captain Fred L. Edwards Jr., USMC
MACV intelligence (J-2) staff
September 1966
Captain Edwards had had passing experience of South Vietnam when, as Marine detachment commander aboard the aircraft carrier Bonhomme Richard, *he made a familiarization tour to help him orient pilots for combat missions. Anxious to do an actual tour of duty, Edwards finagled with personnel officers and arrived in August 1966. A short stint on the top Marine intelligence staff ended when Edwards was detailed to MACV, where he worked for a unit that funneled unusual information from all over South Vietnam direct to the high command. Edwards kept a diary. In Saigon he needed to obtain household items to live independently in the city.*
The local market offers very little that is worth buying, and what it does . . . is prohibitive. . . . For example, tailor-made suits of dubious quality and workmanship are on sale for $60 to $80. The same types of suits can be bought for $30 to $40 elsewhere in the Far East. Shoes are on sale for about $8, but they are made mostly of cardboard. The leather parts have been tanned with urine, and smell like it.

Even if the merchandise was a good buy, servicemen presently are under a continuous curfew, except when traveling to and from American installations. So the only shopping choice is the Army-run PX. Buying at the PX helps staunch our gold hemorrhage.

Today is Sunday, and my "weekend off" starts at [4 *p.m.*]. Since the PX doesn't close until [*eight*], today I will do some much-needed shopping. Because of losses and other results of mismanagement, prices at the PX are scandalous. I write this because officers of all services who were here when the Navy ran the housekeeping chores for Saigon have complained to me that everything fell to pieces when the Navy left. . . .

An Army officer told me that MACV is called "the only Unified Command in the Army." I believe this when I enter a barn-size store in the compound called "uniform sales." The barn is almost filled with Army clothing. One bin the size of a horse-trough contains a jumble of Navy and Air Force items. Marine Corps? Sorry about that.

When I left the States, I expected to wear dress shoes only on the flight to Vietnam and the return . . . so I brought only one pair. Because of daily rains I need an extra pair . . . to give . . . each a chance to dry. Wouldn't it be simpler for the MACV headquarters staff to live in tents outside the city and wear field uniforms with jungle boots?

I find a pair of Army enlisted shoes (they come only in "normal, narrow, and wide" widths) which will have to do. $8.40 for these, which sell for $5.00 in the States, but at least I have a second pair of shoes.

And now on to the main PX building, where I sort through a dozen pairs of wash-and-wear civilian trousers on the shelf. The pair I wore from Oceanside to Travis Air Force Base has long since been frayed and filled with holes. I find [*one*] within my size range, and snatch it, regardless of color or price.

Outstanding! I have a new pair of civilian trousers! I have found no U.S. Navy rank insignia (to wear in place of the Marine Corps ones I also can't find). And I've found no ribbons of the type I rate. But I have a pair of trousers that do not have holes. War is hell.

I search out the beer sales room and buy one of my three authorized cases per month. I notice that beer and soft drinks sell for the same amount per case. I then go to liquor sales, where I buy one of my three authorized bottles. [*The situation with the post exchanges, plus scandals with NCO clubs, diversions from which also fueled the South Vietnamese black market, continued to worsen until PX corruption became a delicate matter between the United States and South Vietnam. Two U.S. generals were demoted and several senior NCOs went to trial in these scandals, which became a subject of congressional hearings. In a huge report released in November 1971, the Senate Permanent Investigating Subcommittee found widespread fraud and abuse in the system.*]

THERE BE TUNNELS!

Sergeant Stewart Green
B Company, First Battalion, Sixteenth Infantry, First Infantry Division
Phu Loi, January 9, 1966
Areas north of Saigon were dotted with Liberation Front strongholds, some of them notorious as "war zones." These had been headaches ever since the French war. Determined to blunt the enemy's momentum, MACV laid on a massive effort, Operation Crimp, to clear away the guerrillas. From the fabled "Big Red One," which at the time had just two months in country, Lieutenant Colonel Robert Haldane's First Battalion, Sixteenth Infantry took part in the sweep,

starting with a helicopter move to Phu Loi. His battalion's mission lay in a
stronghold known as the Ho Bo Woods. For two days Haldane's men patrolled
but encountered nothing more than occasional sniper fire. On his radio net the
commander overheard exchanges revealing that American and Australian units
elsewhere had been finding the enemy in tunnels. On the third day Haldane
decided to retrace his unit's steps, specifically searching for tunnel entrances. One
was soon detected. This discovery marked the beginning of tunnel warfare, a
new type of fighting in Vietnam, which evolved its own tactics and terminology,
starting with "tunnel rats," the brave men who accepted the extreme dangers of
being first into a newly uncovered tunnel. Sergeant Green of Bravo Company was
among the first GI tunnel rats. Green had no idea that this Ho Bo Woods tunnel
formed part of an extensive network that stretched down to Cu Chi and included
Liberation Front command centers and other elaborate facilities. This extract is
from the fine history of the tunnels of Cu Chi by British journalists Tom Mangold
and John Pennycate.

Platoon Sergeant Stewart Green, a slim, wiry 130-pound NCO, hunched
down to relax. Suddenly he leaped up cursing. The country was full of scorpions, huge fire ants, and snakes, and he had just been bitten on his backside, or
at least assumed he had. But as he searched the dead leaves on the ground with
his rifle butt, ready to crush his tormentor, he discovered the bite had come
from a nail. A further, gingerly conducted search disclosed a small wooden
trapdoor, perforated with air holes and with beveled sides that prevented it
from falling into the tunnel below. The first tunnel had been found.

Haldane ran almost gratefully toward it, but as he stood at the entrance he
realized that there were no training manuals to tell him precisely what to do
next. When the battalion had trained for combat back at Fort Riley . . . the
program had not included . . . tunnel warfare. The lessons of the stunning Viet
Minh victory at Dien Bien Phu, if studied, had not been digested. . . .

Stewart Green volunteered to explore the tunnel he had uncovered with his
behind. He leaped in and, with Haldane's encouragement, others joined the
platoon sergeant [*in*] the black depths. The men penetrated a short distance
and found hospital supplies, which were brought up and handed to the unit's
S-2 (intelligence officer), Captain Marvin Kennedy. As Kennedy was analyz-
ing the packages . . . he suddenly heard shouts; he turned and was astonished
to see the tunnel explorers shoot out . . . in breathless haste. Stewart Green was
last out, sweating and covered in dirt. He told Kennedy he had found a side
passage . . . and had suddenly stumbled on some thirty Viet Cong soldiers,
who he could see in the dim light of a candle one of them was holding, which
the Communists had rapidly extinguished. Captain Kennedy, delighted that
he had some thirty enemy trapped under his very feet, called a Vietnamese
interpreter and ordered him to return to the tunnel with the unfortunate

Stewart Green and order the enemy to surrender. The two men reluctantly went back down. Their mission lasted all of a few minutes and they returned embarrassed and empty-handed. Green explained . . . that the interpreter had actually refused to talk to the enemy. The captain quizzed the interpreter, who balefully informed the American officer that he had to "hold his breath" in the tunnel because "there was no air" and he would have "died if he had started to talk." From a military rather than a medical point of view, that last statement might have been extremely accurate. [*Colonel Haldane improvised, dropping smoke grenades into the tunnel, then tear gas. Further exploration led to growing realization that this tunnel was nothing but a small part of a huge network. Tunnel warfare had begun.*]

FIRE ON THE WATER

Lieutenant Commander Don Sheppard
River Division Fifty-One, River Patrol Flotilla Five, Coastal Task Force 116
Bassac River, February 1967
Commander Sheppard arrived on his birthday—though the day was confused by crossing the international dateline. This was Sheppard's first war and he was thrilled—Sheppard had only recently forgiven the World War II Germans and Japanese for giving up too soon for him to fight. A destroyer sailor, he volunteered for riverine forces to get in the action. Sheppard was in the training program at Mare Island when he was pulled out—before he had ever seen a river patrol boat (PBR)—to replace an officer reported as having been killed. With typical Vietnam panache, the supposedly dead river division commander met Sheppard's helicopter at Can Tho. He learned many lessons very quickly. One was relating to the Vietnamese, who had assigned a sergeant as chief of a small group of ARVN soldiers supposed to interface between the Americans and Vietnamese boatmen, villagers, or troops.

I sent for Sergeant Thanh. "Sit down, Sergeant Thanh. What is your sergeant rank? I see no stripe."

He hesitated. "I am equal to a staff sergeant, Thieu Ta."

"Thieu Ta?"

"Thieu Ta, Major . . . Thieu Ta."

"No, Sergeant Thanh, U.S. Navy lieutenant commander."

"Yes, sir, Thieu Ta," he answered, and I guessed that was that.

Sergeant Thanh sat across from me, rubbing his hands nervously.

"Sergeant Thanh, I am new here. Commander Strum told me that you were a very good man, and that you helped him a lot. Will you do that for me?" He nodded yes, answering that Thieu Ta Strum was a great man.

"How long will you be assigned here?" He didn't seem to understand. "How long will you stay here at Tra Noc to help the PBRs?"

"As long as Thieu Ta wants me here and as long as my men and I can do job for you. Policemen not so good—sometimes Thanh had to have good talk with them."

"Where does your family live, Sergeant?"

"I have no family, Thieu Ta. VC kill two years ago in Soc Trang. I join army and have not been back since. No family, Thieu Ta."

"How about your men?"

"They are all from Soc Trang. They do not like VC. They work for you and I work for you."

"Sergeant Thanh, I must be very honest with you. I have no experience with river warfare. I have always been on ships in the ocean. I know nothing about this type of fighting. Will you help me learn?"

"Thieu Ta," he started, then hesitated. "Thieu Ta, I have never known an officer to say he does not know something. Many Vietnamese officers know nothing but they act like they know everything. Many people die because they are ignorant and will not ask if they do not know. Thanh will help Thieu Ta as best I can."

[*A commonality of Commander Sheppard's Vietnam experience is that he was thrown into the middle of a situation to learn on the job. It was also true that Americans left while the Vietnamese stayed behind. For officers the transitions were even starker, since they were typically pulled out for reassignment after six months. As for the mission, Sheppard's two sections—each of a dozen PBRs and sixty-five sailors—were hardly enough to block Liberation Front forces from crossing the Bassac, especially as they kept to the deep center channel. They operated from an anchored landing ship tank (LST) off the mouth of the river, which avoided enemy attacks but also lengthened the time necessary for them to reach any combat position. Commander Sheppard, guided by Sergeant Thanh, tried to make up for weakness and distance by befriending villagers along the river. He helped the villages with aid and tried to get more action for his PBRs. Chagrined, Sheppard watched his first big firefight from shore while supervising a base transfer. Soon enough his moment came, at Khem Bang Co, a canal separating two islands the NLF—and the Viet Minh before them—had dominated since the 1950s. This firefight began with a sampan evading PBRs, which triggered rules of engagement.*]

We were fast approaching the junk. The fire was getting heavier. A machine gun found us; its bullets, like angry wasps, zinged toward us. We kept up a steady stream of fire. Gun barrels grew red as round after round flashed onto the breach.

The cover boat was catching hell. We had taken the enemy by surprise— they were ready for him. He was taking a beating.

"SLOW DOWN! Bryan, wait for Fern" I barked. There was the junk, only fifty yards from us. Our guns kept the Viet Cong pinned down. Our grenades and bullets shattered the hull, tearing it to shreds.

"C'MON! C'MON!" I shouted uselessly to the cover boat. I knew he couldn't hear me.

The Viet Cong overcame their confusion, and the sporadic fire grew more accurate, more intense. I couldn't stay here long. "HURRY . . . goddamn you, Fern. HURRY!" I had stepped in front of the bull. How do I get out of this one?

Romeo Two caught up fast. When he was two hundred yards astern, I yelled, "HIT IT! GET THE HELL OUTTA HERE!" Our PBR jumped ahead but was still too heavy to get on step.

As Fern passed the junk, all his guns concentrated on it. It erupted in a violent roar, catapulting wood, guns, men, and smoke high into the air. It had been loaded with ammunition, or fuel or explosives. It didn't make any difference—we destroyed it. Romeo Two had scored!

The junk, now five hundred yards astern of us, burned beautifully. My eyes and throat smarted from the acrid fumes of smoke and gunpowder. My gunners frantically rearmed their weapons. The Viet Cong guns had stopped. We throttled back. Maybe the battle was over.

[*That would have been too much good fortune. Moments later enemy .51-caliber machine guns opened fire from both banks. Front troops were between the Americans on the canal and safety on the Bassac. Sheppard had no idea what lay ahead of him in the canal or even if it was deep enough to float his boats, but he had no choice. The canal narrowed so much the radio antennas whipped the branches of trees. Finally the Americans escaped. With this baptism of fire, Commander Sheppard began to wean his command away from complaisance.*]

THE WORST DAY OF HIS LIFE

Lieutenant Joseph W. Callaway Jr.
C Company, Second Battalion, Sixtieth Infantry, Ninth Infantry Division
Tan Tru, April 14, 1967
Among the most notable contrasts in the Saigon–Mekong area was the fact that the war raged at full intensity only a few miles away. Staff officers, reporters, and others often commented on how they gathered at rooftop bars in Saigon to see and hear battles in the distance, but for those GIs in the field, Saigon could have been on another planet. Lieutenant Callaway led a platoon assigned to a district of Long An Province, only about twenty-five miles from the South Vietnamese capital. He led with such distinction that just one of Callaway's grunts died while

he held command. That happened on a really bad night when the company commander, Captain Daniel F. Monahan, and the unit's artillery observer also perished. The dead infantryman, Bruce McKee, was someone Callaway had brought out when the company deployed from Fort Riley, Kansas, where the lieutenant had promised parents he would take good care of their sons. What rankled the most was that all this resulted from friendly fire.

Dan Monahan was one of the best men I have ever known. We worked together only seven weeks, but in the environment of South Vietnam it was more like a year, and we got to know each other well. Dan was a burly, bearlike man with an elfish twinkle in his eyes, who constantly tried to make me laugh. . . . Although he said I was too serious and worried too much, he always showed great confidence in my judgment. We would still be good friends today had he lived.

Dan's daughter, Maureen, was born a few days before he was killed. . . . He was concerned about our upcoming combat mission, and as we sat in his base camp tent one night a few days before his death, he specifically asked me to get him out if he was wounded. He also ordered me to take over . . . if anything happened to him, even though I was outranked by Lt. Larry Lawrence, who . . . had no field experience. . . . Dan clearly wanted me in charge if he had to be medevaced.

Late in the afternoon on the fourteenth, after Dan selected the company night defensive perimeter, I argued with him over the location and configuration. We were in the dry season and set up in cracked, concrete-hard rice paddy terrain. A river made a snakelike loop around the entire area, including our position. It also made an identical loop about half a mile downstream. We called this region south of Tan Tru the "testicles."

There was dense undergrowth choked with nipa palm and mangrove swamps adjacent to the riverbanks, and high ground in some sections, where a few Vietnamese hootches were located. I was uncomfortable with the defensive alignment because we were essentially on a peninsula that was accessible to the Viet Cong, and it gave them a number of convenient escape routes. I was very uneasy, almost apprehensive. The Viet Cong could infiltrate a major force into our area quickly. We were almost challenging them to come after us. . . .

Our company defensive perimeter was set up . . . behind the dikes in a middle section of the rice paddy. We dug large but shallow foxholes. . . . The deeper we dug the damper the holes became. The water table was shallow in this area, only about twelve inches down. We got wet just sitting in the holes. The troops not on watch slept outside their foxholes on the dry, hard surface of the rice paddy and behind the surrounding eighteen-inch high dikes.

Dan set up night ambush patrols in the adjacent wood lines to cover the easy river access routes on each side of the peninsula. We had open fields of fire and artillery support on call, so Dan said there was little cause for concern. He may have been ordered to establish the night defensive perimeter in this location by battalion headquarters. . . . He wanted to take some pressure off the exhausted troops, who had been in the field nine of the last ten days. . . . I wish I had argued harder.

At approximately [*10 p.m.*], we began taking sniper fire from the wood line in the 3rd Platoon's area on the opposite side of the perimeter from my position. I was lying down with my back on the ground, looking straight up at the stars, and listening to Dan and Lieutenant Gray call in an artillery fire mission on the sniper. This was Lieutenant Gray's first real nontraining fire mission, and Dan was helping him. It was fortunate for me that I didn't go over and try to help Lieutenant Gray. Again the difference between life and death was often only a matter of luck. . . .

Suddenly, a tremendous lightninglike flash and deafening explosion filled the dark sky. A large piece of shrapnel whistled past about four feet over my head and struck the ground within earshot. . . . It was deathly silent for about thirty seconds, then everyone started desperately calling for a medic. Someone was hit in my corner foxhole position. . . . [*Specialist Four Peter Nero, the best medic in the company, was unable to save McKee, and then was summoned to help Captain Monahan, whose chest had been torn open and who drowned in his own blood. There was no helping the artillery observer, the top of whose head had been completely taken off.*] It all happened so quickly. In one instant they were all dead, and there was nothing I could do to change the painful losses.

ENEMY COWBOYS

Captain Fred L. Edwards Jr., USMC
MACV intelligence (J-2) staff
Saigon, June 1967
A month before his return to the United States, Captain Edwards noted the latest city security scare. It seemed unbelievable, but in that war many things were. The Hondas referred to here were motorbikes, not automobiles.
The latest fad among the VC in Cholon comes right out of our western movies. A Honda driver who is reckless and whom we might call a "hot rodder" in the States is called a "cowboy" in Saigon/Cholon. He might even wear a hat that resembles a sombrero, and attach a picture of a cowboy on a bronco to his rear license plate.

The VC went one step farther and started shooting from the saddle. At least three of them did. The name of the game was for the boy driver to carry a girl passenger who could shoot a pistol. As the innocent-appearing couple on the

Honda went past an American, the girl would shoot, then the driver would speed away. They got two Americans this way. Excellent aim. And they got away. The Americans didn't.

We speculated a great deal about this topnotch female marksman.

Eventually, during a routine police check of an apartment near the Hong Kong BOQ, three VC males were apprehended. Documents found there disclosed that they were the assassins.

The real name of the game was that, each time there was a "mission," one of them would take his turn in rotation dressing like a female and riding as passenger. Another would drive. And the third would stay home.

[*Another Saigon spectacular, apparently carried out at least twice during 1967–1968, was to car-bomb the volleyball court at a different American BOQ. At one time U.S. personnel in Saigon were authorized to carry weapons, but after some Americans, firing from a rooftop bar into the street, intervened in a nighttime shoot-out between police and unknown persons, the permission was revoked.*]

PACIFICATION

Lieutenant Richard Taylor
Division Advisory Team Seventy-Five
My Tho, September 1967

Arriving during the summer of 1967, Taylor was detailed to advise the South Vietnamese Army (ARVN) Seventh Infantry Division. His advisory team was the direct descendant of that led by the legendary John Paul Vann in the early days of the war. Taylor's field assignment was to the Second Battalion, ARVN Eleventh Infantry, part of a task force with another battalion of the regiment plus a ranger unit that operated throughout the division area and sometimes worked in conjunction with the U.S. Navy's Mobile Riverine Force. When not in the field Lieutenant Taylor tried to help ameliorate the social and economic challenges of Vietnamese life—what the U.S. Army called "civic action"—which lay at the heart of pacification. Taylor's experience illustrates the difficulties that made U.S. pacification in Vietnam so problematic. Corporal Thanh was the Second Battalion communications chief, who hailed from the Da Nang area and learned his English selling sodas to American soldiers. Liberation Front guerrillas murdered his father to make an example, in front of Thanh and his mother, so he "hated the Viet Cong with an intensity that was unseen in most other Vietnamese soldiers." Thanh lived in a one-room wooden shack in the NCO housing area in our compound with his wife and three children. He regularly invited me to his home to meet his family, and one day I finally accepted. His children were happy to see an American guest, and I enjoyed meeting them. I believed I could help these enlisted families, especially the children, and I wrote my parents about it. [*Taylor described conditions among the ARVNs and encouraged his parents to start a drive among their church congregation.*]

This was an opportunity that appealed to my parents. They contacted members of their church and soon boxes of clothing, toys, and treats arrived in the mail. I placed Corporal Thanh in charge of distribution, which enhanced his status in the community and made me feel better, too. Maybe, I thought, I can make a difference here after all. I wondered if I should have become a foreign missionary or a Peace Corps volunteer instead of a warrior.

Thanh explained how much good could be done with twenty bags of cement, so I set about getting it. I tried the U.S. Army-Navy base at Dong Tam but found that cement was seldom used for construction. I finally learned that most cement was distributed through the Agency for International Development (AID) and placed directly into the hands of the province chiefs for community projects . . . so I made a courtesy call on the province chief.

The Dinh Tuong province chief was an ARVN colonel who lived in palatial splendor in the largest residence in My Tho. I worked my way through his staff until I found myself sitting outside his office, and then I waited patiently for two hours before being escorted in to see him. In less than two minutes he heard my case, refused me, told me to mind my own business, then dispatched me by the back door. I had no recourse . . . but the little pedagogue had angered me. I refused to give up. Through other channels, I managed to get five bags of cement from Pacific Architects and Engineers in exchange for several homemade Viet Cong flags, which I decorated with a little duck blood to increase their value.

While I was on my humanitarian mission, [*Captain Bobby*] Hurst was on a venture of his own. He met an American nurse . . . at the civilian hospital at My Tho. We cleaned ourselves up as well as we could and drove our old jeep to Edna's apartment, which was comfortable compared with our austere living arrangements at Binh Duc. Situated in an old French colonial hotel, it sparkled with marble floors, large, shuttered windows, and genuine furniture. Edna actually served wine with dinner while she told us of the two little orphans, Oanh and Kim, whom she was thinking of adopting. Hurst invited her to bring them out to Binh Duc for a visit. I didn't understand why they would want to go there, but I kept my mouth shut. Maybe Hurst, a bachelor, was interested in Edna, or maybe not.

Midway through dinner Edna was talking about the orphans. "They're so special. When I get the papers". . . .

She froze in mid-sentence, her eyes opened wider. "Was that what I think it was?"

I hadn't heard it before, but then I did. "Mortars. Sounds like one-twen-ties." We could clearly hear plinking as the rounds popped from the 120mm mortar tubes outside town.

"Got a bunker?" asked Bobby. "We only have half a minute."

"No!" Edna's face was pale.

"Under the table," Bobby ordered.

We crawled under the table, lying flat on the cool marble floor.

My mental clock told me we had a few more seconds before the impact. I scrambled back out. "Anyone want your wine?" I asked as I grabbed my wineglass. Without waiting for a reply, I handed the other two glasses under the table, before sliding underneath.

We listened as the large mortars exploded in the city environs.

"I wonder if I could help them hit the province chief's house?" I wondered out loud. No one else fully appreciated my meaning or sincerity.

SEALs AND PRUs

Lieutenant Robert A. Gormly, USN
Detachment Alpha, SEAL Team Two
Binh Thuy, June 1968

The Navy operated its own elite commando force, which had the stature of the Army's Green Berets or LRPs, the Marines' Force Reconnaissance units, or MACV-SOG. The various formations each had their own specialized training and particular roles. For Navy SEALs (the acronym stood for "sea, air, and land"), typical missions were snatching prisoners, striking, or scouting. SEALs began working in South Vietnam in 1964 and expanded as the Navy sought a ground component to work with its Riverine Force. Bob Gormly was on his second Vietnam tour when he brought his SEAL platoon to Binh Thuy, replacing another unit being sent elsewhere. When he arrived, an intelligence program begun in 1967 to identify and hit the National Liberation Front's village infrastructure was being incorporated into the pacification program. This effort became notorious as Project Phoenix, under which each province was endowed with a Provincial Reconnaissance Unit (PRU), which tried to neutralize persons identified as NLF operatives. In the Mekong Delta area most PRUs were advised by, and often led by, SEALs. As platoon commander, Gormly ran his own SEAL missions and was responsible for SEALs assigned to the PRUs. Here he describes his broad experiences.

Some things had changed in Vietnam since my first tour. Making the rounds of the subsectors, I learned that as a result of the Tet offensive,

North Vietnamese Army (NVA) units were operating south of the Bassac River. There seemed to be more bad guys than when I'd left, and they were more aggressive. I also noticed that their activity had moved further away from the main river. Except for crossings, large units were seldom seen near the Bassac. We'd have to go further inland to get to the areas they considered safe. Except for the fact that we didn't target innocent civilians, we did in fact employ "terrorist" tactics against the VC and NVA—we terrorized them in their safe havens.

I also found out that the VC and NVA knew who SEALs were now— because we were making their lives difficult. When I got to Binh Thuy I heard a rumor that the VC high command (COSVN) had put a price on the heads of what they called "the men with the green faces." I was flattered. This was a sure sign we were hurting them. I went to the IV Corps [*naval intelligence officer*] to see if there was any truth to the rumor. He was surprised I hadn't heard. He said the COSVN was offering the equivalent of $10,000 for any SEAL officer captured. The bounty went down to about $8,000 for a captured enlisted man, and any SEAL was worth about $5,000 dead. Was this true? Who knows? No SEAL was ever captured, and we brought all our dead back with us.

The bounty talk changed how we went on liberty, but not much else. Can Tho, the largest city in the Mekong Delta, was a good place to go for a decent meal. I just made sure we didn't set any patterns. No insignia marked the green jungle fatigues we wore when not in the field. I didn't allow the troops to wear cammies except on operations. Out of cammies, we blended well with the rest of the Navy guys. Usually we wore civilian clothes to Can Tho. And although an edict had come out forbidding U.S. military personnel from carrying concealed weapons, I carried a concealed .38-caliber revolver in a shoulder harness whenever I left the base. I ordered the troops to do the same every time they went off base in civilian clothes. The ban on concealed weapons was a stupid regulation, probably started by some Saigon bureaucrat. It made no sense in a war zone.

Also new since my first tour was the full establishment of the Provincial Reconnaissance Units (PRUs). The "Phoenix" program, established to attack the Viet Cong infrastructure and just getting started when I left in June 1967, was now pushing ahead and achieving great success in the Mekong Delta. The action arm of the program, the PRUs, were being "advised" by SEAL enlisted. Each province in the delta had its own PRU, and with the exception of the one at Chau Doc, they were advised by SEALs. Most SEAL platoon commanders worked closely with PRUs in their operation areas—I was no dummy, I did too. The PRUs were for the most part former VC who had decided life was better on the other side. They knew what was happening in their area, and they always had more information than they could act on, so we often did operations they couldn't.

Because PRU advisers got lonely, being the only Americans in their units, I allowed each of my guys to go to a province for two weeks to work with the PRUs. It was all done unofficially, but it was good for the PRUs and it was good for us. Our guys came back with a wealth of information, and the PRU adviser had company. Another bennie for the PRUs was that we had priority access to the Navy helicopter gunships (Seawolves) attached to CTF-116. When we called they came fast and they were effective. When we operated in squad-sized strength with the PRUs they had that access as well, and it enabled them to take more risks.

However, because there were so many more NVA troops in the delta, I began to run a lot of platoon-sized operations. Not that we often had a full platoon—but ten shooters were better than six. We needed firepower. The enemy's situation had changed, but our self-proclaimed mission remained the same: to kill VC and disrupt their operations wherever and whenever we could. My old operating area was a more target-rich environment than it had been a year before. It was time to kick ass again.

AT THE MICHELIN PLANTATION

Sergeant David Connolly
Eleventh Armored Cavalry Regiment
north of Saigon, "War Zone C," August 1968
One of the heaviest mobile units, the Eleventh Armored Cavalry "Blackhorse" Regiment was equipped with ACAVs, or armored cavalry assault vehicles, either M-113 armored personnel carriers with extra armor and platform-mounted heavy machine guns or M-551 Sheridan light tanks. Sergeant Connolly wrote these two poems to mark one of the Blackhorse's intense combat actions. Connolly later extended his tour to serve as a wireman with the 101st Airborne Division in I Corps. The Michelin Plantation had been a notorious hotbed of revolution back to the colonial period, when labor unrest peaked in 1927; again a decade later; and in the French war, when Viet Minh forces contested the Michelin fiercely. Starting in late 1965, when an ARVN regiment was badly battered by Liberation Front forces in the plantation, its reputation as a sinister NLF stronghold was confirmed. Connolly's incursion took place almost three years later.

Into the Michelin Rubber Plantation

It's the second week of August and I'm not sleeping well at night.
Some years I don't remember, but I just know I'm not all right.
Then it comes and smacks me, where it was I learned to mourn;
and my dreams bring me back the Michelin, and I'm awake to greet the dawn.

"Got two companies of ARVNs," the Lieutenant said;
"we are going to kick some ass.
Every ACAV's up to speed, loaded with ammo and gas.
We've got two tanks and the Recon jeeps. Man, this will be a breeze."
Us Boonierats, we heard "ARVNs" and our blood began to freeze.

What we got was Bouncing Betty mines, mortars and rockets by the score,
from the NVA battalion they said was a company just hours before.
But we hunkered down. We held our ground. "Stand to! Lock and load!"
We fought shoulder to shoulder; the ARVNs, they never showed.

There were burning tracks all over the place and the screams of dying men.
Things looked really bad for us, really bad, and then,
we heard the sounds of incoming rotors and knew we'd be okay,
but too many of the boys I went in there with wouldn't live to see another day.

One Huey was full of officers, there to count the damaged trees,
so the US could pay off Michelin and they tried to ignore our pleas
to get our wounded out of there; see, they had a mission to fulfill.
I still taste the bitterness of that day; you can fucking bet I always will.

Aftermath: The Michelin

The wounded went out first,
then the dead.
The few of us,
who hadn't left in body bags
or on stretchers,
we set up picket lines
as far out as we had the balls to.

The Armorers and Engineers,
flown in after the battle,
they stripped the ACAVs
that weren't still burning
of their guns and ammo,
or began to wire or rig
their hulks to be blown or lifted out.

When they were done
collecting or detonating
Uncle Sam's property,
the next wave of choppers
came in and evac'd
the Armorers, the Engineers,
the tracks, the guns and the ammo.

The eleven of us, the survivors,
we were left there alone,
to wait for the next flight of ships.
I remember shaking
my nineteen-year-old head,
thinking, you have got to be shitting me;
they're going to leave us here,
something you're probably doing
right now.

HELICOPTERS TOO

Specialist Five Al Sever
116th Assault Helicopter Company
Dau Tieng, December 1968

Specialist Sever had transferred to the 116th, the "Yellowjackets," in order to fly helicopters instead of fix them. He was assigned to a ship, Smokey, *that laid smoke to cover helicopter assault landings and so was stuck with the slicks. Sever wanted to be in the action with the gunships.* Smokey *had an installed minigun, but the crew could never make it work reliably enough to change the chopper's status. Sever's longing remained unfulfilled.*

On a mission near the Michelin Rubber Plantation at Dau Tieng, we sat around on Smokey watching our gunships constantly coming in to refuel and rearm. Whatever they were doing, it had to beat sitting and waiting. Late in the afternoon one of the gunships landed with engine trouble and wasn't able to take off, so our crew thought we'd be able to join the guns for the rest of the day. No such luck; the mission was almost over and we'd all be going back to Cu Chi soon. The broken-down gunship would be carried back to Cu Chi by a large Chinook helicopter, as Dau Tieng was not considered a safe place for a helicopter to sit overnight. The VC would probably hit it with mortars or recoilless rifle fire; in fact, some of the infantry sitting around our slicks had just been showing us pictures they had recently found in some bunkers near Dau Tieng of female 75mm recoilless rifle teams. Our [*aircraft commander*] told our fellow platoon members to throw their gear on Smokey and hang around with us for a ride to Cu Chi. "No thanks," was their reply.

They would rather ride in a relatively clean slick than our smelly, oily smokeship. Even our own platoon didn't want to associate with us. Laughing, they headed for the clean slick and the ride home. They never made it. Fifteen minutes after leaving us, the slick fell out of the sky next to an artillery [*fire support base*]. There were no survivors. Witnesses on the ground saw a black puff of smoke come out of the passenger/cargo area moments before the slick fell to the ground. Black smoke meant that a hand grenade might have exploded inside. Maybe it was a lucky hit with an RPG. We would never know.

THE GOODS ON TET II

Lieutenant Colonel William C. Haponski
First Squadron, Fourth Cavalry, First Infantry Division
Di An, January 6, 1969
Colonel Haponski had six months in country when he assumed command of the First Squadron of the Fourth Cavalry in January 1969. With that unit, and as chief of staff (and, previously, operations officer) of the Blackhorse, the Eleventh Armored Cavalry, Haponski became intimately acquainted with the Michelin Plantation. But one of his greatest moments occurred on his very first day with the First Squadron, Fourth Cavalry, in a security operation that illustrates both the realities of village security in Vietnam and the serendipitous nature of intelligence breakthroughs in the war. It all happened as a consequence of the zeal of South Vietnamese district chief Major Nguyen Minh Chau, formerly a Vietnamese Marine officer, who wanted to catch the enemy who had ordered a marketplace bombing in the district. He also wanted vengeance—the Liberation Front chief for his own district, who used the pseudonym Bay Phuong, had tried to assassinate Chau, giving him his fourth war wound. Bay Phuong would be meeting a senior cadre at Tan Dong Hiep hamlet to prepare for attacks during 1969's Tet holiday. Chau got the tip from an ARVN sergeant who had infiltrated the NLF as a double agent. He wanted Americans to help cordon off the hamlet, search it, and arrest the cadres, since his 150 local militia were insufficient for the task. Colonel Haponski summoned B Troop of his squadron and initially supervised from a command and control helicopter hovering above. Under existing standard procedures in a joint venture, the American leader would command. His chopper was swooping above the hamlet and the Vietnamese RF/PF troops were jumping from their trucks when Haponski saw an enemy shooting at his chopper.

I had slipped a round into the M-79 and snapped the barrel shut. I knew the blocking force was far enough off to the north, and my cav had not yet linked up with it, so there was an open pocket, safe for fire. [*The colonel's grenade missed, and the chopper's door gunner did also, but this was good because Haponski and Chau wanted to capture the cadre, not kill him.*] The man below me was frantically running, stumbling, tearing off his clothes as he went. I couldn't imagine why he was doing this, but I fired again and this time the impact was closer. Three or four of the district soldiers were getting close to him as he stumbled again, fell, lost his rifle, got up and ran some more. I could see we had him. . . . [*Haponski radioed Chau's American advisor to get the district troops to cease fire.*] I didn't want the man or us getting shot. Then the soldiers closed in. One of them raised his rifle, and I thought, don't shoot him. Don't shoot. As we landed I couldn't see well what was happening other than the district forces were now dragging the man back toward the hamlet. My God, he is dead, I wondered. But through the high grass blowing apart in the rotor wash, I could see the man kicking his legs.

[*Colonel Haponski caught up to Major Chau as he questioned the prisoner.*] Chau ordered the man's hands to be unbound, and two soldiers helped him to his feet. Another brought out a crude wooden table from one of the thatched huts and two rickety chairs and placed them in the shade of some palms. A Vietnamese beer, Ba Muoi Ba—"33"—appeared from somewhere along with a partial pack of American cigarettes. An RF soldier popped open the beer and put it in front of the prisoner. Chau nodded, and the man tentatively reached out, took the bottle and drank, slowly, looking suspiciously at Chau, and then, growing bolder and showing his thirst, he took several gulps. Chau talked quietly, and the man responded in short phrases.

[*The cadre at first asserted he was a simple soldier. But he had a phony ID card and a rather large amount of cash for a soldier. Later he admitted to being a junior officer with the rear services group supporting the NLF's elite Dong Nai Regiment. Then the man conceded that Bay Phuong had been present and possibly wounded. That led to an intensive search.*]

Sergeant Chu, my jeep driver Bob Towers who had gone with me in the helicopter, and I fell in with one of Chau's PF squads, and I watched as they went carefully up to each house, systematically, and searched inside. I went into the houses . . . with them. When I had first done this six months ago in 11th Cav I had felt self-conscious and guilty like the intruder I was. By now it was second nature. Chau's men seemed thorough, looking for tunnel entrances or other hiding places, and I was watching carefully for anything . . . suspicious. What we found inside, though, was only the common dugout section in the floor into which the family would crawl whenever there was danger. The soldiers . . . [*looked*] under piles of wood, poking long sticks or sections of antenna or rebar rods down into suspicious places to see if they would penetrate into an opening. Nothing. Thus began for me what I came to term our Di An period of "poking around back yards with sticks." This time it was with district forces. Many other times it would be with my American soldiers or a combined team of RF/PF and my guys. At some point that afternoon . . . I must have wondered what kind of mission this was for a cav squadron. An infantry company . . . could have just as well taken the place of my cav troop. In fact . . . an infantry company was much better suited for the task. . . . M-16s were handier in hamlets than 90mm guns.

[*Bay Phuong was never found, though it was learned subsequently that he had been wounded in the legs and had hidden in a loft with a grenade. Later he would be killed, after betrayal by an angry girlfriend. Colonel Haponski heard that his prisoner called himself "Lieutenant Hoang," but he disappeared into the III Corps prisoner cages. Years afterward, Haponski learned from declassified records that "Hoang" had actually been the former commander of the Dong Nai Regiment and was a colonel and the assistant chief of staff of the COSVN subregion. He was questioned intensively by MACV and the CIA beginning on January 16. The Americans were desperate to know if COSVN planned a new Tet Offensive.*]

His real name was Nguyen Van Sau, aka (also known as) Chin Lap. Most enemy cadre knew one another by their aka's and not so often by their real names. After careful examination of all US records and enemy histories I could find, in the context of the circumstances involved, I conclude that Lap at no time under interrogation came entirely clean, and he managed to hide his real rank of lieutenant colonel, a very prestigious rank indeed in an army whose ranks were usually about two grades lower than ours . . . for comparable duties.

From him MACV got . . . confirmation of earlier reports . . . of the entire structure of Subregion 5, locations, personalities, missions; and tactical information such as methods of rocket attack, design and construction of base camps and bunkers.

CIA expert Merle Pribbenow . . . says, "The guy you captured was a real 'honcho,' as we used to call them." The interrogation report says that before being sent to the Dong Nai Regiment he worked for the Combat Operations section of COSVN Military Headquarters.

. . . Lieutenant Colonel Nguyen Van Sau had been in Saigon for several days, planning the attack on Saigon for the 1969 Winter–Spring Offensive, and was on his way back to Subregion 5 Headquarters when we captured him. He ultimately gave the full details of SR-5 and the Dong Nai Regiment's planned actions which, in addition to destruction of Saigon's main radio station, included dropping the Newport Bridge, the critical six-lane structure linking Saigon and the huge [*South Vietnamese*]/American Bien Hoa/Long Binh complex . . . which supported allied operations throughout South Vietnam.

MEKONG BLUES

Lieutenant Colonel David H. Hackworth
Fourth Battalion, Thirty-Ninth Infantry, Ninth Infantry Division
February 1969

At the time perhaps the Army's most-decorated soldier, Colonel Hackworth returned for a second tour in a battalion command, thereby clouding his career chances. "The Hack" found conditions much changed since his time in the Central Highlands in 1965, but quickly set out to solve the problems that entailed. Almost legendary as "Mr. Infantry" in the Army, Colonel Hackworth made it his business to protect his men's lives by giving them the training and tactics to survive. At a time when division commander Major General Julian Ewell was pulling out all stops to push up body counts, Hackworth blotted his copy book by refusing to play. Though reports were that a bounty had been put up for any soldier who killed ("fragged") Hack, after a short time that offer was withdrawn. Hackworth's GIs began calling themselves the "Hardcore."

There was no sense in showing this sorry outfit I was in a state of shock. It wasn't just that the CP group slept on cots inside tents, that they had folding chairs and stateside footlockers, portable radios, and plastic coolers filled with beer and Coke at their fire base out in the field. More than that, it was that they had portable toilets, too (the result, I was told, of my predecessor's philosophy that "for a penny more you can go first-class"), and apparently were blissfully unaware that just nearby their troops were crapping on the ground and not even covering it up. In the sanitation department, the fire base was in even worse shape than the [*South Korean*] defensive position we took over at the Punch Bowl in Korea in 1953.

"It's a pussy battalion," General Ewell had explained when I first arrived In Country, "and I want tigers, not pussies," he'd gone on to say in his characteristic Oklahoma drawl. But he'd gotten it wrong. With the 4th Battalion, 39th Infantry it was not a question of feline degree. As far as I could see, this unit was not even a military organization.

It was total disintegration. Throughout the fire base, amid the shit and the toilet paper and the machine-gun ammo laying in the mud, were troops who wore love beads and peace symbols and looked more like something out of Haight-Ashbury than soldiers in the U.S. Army. All were low in spirit and a few were high, especially on marijuana. There was minimum security. Few men carried or cared for their weapons—most had let them go red with rust as they strolled around without them. Grenades weren't taped, and when a unit moved out, most of the gunners wore their ammo Pancho Villa–style, the ideal way to guarantee an ammo jam sometime down the track, when dirty, dented cartridges were inserted into their M-60s.

The 4/39th's fire base was located in the Wagon Wheel, an [*area of operations*] so named for the five canals that converged there, which, from the air, looked like the hub and spokes of a wheel. The night before I took over . . . I sat up all night in the center of the base, back-to-back with Nev Blumenthal, who'd come along as my handpicked [*operations officer*]. Neither of us was game to sleep (if the VC attacked the battle would be over before it even began, with the position safely in enemy hands), so I spent the time discussing with Nev the things we'd have to do . . . and ruminating on how such disintegration ever could have occurred.

[*A few days after Hackworth's arrival, a new guy set up a Claymore mine facing his own position and killed himself, triggering it upon hearing something in the night. Hack ordered his troops to carry and clean their weapons and wear helmets, and introduced a few changes every day. New positions were dug, poor performers relieved, sanitation transformed. Hackworth began ordering more aggressive patrolling and ambushes. He did everything to give the men the sense they, not the enemy, were in control.*]

The bounty Bravo company put on my head, which ranged from eight hundred to thirty-five hundred dollars depending on whom you talked to, was also fairly easily dismissed. The first I heard of it was when General Ewell (of all people) got the word and came to warn me. He said he was going to insert some [*Criminal Investigation Division*] people into the company to ferret out the ringleaders. . . . Meanwhile he strongly suggested I ease up on the troops. I wasn't going to ease up and told the General so; besides, there was a simpler way to call Bravo's bluff. Before long we were conducting operations, and on one of them I found myself with fractious B Company, all of us approaching in a skirmish line a small enemy force in a clump of the Delta's ubiquitous nipa palm. A fight seemed imminent, and since my experience told me that soldiers in a firefight are generally too busy, too scared, and place far too much faith in their leader's ability to get them out safely to knock him off, I felt it was a perfectly unperilous opportunity (for me) to shit or get off the pot. So I moved up well in front of the advancing skirmish line, with my back an easy target for even the sorriest rifleman in Vietnam. And I was right. Thoughts of wasting the battalion commander were forgotten as the little fight heated up; working for a common purpose, we killed a few VC in exchange for not a single B Company casualty, and I don't think I heard much about a price on my head ever again.

[*This late-war Army intrigued Hackworth, in spite of his own traditionally "Airborne All the Way!" stance.*] Even when they pissed me off, I had to admit there was something I liked about the draftees who didn't want to be there and made no bones about it. I liked draftees in general, even with the attendant attitudes. Historically draftees have kept the Army on the straight and narrow. By calling a spade a spade, they keep it clean. Without their "careers" to think about, they can't be as easily bullied or intimidated as Regulars; their presence prevents the elitism that otherwise might allow a Regular army to become isolated from the values of the country it serves. Draftees are not concerned for the reputation of their employer, the Army (in Vietnam they happily blew the whistle on everything from phony valor awards to the secret bombings of Laos and Cambodia); a draftee, citizens' army, so much a part of the history of America, is an essential part of a healthy democracy. [*Henceforth Hackworth made it his primary mission to ensure that his men left for home in one piece.*]

SEVEN MOUNTAINS ATTACK WITH THE SOUTH VIETNAMESE

Captain Robert L. Tonsetic
Military Region Four Ranger Advisory Command
Can Tho, September 1970–May 1971
Tonsetic returned for a second tour as a seasoned veteran of the Vietnamese low-lands. In 1968 he had witnessed both waves of the Tet Offensive as commander of Charlie Company, Fourth Battalion, Twelfth Infantry of the 199th Light Infantry Brigade. That was around Long Binh and Xuan Loc, and in Saigon–Cholon during "second Tet." Now he went to the Mekong Delta as an advisor to the Biet Dong Quan (BDQ), the South Vietnamese Rangers. The Delta—Military Region Four—may have been the best-pacified section of the land, but Can Tho still showed signs of the tough fighting at Tet. The advisory unit sent Captain Tonsetic to the ARVN Forty-Fourth Ranger Battalion at Cai Rang. It was one of four South Vietnamese regular army (not montagnard "border ranger") units of this type in the region. The men wore elite "Black Panther" designs on their helmets, tailored camouflage fatigues, and red berets in camp.

The 44th Ranger battalion typically fielded about 400 men, but the number fluctuated depending on the casualty rate. . . . Each company was authorized a captain, but most were senior lieutenants. In the 44th, many . . . troops were ethnic Cambodians and easy to spot, since they tended to be slightly taller than the Vietnamese with somewhat darker skin. They also tended to have less Mongoloid eyes and wavy hair. Most were fierce fighters, and imbued with beliefs and rituals of their own, usually preferred to serve in the same squad with other Cambodians.

In accordance with their religious beliefs, most had tattoos on their chests meant to protect them in battle. When a Cambodian was wounded, he blamed the tattoo artist for a faulty design. There were also a number of Chinese. . . . Most came from the urban centers, such as Saigon's Cholon section, or . . . Can Tho. Even though Chinese families weren't eager to see their sons enter the army, they were in no position to resist—especially the ones who didn't have the money to buy their way out of the draft. As far as I could determine, there was no hostility between the diverse groups represented in the battalion.

[*Instead hostility festered among the leadership, between those who saw the Forty-Fourth's commander, Major Thi, as incompetent, favoring a senior lieutenant, a Cambodian; and those in the major's camp. The deputy American advisor, whom Tonsetic saw as reflecting short-timer attitudes, disliked Thi. Tonsetic himself, spending more time with the major, concluded Thi was a good ARVN officer. Not long after Captain Tonsetic's arrival the Forty-Fourth was alerted for an attack into the Seven Mountains area, against a pair of peaks known as Nui Ba Voi, controlled by the Sixteenth Regiment of the ARVN Ninth Division, which had a very poor reputation. Major Thi consulted with its commander at headquarters. ARVN artillery, Vietnamese and Australian air strikes, and U.S. Navy Seawolf gunship helicopters would support the attack.*]

Intelligence sources reported that a VC regimental headquarters and two infantry battalions were holed up in a labyrinth of caves and rocks in the two mountains. The attack was scheduled for the following night. A final helicopter reconnaissance was planned for the following morning, and we were invited to fly along. . . .

Based on enemy strength, the terrain, and the numbers of friendly forces, the chances . . . didn't look favorable to me. U.S. infantry tactical doctrine specifies that the attacker should have at least a 3 to 1 advantage in numbers . . . to ensure success. In this case, we didn't even come close. Given the nature of the terrain, the ratio . . . should have been even higher.

I asked the [*U.S. senior advisor to the ARVN regiment*] if ropes, grappling hooks, and other mountain climbing items—as well as flamethrowers to flush the enemy out of the caves—were available for issue to the Rangers. He said that he'd have to ask his ARVN counterparts. That didn't give me a warm and fuzzy feeling.

[*The following morning Thi and Tonsetic returned to the ARVN headquarters, where the captain asked the Sixteenth Regiment's deputy advisor whether his boss had requested the special equipment for the assault. The objective, Nui Ba Voi, had some near-vertical cliffs, and the ARVN Rangers had no training at all in mountain climbing.*] "Yeah, he did," Drinkwater replied. "The Regimental commander doesn't think you need flamethrowers. He said they were too heavy for the Vietnamese soldiers to carry, and besides, the regiment didn't have any on hand. They'd have to requisition them through Division, and that would take weeks."

I recalled an incident in 1968, when an NVA flamethrower detachment conducted an attack on a montagnard village near Dak To. The North Vietnamese had no problems carrying heavy flamethrowers. Now I began to understand why the 9th ARVN Division had such a poor reputation.

"Nice," I said sarcastically. "How about the ropes?"

"The regiment doesn't have any of those either," he answered, and then added, "Tell your battalion commander he might be able to buy or requisition some in town." [*Major Thi did no better on his end. He warned Tonsetic that the plan would fail and many Rangers would die. Thi wanted a B-52 bombing to soften up the enemy. Tonsetic passed along the appeal but knew there was zero possibility of it happening. The attack was timed for two in the morning.*]

Sheets of rain blew across the darkened landscape as the column of ACAVs turned off the main road and rolled south toward the Ranger assembly area. It was about 10 p.m. when the ACAVs arrived. . . . Major Thi's plan . . . called for two Ranger companies to [*march*] . . . while the remaining two companies and the headquarters group would follow mounted on the ACAVs. . . .

The column moved out at a crawl as the tracks churned through the glutinous mud of the swampland toward the final line of departure. The rain that had slowed to a drizzle began to pour . . . again, and Bui, my radio operator, offered me a corner of his poncho. The other forms on the deck of the ACAV were also huddled under their rain-soaked ponchos. A voice that spoke from a poncho beside me turned out to be an American sergeant. He [*was*] an NCO adviser to the armored cavalry troop, and we exchanged a few words over the roar of the engines.

The sergeant advised me in a fatherly manner, "Don't you go into any of them caves, cap'n. There's people went in there last year, and never came out." I could tell by the tone of his voice that he was well meaning and dead serious.

[*Captain Tonsetic thought of the Pacific island battles of World War II, when enemy-held caves had become meatgrinders for U.S. Marines. The bombing and artillery had no discernable impact, the troops became mired in mangrove, and the timetable was hopelessly set back. Once rock climbing did start, the enemy spotted the Rangers immediately and began tossing grenades down the cliff. Medevac helicopters were impossible in the swamp, and moving wounded aboard ACAVs was no substitute. The Forty-Fourth Rangers eventually gained a foothold in a saddle on the slope of Nui Ba Voi, then a position atop the cliff, but the "assault" turned into a monthlong siege. A quarter of the battalion was lost.*]

It was later determined that the Rangers entered one of the main entrances of the Mo So cave complex that housed the VC headquarters in the Kien Luong District. In addition to the main entrance, there were numerous small [*cave mouths*] located all over the mountain that were connected to tunnels leading to the inner recesses of the mountain. Therefore, the enemy was able to pop up in any number of locations . . . to engage the Rangers at will. Under the cover of darkness it was not difficult for small groups of enemy soldiers to escape . . . and similarly it was possible for reinforcements to slip undetected into the cave-riddled mountains.

The caverns were large enough to accommodate a VC regiment, and the caves were fully stocked with enough supplies and food, including live poultry and hogs, to sustain a large force for months at a time. The cave was recognized as a historic relic in April 1995, by the Vietnamese Ministry of Culture and Information. A modern-day tourist guide now invites [*visitors*] to take "a two-hour, five-kilometer walk through shrimp breeding grounds, paddy fields, and canals to reach the magnificent cave." . . . We had no idea of the size and complexity of these caves in 1970, but the Communists certainly did.

5

Eye Corps

THE FIRST MEDAL OF HONOR

Captain Roger H. C. Donlon
Special Forces Detachment A-726
Nam Dong, July 6, 1964

Roger Donlon had knocked about in the 1950s, though the uniform kept beckoning. Donlon enlisted in the Air Force and served in the Army, and gained—and regained—admission to West Point, though he resigned from the Corps of Cadets in the spring of 1957 fearing he could not hack it. Donlon finally made second lieutenant through Officer Candidate School in 1959. He joined Special Forces in 1963. Detachment A-726 formed at Fort Bragg in January 1964. A dozen Green Berets, each with an important military specialty, cross-trained in other ones; the team drilled together and deployed as a unit to South Vietnam through Tan Son Nhut. They were sent to Camp Nam Dong in the Central Highlands. Also there was Gerald C. Hickey, an anthropologist whose forte was knowledge of montagnard tribal cultures.

Donlon originally planned to spend only a few weeks at the camp, preparing montagnard local forces, and then move on to set up another border camp. Nam Dong would be defended by three companies of Civilian Irregular Defense Group (CIDG) strikers, led by a six-man ARVN Special Forces team. A sixty-man Nung unit worked directly for the Americans. Donlon and his Green Berets had less than two months in country when NLF guerrillas attacked Nam Dong. One day earlier, a dispute over a girl in the village had triggered a nasty fight between montagnards and Nungs, who now distrusted one another. Captain Donlon worried the ruckus had been started by a Liberation Front agitator infiltrated in one of the CIDG units. At a meeting that night, leaders tried to talk out the problem. The enemy attacked shortly before 2:30 a.m., when a white phosphorous mortar shell exploded on the roof of the mess hall. Buildings crumpled under bombardment, one after another. The NLF assault troops overcame one of the CIDG companies in the outer works and reached the inner perimeter. Donlon had several wounds but refused treatment and continued leading the defense.

Then the heavens lit up. It was just after four. Finally, the flare ship was on top of us. Welcome as the illumination was, that flare ship brought more than light. Now we had a glimmer of hope. And the VC must have seen the flare ship as a bad omen. Little by little the intensity of their firing diminished. They knew an air strike almost always followed a flare ship. It seemed they might be withdrawing, but they were far from through with us.

Then, in front of Brown's pit, a loudspeaker crackled. We heard a man speaking excited, high-pitched Vietnamese. The sound was incredibly strange amid the booming battle noises and it startled both sides into silence. Not a shot was fired as the voice carried across the camp.

Dan turned to Tet, the interpreter. "What's he saying?" he asked. Tet was shaken.

"He say lay down weapons. VC going to take camp and we all be killed!"

Dan, Gregg, and Brown were unimpressed.

"Over my dead body," Dan declared.

"We'll lay down our weapons when we're too dead to pick them up," Gregg added.

The silence continued. Not a shot was fired in that sector. The silence was unnerving. And all at once it was broken again by the loudspeaker. This time the voice was in English.

"Lay down your weapons," it urged. "We are going to annihilate your camp. You will all be killed!"

"Can you pick it up by the sound?" inquired Gregg.

"I think so," Brown said. He was adjusting the elevation on his mortar. "Where do you think it is?"

"Over here," Dan answered, pointing.

[The Americans loosed a barrage of a dozen mortar rounds. The NLF answered with their own mortars, including ones seized from the montagnard strikers. But the Americans held on and lobbed shells into the area where the loudspeaker seemed to be when it spoke again. The enemy fire slackened. Captain Donlon began to run to the positions where his team members were isolated. Two Green Berets had been killed. The mortars, which had had as many as 350 rounds available when the battle started, were almost used up, some down to a dozen apiece. Finally Donlon permitted his wounds to be treated. The Americans began

looking for enemy bodies and stragglers. They almost blew out one position where they saw movement but realized the supposed enemy was a goat. Finally a relief column arrived from another CIDG camp.]

At eight o'clock we were treated to a wonderful sight. *Trung-uy* Lu came marching down the road and into the camp with about seventy-five of his men. He had brought them through the valley from Khe Tre. When he reached my cinder block CP he found me sprawled under the parachute canopy, looking like an oriental potentate.

[*Captain Donlon was awarded the Medal of Honor for his defense of Nam Dong.*]

THE BEGINNING OF THE SURGE

Lieutenant Philip R. Caputo
C Company, First Battalion, Third Marine Regiment
Da Nang, March 1965–July 1966
Lieutenant Caputo landed on China Beach with the initial waves of U.S. Marines sent to South Vietnam. The Marines, packed for an amphibious assault, were met by Vietnamese girls with strings of flowers and newsmen with cameras. This beginning to their war became only the first oddity of the Vietnam experience. At the time their mission was merely base defense—President Lyndon B. Johnson had yet to decide to commit Americans to ground combat. But the rules of engagement changed, literally under Caputo's feet.

America seemed omnipotent then: the country could still claim it had never lost a war, and we believed we were ordained to play cop to the Communists' robber and spread our own political faith around the world. Like the French soldiers of the late Eighteenth Century, we saw ourselves as the champions of "a cause that was destined to triumph." So, when we marched into the rice paddies on that damp March afternoon, we carried, along with our packs and rifles, the implicit convictions that the Viet Cong would be quickly beaten and that we were doing something altogether noble and good. We kept the packs and rifles; the convictions we lost.

The discovery that the men we had scorned as peasant guerrillas were, in fact, a lethal, determined enemy and the casualty lists that lengthened each week with nothing to show for the blood being spilled broke our early confidence. By autumn, what had begun as an adventurous expedition had turned into an exhausting, indecisive war of attrition in which we fought for no cause other than our own survival.

Writing about this kind of warfare is not a simple task. Repeatedly, I have found myself wishing that I had been the veteran of a conventional war, with dramatic campaigns and historic battles . . . instead of a monotonous succession of ambushes and fire-fights. But there were no Normandys or Gettysburgs for us, no epic clashes that decided the fates of armies or nations. The war was mostly a matter of enduring weeks of expectant waiting and, at random intervals, conducting vicious manhunts through jungles and swamps where snipers harassed us constantly and booby traps cut us down one by one.

The tedium was occasionally relieved by a large-scale search-and-destroy operation, but the exhilaration of riding in the lead helicopter into a landing zone was usually followed by more of the same hot walking, with the mud sucking at our boots and the sun thudding against our helmets while an invisible enemy shot at us from distant tree lines. The rare instances when the VC chose to fight a set-piece battle provided the only excitement; not ordinary excitement, but the manic ecstasy of contact. Weeks of bottled-up tensions would be released in a few moments of orgiastic violence, men screaming and shouting obscenities above the explosions of grenades and the rapid, rippling bursts of automatic rifles.

Beyond adding a few more corpses to the weekly body count, none of these encounters achieved anything. . . . Still, they changed us and taught us, the men who fought in them; in those obscure skirmishes we learned the old lessons about fear, cowardice, courage, suffering, cruelty, and comradeship. Most of all, we learned about death at an age when it is common to think of oneself as immortal.

BATTLE JOINED

President Johnson initially accepted a MACV strategy of defending "enclaves" around major U.S. bases while holding some forces (principally the Army's 173rd Airborne Brigade) in readiness to respond to emergencies. But the U.S. command pressed for—and received—permission to patrol outside the enclaves, then operate as far out as they could be covered by artillery. In late July the president approved full-scale operations and ordered major ground forces to South Vietnam. The first major battle took place southeast of Chu Lai in mid-August. It resulted from Operation Starlite, a Marine effort to break up a suspected attack on Chu Lai base by the Liberation Front First Regiment. Otto J. Lehrack, though not a participant here (he commanded a Marine company in 1967–1968), has written the most extensive investigation of Starlite. He notes that Marine radio intelligence units first discovered and located the NLF and then describes the origin of the operation, which began on August 15, 1965, with U.S. Marine commander Lieutenant General Lewis L. Walt and his ARVN opposite number.

[*Major General*] Nguyen Chanh Thi, the ARVN commander of the I Corps Military Region, had urgent news for General Walt. A captured VC, Thi told the Marine commanding general, revealed that the notorious 1st VC Regiment was massing south of the Tra Bong River, near the village of Van Tuong, on the Van Tuong peninsula, in preparation for an assault. . . . Numbering about two thousand troops, this force was to attack and destroy the main [*Marine*] air station facilities and aircraft while local guerrilla forces pinned the defenders in place with relatively minor but noisy and potentially dangerous activities. The defector was a seventeen-year-old named Vo Thao, who had been abducted by the VC. . . . After a few weeks of training Thao had been assigned to the 40th Battalion of the 1st Regiment. Typifying many Vietnamese, he had relatives on both sides of the fight. His paternal uncle was a member of the VC, three other uncles worked for the ARVN or the Americans, and his stepfather was an ARVN sergeant. When his Viet Cong commander refused permission for Thao to visit his family, he had filled out false leave papers and deserted.

General Thi told Walt that he thought this was the best, the most reliable, information he had received about the enemy during the entire Vietnam War. Walt considered his reaction and, apprehensive about leaks . . . asked Thi not to share this information with other Vietnamese commanders. Walt then set out for Chu Lai to discuss the situation with his commanders on the ground there.

General Nguyen Chanh Thi's information was only partially correct. Part of the [*NLF*] regiment, the 40th and 60th battalions, and elements of the 45th Weapons Battalion, were at Van Tuong. The remaining units were . . . farther south. And the VC force was not preparing for a regimental-size attack on Chu Lai. The enemy commanders had already decided to limit attacks on the Marine base to small, highly mobile, and suicidal sapper attacks.

[*General Walt sent several Marine battalions against the NLF and in a two-day action claimed to have killed more than six hundred enemy. Some fifty-four Marines died in battle. The Americans believed they had destroyed the enemy regiment, but a few months later the Marines encountered it again, then again after that. From early 1966 the First Regiment belonged to the Second Division of the People's Liberation Armed Forces and later the Vietnam People's Army. It was never destroyed. That was Vietnam.*]

ENVY

Captain Alex Lee, USMC
Headquarters staff, Second Battalion, Seventh Marines
Qui Nhon, August 1965
Both other battalions of the Seventh Marines participated in Operation Starlite. Captain Lee's unit, the Second of the Seventh, did not, working instead as a

special landing force, a Marine unit prepared for contingency amphibious operations that could storm ashore at any point along the Vietnamese coast. The Marines were unhappy to be left out.

The news from the north during late August of 1965 caused the men of 2/7 some bitter feelings. From the *Stars and Stripes* newspaper, we learned of our being left out of the war being fought by the other battalions of our parent regiment. . . . During August, a large Marine Corps formation, one that included our two sister battalions, 1/7 and 3/7, conducted Operation Starlite on the Batangan Peninsula in Quang Ngai Province to the south of the Chu Lai enclave. Reports came to us, perhaps greatly enhanced before their arrival, that six or seven Marine battalions had been committed and that more than one thousand Viet Cong had been killed by the Marines who had taken part in Starlite. The operation was hyped in some elements of the press as a great victory and as proof that the tide was turning in the war. Our officers and enlisted Marines were still naïve enough to be a bit sad when they learned that the units to the north were getting solid contacts with the Viet Cong. BLT [*battalion landing team—the acronym for a unit assigned as a special landing force*] 2/7 Marines were somewhat disheartened to find that when a large, tough operation had been conducted, we had been left, under Army command, to languish as guardians of our little area around Qui Nhon.

DOUBT

Captain William Van Zanten, USMC
Third Battalion, Seventh Marines
Chi Lai, August 1965
Captain Van Zanten, in contrast to the Marines of 2/7, was actually with one of the battalions in Starlite. Like Captain Lee he was then with battalion staff and had a bigger picture of the action—and like the Marines at Qui Nhon he came away convinced that Starlite had been a victory. But as a direct observer he had a different perspective on the cost of this operation.

We spent a few days back aboard the USS *Iwo Jima* after OPERATION STARLITE while the Marine Corps decided where to drop us on a more permanent basis. Initial intelligence reports indicated that the operation had been a clear victory for the good guys. The hard core North Vietnamese troops had been hurt real bad. What remained of their fighting force had scattered to the wind. . . . Marines from Okinawa and Camp Pendleton spoiled their party. We beat them to the punch. Surely this nonsense would soon be over and we could get back to our life in the real world. . . .

We wanted to be pampered a little and by Navy standards it sort of worked out that way. If we felt like a hamburger at 2:00 a.m., we got one. If we wanted laundry done, it came back in three hours instead of three days. Somehow meals were bigger and loaded with more good meat and potatoes than usual. Was this a coincidence or were they trying to tell us that they knew we had done a good job? Who cared? We accepted the newly found hospitality without complaint. The troops got treated well too. . . . We were fully aware of the negatives involved in our recent experience, even though we didn't necessarily want to face them head on. We talked little of our wounds. In a strange way, we didn't realize we had anything to worry about.

We should have been frightened beyond description. Our battalion had lost 27 marines to wounds and death. This was about 1.5 percent of the troops aboard this floating war machine. Anyone could live with those odds. One in a hundred. No problem. What we didn't calculate, of course, was that over a year of combat, this projected to a 100 percent casualty rate. Those kind of numbers had no meaning, even in our wildest imagination. No one expected a full year of action.

What we also did not, at least openly, discuss at great length was a more telling statistic, one that struck closer to home. Our battalion, like all battalions in the Corps, had 27 lieutenants on the payroll. In four days we had lost two of our 27. We had lost 8 percent of our company-grade officers in four days. This should have been extremely concerning. Dale Rutherford had taken a bullet between the eyes. Very dead. Phil Avila caught a bullet in his left leg. He lived. The leg didn't. . . . Dale and Phil were part of an eight-man group of lieutenants that I lived with prior to leaving for Vietnam. There had been eight of us who shared two adjoining houses on a beautiful, sand-lined beach a mile north of San Clemente. Serious bachelor pads. Serious bachelors. Twenty-five percent of our little fraternity in San Clemente was now dead or maimed for life. Twenty-five percent in four days. This had better be a statistical blip.

THE OTHER SIDE OF THE HILL

General Tuan was emblematic of many Vietnamese who fought the Americans. He had joined the Viet Minh in 1945 and fought, first the Japanese, then throughout the French war, rising steadily through the ranks. He lost one eye to Japanese shrapnel and took a bullet in the leg from the French. At forty he began fighting Americans. Here Tuan is interviewed by William Broyles, who as a young lieutenant with the Americal Division had fought Tuan's troops west of Chu Lai in 1969.

"When the Americans entered the war, we spent all our time trying to figure out how to fight you. The incredible density of your firepower and your mobility were our biggest concerns. I myself saw the first B-52 raid. . . . I will never forget it. Twenty-six B-52s dropped their bombs four kilometers from me. It was horrible. Two or three hectares of land were simply blown away. Our losses were huge.

"And then after several battles—near Chu Lai south of Da Nang, in the Ia Drang Valley in the Central Highlands—it came to us. The way to fight the American is to grab him by his belt . . . to get so close that your artillery and air power were useless. The result was interesting—our logistics forces, which were farther from the Americans, took greater losses than the combat units."

I asked him about the Tet Offensive of 1968, when the Communists launched attacks on cities and towns throughout South Vietnam in an enormous surprise attack that was the turning point of the war.

"In the spring of 1967 Westmoreland began his second campaign. It was very fierce. Certain of our people were very discouraged. There was much discussion on the course of the war—should we continue main-force efforts, or should we pull back into a more local strategy? But by the middle of 1967 we concluded that you had not reversed the balance of forces on the battlefield. So we decided to carry out one decisive battle to force LBJ to de-escalate the war." . . . I asked General Tuan if they knew they had won the war in 1968.

"Yes and no. Nixon began the withdrawal, but Vietnamization was a difficult period for us, at least in the beginning. Your years here [*referring to Broyles's own time in country*], 1969 and 1970, were very hard for us. The fighting was very fierce. We were often hungry. I was the division commander, and I had no rice to eat for days."

A FIGHT OF THEIR OWN

Captain Alex Lee, USMC
Headquarters staff, Second Battalion, Seventh Marines
Tam Ky, December 1965
Even in their role as a special landing force, the Marines of 2/7, who had complained of being left out of Operation Starlite, soon found their way into battle. In the two-week-long battle Lieutenant Colonel Leon D. Utter's battalion made a heliborne assault into an LZ, dubbed "Spruce," which then served as base for a large task force to chopper into action throughout the area. Utter's battalion fought the People's Army and NLF wherever they found them. This would be called Operation Harvest Moon. With a few weeks of this they were near to exhausted. Captain Lee reflects on the campaign.

After another day of sloshing through the muck while remaining constantly vigilant against Viet Cong attacks, the lead elements of 2/7 arrived at National Route 1. . . . Movement east had been assisted by a fifty-foot bridge erected by the engineers over a large stream and the constant cover of helicopters and artillery, ready and willing to fire on any Viet Cong who popped up his head. As the troops finished loading up the trucks, mortar fire fell on the convoy. The 2/7 Marines and the helicopters returned a murderous level of fire, and the mortars ceased. . . . After that bit of excitement, the convoy of trucks returned to the Chu Lai enclave without incident.

Instead of another night in the rain, the Marines of Company F were sent on board an LST, the USS *Kemper County,* which was commanded by [*Lieutenant Commander*] Bill Stockton. On board the LST, the Marines . . . got a number of remarkable surprises. The sailors took their torn and muddy clothing and gave them dry clothes to wear while the torn field uniforms were washed and dried. The ship's cooks fed every Marine fresh food, all anyone could eat, the first fresh food the Marines had seen since July. The sailors slept in the passageways, giving their bunks to the tired infantrymen. The senior medical corpsman of the *Kemper County* came to [*company commander*] Captain Nolan the next morning with tears in his eyes. "I'm sorry Captain, I put half your company in the hospital with immersion foot last night." The unlimited good will of the men of the *Kemper County* has never been forgotten by the Company F Marines. As recently as a reunion in 1997, the men of Company F have feted the [*skipper*] of the *Kemper County* to offer their thanks for what he and his men did to renew the morale and physical well-being of the worn and weary Marines and corpsmen. On the morning of 20 December, Captain Jim Nolan put his entire command, all the men of Company F and its attachments who could be returned to duty, on two trucks. The trucks were not crowded.

As an operation, the conduct of . . . Harvest Moon left a great deal to be desired. Marine backpack communications equipment was deemed to be utterly unsatisfactory in the monsoon weather, and the radiomen . . . had clearly been the targets of the Viet Cong. Nine casualties—three dead and six wounded—were taken by the battalion communicators, a heavy toll. Lieutenant Colonel Utter noted that nothing worked very well in the rain and that having the Marines carry three days of rations was unrealistic when they were constantly moving over arduous terrain in the driving rain. He also noted that the casualty reporting system was not adequate . . . with some 2/7 casualties still not located seven days after . . . the operation. All that was known about those men was that they had been lifted out of the battle; where they had been sent to recover could not be learned. [*The battalion suffered ninety-five wounded and twenty Marines killed but many nonbattle casualties were not counted—on*

*one day alone fifty-one Marines left the battle area with noncombat injuries or
sickness, especially immersion foot.*]

COMBINED ACTION PLATOONS

Corporal Robert A. Beebe, USMC
C Company, First Battalion, Seventh Marines
Binh Nghia village, Quang Ngai, June 1966
*Complementing the big unit war was the village war of pacification. Many argue
that the struggle for the villages was in fact the more important. Certainly, in
guerrilla warfare, gaining the support of the people had to be a central aim. Many
tactics were employed in pacification. In I Corps the most innovative was the
creation of Combined Action Platoons (CAPs), in which handpicked squads of
U.S. Marines joined directly with South Vietnamese Popular Forces (PF) militia
to constitute joint units that had local knowledge plus the Americans' ability to
draw upon the larger resources of U.S. forces. The first of these CAPs formed in
June 1966 to defend Binh Nghia at the initiative of Major Richard Braun, an
American district advisor, and Vietnamese police officer Ap Thanh Lam, who
had taken the initiative to kill an NLF leader in his home village. The story of the
inception of the CAP program is narrated by Bing West, a young Marine officer
who became involved a little bit later. The first CAP worked in this village for
almost eighteen months.*

Braun's reputation for effectiveness attracted senior officers. In early June of
1966, Lieutenant General Lewis W. Walt visited Braun. Walt commanded the
Marines in Vietnam, a battalion of whom were working in Braun's district,
which was called Binh Son. . . .

Braun told Walt that the Marines would be more effective if they worked
with the Vietnamese instead of just beating the bushes on their own looking
for the VC. Walt asked for a specific recommendation.

"Well, General," Braun replied, "I'd like to see us try a combined unit,
a group of Marines and Viets who would eat, sleep, patrol and fight as one
unit—not two."

"If you had them, where would you put them?" Walt asked.

"There's a big village not far from here. It sits along a river which the Cong
use to move supplies. . . . As a matter of fact, it's just south of Chulai airfield.
The government forces were chased out . . . a couple of years ago. A platoon
of Cong live there regularly now, and sometimes a company or more come in
to resupply or rest."

"Why pick there to start?" Walt asked.

"I didn't, sir. The district chief did. He has this outstanding police chief who's being bad-mouthed by some of the local politicians. These pols make the mafia look like a bunch of Trappist monks. The district chief's afraid he will say the hell with it and transfer to another district. But his family's from this village and his mother still lives there. The district chief says he'll stick around if we make a play for the village. . . . " [*General Walt agreed to try the idea.*]

To the men of the 1st Marine Division who were stationed in the district, Binh Nghia was just another village. . . . If the Marines approached on a large-unit sweep, they would find no traces of the enemy. If they happened to pass through . . . on a small patrol, they would likely receive some harassing fire from distant treelines. The villagers were uncommunicative but not sullen. Among the Americans, Binh Nghia had no special reputation.

Still, when the call went out for volunteers to live with the Vietnamese forces in the village, the response was enthusiastic. General Walt had asked the commander of the Marine battalion in the district to select twelve men. The first rifle company polled produced over one hundred volunteers. The primary reason was comfort. For Marine riflemen, assignment to the village would be an escape from the routine harassments of duty. . . . Many thought they would be out of the dust or mud. They would sleep on cots instead of the bare ground. There would be no more jungles to hack through or mountains to climb—no more leeches, vipers, or trench foot. There would be no first sergeants barking at stragglers. Life in the village would be sweet and easy. Or so it was rumored.

General Walt had laid down two stipulations concerning the volunteers. First, they had to be seasoned combat veterans. That was not . . . difficult. . . . Second, Walt asked the battalion officers to send only men who could get along with the villagers. Major Braun had been emphatic on that point, and it slowed the selection procedure. It took eight days to pick twelve men. The officers were aware from their own surveys that over 40 percent of the Marines disliked the Vietnamese. The problem was particularly acute among the small-unit leaders—the lieutenants and sergeants—whose opinions had considerable effect on their men. . . .

The noncommissioned officer chosen to lead the volunteer squad was known to like the Vietnamese. His name was [*Robert*] Beebe and he was a career Marine . . . in the service for four years, although he was still a corporal. . . . Beebe was a scrapper and a stickler for alertness in the field . . . [*with*] another side. He disliked rules and details, and somehow he could not imagine himself making out pay rosters and guard rosters and equipment rosters. . . . The village volunteers thought they had the right kind of leader in Beebe. [*It turned out the Marines did sleep on the ground, had to construct a whole new police fort with the Vietnamese, and set out on a mission with Police Chief Lam that greatly affected the security status of Binh Nghia. They also set the standard for what became a vigorous CAP program, which was, however, continually viewed with suspicion by conventional-minded Marines.]*

ELEPHANT CHESS

Lieutenant Colonel William R. Corson
Third Tank Battalion, Third Marine Division
Phong Bac district, Quang Nam Province, fall 1966

The success of the early CAP experiments was replicated more widely. The units expanded to companies, first tried around Phu Bai. By early 1967 there were dozens of Combined Action Platoons throughout I Corps, and they were considered to have full combat capability, in the military jargon, "unit integrity," unusual for mixed groups of Americans and Vietnamese. So long as he headed III Marine Amphibious Force, General Walt was a strong supporter. At a certain point he asked Colonel Corson to take charge of combined action. The assignment resulted from Corson's own success with a different experiment using his Third Tank Battalion in Phong Bac district. Corson incorporated several elements in his approach. He tried to avoid giving any impression the U.S. troops were there to enforce landlords' demands for rent; he assumed what he called "hamlet nationalism," which acknowledged peasants' tacit approval for the NLF but tried to wean them away by substituting entrepreneurial values; cash could beat ideology. And Corson capitalized on the villagers' fear of hunger—greater than their fear of the Liberation Front. Dropping hand grenades into the fish pond, which suddenly yielded a huge catch (and profit), became a way to win political acceptance if not loyalty.

Initial rapport with the peasants of Phong Bac was established by utilizing an aspect of their culture never hitherto exploited by Westerners: the game of *co tuong*, or, as it is sometimes called, "elephant chess." Elephant chess is the most ubiquitous game in the world, being played by approximately 800 million Orientals. It is similar to draughts or conventional chess but it is still uniquely Oriental in origin. The Chinese, the Vietnamese, and the Thais all claim to have invented it, but regardless of where it came from, it is the single most pervasive activity in Vietnam. In any hamlet 95 to 98 per cent of all males over fifteen play it. "Elephant chess" is more than a game to the Vietnamese; it is a status symbol wherein skill in playing is considered a mark of a man's cultural prowess.

We therefore organized a *co tuong* tournament. . . . Each of the villages held a separate elimination tournament to determine its local champion, who would then compete in the championship held in Phong Bac at the time of the harvest festival. On the night of the festival some 1,200 persons came to watch the . . . match. The champion received . . . as his prize a $55 transistor radio which had status appeal as well as considerable monetary value. I presented [*it*], and the people were impressed by the interest we had shown in the game.

After the prize had been presented and the crowd was beginning to disperse, I quietly challenged the champion to a game. He was taken aback . . . but with some condescension agreed to the game. We began to play, and the crowd . . . to observe the Occident vs. the Orient. The game was interesting and went as planned—a draw. That night when the peasants returned to their homes they had a further item to discuss, and discuss it they did.

Prior to the tournament I had trained a dozen Marines who were assigned to the Civic Action Team in the intricacies of *co tuong*. After [*news of*] the tournament and the subsequent challenge match had filtered down through the hamlets, the marines went forth to play. . . . No matter where they played the game a crowd would gather and the barriers began to crumble. The Marines' challenges had to be accepted, for to the peasant a challenge at *co tuong* was a matter of face. At the *co tuong* table much was revealed about the opponent's personality and character, but most importantly the barriers of language and cultural differences were breached. . . . and the Marines were "in" the social structure of Phong Bac.

DOG AND PONY SHOW

Bronson P. Clark
American Friends Service Committee
Quang Ngai, February 1967

The CAP Marines and other units in I Corps were only one part of a large apparatus that struggled with issues of pacification with the goal, as the phrase (coined in the Vietnam War) went, of "winning hearts and minds." For the State Department pacification was the primary mission in Vietnam other than relations with the Saigon government; for the CIA it was the first or second priority of perhaps four. An array of private organizations that worked for simple humanitarian purposes—from Catholic Relief Services to the International Rescue Service, International Voluntary Services, American Friends Service Committee (AFSC), and others—indirectly contributed to the pacification program.

Meanwhile, at the same time, the large-scale military operations devastated the countryside, driving thousands of people from their homes into resettlement camps. In 1967 there were nearly three hundred thousand Vietnamese in these camps and five hundred thousand who had recently left them. A major inves-

tigation by a U.S. Senate Judiciary subcommittee in 1971 to 1972—when the pacification of South Vietnam was supposedly complete (and successful)—found hundreds of thousands of people still in camps. Official figures at that time showed 213,000 in the camps and about the same number "in the process" of being resettled. These were constantly floating numbers—and the statistics were massaged to minimize the problem. It was never solved.

Humanitarian organizations, among them the AFSC, were hugely concerned about the refugee situation. Bronson Clark, an electronics industry executive and AFSC board member who had gone to prison in World War II for his Quaker pacifist beliefs, visited South Vietnam in January 1967 to review AFSC programs. In Saigon he had several meetings with expert Bernard B. Fall, livid on refugees, who repeatedly called Clark's attention to those being generated by the big "Cedar Falls" and "Junction City" operations then in progress north of Saigon. Clark decided to see refugee camps in I Corps.

Our visit to Quang Ngai was memorable in every sense. Our early dawn Air America . . . flight to Da Nang was made in a plane holding 18 people, two Green Berets and the rest USAID types, mostly agricultural experts going up-country. It flew at 7500 feet to avoid ground fire. One USAID person said "I feel very safe with the Green Berets on one side and the Quakers on the other." At Da Nang we changed to a C-47 carrying . . . milk powder for Quang Ngai. We flew over the coast at 200 feet, seeing junks at sea for the last ten miles. Quang Ngai was in every sense a rural city, but its airport was an armed camp.

The Quang Ngai program had two parts, the Prosthetic Center and the Day Care Center. Two volunteers . . . helped . . . at the Prosthetic Center. Everyone else connected with this operation was Vietnamese. We witnessed the expressions of delight when Vietnamese could steady themselves on parallel bars and walk a few steps with a new prosthetic device. At the Day Care Center, it was good to see children separated for a brief time from the rigors of war, eating a proper lunch and beginning a pre-school education routine. . . .

Next, we visited some of the ten large regroupment camps, which I had lobbied so vigorously against in Washington, D.C. In one we talked to Phillip Thomas, a CIA operator who worked to instruct the Vietnamese on "how to live" . . . in this insufferable situation. He gave the standard justification for burning villages and rounding people up in these camps. Ironically, he could not stay in his own camp at night, nor could any other American, because the place was not safe.

[*Clark discovered that Liberation Front cadre circulated freely through the camps at night, and when he visited civilian hospitals, Vietnamese medical personnel told him that 90 percent of their patients were civilians. Only a few weeks after Clark's visit, Bernard Fall followed him to I Corps and died tragically, inadvertently stepping on a mine while with a Marine patrol.*]

ARC LIGHT

Lieutenant James J. Kirschke, USMC
H Company, Second Battalion, Fifth Marines, Third Marine Division
Con Thien, September–November 1966

Nestled up against the demilitarized zone (DMZ), Con Thien was among the bulwarks shielding South Vietnam from attack across the DMZ. In 1967 it was incorporated into a formal defensive barrier—and subjected to a lengthy siege by the North Vietnamese. But by 1966 it was already a place of deep suffering and steady attrition. The Second Battalion of the Fifth Marines held Con Thien for two months toward the latter end of the year, and for the last quarter of 1966 the Second Battalion of the Fifth Marines suffered some 425 battle casualties, over two-thirds of the strength of its field companies. Lieutenant Kirschke led an H Company platoon, with a standard strength of sixty-three men but typically numbering thirty to thirty-five Marines. Moreover, Kirschke's unit averaged four nonbattle casualties a day—everything from colds and bronchitis to trench foot, malaria, hepatitis, and scorpion or snake bites. And the monsoon rain was fearsome—ninety-seven inches in three months.

For several nights . . . B-52 strikes pounded the area just west of us where the southern line of the DMZ swung south. . . . On those nights the first sounds we heard were loud, buzzing noises as the planes approached. On the first night they came, as tired as I was I bolted awake. . . . Then they released their bombs, five-hundred pounders. Each strike seemed to deliver hundreds of the bombs, so for the duration of each attack the earth shuddered continually beneath us. The din was deafening. When I thought of the devastating effect the strikes could be having on enemy soldiers who might have been attempting to infiltrate, however, after the first night I found both the noise and the ground shaking . . . consoling. I believe I slept more soundly on the nights when the B-52s thundered in. Except for the night a five-hundred pounder was dropped by accident less than two hundred meters from our platoon "CP." . . .

On October 19, I received word from our CO that our company would be running an ambush along the "elephant trail" that night and that 3rd Platoon would be on the point while moving to the ambush site. The Marines in our battalion . . . called the track the elephant trail because Company F had seen evidence that the NVA had sent supply-laden elephants down it. . . . I arranged to have our guide, Sergeant Hoole . . . familiarize himself with the terrain during daylight hours.

Sergeant Hoole had an excellent terrain memory, but as always I checked his guidance . . . periodically with my luminescent compass dial. Several hours after our patrol had left Con Thien . . . we reached the trail. In the growing darkness Hoole signaled for us to hold up and [*beckoned*] me forward. When I approached, he whispered, "This is the elephant trail, sir."

"Are you sure?"

Pointing to a huge pile of dung on the deck at our feet, he said, "Yes, look."

Sensing on some level how he would respond, I said, "How do you know it's elephant dung?" With a note of exasperation in his raspy whisper, he replied, "See how big it is, Lieutenant!"

The terrain . . . was more desolate than any I hope to see again. The ground was churned up . . . with craters gouged out by the B-52 strikes. The air surrounding the trail was fetid with the smell of rank vegetation, blasted trees, decomposing NVA bodies, and blasted elephant carcasses, their bodies scattered around the rims of the craters. Arms, legs, trunks, hooves, tusks, and other body parts could be seen rotting in the dank jungle on either side of the trail. The mostly intact NVA bodies I was able to see seemed swelled to one-third more than life size. I have always had an exceptionally strong stomach, and yet the smell . . . was almost overwhelming to me and many of the men. . . .

We set our ambush about 10 p.m. Not too long after this a merciful breeze began to blow so that enough of the fetid smell around our positions drifted away to make the air at least bearable. Before long all was silent except for the sound of the wind running through the torn trees.

We made no contact with a living enemy that night. As we were moving around one crater when going back in, however, the ground gave way under my feet. To stop myself from sliding in I fell sideways against the inner rim of the crater, where my hand made contact with a slimy object that I could not, perhaps fortunately, make out. The heavy smell of death stayed with me for many hours afterward.

RECON ON THE DMZ

Captain Timothy Huff, USMC
C Company, Third Reconnaissance Battalion, Third Marine Division
Dong Ha, March 20, 1967

Tim Huff was on his second Vietnam tour, back leading a company of the Third Reconnaissance Battalion, a storied outfit. On this day he briefed top Marine commander General Lewis Walt, visiting the Third Division's forward headquarters at Dong Ha. Captain Huff explained how almost half his seven scout patrols around Khe Sanh had had recent enemy contact. There were numerous reports of People's Army troops out there. General Walt complained of this level of effort and demanded more scouting below the DMZ. He wanted to show MACV the North Vietnamese were not pushing across the demilitarized zone. Huff was cut off when he tried to continue. Afterward he was pulled into a back room and the exchange reprised. Walt directed Huff to insert patrols by truck, not chopper, and do it near the post known as the Rockpile. Despite qualms, Huff followed orders. So at about three a.m. the next morning, my driver and me in our jeep, and a six by [*medium truck*] with two patrols in it, headed out of Dong Ha for the Rockpile. It was about a fifteen-mile one-way trip in the dark. I kept telling myself this was stupid—nobody drives out at night along Route 9. The only way we could make it is if the NVA thought we were one of their trucks. I couldn't understand Walt. Charlie owned the place out there.

So we made it past Cam Lo, and about halfway from there to the Rockpile, we dropped off the first team, trying to keep the trucks rolling so that no one would think we had stopped. Then we kept going for that one big hill that rose up out of the valley in the moonlight all by itself. It was off to the northwest of us. Hell, I was banging on my M-16 and praying my Hail Marys. I know what Ichabod Crane felt like in Sleepy Hollow.

I couldn't believe that we made it . . . but we hadn't had any problems yet. It wasn't easy to drop off a patrol, go away further, and turn and head back without [*revealing that*] that's exactly what you were doing. Anyway, we then got pointed back in the direction of Dong Ha and moved as fast as trucks can on Route 9 at three a.m. without lights.

I knew the patrols would be working their way . . . north and trying to hide for the rest of the night, but after we had passed the place where we had dropped off the first team, gunshots broke out—[*they were*] in contact. [*Captain Huff raced for Dong Ha to get a helicopter.*]

I had some ammo resupply tied down on pallets with the intent to drop them . . . if that was what we needed to do. We went out in a CH-46. The pilot was in contact with the patrol, and I was talking with him from the rear of the bird, but I had no radio contact myself with the team. My gunny was with me. When we got near the team, apparently it had been clear of the enemy for a little while, but the pilot was talking with the team leader, not me. It was difficult for me to really be sure of what was going on. The pilot called for yellow smoke to spot the team's location so he could go in to pick 'em up. They were not in sight yet. Then the smoke popped, and . . . we quickly dropped down. Thank god we hadn't started to hover, because it wasn't our team. The NVA must have had our radio frequency, and it was their smoke grenade suckering us down. The chopper flashed through a hostile LZ with .50-caliber machine gun fire raking its bottom. We were about fifty meters up and the pilot was hauling ass. The gunny yelled that he was hit in the foot. [*Captain Huff also suffered a leg wound, but felt it merely as a sting until he tried to walk. His Vietnam tour was over. Huff never did figure out why General Walt was so determined to prove the People's Army was not infiltrating across the DMZ.*]

ARTILLERY ON THE DMZ

Lieutenant Jim Brown, USMC
C Battery, First Battalion, Twelfth Marines, Third Marine Division
The Rockpile, June–July 1967

Lieutenant Brown volunteered as an artillery forward observer and was assigned to the Marine battery stationed at Camp Carroll. He was then sent to the Third Battalion, Third Marines (3/3), operating from the base known as "the Rockpile." This position was designed to protect the road, Route 9, that connected major U.S. facilities around Dong Ha, near the Vietnamese coast, with Khe Sanh, out toward the Laotian border. The Rockpile was unusual not only because the road bisected the camp but also because the Marines placed only an observation post atop the hill rather than locating their strongpoint on the height.

This base differed from any that I had seen in 'Nam in that it had a wilder, rougher appearance. Here was the ever-present barbed wire, but the location, sitting as it did down in the valley, seemed vulnerable. Adding to this insecure feeling was the fact that the elephant grass grew much closer to the perimeter than it had at Camp Carroll. Inside the barbed wire there were no orderly rows of tents, only low bunkers and trenches . . . with a few random tents scattered about. One of the latter served as the kitchen and another as the mess hall. A third was . . . the first-aid station, and all had dirt floors with the canvas sides rolled up. The dining tent had no chairs or tables; instead long planks were positioned a little over waist high so people could stand and eat. This makeshift chow hall was . . . right next to the dusty main road that went through the middle of the camp, and whenever a vehicle came by during meal time, clouds of dust would roll across the food. That is just what happened when we arrived during the noon meal. We did not seem a bit appreciated by those eating.

The dust was not something I had anticipated before coming to 'Nam. I had envisioned humid jungles, not the dry heat I was finding. In these hot summer months the base camps up on the DMZ were dry dust bowls, and grit was everywhere. It got in everything you ate and burned your eyes. There was no way to keep clean, and our weapons had to be constantly tended. . . .

That first week passed quickly. . . . As a new FO, however, I was not exactly greeted with open arms. These infantrymen had seen a lot of FOs come and go, and until the new man proved his competence, they did not get too friendly. There had been less-than-perfect fire missions, and maybe someone had lost a buddy as a result. It was one thing to have trained as a forward observer but another to have the personality and skill to get the job done. . . .

[*After a time Lieutenant Brown was sent to the hilltop observation post, where, among other things, Marines were nearly killed by an errant U.S. bomb during an air strike.*] I was calling in fire missions more frequently now, and enemy activity had begun to pick up. One morning a unit on patrol over on Mutter's Ridge started taking mortars, and because we could easily locate the enemy movement, we were directed to call in artillery until the patrol could pull out. I spent most of the day firing away, and was that satisfying! Bringing the adjusted rounds in on target and firing for effect when you knew the enemy was there created a real high. All this was happening while sitting abstractly on top of the world and controlling things down below. I could imagine how Zeus must have felt on Mount Olympus when he hurled his thunderbolts at the mortals beneath him. It also did not hurt . . . that we were not receiving any incoming ourselves. This was the way to fight a war.

TIME IN THE BARREL

Captain James P. Coan, USMC
A Company, Third Tank Battalion, Third Marine Division
Con Thien, September 1967
Captain Coan led a tank platoon during the most sustained combat of 1967, the siege of Con Thien. The companies of Coan's battalion were constantly in the thick of action as they helped Marine infantry hold Con Thien combat base and clear the surrounding terrain. Some 340 Marines died and almost 3,100 were wounded during the most intense months, and American commanders estimated they had wiped out over 1,100 Vietnam People's Army soldiers.

I have a deeply personal perspective about that red clay bull's eye known as "The Hill of Angels," having survived the attempted siege. . . . Hundreds of rounds of incoming artillery, mortars, and rockets pounded our beleaguered outpost daily. Monsoon downpours turned the laterite clay soil into oozing mud, flooded bunkers and trench lines, and made Con Thien a living hell. As our casualty list grew steadily . . . the news media latched onto our ordeal, referring to it as a "little Dien Bien Phu." We Marines knew otherwise, but we had the full attention of the entire military chain of command up to and including . . . President Lyndon B. Johnson. . . .

Life on The Hill was growing increasingly hazardous. Intermittently throughout the day on September 12, Con Thien was shelled by more than one hundred 60mm and 82mm mortars. A dozen Marines were hit by flying shrapnel, but none were killed. The first round in the salvo was the most deadly because by the time one heard it whooshing down, it was too late to duck for cover. . . .

Each night one of the tanks took a turn on the northern side of the perimeter aptly named "Dodge City." At least one, sometimes two, NVA recoilless rifle teams were hidden among the bamboo thickets and hedgerows some-where outside the northern perimeter, and they loved to snipe at tanks or other lucrative targets that presented themselves. Somehow they were able to hide the backblast dust and smoke from searching . . . eyes.

A-12's driver, Lance [*Corporal*] Bert Trevail, a former Canadian with mischievous blue eyes and a red-orange mustache, settled his fifty-two ton iron monster into its predug firing slot facing north. Each of the four crewmen stood a two hour watch . . . commencing at ten o'clock. Corporal Sanders was scheduled for first watch, but he was feeling drowsy. The tank platoon leader, Second Lieutenant Coan, agreed to swap. . . . That way he might get an uninterrupted four or five hours of sleep after his watch ended at midnight.

Unusual reports began arriving at the battalion CP shortly before mid-night. Mike Company [*of the Third Battalion, Ninth Marines*] reported some harassing sniper fire and movement to their front on the northeast perimeter. About the same time [*a forward observer saw*] lights moving south across the Trace [*a swath of terrain below the DMZ that had been cleared to reveal enemy maneuvers*] three klicks east of Con Thien and blinking lights on the southern edge of the Trace. An artillery fire mission was called in, and a spectacular fireworks show of twenty secondary explosions resulted in brilliant orange and red bursts of fire shooting hundreds of feet into the air. A follow-up [*radar-directed*] air strike in that same area ninety minutes later resulted in two more secondary explosions. . . .

Lieutenant Coan was startled awake about three in the morning by the snapping and popping of glowing green tracers barely clearing the top of the tank turret. An NVA heavy machine gun northwest of Con Thien was spray-ing the slopes. [*Coan put the weapon out of action with his main gun.*] Shadowy figures silhouetted by exploding mortars and flare light sprinted toward the outer perimeter wire. Coan's tank spewed .30-caliber bullets at the charging enemy. "Fire more HE at 'em!" Six more 90mm cannon rounds split the night air with their high velocity *KRACK!* [*A quad .50-machine-gun truck and many M60 machine guns joined in the fireworks, and the VPA evidently decided not to make a final assault, launching RPGs instead.*]

At dawn, daylight revealed the devastation wrought earlier. Great gaps had been blown in the . . . perimeter wire, and numerous fresh craters pock-marked the minefield. But to everyone's amazement, not a single enemy body was lying in sight. Had their eyes played tricks on them during the attack? Many a Marine began to doubt his own perceptions. [*No actual attack would ever be made at Con Thien. Instead there was a steady beat of bombardments plus numerous firefights throughout the surrounding area.*]

AFTER TET

Lieutenant Colonel Charlie A. Beckwith
Second Battalion, 327th Infantry (Airborne), 101st Airborne Division
A Shau Valley, spring 1968

While running his renowned Project Delta scout teams, Colonel Beckwith had been wounded during preparation of an air assault in Binh Dinh Province in January 1966. Beckwith returned for a second Vietnam tour with the 101st Airborne Division when President Johnson sent a brigade of the paratroopers to South Vietnam shortly before the Tet Offensive. With battles at Hue and Khe Sanh still raging at full intensity, Beckwith was assigned to another I Corps hot spot, the A Shau Valley, the favorite North Vietnamese approach to Hue. Beckwith assumed command on February 10, 1968.

This was straightforward infantry work; pure yes, sir, no, sir, three bags full; square the corners, straighten the lines, sweep the fire base, search and destroy the enemy. This is chain of command administration, don't stop and talk to the old man, take it to the first sergeant.

The tempo of the war at this stage was much faster than when I was here last. There were a lot of bad guys running around now. You could get killed very easily. I felt it was my job as a battalion CO to come to grips with the enemy and destroy him. I went looking for fights and anybody didn't feel the same way shouldn't be around me. When [*Colonel*] "Rip" Collins commanded the 1st Brigade, each of the division's battalions shared equally in the hard jobs. Later, when "Doc" Hayward had the brigade, I felt that whenever there was a nasty job to be done the 2/327 got it. I liked that. We were known as the "No Slack" battalion.

After Hue, we cleared the area around the Division headquarters in what was known as Operation Mingo. Then came action while the 2/327 was attached to the 1st Cav for Operation Jeb Stuart. Operation Nevada Eagle cleared the Hue-Phu Bai area. Somerset Plain swept the southern portion of the A Shau valley. The toughest job the battalion had was clearing a seven kilometer stretch along Route 547, which ran west from Hue. There were no VC here, just NVA regulars! The road faced steep mountain and thick, nearly impenetrable jungle. The cost was high. We got clawed and we clawed back. Eventually the road was won and Fire Support Base Bastogne established.

I learned if you command [*a*] battalion in combat in Vietnam for nine months it's going to grind you down. . . . All losses are bad. Some still stay with me. Much of what happened haunts me to this day.

Toward the end of the tour I became very tired. I was offered the Division's operations shop but turned it down. I did that for several reasons. The bombing of North Vietnam had been discontinued and that turned me off. If we were going to hang our ass out over there and they were not going to continue the bombing, then I was confused.

I'd also learned that [*Major General*] Melvin Zais was replacing [*General*] Olinto Barsanti as commander of the Division. Barsanti, whose call sign was Bold Eagle, was a wild man. He literally terrified his battalion commanders—ate lieutenant colonels for breakfast. Hard as he was on officers, Barsanti was always good to the troops. I somehow got along with him just fine. Mel Zais was a different story. In my opinion he didn't trust his subordinates. The 2/327 was being extracted from the A Shau Valley. The weather was bad, heavy fog drifted across the valley floor, and because of the timing necessary to lift the troops, my plate was full. It was a complicated but not impossible job. I'd done it numerous times before. What I didn't need was someone else on my radio net offering advice. Mel Zais came on my frequency and began to tell me how I should do my job. So when my tour was up, I felt it was best for me not to return to the 101st. I had paid my dues. . . . It was time to go home.

PATHFINDERS IN THE A SHAU

Corporal Richard R. Burns
Pathfinder Detachment, 101st Airborne Division
Camp Eagle, March 1968
In World War II "pathfinders" were the brave paratroopers who jumped first into a drop zone, with no protection at all, and marked it with lights and navigational aids to guide transport aircraft to the right place for accurate parachuting of GIs. The Vietnam adaptation was that pathfinders went first into an LZ, monitored conditions on the ground, and guided choppers into the place, like a combination of scout infantry and a mobile airfield control tower. Pathfinding was a unique capability, and pathfinders were so rare that special requests were made for them. A clear requirement for pathfinders developed in Operation Somerset Plain, when Colonel Beckwith's 2/327 cleared a broad hilltop near the mouth of the A Shau, where commanders intended to install a firebase big enough to emplace 175-millimeter, 155-millimeter, and 105-millimeter artillery. The place would be known to U.S. soldiers and Marines as Fire Base Bastogne, named for one of the 101st Airborne's most famous World War II battles. Corporal Burns was one of two pathfinders sent to Bastogne. They were thrilled to meet Colonel Beckwith, a widely admired officer.
We needed a location high enough to control aircraft and, luckily, found a spot right at the uppermost point on the hill. For the next two hours, one of us remained there at all times so nobody could claim it from us.

Eventually we got in a pissing contest with a group of battalion head-quarters staff who wanted the site. As we argued over land rights, a stocky, well-built, older soldier in an [*officer of the day*] T-shirt approached us. His dog-tags dangled outside his shirt. The headquarters people fell silent as he stepped up to us.

His voice was gruff. "What's the problem here?"

A senior NCO just about snapped to attention. "Hello, Sergeant Major! We were trying to tell these guys that we need this location to set up a two-niner-two [*radio antenna*] and some other equipment."

The sergeant major eyed us for a moment. I felt like I was being inspected. "You the Pathfinders?"

Ron cleared his throat. "Roger that, Sergeant Major!"

The sergeant major had a thick neck and a barrel chest. Although shorter than Beckwith, he looked just as tough. "Well, let me hear your side."

Both Ron and I explained that it was essential that we be able to maintain eye contact with all the aircraft in and around Bastogne. As the firebase grew in size, it would be crucial. Besides, we had laid claim to the site first.

As the sergeant major appeared to be rigid and uncompromising, we assumed he would side with his own people. Instead he said rather cordially, "The Pathfinders will go ahead and set up here. We're going to have a lot of aircraft coming in and out of this firebase. You men can set up your antenna and the rest of your equipment over by the TOC."

The group grumbled but immediately unassed [*left*] the area. The sergeant major introduced himself. "I'm the battalion sergeant major, Command Sergeant Major Gergen. You men need anything?"

Ron and I replied simultaneously, "Negative, Sergeant Major."

"Well, if you two need anything, let me know!" Sergeant Major Gergen politely turned and walked away.

Ron knelt beside his ruck and looked up at me. "You've heard of him, haven't you, Richie? That's 'Bull' Gergen."

Son of a gun. I didn't put that name together. Bull Gergen was something of a legend himself. "Damn, I can see how he got his name. He looks just like a bull! He and Beckwith must make one hell of a pair!"

[*The pathfinders had barely time to set up their radios before they had their hands full.*] Within thirty minutes of our arrival . . . scores of helicopters and Chinooks flew in with backhoes, sandbags, steel culverts, mechanical mules, and other materials to build bunkers, LZs, and fighting positions. Ron and I had to set up a POL (petrol, oil, and lubricants) refueling point, establish two supply LZs, and oversee the VIP LZ. One of us controlled aircraft while the other supervised all the LZ preparations.

Most of the air traffic ceased as nightfall came. Just about everyone had some kind of cover to protect them except Ron and me. We'd been too busy to fill sandbags or dig a hole, so we laid our ponchos out on the ground and fell asleep. Around midnight we woke to gunfire as enemy soldiers probed the perimeter. Around an hour after first light, enemy mortars exploded on the far side of the hill, overshooting the hilltop. Just as the mortar fire ceased, aircraft began calling for instructions.

Around midmorning, Ron was on the radio while I was popping smoke. I heard a loud whiz zoom right by me. A few minutes later, bark exploded off a tree to my left. [*A sniper had made the pathfinders his target.*] Ron and I crouched behind our rucksacks, and he reported the danger to all the aircraft. I yelled to other soldiers standing around. A few men looked at me kind of bewildered until a round kicked up dirt in front of them. They immediately scrambled for cover.

Throughout the day and into the next, the sniper fired a round every five to fifteen minutes. One soldier was grazed in the head. It was soon discovered that the weapon sniping at us was an enemy .51-caliber machine gun. It made a distinct sound. Like our .50-caliber, this gun could fire an aimed round from over two kilometers away. The bullet was huge. Even though it wasn't super-accurate at that great a distance, it scared the hell out of anyone on the receiving end. Again, I thought about Charlie Beckwith's taking one of those monsters in his side.

[*That had happened to Colonel Beckwith during 1966. Officers, of course, were special targets for the enemy, as they were for superior officers on their own side, Regular Army men making their mark in Vietnam. Beckwith himself had observed (above) that the division boss, General Barsanti, ate battalion commanders for breakfast. But Beckwith protected his men. Corporal Burns saw that too.*]

By midmorning air traffic was really hectic. Ron and I had to make sure that all the aircraft remained at a safe distance from one another and also stayed clear of whatever direction the mortars were firing [*plus many more tasks*]. In addition to doing all that, while monitoring the radio I received a call from General Barsanti's pilot requesting landing instructions.

After relaying the information, I cleared the pilot to land out at the VIP pad. Ron and I were flipping a coin to see who would have to physically guide in the general's bird. Unfortunately, I lost.

I was getting ready to turn the handset over to Ron when a voice boomed over the radio, "Bastogne Control! This is Bold Eagle!"

It was General Barsanti himself. "Bold Eagle! This is Bastogne! Over!"

"What the hell are all those soldiers doing down there with their shirts off? Over." I glanced around. Most everyone without a shirt had been laboring in the hot sun for hours. Surely the general knew how hot it was.

Maybe I'd misunderstood his transmission. "Bold Eagle! Say again. Over!"

"You heard me. I want the battalion commander to meet me when we land. Is that clear?"

"This is Bastogne. Roger!" I gave the handset to Ron. "Barsanti doesn't like the troops having their shirts off. He wants Colonel Beckwith to meet him when he lands."

Ron frowned. "You've got to be kidding. It must be over a hundred degrees out here."

I wondered if Barsanti knew we were fighting a war. I ran over and relayed the message to Colonel Beckwith, who didn't seem overly concerned. I then stood in front of the VIP pad and raised my hands above my head, giving the pilot the signal to guide in on me. The general's helicopter slowed to a hover. The chopper's blades made their loud *whopping* sound over my head while gravel and dirt blasted my face and chest. Even the wind created by the helicopter was warm instead of cool. I crossed my hands, giving the signal to land. With the skids firmly on the ground, Barsanti hopped out of the cabin, followed by the tall and lanky General Clay, the assistant division commander.

Suddenly Barsanti stopped in his tracks like someone had kicked him in the chest. He had a perplexed look on his face. I was so busy landing the helicopter, I hadn't noticed anything behind me. I turned around, and there was Colonel Beckwith waiting to greet the general, shirtless. [*Burns heard none of their conversation, but Beckwith never ordered his GIs to wear shirts. And Barsanti, as his chopper flew off, hit back with a new demand that the grunts pick up shell casings and other debris he saw. On subsequent visits the pathfinders took to "mistaking" Barsanti's call sign as "Bald Eagle." No amount of ass chewing dissuaded them from this deft bit of GI push back.*]

TREACHERY IN THE DARK

Major Dang Ngoc Mai
Fortieth Battalion, First Regiment, Vietnam People's Army Second Infantry Division
Ngok Tavak, May 10, 1968
South of the A Shau and west of Da Nang lay another border post that MACV used to launch scouts into "Indian Country." That was the base at Kham Duc. Once the People's Army invested Khe Sanh, Kham Duc became the northernmost place from which reconnaissance teams operated against the Ho Chi Minh Trail and gathered intelligence on the threat to Da Nang. One important question was the status of the People's Army Second Division, believed to have been chewed up in a series of engagements with Army and Marine troops in late 1967.

Suddenly there were indications not only that the Second might be active, but that the VPA were rushing to complete a road that would greatly increase their supply capacity. In March 1968 the Eleventh Mobile Strike Force Company, a CIDG unit under an Australian officer, Captain John D. White, was sent to Kham Duc to investigate. The commander at Kham Duc ordered White to set up a laager position at Ngok Tavak. From its beginning as a patrol base, Ngok Tavak quickly morphed into a satellite position for Kham Duc, less than five miles north. White's company was reinforced by a platoon of Marine 105-millimeter howitzers and a montagnard unit. The Australian and his strikers believed the latter was peppered with enemy spies when they found telephone and mine control wires cut. A mutiny among the montagnards only added to the ominous signs. Unknown to White or to Kham Duc commander Captain Christopher Silva, who came to help resolve the montagnard mutiny, the North Vietnamese very much intended to strike. Their attack began with a firefight inside the camp, between NLF infiltrators and the rest of the garrison. It illustrates a continuing feature of the Vietnam experience—the fear of betrayal. This account is by an Australian Vietnam veteran.

Major Mai, Commanding Officer of the 40th Battalion, had got his assault troops into position ready for the attack on the fort; it was [2 a.m.] on 10 May, a delay of five days from their original plan, but the regimental commander had agreed not to go ahead without their support weapons. A Montagnard–Local Force unit assisted the 40th Battalion. The [locals] would remain in place when Mai's unit moved to its secondary mission. All was ready; they now waited for the moon to set so that their first moves would be covered by darkness. The official report for the weather listed moonset for [3 a.m.]; they were prepared with time to spare. Just prior to this, at [2:45], Kham Duc came under heavy mortar and recoilless rifle fire, with approximately 68 mortar rounds exploding in the camp area. Special assault squads were assembled to breach the Ngok Tavak defenses using explosives, which would allow the second wave, who had flame-throwers, to fan out and destroy the guns. Major Mai probably had about 350 men . . . for the attack. This group would have been a mixture of northerners and South Vietnamese with some Montagnard[s] . . . as well. Facing them was a conglomerate [under] Captain White with Lieutenant Bob Adams, who was White's direct support artillery officer, in command of the Marines. Although it was an allied group, it was not a comfortable bond of fighting men. . . .

When the moon went down, the North Vietnamese force screened by the CIDG at the bottom of the eastern track began their move toward the top of the hill. It was just after three o'clock. . . . The [montagnards] from Kham Duc had turned on the allies, the first double-cross of the battle. Marine Paul Czerwonka was on the .50 calibre machine gun at the top of the track. Joseph

Cook was the loader and Greg Rose said he was there as well. [*Rose*] said they let the first CIDG through the outer defence and into the position:

> [*He was saying*] don't shoot, don't shoot, friendly, friendly, after looking toward the Nungs on the other side . . . on the .30 calibre machine gun. The second CIDG doing the same a few seconds later, made us very suspicious. Czerwonka gripped the handles of the .50 and [*got to*] his knees and leaned forward. Cook . . . moved behind us to put on his flak jacket and gather more grenades. I took my M-16 off safety and lay down pointing it down the road where the CIDG were. As we heard an explosion behind us, the .30 calibre and two Nungs copped a satchel charge. Within . . . seconds a deafening explosion erupted to my right. . . . I saw a group of the enemy run by with flamethrowers lighting up the perimeter.

[*Both of Private Rose's comrades died as the enemy erupted into Ngok Tavak. In fact, every one of the thirty-three Marines was either killed or wounded, as were captains White and Silva and many MSF Nungs. The eastern defenses collapsed first, then the fort fell bunker by bunker.*]

Major Mai's battalion continued to rush up the track and spread into the fort throwing grenades and firing rapidly with AK-47s, although some carbines were also heard. These belonged to the CIDG traitors. At the same time, [*Mai used*] secondary assaults . . . to test the strength of the defenses in the southern and western quadrants held by [*the Nung company's*] 1st and 3rd Platoons. Accurate 60mm mortar fire hit the camp . . . from the ridgeline to the south. . . . Rocket-propelled grenades (RPG) struck the area around the [*Australian*] and U.S. Special Forces positions. These . . . had obviously been spied by the 1st Regiment's reconnaissance parties in the weeks preceding. . . . The assault soon concentrated on the track up from the old vehicle park [*the CIDG's traitors' position*], and it became the main . . . conduit that funneled the NVA into the position. This is when scattered and uncoordinated [*Marine*] artillerymen probably destroyed the North Vietnamese momentum. There was no center of gravity, no fixed line on which the attackers could concentrate.

[*Fighting by ones and twos, caught wherever they had been when the attack started, the defenders never employed their howitzers, but the Marines nevertheless stalled Major Mai's attackers. Like in an Old West shoot-out, or a bitter city fight like that at Hue at Tet, Mai's soldiers had to go after the defenders one by one. Presently, morning came, and Captain White rallied the remaining troops and retreated into the jungle rather than toward Kham Duc. Helicopters picked up the survivors later that day. The U.S. command sent a full rifle battalion to reinforce Kham Duc but decided the place could not be held and began to withdraw by airlift under fire. Kham Duc's last positions were abandoned about noontime on May 12.*]

FROM THE AIR

Lance Corporal Ronald D. Winter, USMC
Marine Medium Helicopter Squadron 161, U.S. Marine Corps
A Shau Valley, November 1968
A crewman aboard one of the CH-46 helicopters of HMM-161, a transport squadron that only arrived in the spring of 1968 but set records in I Corps for sorties flown and hours spent in the air, Winter participated in all the hairy operations. Though HMM-161 was stationed near Quang Tri—in fact its home was closer to the DMZ than any chopper base in South Vietnam—its ships ranged widely.

We were skimming the treetops at the head of the A Shau Valley, doing about 120 knots, coming in fast for a strafing run. As sometimes happened when the younger lieutenants were flying, a rock 'n' roll station was playing in my headset, and the Stones were blasting out, "Hey, hey, you, you get off my cloud."

It was mid-November and the war had established itself as "Rock 'n' Roll— Lock and load!" We had seen so much death and destruction, fighting, and dying in the past six months that my emotions had taken on an unreal quality, a hardness, necessary to protect me from the reality of war.

Sometimes I really wanted to be able to feel something, anything, other than anger. But I couldn't, and it didn't even bother me. Flying became an escape for me, and if I could mix the roar of battle with hard-driving rock, so much the better. I no longer cared if someone out there died; it was the luck of the draw.

Sometimes I didn't even care if I died, and figured if my time was up, it was up; otherwise there was no sense worrying about it. I looked at it with a "kill or be killed" attitude. Too many of my friends were getting killed there for me to have any sympathy for the North Vietnamese.

We approached the target area, I opened up, and the beat from the Stones was joined by the metallic thunder of my .50-caliber. I knew what was coming ahead of time, so I had dispensed with the 50-round box and had loaded a string of ammunition directly from a 500-round box.

Six- and eight-round bursts kept roaring out of the barrel, and I watched with a kind of detached satisfaction as the tracers went directly into the target. I kept firing until we had passed over the zone and the pilots radioed to cease.

I felt a sense of relief, sweating in the cool air, and reached for a cigarette. Strafing runs had become part of our routine now that the North Vietnamese were back in force, and aside from flying reconnaissance insertions, they were my favorite missions.

There was a sense of power in those actions that far exceeded anything I have ever felt since. I was twenty when I got there and had turned twenty-one in October. I had, at that point in my life, direct control over everything I saw outside that helicopter and its effect on my life. When the engines began their high-pitched scream and the rotors began turning, I'd feel a sharp sense of excitement and my blood began pounding. I'd lock and load as we flew over the perimeter . . . then hold back as long as was necessary, keeping the excitement just below the surface.

Then we'd get a call for assistance, or take fire in a zone, and I'd explode with all that pent-up frustration, spewing bursts of destruction out the end of the .50. I solved every problem I had right there on the spot—at least until the next time.

Life was harsh, not only in Quang Tri, but throughout northern I Corps in November 1968, and there were three ways to deal with it. You could fly forever, immersing yourself in the work and the war to a point of exhaustion, leaving little time for reflecting on the heat, or the rain, or the death.

If nonstop work and fighting weren't your way of dealing with unpleasantness, you could find a way to make music part of your life, and do your best to lose yourself in its rhythms as much as possible.

Or you could turn into a booze scrounger, trying to drink yourself into oblivion each night and spending half the next day recovering before starting all over again. In reality, many of the Marines in HMM-161 took on portions of all three of those choices.

6

Vietnam Days

IN THE FIELD

Captain Colin L. Powell
U.S. advisor, Second Battalion, Third Infantry, First ARVN Division
Camp A Shau, February 1963
Among the small minority of Americans who first arrived in Vietnam as advisors to the South Vietnamese army (ARVN), Colin Powell was also exceptional in having that initial tour during the early days, before the major U.S. intervention. He went to the upper part of South Vietnam, to Camp A Shau, a base the ARVN would not be able to hold much longer. Powell's experiences in field operations would be quite typical of what GIs faced in the boondocks, except that the danger from the enemy was far less intense during this period. Later, patrols would often hesitate to follow a trail for fear of ambush, and they would not halt so often to deal with vermin. Here Powell recollects an early-war patrol.
On this march, I discovered the reality of a triple-canopy tropical forest. The lowest stratum consisted of saw grass, bushes, vines, and small trees struggling for air. Adolescent trees formed the second canopy, densely packed, rising thirty or forty feet. The third canopy consisted of mature hardwoods, some over one hundred feet high. Unless we broke out into a clearing, we could go all day long without seeing the sun. Even in the shade, sweat bathed our faces and our uniforms turned soggy. The salt from our perspiration formed gray-white semicircles under our armpits and blotches on the backs of our fatigues. We constantly popped tablets to replenish our bodies' salt supply. A distinctive smell clung to us, a pungent mixture of mud, dirty bodies, and

rotting vegetation. Every day was an endless obstacle course, as we tried to make contact with the Viet Cong. We were constantly going "cross-compartment," following trails down one steep valley and up the other, clambering over craggy rocks and fording streams. . . .

We moved in a cloud of insects. Worse were the leeches. I never understood how they managed to get through our clothing, under our web belts and onto our chests, through our bloused pants and onto our legs, biting the flesh and bloating themselves with our blood. We stopped as often as ten times a day to get rid of them. It did no good to pull the leeches off. Their bodies simply broke and the head remained biting into the skin. We had to stun them with bursts of insect repellent or the lit end of a cigarette, which made a hissing sound on contact.

The trails . . . had been sown by the VC with snares and punji spikes, bamboo stakes concealed in a hole, the tip poisoned with buffalo dung. The first casualty I witnessed was a soldier who stepped onto a punji stake. For all the hardship, I was still excited to be on the trail . . . feeling especially alive as strength and fatigue flowed alternately through my limbs.

STILL THERE

Corporal Roger Hayes
First Battalion, Fifth Infantry (Mechanized)
Cu Chi, fall 1967
Observant and perceptive, Corporal Hayes was close to the ideal the Army sought for GIs, and he would become a squad leader before his year was up. His recollections show that pests persisted over time, and many of the same ones were present everywhere. Rats, snakes, and leeches appear in most veterans' Vietnam stories, wherever stationed. Tigers, elephants, and monkeys were more common in the jungles of the Central Highlands or I Corps. The ants and bees Corporal Hayes remarks on were often found in the plains and paddies.
The area of Vietnam in which we operated, between Saigon and the Cambodian border to the west and northwest, did not have a large population of tigers or snakes, which would have made life unpleasant. Or, if those critters were around, we didn't encounter them regularly. There was, however, a healthy population of voracious insects.

Aggressive fire ants occupied much of the area and seemed to dislike intruders. When we came too close, dozens of them, if not hundreds, attacked and bit. Each one felt like a bee sting, although the pain dissipated once the attack ended or the insects were brushed off. Trees often had a line of fire ants going up or down the trunk. It was common to see GIs who were taking a break examining the bark prior to sitting down and leaning back against the tree.

The ants made us miserable when we invaded their territory. The only way to get rid of them was to get out of their immediate area, then strip off clothing as quickly as possible and brush them off.

On more than one occasion when trying to escape enemy fire, we unwittingly dove into an area populated with these ants. Suddenly priorities changed: Viet Cong or NVA rifle fire became a lower priority when compared with attacking fire ants. The unfortunate victim would stand up—exposing himself to enemy fire, drop his weapon, rip off his clothing as fast as possible, and brush away the ferocious attackers.

I knew of no soldiers enduring the fire ant attacks who were shot by the NVA or VC. I always presumed that the enemy was laughing too hard at the GI's predicament to take proper aim.

Ants were not the only pests we encountered. While our tracks [*armored personnel carriers*] were moving through an area one day, our driver chose to pass between two trees about six inches closer together than the width of our vehicles. The trees bowed to one side as we passed between them. No one saw, until it was too late, the beehive in one of the trees. The bees had the same disposition as the fire ants. They attacked with a vengeance that I'm sure the enemy would admire and possibly emulate.

Some of the guys under attack by the bees yelled and waved their arms wildly. This attracted the attention of the bees, who were searching for tactical targets, much like a jet fighter pilot whose home base had just been bombed. With identified targets, the bees homed in. I and a few others took a different tactic. We slowly pulled our collars closed and sat still. Several bees stopped in front of my face and inspected me, then went on. I was evidently identified as a noncombatant and was not stung.

Finally the insects broke contact and withdrew. Welts covered the faces and arms of those who were attacked. Several of them required medical evacuation. One or two of them had such swollen faces that they were difficult to recognize for awhile. If I had been in command, I would have made sure that these soldiers received a Purple Heart.

The insects that caused us the most misery were mosquitoes. The area where we operated seemed like the world's optimum mosquito habitat, with warm temperatures, high humidity, and plenty of standing water. They weren't too bad during daylight hours, but they were a constant menace at night.

One evening as we were en route to an ambush site, we paused along a road near a rice paddy to wait for full darkness. As the daylight faded, we heard a distant buzz, which grew steadily in volume as thousands if not millions of bloodsucking pests descended on us. There was nothing we could do.

RAIN

Lieutenant David G. Fitz-Enz
Sixty-Ninth Signal Battalion, 173rd Airborne Brigade
Bien Hoa, October 1965

Lieutenant Fitz-Enz's battalion, one of those that crossed the Pacific as part of the great wave of 1965, landed at Vung Tau after the Navy had kept them aboard ship for most of a month. The GIs were desperate to get land under their feet again, but after only a few hours ashore they were crammed into C-130s for the flight to Bien Hoa, the rear base of the 173rd Brigade. There they pitched tents and settled in. Their initiation came, after dark, that very day.

During the night we had our first experience of the rains common to Southeast Asia. I was lucky; the other half of my tent came from the chaplain, who had been invited to share the battalion commander's roomy quarters. Lying on my air mattress with my raincoat covering the windward opening above my head, I was snug. The rain hammered without letup and a river formed down the middle of my dirt floor. It ran and swelled until I felt movement, just a little at first and then, with a rush, I was buoyant and moved quite quickly out the other side of my tent and into the company street. I was not alone at midstream; my neighbors were there as well. Clad in shorts and combat boots—we slept with them on—we chased each other into the mess tent. As we organized in the dark, a great gust of wind inflated the canopy and, with the tension released, the large heavy ridgepole fell to one side. We looked up in disbelief as the sodden canvas roof settled gently on our heads.

In the morning things looked no better. It heated up rapidly and I experienced Kipling's "thunder in the sun." Our uniforms were designed for warfare in Central Europe. Vietnam had come on too quickly, and the "jungle fatigues" that became so popular were only in the hands of line infantry units. Our work clothing had become recruiting poster material because we were tailored down to skin-tightness. In order to roll up my sleeves I had to cut the seam free to just above the elbow and roll it to the middle of my biceps. The pants were just as tight but nothing could be done with them. On the olive drab fatigues, all our markings were in bright colors, just the thing for a parade. In Vietnam they were target material.

GUARDING THE BASES

Lieutenant Colonel David H. Hackworth
on assignment from the Pentagon, October–December 1966

After an initial combat tour in Vietnam, Colonel Hackworth returned with military historian S. L. A. Marshall, who had been asked to teach Army officers his methods for interviews recording lessons learned in battle. The two first visited the Cav in the Central Highlands, then moved on to the headquarters of the First Infantry Division.

We said goodbye to [*General*] Jack Norton and his luxurious An Khe home and flew off to the equally luxurious 1st Division base camp at Di An. The base camp mentality in Vietnam was an outgrowth of the static days of the Korean War. Back then the Vietnam-era generals had been majors and lieutenant colonels on the outside looking enviously in; no doubt many of them had thought, *When I'm a general I'll have that, too,* and now that they were, they were going to, even if the base camps had even less place in this war than they had in the last. In Vietnam, a frontless war, the security requirement alone at these base camps was massive. At the 1st Air Cav, an entire brigade— fully one third of the division—was engaged solely in protecting the unit's An Khe home. Similarly, by the time I'd left the 1/101st in June, one third of its combat power was tied up guarding Phan Rang. In the 1/101st this was particularly significant, in that when we'd originally gone to Phan Rang, the position was almost Charlie-free. But the longer we stayed, the more interest the enemy took in the place. By the time I left, they were regularly blowing up vehicles, lobbing an occasional mortar shell, and doing selective sniping. So, almost by design, the base camp invited enemy activity, and then drained the fighting strength of a unit in the effort to counter it. Frontline troop strength was continually drained, too, by the number of men needed to stay behind simply to service the base camps as they grew bigger and more plush. And in that the camps created an extra layer of diversion in which a trooper, fresh out of the hospital or back from R&R, could lose himself before returning to his unit, it wasn't long before these massive installations were really as much the enemy as the enemy himself.

ASSIGNMENT

Lieutenant Jim Brown, USMC
C Battery, First Battalion, Twelfth Marines, Third Marine Division
Camp Carroll, 1967–1968
Jim Brown, a young Mississippian who graduated from the University of the South in Tennessee, had long aspired to be a marine and in due course signed up for Officer Candidate School. Arriving in South Vietnam at Da Nang on June 6, 1967, Lieutenant Brown experienced that rite of passage—assignment—that

*every American coming to this war endured. He feared assignment to a rear-
area service job that would leave him a REMF—a "rear-echelon motherfucker."
Brown's simple patriotism and desire for combat put him in a very hot spot.*

On reporting in at division headquarters, I learned that I would be meeting
with a full colonel in charge of filling billets throughout the division. After I
waited a long time, the colonel finally called me into his office, and I made
my first mistake. . . . Full of dreams and ideals, I had the misguided fear that
I might get stuck in some rear area and never have an opportunity to see war
firsthand. . . . I put on my most sincere manner and said to the colonel, "Sir,
if there is any way possible, I would really like to be a forward observer in the
field with an infantry company." The colonel calmly laid down the papers
he was studying, rocked back in his chair, and placed his hands behind his
head. He looked me hard in the eyes and seemed to be studying me for an
interminably long time. Without any change of expression he finally said,
"1/12 supports 3/3 [*Third Battalion, Third Marines—an infantry unit*], and I
think they can use you up there." With that, he stamped 12th Marines on my
orders while telling me to catch the next plane to Dong Ha, which was near
the actual demilitarized zone (DMZ). He further instructed me to report to
the commanding officer there and repeat my request.

GOD'S WARRIORS

Chaplain Claude D. Newby
Second Battalion, Eighth Cavalry, First Cavalry Division (Airmobile)
Bong Son, March 1967
*The Army tried to provide for almost all aspects of soldiers' physical and spiritual
needs, including religious worship. Chaplains were assigned to every battalion
in country and had their own chain of command through the divisions and
ultimately to USARV, the Army's administrative headquarters for Vietnam.
Captain Newby, though of the Latter-day Saints (LDS)—the Mormons—gave
services for all denominations. But his LDS faith was a minority persuasion and
caused difficulties for him with the religious chain of command. In the meantime,
chaplains confronted such staples of the war as dealing with the media.*

I rejoined Alpha Company in the early evening because it was again engaged
in a prolonged battle and had sustained casualties. . . . I remember this fight in
particular because it occurred on Good Friday, and because of what happened
to the mortar sergeant.

Sergeant Theberge had been wounded earlier in the day and evacuated. A
sniper had shot him in the back of the head, the shot had passed through a
light-colored bottle of insect repellant on the back of his helmet. Theberge

returned to duty a few days later with his head swathed in white gauze—even better markings for an enemy sharpshooter.

That morning, moving from the helicopter after it dropped me off, I headed for the company CP. In passing, I asked [*Private*] Smith, Smitty, a slender black soldier from St. Louis, to sing a solo in the worship service I intended to conduct as soon as conditions allowed, likely after nightfall.

Later, right after dark, those who wanted to and could do so gathered to worship near the center of the FOB. I commenced the service, held at a whisper, and at the appropriate moment I announced Smitty's solo. Strained silence met this announcement, and then from the dark came, "Chaplain, Smitty was medevaced, shot in the stomach."

Smitty had grasped a buddy's M-16 to help the buddy up a muddy bank, and the weapon discharged accidentally. Smitty's former girlfriend wrote me sometime later. She said Smitty collapsed and fell dead while he danced with her, a month after he was released from the hospital.

Easter morning I joined with Chaplain Dowd, to provide concurrent Catholic and general worship service to all elements of my battalion. An ABC television crew accompanied us to film Chaplain Dowd in action for a television special, *The Combat Chaplain*. A helicopter was at our disposal for the whole day, as we were supposed to be in an Easter cease-fire.

Beginning at LZ Santana and going from company to company, we celebrated Easter, conducting services concurrently, usually within 50 feet of each other. The services were strikingly dissimilar.

Chaplain Dowd's masses, even in the field, were formal and traditional, with bright-colored alb and other priestly garments. My services, on the other hand, were informal and included more singing.

Before our third set of services, the television crew prepared to film my congregation. "We'll shoot your congregation singing and splice it into a mass to improve the show," the camera operator explained—a little journalistic license there.

THE BURDEN OF THE WAR

Lieutenant Joseph W. Callaway
C Company, Second Battalion, Sixtieth Infantry, Ninth Infantry Division
Long An Province, spring 1967
Despite all the discussions of such Vietnam War practices as "search and destroy," "clear and hold," or their permutations, the reality of combat tactics devolved into efforts by little bands of men to find the adversary and somehow fix him in place until U.S. firepower could be brought to bear. This made for great

disparities in risk for soldiers of different ranks. Tactical methods were, of course, the province of field commanders.

Many American field-grade officers, majors and colonels, let the line company-grade officers, captains and lieutenants, bear a disproportionate risk in Vietnam, leaving these inexperienced officers with the important and crucial battlefield decision making and, therefore, the true burden of the war. If you had power in Vietnam, it was an easy war in which to hide, particularly for the many field-grade staff officers. The Vietnam War meant career development and enhancement. . . . Killing communists was just a task mission. Few senior officers showed motivation from overwhelming patriotism or a righteous cause. Most knew that this was a meaningless conflict, and except for personal advancement most showed little passion for the war.

Some field-grade officers worked on the macho nature and ambition of the unknowing, inexperienced, and gullible young junior officers. These senior officers on occasion awarded themselves medals while sending junior line officers into the breach and often to their deaths. In my experience, senior officers usually took little risk themselves. In all fairness, the war was a series of small unit battles that did not warrant a field-grade officer's participation. The junior . . . officers had to learn the combat game and the art of survival on their own.

In Vietnam we eventually learned we were nothing but human bait sent out to make contact with the VC and NVA so we could respond with overwhelming artillery and airpower. Vietnam infantry grunts were sometimes used as expendable people—just part of the strategy.

RACISM ON THE WATER

Lieutenant Wynn Goldsmith, USN
534th River Section, River Patrol Flotilla Five, Coastal Task Force 116
Nha Be, April 6, 1968
It was the inbred attitudes of Americans, yet to be reconciled by civil rights protests and social upbringing, that fueled racial incidents in the combat zone. This was true across all the armed services. Here Lieutenant Goldsmith, skipper of a river assault unit of patrol boats (PBRs), confronted a nasty incident that furnishes a stark example of what kept men at odds. The day brought a counseling session for one of Goldsmith's boat captains and the end of flags on the boats—including the Jolly Roger and several state ensigns.
For me, April 6, 1968, was basically a quiet day on patrol in Area 2. A couple of sweeps down Ambush Alley with everyone at general quarters followed by a couple of hours of searching sampans, water taxis and junks headed to Ben Tre from the south. The boats on patrol in Area 1 got into a fight and killed one Viet Cong who was evading a [*militia*] sweep. My boats did not even test

fire their weapons. It was just another hot, sticky, long day on the river until late in the afternoon.

The memorable happening was not due to any action on the river. The boat captain (a seasoned veteran whose name will not be mentioned here) was listening to his little AM transistor radio in the coxswain's flat as we buttoned up and made ready for another run past the Mo Cay Canal before running Ambush Alley. I was pulling a drink of ice water from the five-gallon insulated jug beside the small-arms locker . . . as some sort of newsbreaking announcement came over the little radio. I did not hear the radio report but I sure remember the next words from the boat commander.

"Hip, hip, hooray! That black nigger Martin Luther Coon has been killed!"

I was dumfounded. [*Seaman*] Willie Brown, a slight, nineteen-year old African American, was the forward gunner. He reacted immediately to that obscene exclamation as he would to enemy fire from the bank. Willie jacked rounds into his fifties and swung the mount around as fast as he could. Fortunately the stops built into the gun mount held. I rushed forward to keep Willie from grabbing the M-16 he kept at his feet. By the time I reached him he was a sobbing little boy and not the fraternal killer he well could have been.

I spent the next half hour alternating between crying with Willie Brown and getting that boat commander to make apologies to him. The boat captain was distraught himself after he realized what his words had done. He was the type of guy who would have sacrificed his life for Willie Brown if need be. PBR crews were that bound together. Now the boat captain did not know how to approach his young gunner. I suggested to him that he could begin by cutting down the Confederate battle flag flying under the national ensign from the jackstaff. . . . He did that and then went over and hugged Willie Brown. While the two of them, one a quiet young black seaman from inner-city Baltimore, the other a tough, profane, white, first-class petty officer from hardscrabble rural Mississippi, cried and consoled themselves, I took the boats back to base. I was still shaking when I made the landing.

MONSOON

Lieutenant Lynda Van Devanter
Seventy-First Evacuation Hospital
Pleiku, October 1969
Lynda Van Devanter had not wanted the Pleiku assignment, but as a soldier she had little choice. Rocket attacks happened almost every night. Van Devanter worked at the 71st Evacuation Hospital for inhuman hours when the casualties poured in, but found time to try to expose the hospital's self-appointed "moral guardian," who objected to women's relationships with GIs but had her own

lesbian affair. Lieutenant Van Devanter had four months in country when the monsoon hit. The staff could not keep up with the mud that invaded their hospital, mixing with blood "in ways that were reminiscent of a fifties horror film." They struggled to clean at least the neurosurgery room, on grounds that germs in the brain were more dangerous than in other places.

One of the clearest, most oppressive memories of that year . . . was the fall monsoon season. The unrelenting rains and violent winds began in early October and lasted until January with hardly a break. Together those four months felt longer than any other full year I've lived before or since. The people who had warned me about the season were right: These were the "real monsoons." The red mud was everywhere—on the buildings, in our rooms, on our clothes, and on every casualty the choppers brought. The surgical-T [*theater*], which was located at the base of a hill, filled with mud and water that came through the swinging double doors. We spent hour after hour sweeping and shoveling mud back outside. However, that problem was not half as serious as the ones we faced in the [*operating room*].

The fall monsoons brought our greatest number of casualties. It was a good time for the V.C. because they knew the country and were at home with its seasons. To our soldiers, the elements were merely another enemy which, in combination with the V.C., proved unbeatable. If we at the 71st Evac had previously thought we were pushing ourselves to the limit, we were wrong. Before the monsoons, it would have seemed impossible for us to work any harder, but when the casualties increased, we kept going until we dropped. Then, after a couple hours of sleep, we'd start again. Overworked doctors, nurses, and technicians were falling into almost deathlike sleep at the operating tables. The anesthetists were always the first to go since they were usually sitting and were breathing the leaking gases from their own anesthesia machines. We tried to sleep during every spare moment, taking our rest on floors, chairs, and even on empty gurneys. At one point, I was so exhausted, I took a nap in the expectant area, on a gurney that had previously been occupied by a soldier who had died only moments earlier. It was still stained by his blood. I was so tired I could have slept there even if the dead body had been lying with me. As the weeks passed I began to feel like I needed a break or I would crack. . . . But that break wouldn't come for a long time. Instead, we got more casualties and rain.

FUCKING NEW GUYS

Private First Class Ches Schneider
Delta Company, Second Battalion, Sixteenth Infantry, First Infantry Division
Tan Son Nhut Base, December 4, 1969

Private Schneider, an eighth-grade teacher in civilian life, had seen his draft deferments expire in 1968, gone through draft classification appeals, and run out of options. Though he had previously taken and passed the entry test for Officer Candidate School, Schneider elected to become a plain infantry grunt. Here he records his arrival in South Vietnam, at the huge air base complex outside Saigon. Newly arrived soldiers were uniformly known as "fucking new guys," or FNGs. Those nearing departure were "short-timers," watching their DEROS—or "date eligible to return from overseas" date—with almost religious mysticism. These crowds inevitably collided at the port of entry, here Tan Son Nhut, where FNGs came off the plane and those bound for "The World" boarded their Freedom Bird.

A tin shed served as the airport terminal for Tan Son Nhut. This terminal was the main corridor to the war in the southern part of Vietnam. An Army guide greeted our group with a welcoming speech. He apologized for the shed, but assured us that by the time we left, Tan Son Nhut and Saigon would have an airport facility to rival that of most major American cities. It was under construction just then. His greeting helped quash any hopes we had for an early end to the war. It simply wouldn't make economic sense to end a war before the United States had extracted its money's worth from the new airport terminal.

We were FNGs, fucking new guys, and sat in the FNG section of the shed. A roar went up from a group of soldiers that equaled our number. They sat in a section marked DEROS. I realized that "DEROS" must mean "going home" or something to that effect. I fully understood why they were happy to be going home, and of course, I envied them. But I couldn't comprehend the meaning of the insult they hurled in our direction. "Short!" they yelled. "Short!"

"Beaucoup short!" they screamed, and made a sign with their index finger and thumb to indicate just how short they meant. They were a rowdy, unkempt, and undisciplined group. Some carried souvenirs, weapons captured from the enemy. All wore smiles that couldn't be ripped from their faces. They were going home, and we were just starting.

It seemed so unfair. It was very depressing. As we marched out to the buses that would transport us to our next destination, I turned to see that undisciplined herd stampede toward *our* plane. They didn't march. They didn't even walk fast. The undignified, unmilitary, obnoxious rabble stormed our airplane. . . .

We in-processed at the 93rd Replacement Battalion. Rumor had it that the bus in front of us had received sniper fire as it passed through the crowded streets. Rumor had it that our bus had been the target, because we had officers on it. Rumor also had it that we would be going home soon. Rumor had it that we wouldn't be staying the mandatory 365 days. Rumors are a staple of the Army diet, and like Army chow, should be ingested with care and patience.

THE BOB HOPE SHOW

Lieutenant Christine McGinley Schneider
Ninety-Fifth Evacuation Hospital
Da Nang, December 25, 1970
Ms. Schneider, whose mother had been a Navy nurse in World War II, under-
stood the need for nurses in Vietnam and wanted to go but felt she lacked the
experience coming out of school. She worked in the jail ward of her county hos-
pital for a year, then joined the Army, which sent her to the Ninety-Fifth Evacu-
ation Hospital at Da Nang. From the moment of her C-130 flight up-country,
Schneider, as an American woman, began to realize she had a special VIP status
in Vietnam. That led to anguish for her as a result of The Bob Hope Show.
Schneider then had six months in country.
One of the most incredible stories—this is a true story. I had gone to the Bob
Hope Show on Christmas, and of course I was excited to be able to see it; I
had watched it on television so many years. There weren't many girls there,
of course, and they roped off all the women from the guys; there were MPs
standing there. All these GIs were taking our picture, and that sort of jarred
my world, because you didn't go out much. My whole world was the hospital,
but even when you went to the PX, people were always taking your picture. So
the same thing happened here. Most of them were grunts; they brought them
in from the field, and they were going right back out when the show was over.
It didn't seem much longer than it takes to get your pictures developed when
this guy came in [*to the Ninety-Fifth Evacuation Hospital*] just shot up really
bad, and he died, but before he died, he told me that he had my picture. It was
the one picture he had in his pocket—my picture from the Bob Hope Show.
To think that of all his worldly possessions he would carry my picture . . . and
I have that picture now. He wanted me to have it. . . . He knew he was dying.
. . . It was just the eeriest thing. Those are the kinds of things that make me
know that my being there did make a difference to a lot of people, to a lot of
guys who probably don't even know my name but will always remember that
someone cared.

FNG AIRMAN

Lieutenant Michael Jackson, USAF
Twentieth Tactical Air Support Squadron, 504th Tactical Air Support Group
Camp Eagle, July 1971
It was not only GIs and jarheads who counted the days of their tours. Airmen did
too. This account by Mike Jackson, a forward air controller, captures the essence

of the exchanges between FNGs and comrades who had more time in country. Jackson also gives a feel for life on base in South Vietnam's heat and humidity. So maybe I had a little adjusting to do. And maybe the other guys didn't go out of their way to treat me with the kind of deference I'd come to expect . . . In retrospect, I went through a clumsy adjustment period, but everyone does. Unless you were raised in a war zone, it was inevitable. . . . I'd had my share of people to boss around. Not so in the 'Nam, where I was currently low man on the totem pole. I barely had a name save for the familiar FNG label that grated on my nerves more and more with each passing day.

"Hey, Jackson! Man, if I had three hundred and forty-three more days in this hellhole, I'd slit my wrists. It's rough bein' the FNG, eh?"

"C'mon guys, go easy on the FNG. The poor bastard is still forty-nine weeks away from DEROS. . . . Jesus, that sounds like a lifetime."

I'd fire off a cold smile before refocusing my attention on the various discomforts and annoyances of my new lifestyle. For starters, I was always dirty, always wiping away the sweat that beaded across my forehead and trickled down my neck. My body felt as though it had been dipped in cornmeal batter and deep-fried in a vat of tropical bacon grease. I suppose I should have counted my blessings. Despite our limited water supply I could manage to grab a quick shower every day. Anyone with any sense of cleanliness almost had to. It wasn't a case of hygiene overkill; it was absolutely necessary if you wanted to be able to stand yourself, let alone have others stand you. Returning from a mission I'd be blinded by my own sweat as my flight suit squished with pore juice every time I took a step. [*For grunts on patrol, even more for lurps or SOG troopers in the boonies, the wonders of the mere concept of a daily shower can be imagined. There were real differences that flowed directly from what a person did in the war.*]

INTEGRATED ARMY

First Lieutenant Tracy Kidder
509th Radio Research Group
Chu Lai, Landing Zone Bayonet, 1968–1969
Harvard-educated and, after the war, a Pulitzer Prize–winning author, Tracy Kidder joined ROTC while in college to choose his arm of the service instead of leaving it to the draft. He decided on intelligence and trained for the Army Security Agency (ASA), which intercepted enemy communications and fed them to the National Security Agency. Kidder arrived in the summer of 1968, at a point when racial tensions among troops were becoming pronounced. His own ASA detachment, by definition a REMF unit, was among those that could be expected

to be the most afflicted—except that his detachment of the 509th had no blacks in it at all. Kidder's handling of his first black serviceman illustrates the dilemmas of race relations in Vietnam.

The confidence that came from warm shaving water! Confidence bred certainty, which was always useful, as on the day when my one essential man, Spikes, came to me and said, "Lieutenant, they're sendin' us a nigger."

Racial strife, like combat, was an issue I hadn't had to deal with. The vast majority of young Americans sent to Vietnam and assigned to the combat arms came from the country's lower economic tiers, but a recruit with black or brown skin stood the greatest chance of being assigned to fight. The Defense Department's own statistics would later prove this. Black enlisted men made up about 8 percent of the armed forces and suffered about 15 percent of the casualties. But it was already obvious enough to everyone in Vietnam. There weren't many African Americans assigned to safe jobs like radio research. None was assigned to my detachment, and so it had been easy to ignore Spikes's habit of calling people in his drawl, "Boy," then adding jocularly, "I don't mean Roy." I had never been to a civil rights demonstration, not even in the North. I knew only a few black Americans personally. But I knew I should be on their side. Without question [*friends would have insisted*] that I stick up for a black soldier under my command.

"Stoney," I said to Spikes, "you can't use that word again."

His jaw was set. I appealed to his sense of community. "This guy is going to be part of our detachment." I appealed to his patriotism, which I knew was strong. "He's an American, just like us."

"Where's he gonna sleep?"

Pancho was sitting nearby. "He can sleep in my place."

Spikes shrugged. So far as I knew, he never mistreated the new guy. I think that after a week or so he actually thought of him as one of us. Melvin Harris. It would have been hard not to like him, even though he didn't drink. He was small and quiet and didn't shirk the communal chores. I think he believed first in staying alive. When he went outside our hootches, he always wore his steel pot, with the two chin straps dangling. I had several long talks with him, alone at night in operations when he was on duty. He told me a little of his past, a sad story of an alcoholic father in the slums of Philadelphia, a familiar story but one I'd never heard firsthand before. I remember arguing with him about the Black Panthers, who seemed menacing to me, and trying to get him to denounce them, but he wouldn't. Like Spikes, he seemed to feel he'd ended up in the wrong place, in his case because everyone else was white. He didn't want to be "Tomish," he'd say. He didn't want to be a "gray." But he fit in at my detachment.

FROM THE OTHER SIDE—AND WHAT ABOUT THE VIETNAMESE?

First Lieutenant Ezell Ware Jr.
Second Aviation Battalion, Second Infantry Division
detached for special service, Utapao, Thailand, late 1969
An African-American born and bred in Magee, Mississippi, Ezell Ware believed in the war, before and after his service. After some college, Ware decided to enlist in the French Foreign Legion, but a Marine recruiter who shared its office convinced him to join the Marines instead. After serving a full enlistment and serving briefly with the San Diego police, Ware joined the Army so he could fly helicopters, which the Marines at that time would not let a black man do. Ware became a warrant officer in 1967, in time to be sent to South Vietnam before the Tet Offensive. Later he advanced directly to first lieutenant—and was sent from his duty station in South Korea to Thailand, where he flew AH-1 Cobra gunships for a shadowy organization that may have been the CIA. He crewed with Captain Ronald G. Burdett, an officer who hailed from West Virginia and, unknown to Ware, had been a grand dragon in the KKK. On the mission Ware recounts, their gunship was downed. The black man nursed the badly injured white through a lengthy escape from the enemy. The KKK connection only came out during their ordeal.

In Vietnam it's sometimes hard to tell which war I'm fighting. I know who the enemy is down there, in the jungle, and I know I'm supposed to be on the same side as Burdett, the man just behind me in the cockpit, but I also know he hates me just as much as Charlie does. Probably more. Charlie doesn't really hate me; he just wants me dead so I can't kill him. But if he does hate me, it's because I'm an American, and Charlie hates all Americans the same—white, black, yellow, and brown. That's a rational hatred—a hatred for your wartime enemy. Burdett's hatred is personal.

Burdett here, he doesn't think of me as an American. He thinks of me as a Negro—something less than he is—and he tolerates me because those are his orders. He's stuck flying missions with me, the two of us sent way out in the jungle for hours, but he still can't figure out how the Army let a black man into the cockpit of a helicopter gunship and taught him to fly into battle. Every time we get back to camp in Thailand, he runs out of there like a guy who's been holding his nose around a stink. That's all right; I'm in no hurry to share a laugh and a smoke with him, either. I'm here for me, and for those guys down there, not for him. I don't like flying with him any better than he likes being paired with me.

[*The two men miraculously survived many days in Indian Country, recovered, and became friends. Meanwhile, Ware also reflects on the somewhat similar*

racial aspects of the American-Vietnamese relationship, epitomized in an inci-
dent that had occurred during his previous Vietnam tour with the Sixty-First
Assault Helicopter Company of the 101st Airborne Division in 1968, when his
unit had been at Qui Nhon, where it worked out of Lane Army Airfield at the
camp of the South Korean White Horse Division.]

The Koreans had bought out everything in the PX again, so on a day we
weren't on standby Somers and I rode a jeep to Qui Nhon, to shop at the much
bigger PX [*there*]. I hadn't spent any money on anything except Cokes [*so far*],
so I had plenty of money to spend on gadgets and cigarettes and whatnot.

I drove. We parked along the side of the road near the PX and did our shopping inside. When we came out I absentmindedly laid a carton of cigarettes
I'd bought on the jeep's hood and reached into my pocket for the keys. Just
that fast, a Vietnamese kid—not more than twelve—grabbed the cigarettes
and ran off. In Vietnam, American cigarettes were more valuable than gold.

Without thinking, I unholstered my .38[-*caliber revolver*], raised my arm,
and aimed at him. Somers said nothing, I think because he couldn't believe
I'd actually pull the trigger. But I almost did. I was that close. And then I came
to my senses.

This was what battle did to you. Or to me. Life wasn't even worth a carton
of cigarettes anymore.

CONTACT WITH THE VIETNAMESE

Specialist Five Al Sever
116th Assault Helicopter Company
multiple locations, 1968–1972
Originally a maintenance mechanic, Al Sever transitioned to flight as a door gun-
ner and later a crew chief. Starting with the 116th, stationed at Cu Chi with the
Twenty-Fifth Infantry Division but operating throughout the Saigon–Mekong
area, Sever repeatedly extended his tour until his latest extension request was
denied. He went home after thirty-one months in country. Along the way Sever
served in every region of South Vietnam from the Mekong to the DMZ. Here he
comments on the policy the United States adopted after Tet of restricting Ameri-
cans to their bases.

We really didn't have much contact with ordinary Vietnamese, either civilian
or military. We had a lot of contact with Viet Cong and North Vietnamese,
but we did our talking with bullets. Other than our hootch maids and kitchen
help, we did not have the opportunity to meet local people. I always wondered
how [*a comrade who married a South Vietnamese woman*] managed to meet

his fiancée, but I suppose they met prior to Tet '68, when soldiers were allowed to go off base and mingle with civilians.

I thought the people in charge made a wrong decision when they limited our access to the civilian population. By restricting troops to the base and not [*permitting*] any contact with the Vietnamese, the military was allowing the troops to form a "Fort Apache" complex. We were isolated behind our barbed wire fences in a foreign land and literally surrounded by the enemy. After months behind the wire, most troops started to view all Vietnamese as the enemy. Of course, keeping us penned up lessened the chance of terrorist assassinations off base, but I wonder if we would have lost any more troops overall. Surely we were losing troops to Vietnamese who might not have supported the Viet Cong as much if they had a chance to meet and work with Americans. Granted we Americans were, on the whole, barbarians. But maybe they could have civilized us a little.

Having no real contact with the population, our troops passed on stories and rumors about the local people until they became . . . myths. Base camp barbers were found dead after assaulting the bunker line; hooch maids paced off the distance from last night's mortar impact to better targets for tonight's mortars; boys sold soft drinks along the road with ground glass in the ice, little boys threw hand grenades into parked jeeps, et cetera. Maybe such things had happened at one time somewhere in country, but they didn't happen everywhere or every day. We had no idea what the average peasant thought of us, but it was rare to see anyone waving and smiling as a gunship crew flew several meters above their heads.

We had myths about ourselves also: troops who told their friends that they were fed up and walking home, then left and weren't seen again; the bunker at the Ann-Margaret Bridge where sleeping guards would be periodically found dead with a sign on them reading, "GI sleep, GI die"; a bunker guard shooting his best friend by mistake in the dark; helicopters landing with the whole crew dead. This last story happened at least once, because I saw it.

LETTERS FROM HOME

First Lieutenant Larry Rottmann
Twenty-Fifth Infantry Division
Cu Chi, 1967–1968
Lieutenant Rottmann served through the period of the Tet Offensive in one of the most crucial areas of Vietnam. The Tunnels of Cu Chi, National Liberation Front underground installations that the Twenty-Fifth Division never quite succeeded in

*neutralizing, housed not only NLF troops but also certain of their regional com-
mands and, for a time, the Central Office for South Vietnam (COSVN), the adversary's top headquarters for the entire zone from below the Central Highlands to the
southern tip of Vietnam. Rottmann penned this telling poem about writing home.*

APO 96225

A young man once went off to war
in a far country.
When he had time, he wrote home and
said, "Sure rains here a lot."

But his mother, reading between the lines,
Wrote, "We're quite concerned. Tell us
what it's really like."

And the young man responded, "Wow, you ought
to see the funny monkeys."

To which the mother replied. "Don't
hold back, how is it?"

And the young man wrote, "The sunsets here
are spectacular."

In her next letter the mother
Wrote, "Son, we want you to tell us
everything."

So the next time he wrote,
"Today, I killed a man.
Yesterday, I helped drop napalm on women and
children. Tomorrow we are going to use gas."

*   *   *

And the father wrote, "Please don't
Write such depressing letters. You're upsetting
your mother.

So, after a while, the young man wrote, "Sure rains a
lot here . . . "

DEAR JOHN LETTER

Corporal William D. Ehrhart
intelligence section, First Battalion, First Marines, Third Marine Division
Thua Thien Province, circa October 1967

A member of, and then assistant to the chief of, the intelligence section, Corporal Ehrhart went on many scouting missions because his unit included the battalion reconnaissance team. His battalion fought at Con Thien, in Quang Tri Province, and in a variety of other operations. Ehrhart was a very short-timer when wounded at Hue in February 1968, with his tour in country set to expire in March. But, earlier, Ehrhart was powerless to prevent the personal setback that arrived, as it did for so many in Vietnam, in the form of a "Dear John" letter.

I walked out of the battalion mailroom holding Jenny's letter as though it were the Host. I hadn't heard from her in more than a month of twisting, turning nightmares and vivid daydreams played out in slow motion: automobiles wrinkling like tinfoil under the force of high-speed impact, trapped bodies screaming, sirens and ambulances, hospitals, the deathly stillness of white sheets and nurses, cancer, leukemia, knives and threats in dark alleys on moonless nights. I walked slowly to the intelligence shop in the command bunker and sat down. I opened the letter.

"Dearest Bill," it began, "I guess you're wondering why I haven't written. I just don't know how to explain." What followed was less an explanation than a simple farewell—brief, alien, and distant—less than half a page. "Please forgive me," it concluded. "I pray God will protect you and keep you safe. You'll always be special to me. Jenny."

I couldn't make sense of it. I was prepared for bodily injury, had already imagined myself spending a life caring for a woman with one leg, a blind woman, a woman confined to a wheelchair. Death I could have understood. Anything. But this. This isn't possible, I thought. This isn't *possible*! Eight fucking months! Long letters. Passionate letters. Filled with every imaginable endearment. A perfect chain, like a rosary, a lifeline, a beacon. Something beautiful in the midst of the inescapable ugliness. Gone just like that? This isn't possible, I thought.

"What'sa matter, Corporal Ehrhart?" asked Gunny Johnson. I looked up. He and Lieutenant Kaiser were both staring at me.

"What? What? Nothing."

"You're white as a ghost, boy," said the lieutenant. "You look like you got the DTs. Are you feelin' okay?"

"What? Yeah, sure. Nothing."

"What is it?" the lieutenant persisted. "Bad news from home?"

No! No! No! *Please*, no! "What? I don't—what sir?"

"Go lie down, boy" said Lieutenant Kaiser.

"What?"

"Go lie down," said Johnson.

I got up and walked out into the bright hot light. . . . I started across the sand toward the tents, stumbled, righted myself, turned toward the high berm that surrounded the perimeter, walked to the top, and sat down, staring up Highway 28 toward Danang, where the big Freedom Birds took off every day heading for the World.

SAIGON FUN

Captain Robert L. Tonsetic
Mobile Training Team 162
Tan Son Nhut, May 1971

Captain Tonsetic was senior advisor to the Second Airborne Battalion of the ARVN's Airborne Division, based at Tan Son Nhut. He was seven months into his second tour in country. This time around Tonsetic, after a hard campaign with the South Vietnamese Rangers (see p. 81), was reassigned as an American with the Airborne Division. He needed to blow off some steam, and his recollection illustrates Saigon, circa 1971.

The Team 162 Airborne Division advisors were billeted at the Missouri BOQ in Saigon near the airbase. The BOQ had several floors of rooms that opened onto a balcony that overlooked the parking lot where we kept our Jeeps. A sandbagged checkpoint manned by Vietnamese guards was the only security at the facility, so we kept our weapons close at hand in our rooms. . . .

Since it was Saturday and we didn't work on Sundays, when our battalions were at home station in Saigon, Ed [*Donaldson, Tonsetic's sponsor and friend*] suggested that we sample Saigon's nightlife that evening. After enjoying a Saturday night steak dinner in the BOQ's dining facility, we were ready to head downtown. I assumed we'd be driving in Ed's jeep that evening, but he said we'd be better off taking a Vietnamese taxi. A Jeep parked on a Saigon street was likely to be stolen minutes after it was parked, even if the steering wheel was secured with a heavy chain and lock. In Saigon, crime was normally more of a threat than the acts of terror perpetrated by the Communists. So called "Saigon cowboys" riding on Honda motorbikes sped down darkened streets and alleyways in search of drunken and disoriented GIs to mug. Without even slowing down on their Hondas, they could snap a Rolex off your wrist or snatch an expensive camera off your shoulder in a nanosecond.

Our first stop was the *Hoa Binh* Bar on Le Loi Street, a favorite hangout of the airborne advisors. By 8 p.m. the bar was crowded with American and Vietnamese paratroopers along with Marine advisors. After downing a *Ba Moi Ba* beer, I spotted a couple of black soldiers wearing airborne camouflage fatigues at the end of the bar. I walked over to introduce myself to the pair, and was surprised when they greeted me in Vietnamese. I thought they were pulling my leg, but I smiled and bought them a beer anyway. When I returned to my seat . . . Ed laughingly explained to me that the men were Vietnamese airborne troopers who were the offspring of French African Colonial troops who fought in the first Indo-China War.

After quenching our thirst at the *Hoa Binh,* we hailed another taxi and headed for the well-known Pink Pussycat Bar. Ed warned me not to buy any Saigon tea for the bar girls. That could set you back ten or more dollars per tea. We had no trouble enticing a couple of bar girls to our table after we ordered our drinks. We ordered them a couple of cokes, but they began to lose interest when we refused to follow up with . . . Saigon teas. When we got up to leave, one of the girls suggested that if we returned at closing time they would, "love us longtime" when they got off duty at the bar. They'd go for a one-night stand for a price, but what they really wanted was a long-term relationship with an apartment and unlimited privileges out of our paychecks.

It was approaching the curfew hour so I suggested to Ed that we head back to the BOQ, but he assured me that we wouldn't be apprehended. . . . The 716th Battalion MPs never bothered the Airborne Division's advisors after they fought side by side with the Airborne during the Tet Offensive of 1968, and the Vietnamese White Mice (Vietnamese civilian police) knew better than to try to arrest any American wearing the uniform of the Vietnamese airborne. Our final stop was Mimi's Bar Lounge and Restaurant where we had a few more drinks and a late night supper. I was glad that we could sleep in the next morning since I could already feel the effects of the formaldehyde in the Vietnamese beer.

REST AND RECREATION

Private First Class William Goshen
India Company, Seventy-Fifth Infantry (Ranger), First Infantry Division
February 1969
The tour of duty in Vietnam followed a defined trajectory, twelve months for soldiers and airmen, thirteen for sailors and Marines. Arriving in country, the soldier would be processed through one of a few main receiving centers, given an assignment, and moved to a unit. Personal fears revolved around making the grade, fitting in, and the mysteries of combat. Toward the end, when the grunt had become a short-timer, concerns centered on staying alive long enough to catch that "Freedom Bird" home to "The World." Somewhere in between these stages was the moment for "R&R," literally a vacation from the war, to which all were entitled. The military offered the venues, men took their choice among what was available at the moment. A certain amount of negotiation took place. The fleshpots of Bangkok were a destination for many on R&R; married personnel or

officers might meet their mates in the Philippines or Hawaii. Some went to Hong Kong, a few to Australia, and others to Singapore, Taiwan, or Japan. The R&R moment for Private Goshen came after graduation from the arduous training of the MACV Recondo School, making him one of the skilled Rangers with the First Infantry Division. At the time the Army was reorganizing its special operations as units of an independent Ranger regiment attached to divisions in the field.

Things really began to heat up for us after our unit was redesignated. We began to get more missions at the same time we were getting a lot of replacements . . . and they needed a lot of training. We had to cannibalize downtime teams just to get full teams together for mission assignments, which meant . . . seasoned Rangers were getting . . . less time between missions, and there were fewer people in the company area qualified to train the new men.

Typically we were given three days between a warning order and an upcoming mission, but in early 1969 that was cut to one or two. . . . At times, we were given only a one- or two-day turnaround . . . which was not enough time to get ourselves physically or mentally prepared for another launch, especially for those of us who were walking point on the patrols. Giving up downtime was a price that few of us could afford to pay.

One day, I received a big surprise. Lieutenant Davis walked over and handed me a piece of paper. He told me that he knew things had been rough lately and that I needed to take some time off to get a little rest. I didn't know what he was talking about until I looked at the paper and saw that it was a seven-day leave to Japan. I couldn't have been happier if he had told me the war was over. . . .

[*After a flight to Tokyo and an orientation on behavior acceptable in Japan, Goshen, who wanted to see Mount Fuji, traveled to Atomi, the town at the foot of the mountain.*]

Several of us made our way to the train station to catch a ride on the bullet train, which was capable of speeds of nearly two hundred miles an hour. As we climbed aboard, I made my way to the dining car to consume my first full meal outside since arriving in Vietnam. . . . I finally decided to order curried chicken. It was absolutely wonderful. After several months of dehydrated LRRP rations and canned C rations, the meal was simply exquisite.

The best part of dining aboard the train was being able to observe the countryside. . . . The only problem was that at two hundred miles an hour, everything closer than a mile was only a blur. But I could see that Japan was indeed a beautiful country, and I was even more impressed when we finally arrived at the town of Atomi. . . . [*Goshen marveled at the view from a palace he visited at the eight-thousand-foot point on Fuji—"It reminded me of the beautiful oil paintings I occasionally saw in Oriental restaurants back in the States." And he was even more taken with the vista from the summit.*]

At the top we found that some inspired soul had erected an indoor ice-skating rink, which several of the guys wanted to try. I told them I didn't know how to ice-skate, but I was a pretty fair roller skater. They finally talked me into making an attempt, and skating was really great. With a little practice I could glide around with ease. . . . However, stopping remained a different story altogether. All I could do to brake to a halt was to slam into a wall. . . . At least the ice-skating got our minds off the war. [*As the days flew by Goshen thought about home and then, increasingly, about what still awaited him in country. Soon he found himself returning to base camp at Lai Khe, South Vietnam.*]

7

War in the Plains

EARLY DOUBTS

Private First Class Jan Barry
U.S. Army Support Group, Vietnam
Nha Trang, 1962

Jan Barry started with hopes for an Army career and organized a petition campaign in his hometown of Interlaken, New York, to secure an appointment to West Point. In the meantime he enlisted. Upon learning he was headed for South Vietnam, Barry went to the library to read up, but the only books there concerned French Indochina. In the field he met a Special Forces sergeant who told Barry we were on the wrong side, backing a dictatorship, and that the Liberation Front were really the ones protecting villagers from a Saigon police state. He heard similar things from other military professionals, men who had been through World War II and Korea. Barry's encounters sowed seeds of doubt, and his Vietnam experience—long before the high days of the war—fertilized them. Private Barry's early tour was vintage U.S. Army.

When I got to Saigon, Tan Son Nhut airport, the reception area was a bunch of World War II tents in a palm tree grove that looked exactly like a south sea island setting in World War II. There was no propaganda or . . . training, so people were thrown out into this country and had to find out for themselves what was going on.

The headquarters of my unit was in Nha Trang. It was an aviation unit that flies Canadian DeHavilland [*C-7 Caribou*] bush pilot planes that land and

— 139 —

take off in a very short space. It was also the Special Forces headquarters. We were the air force, in essence, for many of their operations.

I was to keep the radios working, which is not what I was trained to do. I was trained in infantry radios. Typical Army—you train in the infantry and they send you to an aviation unit. So I had on-the-job training.

Airplanes were held together with spit, baling wire, and chewing gum. People flew them until they crashed. You also realized that we were left with all the leftover equipment. You had helicopters, the banana-shaped helicopters from Korea, that literally came apart in midair. . . . We were using bombers left over from World War II that crashed because the wings came off in these dives. The most sturdy planes in this crazy arsenal were these little bush pilot planes that were not designed for military use.

This unit had airplanes stationed on airfields all over South Vietnam and in Thailand. They flew in and out of the airfields for repairs, R and R, beer runs. It was a combination of half serious military missions and totally frivolous things like beer runs and taking nurses up for rides with officers. In the middle of all that, people like me, who are enlisted men, have to pull night guard duty to supposedly protect all these people.

You had orders that you couldn't keep any ammunition in your rifle. They were locked up because I was told that guys had previously gotten drunk on Saturday nights and got into shoot-outs in the barracks. They never said this, but what became clear was that they were afraid we would shoot the officers. I think they were also afraid that somebody would shoot a civilian and it would be an international incident. So there was some practical reason, but there was also the problem of being in a war zone and not having access to your weapons.

You were in this ridiculous Mickey Mouse situation, like play acting, in which you're on guard duty but your weapon isn't loaded. This is an M-1 . . . a World War II rifle.

We got blown out of bed one night, about 3 a.m. It turned out that [*the Liberation Front*] had come through the wire and were blowing up airplanes. There were Vietnamese guards outside the perimeter and American guards on the interior perimeter where our airplanes were. All the guards started shooting like crazy, although they had no idea what they were shooting at. It sounded like you were in the middle of World War II. We couldn't get access to our weapons because it was Saturday night and the person who had the key to the conex box—which was a big steel box where all the weapons were locked up—was downtown shacked up with his girlfriend.

[*Barry was ten months in country when he was summoned to the West Point Preparatory School. His efforts to get into the Point bore fruit—Barry entered the class of 1968, which was told they were preparing to lead platoons in Vietnam. But he was the only cadet with actual experience there. The contrived Gulf*

*of Tonkin Incident disturbed Barry, and other things he learned bothered him
equally, to the point that he resigned from the Corps of Cadets in November 1964.
According to Barry, he was the tenth of fifty of that class to resign. Barry went on
to become a founder of Vietnam Veterans Against the War. This poem captures
his thoughts from that early tour of duty.]*

IN THE FOOTSTEPS OF GENGHIS KHAN

There, where a French legionnaire
once walked patrol
around the flightline perimeter of the airfield
at Nhatrang
occupied even earlier
twenty years before
(a year more than my nineteen)
by the Japanese

Unhaunted by the ghosts, living and dead
among us
in the red-tile roofed French barracks
or listening in on the old Japanese telephone line
to Saigon
we went about our military duties
(setting up special forces headquarters
where once a French foreign legion post had been
oblivious to the irony
of Americans waking in the footsteps
of Genghis Khan)

Unencumbered by history
our own or that of 13th Century Mongol armies
long since fled or buried
by the Vietnamese
in Nhatrang, in 1962, we just did our jobs
replacing kepi's with berets, "ah so" with "gawd!"

OPERATION DAVY CROCKETT

Lieutenant Larry Gwin
A Company, Second Battalion, Seventh Cavalry Regiment, First Cavalry
Division
Bong Son, May 1966
*After some months in the Highlands, the Cav leaped into the coastal plain as
part of a concerted offensive to corral enemy forces reported in the foothills.
Gwin's unit air-assaulted into Binh Dinh Province with his brigade, now under*

Colonel Hal Moore. Binh Dinh had long been a center of National Liberation Front strength. Intelligence confirmed the presence of the People's Army 325th Division—the same adversaries the Cav had fought at Ia Drang—in Binh Dinh. Alpha Company took the field with replenished ranks, but Gwin notes, "We didn't last at full strength very long." His troopers donned gas masks for the attack. Gwin encountered terror of a new kind.

I knew we'd run into something. Bong Son was VC country. It had been crawling with the bastards back in February, when Alpha company had fought at LZ 4. . . . [*Major General*] John Norton, our new division commander, whom I'd remembered as the commanding general of the 82nd Airborne Division back at Bragg, wanted to find them.

Yes, this was going to be a hot one. I could feel it. Something was gnawing at my stomach, too. (I didn't know it was worms.) Would the new CO keep his cool if we ran into something? How good was the new guy, Polli [*fresh leader of the company's mortar platoon*]? Were we headed for another blood bath?

We flew into a mustering area north of Bong Son and camped in a secured airfield beside the choppers that would rev up in the early morning and carry us farther north. We rested, cleaned our weapons, ate hot Cs, and absorbed Captain Davison's orders that night. He'd flown over the target that afternoon—a razor-back, rock-strewn ridge overlooking a village ten clicks north. After an artillery and tear-gas prep, we would assault the ridge, four ships at a time. A simple dawn air assault—routine but for the tear gas. Enemy units were suspected . . . but Davison had seen nothing suspicious that afternoon.

I slept on my poncho on the hard dry ground near the airstrip. Despite the cool air and the quiet night, I slept badly. . . .

The sun blazed as it rose from the South China Sea. We flew at eighty knots, a thousand feet up. After just a few minutes in the air I could see the objective. . . . Our choppers dropped faster, swooping in behind the gunships that had blasted the ridgeline. I leaned out the door and watched the first wave land. Troops were dropping from the Hueys as they hovered over the hilltop. They had to jump. There was no place to land!

"Gonna have to jump!" I yelled, my words muffled by the mask, the roar of the Huey's turbine, and the wind whipping through the bay. First Sergeant Miller's goggle-eyed visage nodded acknowledgement, and he spread the word. A hundred meters out, I felt the rotor blades change pitch as our ship flared its nose for the approach.

Boone (my new RTO), who'd been monitoring the radio, tapped me on the shoulder. "PAVN in the village!" he yelled.

Oh, Jesus, here we go again, I thought, looking back out the door at the hilltop coming at us fast now, exposed, rocky, and bright with sunlight. White tracer rounds caromed crazily into the air from behind the ridge. I heard a vague *whump* in the distance. Another hot LZ.

The ship continued steadily. . . . I had my right foot on the landing strut, and was holding on to the cargo-bay pole with my right hand. The door gunners started pumping rounds down the hillside. As we hovered over the ridge, I jumped. Too soon.

Crashing into the rocks on my back, I was momentarily paralyzed with pain. I couldn't breathe. I looked up. The chopper's landing strut and underbelly were coming down slowly, inexorably, the strut across my chest. I'm gonna get crushed, I thought. Then the other men jumped, masked grotesques from outer space, crashing all around me, falling, grunting, and cursing. The chopper suddenly stopped its downward course, stabilized, lifted slowly, then dipped its nose and fell away, down the far hillside toward the village.

[*Lieutenant Gwin survived three days of battle and another assault landing before leg injuries forced him to seek medical care. During that short time Gwin suddenly realized he no longer knew some of the wounded and dead loaded into the choppers. This war chewed men right up.*]

MARINE SNIPERS

Gunnery Sergeant Thomas Casey, USMC
Sniper Platoon, Fifth Marine Regiment
An Hoa, January 1967

Tom Casey was an excellent shot and became a Marine sniper. The Fifth Regiment sniper platoon was provisionally created near Chu Lai in July 1966. Casey led it intermittently through 1966 because a number of the men were constantly detached for security duties at U.S. bases. That November the platoon reassembled and Casey became permanent commander. Two months later a pair of two-man sniper teams were sent on mission to An Hoa. The sniper, assisted by a spotter, used an M1D rifle. Sergeant Casey, a competition shooter on Marine rifle teams, served as the sniper on this outing. Line officers frequently looked askance at specialized sniper units, seeing them as diverting fine marksmen from their companies. Tom Casey's experience with Sergeant Manuel Ybarra's patrol of H Company, Second Battalion, Fifth Marines, shows the value of snipers in the boonies. Casey's spotter was Corporal Ron Willoughby.

Willoughby's elbow nudged Casey out of his moment of reflection as a file of soldiers stepped out of the tree line and turned away from the snipers' hillside lookout to follow the Marines of Sergeant Ybarra's patrol. Casey whispered, "Man, those guys are armed, and I can see weapons even at this distance. We got to warn the patrol or those bastards will sneak up on their rear and cut them off from us."

Willoughby had his binoculars clasped tightly in his fists, and he stared along the edge of the rice fields at the column of Viet Cong. He put his glasses down and spoke in a muted tone. "I make them about five hundred meters at the rear and six hundred meters when their point man crosses that big dike up ahead. See if you can target the length of their column, and you'll hit somebody and then Sergeant Ybarra will be forewarned. What do you think?"

Casey looked at Willoughby like he'd just farted and replied, "I think it's a great fucking idea. What did you think I'd think?"

Willoughby, who was just getting to know Casey pretty well, looked hurt. "I think you better shoot now, Sergeant Casey, 'cause those bastards are moving up pretty fast and in another minute there ain't gonna be anything left to shoot at!"

Sergeant Casey didn't look back. . . . He took the towel off the scope, raised the Remington to his shoulder, and laid the barrel across a thick branch. . . . The Viet Cong [were] well past the six hundred meter dike marker that Willoughby had earlier range-estimated. Casey took the rifle off his shoulder and dialed in six hundred meters of elevation. The wind was in his face and negligible. He held dead on the lead VC, figuring the bullet drop would take out the second man in the file. At seven hundred meters the bullet would drop maybe forty-five inches, but he was shooting downslope, so the target would appear closer than it actually was, perhaps as far away as eight hundred. . . . The column had seven soldiers and a black-clad person who might have been a female Viet Cong nurse. Casey figured it didn't matter because they were all armed and the woman was a combatant and subject to all the same harsh rules of survival that applied to everyone in this crazy fucking war.

The crosshairs settled on the point man's tunic, and Casey took up the slack until the rifle discharged. Willoughby thought the blast and concussion . . . was so loud . . . that everyone in the world would know where he and Casey were emplaced.

When the rifle barrel settled again onto the point man, there was a gap behind his position and a soldier lay sprawled on the trail. The other members of the Viet Cong patrol scattered into the tree line. . . . An hour later Manny Ybarra and the patrol from Hotel Company came toward the hill and waved for the snipers to join up. Casey noticed that Ybarra had approached the sniper hide from the other side of the rice valley. Later, Ybarra would point out that the surest way to get ambushed is to come in from patrol using the same trails you went out on.

CALLING IN THE FIRE

Second Lieutenant Paul R. Young, USMC
First Reconnaissance Battalion, First Marine Division
Duc Pho, March 1967

Our turn for Duc Pho came in March.

Duc Pho was the southernmost district of Quang Ngai Province, an area that had been under Communist control for years. Large Vietcong units operated freely throughout the heavily populated coastal region, levying taxes, recruiting party members, and developing a network of fortified villages and underground hospitals. There were so few ARVN and civilian officials in Duc Pho that most . . . people living there had never seen nor dealt with a representative of the South Vietnamese government. For them, the Vietcong was the government. . . .

As we approached Nui Dang, we flew over a large, triangular-shaped fort built long ago by the French—a landmark to bitterness and failure. There was a message in that fort, but we were Americans and wouldn't hear it if it jumped up screaming. So now the fort was ours, part of 3/7's growing perimeter, where artillery fired, helicopters came and went, and Marines on foot moved everywhere. It was a regular city down there.

We landed in a cloud of red dust and filed off the birds to be met by a sergeant from the liaison section. . . . Sergeant Below and I left the men in the paddy and followed . . . to the battalion CP, where we were told we would be going out later in the day and shown on the map where our insertion would be. We sat on a stack of 105 ammo crates and began outlining the assigned grid squares. . . . We would be changing places with a patrol already in the area, which was not good. . . . Other Marines would be operating in the vicinity, but none close enough to lend a hand if we got into trouble. Our insertion was scheduled for late afternoon. . . .

Our LZ was down low in the foothills, not far from a large village. The insertion would go down about as unnoticed as a setdown at Hollywood and Vine. We went in without incident . . . and headed in the direction of a more distant hill. . . . The vegetation was tall and thick enough so we could travel most of the distance . . . without being seen. Within an hour we were on the side of the hill establishing an OP among some boulders screened by trees and heavy brush. I got out my binoculars and climbed a tree to look for Charlie Cong and his cousins from the north.

The area was loaded with them.

A thousand meters away, uniformed bearers moved up and down a trail, carrying weapons and supplies like a regular conveyor belt. Most of the bearers kept to disciplined intervals of one hundred feet or more, but a few of the careless ones tended to bunch up along the steep places. . . . I reported our sightings to 3/7, then read off the coordinates and azimuth of the target to the 105 battery at Nui Dang. . . .

I called shots until dark . . . for the time being playing havoc with the supply line. But soon after dark, they were moving by lantern light, and it was difficult to keep the rounds on target. Finally, I told arty to blast the trail every hour or so in the hopes of hitting something and climbed down from the tree. [*Young's patrol kept up the game into the next day, when they returned to base, then immediately went on another mission.*]

A RECURRENT NIGHTMARE

Sergeant Alan G. Cornett
Long-Range Reconnaissance Patrol Detachment, First Brigade, 101st Airborne Division
Duc Pho, June 1967
After an initial raid to capture prisoners, Cornett's unit received orders for another operation of the same sort.
I can't remember the name or location of the village, but I still wake up at night thinking about it.

The mission would be the same, the taking of prisoners. I was once again the chief medic and was assigned to the headquarters fire team. Lieutenant McIsaac would be in charge of the fire team and the whole raid.

On the line we moved toward the village, at the ready. As we entered the tree line, we started taking incoming fire. The enemy had been taken by surprise but was quickly mounting a defense. Outside one of the hootches . . . we came to two rucksacks that looked to be VC. As we got closer to the hootch with the rucksacks, two young women who had been herding cattle and were caught in the open paddy when we landed were between us and the hootch. Weems, one of the fire-team leaders, told them in Vietnamese to stop, but they kept moving. Weems then grabbed one of the girls and put her on the ground. The older girl went to her belly, and both girls started praying for us not to kill them. Another Lurp and I reached the hootch with the rucks and proceeded to check it carefully. We could hear a child crying from inside. I yelled into the hootch, "Lai Dai!" (come out), but the crying grew more intense, almost to a scream. I looked inside where a child, a girl about two years old, was clinging desperately to what must have been her mother, who was sitting up in the corner with her arms around the little girl, as if trying to protect her from harm. There wasn't any visible blood, only a small hole in the mother's head. She was dead. A stray round had killed her. I pleaded with the child to come out, but the more I talked the more terrified the child became.

In a crouch I moved into the hootch as another Lurp covered me; I didn't know if the owners of the rucks were still inside, waiting to blow us away. There were two other small rooms. . . . Most hootches had a trapdoor in the floor that concealed an area that could house an enemy. That hootch had a trapdoor, but after carefully opening it, I found it contained only pottery filled with rice. There was nothing in either room. By the time we finished checking . . . the other guys had checked the rucks that were sitting outside. They contained demolitions and things that a man living in the jungle needed to survive.

Meanwhile, the platoon's mission to capture prisoners had deteriorated into a running gun battle. With the enemy gaining strength by the minute, Lieutenant McIsaac decided to extract us while we still had the chance. . . . He called in the slicks. . . . We ran back out of the tree line and jumped into the helicopter. . . . By that time the enemy was shooting at us with a heavy machinegun (.51 caliber), and tracers were flying everywhere, several of them coming in one door and going out the other. One round smacked heavily right over my head. . . . Suddenly my helicopter started bucking and shuddering terribly. The pilot turned around and gave us the thumbs-down. . . . Our pilot was very good and was able to control the helicopter until we slammed into the ground. Fortunately it stayed right-side up, and nobody was hurt.

[*Sergeant Cornett and his buddies were rescued by another chopper and decompressed at base camp, but in his mind he could still see the dead woman and hear the child screaming, and worried that the young girl had no family.*]

SHAME

Specialist James W. Walker
Long-Range Reconnaissance Patrol Detachment, First Brigade, 101st Airborne Division
Duc Pho, central coast, June 1967
Specialist Walker, a Britisher who enlisted in the U.S. Army, transferred from military police to the storied lurps (LRRPs). The mission he records formed part of the same campaign as that above. In it Walker came face-to-face with the underside of pacification.
We had another mission to prepare for, and it wasn't much of a surprise . . . that it was not going to be a Lurp mission. We would be going back into the Song Ve Valley in detachment strength—another misuse of our talent by higher command. Our detachment and elements of a nearby ARVN Ranger battalion were to conduct sweeps of the valley floor and to evacuate all civilian inhabitants along with their personal possessions, including livestock. I wanted to ask Lieutenant McIsaac if the operation would qualify us as cowboys, but sensing his mood . . . I decided to keep my mouth shut.

Our unit was about to participate in what was being called the largest single civil-affairs project to date. With the rest of the brigade roaming the mountains and jungles around us . . . we didn't really expect to have a lot of trouble with Charlie, who had only three options. He could take us on in the open; he could go after the rest of the brigade in the bush; he could shag his ass before his escape routes were shut down, then come back to fight on a better day.

At the briefing we were told that the Vietnamese civilians occupying the south end of the valley would be waiting for us outside a ville, ready for evacuation. Anything north of that point was in the designated free-fire zone. Free-fire meant just what it said—we didn't have to wait until something declared itself a danger to us, but could blow it away without provocation. Nothing was safe in the free-fire zone. Dogs, cats, chickens, ducks, people, trees that moved in the wind. . . .

We touched down just outside the ville and spread out across the paddies, then we sat down propped against the paddy dikes, waiting to move out. Two hours later we were still waiting. It was the army way. . . .

I watched as the Vietnamese civilians to our rear jabbered their heads off. Behind them, over a thousand head of cattle trudged along, probably every bit as tired and hot as we were. Where was Rowdy Yates when you needed him? "Head 'em up, move 'em out, Rawhiiiiiiiiiiide."

Finally, nearly three hours into the mission, the ARVN Rangers showed up. They came in by Chinook helicopters. . . . It was a real comfort to see them stumbling around, bumping into each other, chattering, and holding hands. The Keystone Kops couldn't have been any more hilarious. If they had been our support we would have been in deep shit, yet they were supposed to be the cream of the Vietnamese Army! I turned to Boss for a little support and understanding and saw him nodding toward a hootch perhaps a hundred meters away. "Limey," he said, "I've been watching that hootch for over two hours and nobody has come out." Before I could respond, automatic fire broke out to our rear. Expecting to have to open up on an assaulting wave of enemy troops, I grabbed my weapon and spun around. Instead I was met with a sight that I will never forget: the ARVNs were shooting at the cattle. The Vietnamese civilians looked on stoically as their own military, their protectors, systematically destroyed their wealth. Winning the hearts and minds of the people! Yeah.

I was shamed by what I saw. We all were. We self-consciously shied away from the South Vietnamese Rangers, not wanting any part of the slaughter nor to be seen to share their guilt. In the background, Lieutenant McIsaac was screaming at the ARVNs to stop. . . .

Suddenly, less than a hundred feet away, a hootch disintegrated with a roar and a blinding explosion. I dived to the ground. Obviously the enemy had hidden explosives in at least one of the buildings. It was the only proof we needed. Not having the time to conduct a more thorough search, we started to set fire to the entire village.

It wasn't long before we received a call from a C&C chopper to stop the torching. A few minutes later, the call came in again. . . . What a bunch of shit! We were furious. I guess the order of the day had been changed . . . and that "clear the valley, but don't mess it up any" superseded the original orders. Well, none of us bought that line of thinking. The Zippos stayed busy and so did the guys. And other secondary explosions detonated around us, confirming our suspicions. With half the ville ablaze, a Huey helicopter hovered about four hundred feet overhead. I could see the unhappy officer . . . talking on the radio, his arms flailing madly. We all prayed the moron would lose his balance and join us on the ground. Eventually Lieutenant McIsaac, tired of getting his ass chewed out, told us to knock it off and move out.

[*In a six-day operation the LRRPs found a wounded guerrilla in that first village, observed an enemy squad running away, encountered a dead body floating in the river, and had a single contact—with guerrillas in bunkers, whom they neutralized. Walker records that the 1/101st's after-action report claimed it had relocated 6,256 villagers with 1,341 head of cattle and, by body count, killed 470 of the enemy.*]

Second Lieutenant Frederick Downs Jr.
First Battalion, Fourteenth Infantry, Fourth Infantry Division
Duc Pho, central coast, September 1967

A newbie just out of Officer Candidate School, Downs conducted patrols carefully.
My first days on combat patrol introduced me to the vicissitudes of war: ten-foot deep punji pits; wait-a-minute vines that collected around the feet and legs until their combined strength stopped you and you had to say "wait-a-minute" while you untangled or cut yourself loose; the hot sun beating down on us as we marched with seventy-pound packs, the sweat pouring off us; bugs so thick around our faces that we sometimes inhaled them; and the physical agony of forcing muscles to keep on going.

It was a search-and-destroy mission, which meant we searched all the hootches we found and then burned them down. Whether a single farmer's hootch or a whole village—all were burnt. The few Vietnamese we found in the area were women, children, and old men who had been left behind. When we started to burn their particular hootch, they would start wailing, crying, and pulling at our clothes. We didn't harm the people, but the orders were to destroy all the dwellings, so we did.

The first time I saw a Vietnamese family go into hysterics when their hootch was set on fire I was unsure of whether burning down their home would accomplish our mission. The mission was to deny the enemy the use of the hootches, to destroy any food we found, and to teach the people a lesson about supporting the enemy. But I quickly got used to it and accepted that this was one way to win the war.

I was fired at by a sniper shortly after we had swept through one small hamlet. I always thought the sniper was firing at us because we had just set fire to his hootch and, unfortunately, he picked me as a target.

MOMENT OF TERROR

Warrant Officer Thomas A. Johnson
A Company, 229th Assault Helicopter Battalion, First Cavalry Division (Airmobile)
An Lao Valley, September 5, 1967
Flying a slick for the Cav, Tom Johnson achieved full pilot status (aircraft commander) barely two weeks before this, his first night resupply mission, which turned into an emergency extraction when the LRRP team he was to help came under attack. The lurps had simply hacked their LZ out of the nearest forest clearing, with barely the diameter of Johnson's UH-1 rotor blades. It turned out to be a slope pockmarked with tree stumps disguised by vegetation. This was a hairy extraction—at night, no light, not daring to use flares, with the lurps under fire to boot. Johnson's recollection gives a feel for the problems of flying helicopters in Vietnam. Warrant officer Johnson was later awarded the Distinguished Flying Cross.
Tall trees, silhouetted by the fires, pass only a few feet underneath the aircraft, dancing violently from the hurricane force winds generated by the Huey's blade system. I remind myself that we are in a tail-low attitude—the tail rotor must clear the trees before I descend any lower.

"Tail rotor clear, sir," Thompson yells on the intercom. He is leaning out of his cubicle and has a plain view of both the tree line we have just crossed and the tail rotor itself.

At near zero forward speed, 30 feet up in the air, I smoothly push the collective pitch control down, and we begin to settle vertically into the small clearing.

Alternately looking straight ahead and through the chin bubble . . . I size up the conditions in the LZ. It slopes alarmingly . . . toward the valley floor and is filled with stumps and mortar craters. If we maintain our current direction, the hover will be so high that it will be impossible to take the [*lurps*] aboard.

"Stop fire—left turn!" I call over the intercom.

"Tail rotor clear, sir," is the reply as the guns go silent.

Both [*crewmen*] Thompson and Denning are leaning dangerously . . . for a clearer view of the main and tail rotors. Striking any object with either will mean certain death. On this much of an incline, we would fall . . . and roll downhill in a fiery ball.

As I press the left pedal to rotate the fuselage . . . on its vertical axis, I repeatedly cross check the engine and rotor system tachometer for any sign that we are running out of power. This would be a disaster of the highest magnitude, since we are now inside the LZ's walls, with nowhere to go except up or down. If we run out of power, the aircraft will begin a slow settling to the ground, and with the degree of incline on the LZ floor, the first part of the helicopter to touch the ground will be the tips of the main rotor blades. If this happens the rotor system will separate. . . .

I am oblivious to the carnage within the LZ and the gunfire around me. My fear level has increased dramatically. At the moment I am far more afraid of dying from some miscalculation in my flying than I am . . . of my enemy. I concentrate on the trees directly ahead, with occasional glimpses downward. . . . We continue our descent.

[*Thompson managed to hover at a few feet, but that means the rotors, as they pass on the uphill side, are barely three feet from contact—and a crash. He is challenged to maintain the chopper's stability as his crew moves around and then the first of the GIs jumps on the skids to climb into the ship. He adds power as the lurps board the slick.*]

How many survivors are there? Will there be more than I can get out? Who will be left behind?

Helicopter lifting capacities are critically limited by density altitude, an equation that adjusts current altitude for factors of temperature, humidity, and barometric pressure. All helicopters can lift more when the air is colder and drier and thus denser. In the States, the Huey could easily transport a crew of four plus as many as ten soldiers, depending on how heavily loaded they were with packs. In Vietnam, the tropical heat and humidity reduces the maximum safe capacity to six troops with packs. Any more than six or seven can be a real problem. It's to our advantage that these survivors will have nothing but their shirts and trousers, and that it is the coolest period of the tropical day . . . just before daylight.

The scuffling in back continues, and I [*increase*] power and fearfully glance at the main rotor rpm gauge on the dash. The needle is steady at 6600 rpm.

For the first time I think of the possibility of being shot. I am less than one-third of the way through my one-year tour. At first, I felt invincible. It only happens to the other guy. Now—reality. We have been a sitting target for over 60 seconds of my life. It seems more like an eternity. [*Explosions of rockets from supporting gunship choppers startle Johnson. Then his crew chief tells him the lurps are aboard, and he begins to climb out. The ship responds sluggishly. At thirty feet, near the treetops, the engine whines as the pilots demand more power than it can deliver. Johnson's ingrained response to this situation puts the chopper into a spin.*]

[*Copilot*] Johansen mutters without keying his mike. I can't tell if he is giving me words of encouragement or praying. At the moment, either would be suitable.

Halfway through our rotation, the low rpm warning light on the dash comes on, illuminating the whole. The audible alarm shrills in the intercom—the third time I've heard it in flight. [*Johnson attempts a corkscrew climb and gets a little power, but finally is forced to head directly into the hill, where his skids drag across the branches. But as the chopper begins to fall, its forward motion is regained.*] We've made it—our apocalypse will have to wait.

FRIENDLY FIRE

Warrant Officer Chuck Carlock
Seventy-First Assault Helicopter Company, Fourteenth Aviation Battalion, Task Force Oregon
Chu Lai, coastal base, October 1967
Flying a gunship helicopter, Carlock carried out many missions in the I Corps area. He found the South Vietnamese almost as dangerous as the enemy.

The ARVN . . . was a great source of friendly fire. One of the first night missions I flew in Vietnam, we passed over the province capital, Tam Ky, at around 1,500 feet. The friendly South Vietnamese soldiers (ARVNs) shot about 100 friendly tracer rounds at us. McCall said that they did this every night. The ARVNs always claimed to be clearing their rifles. I asked him why didn't we shoot back? He said that if they ever hit him he would, that he didn't give a damn if they court-martialed him or not. On clear nights, we flew around the town. We always turned our lights off, so they could only shoot at the sound.

Eventually, I had enough of this. One night (after I made aircraft commander), I was flying a single gunship along Highway One to Chu Lai. In a foul mood as I approached Tam Ky, I told my [*copilot to arm the guns*], "Put it on hot and get ready." When the ARVN soldiers unloaded on us . . . we returned about 2,000 rounds of miniguns right back at them. Miller said he was about ten miles behind me and saw me go low level with no lights and land at Chu Lai without calling the control tower. This ensured there would be no record of the time I landed. As far as I know, the ARVNs never shot at a helicopter at night again. . . .

Tam Ky also had a lot of VC. Several weeks after I arrived at Chu Lai, a Chinook (large two-rotor helicopter) accidentally dropped a sling-load of artillery shells there and started a fire which ignited a VC grenade factory in the town.

One day I took a hit as we flew across Tam Ky, and my gunner saw the muzzle flash at the back of the Catholic church in town. I assume that some Charlie decided to use the church for cover. The round tore up a bunch of the electrical equipment in the chopper.

The most frustrating kind of "friendly" fire was that we received from the VC who would fire at us from "friendly" areas, knowing we wouldn't shoot back. Many times as we came in on the final approach at night to the refueling point at Tam Ky, the VC would sneak . . . into an area of hooches near the perimeter to shoot at us. I always refused to let Bruce or Aker return fire because we were so close to the provincial capital headquarters building. One day, as we were coming in on final approach . . . I felt the helicopter lurch. Bruce and Aker, frustrated at being shot at and not being able to shoot back, began to laugh as they told me they had shoved a large hunk of metal out the door. . . . It was a link from a tracked vehicle's drive train and was extremely heavy. Bruce made a perfect hit on the hooch . . . and it caved in the entire roof.

Second Lieutenant Frederick Downs Jr.
First Battalion, Fourteenth Infantry, Fourth Infantry Division
Duc Pho, central coast, November 1967
Lieutenant Downs found the low field strength of his rifle platoon problematical whenever it came time to set up night defensive positions.
Evening was drawing near as we reached a relatively flat top on a ridge which would make a good night location. The only formation for a night position, or any defensive position in the jungle, or an area without definite lines of battle, was a circle on high ground with everyone facing outward. An attack could certainly come from any direction or from many directions at once.

My platoon fluctuated between twenty-three and thirty men. I always put three men in a foxhole so they could build a hootch and set up a proper guard at night. This meant we could have seven to ten positions to form our circle. The medic, radioman [RTO], and I represented the hub in the middle of the circle. We were not in the middle for protection but to maintain control. If our position was in the line when an attack started somewhere else, I would have had to pull out to where the fighting was to direct our defensive efforts. My RTO would have to stick with me like a shadow with his radio, and, of course, the medic would be needed when someone was hit. With all three of us out of position there would have been a gap in the line.

My position in the middle provided better control and a roving reserve of two extra rifles to add strength where needed. The medic carried a rifle, but after the first man was hit the medic's firepower was cut as he attended to the wounded.

Every American defensive position in Vietnam was set up on a similar basis, whether it was my small platoon in the middle of the jungle, a battalion firebase, or a main base camp such as the one at Pleiku which was composed of three or four brigades.

The trouble with Nam was that we didn't control anything that we were not standing on at the time. Anything that moved outside our perimeter at night was fair game because the night belonged to the enemy and both sides knew it. The reality of only owning the ground you stood on meant making sure you continued to stay on that ground.

Major Colin L. Powell
Third Battalion, First Infantry, Eleventh Infantry Brigade, Twenty-Third Infantry (Americal) Division
Duc Pho, July–October 1968
Major Colin Powell, returning for a second tour, was assigned as executive offi-cer (XO) of the Third Battalion of the First Infantry under Lieutenant Colonel Hank Lowder. Though the XO functions as a deputy commander, his main job is to keep the unit running smoothly, ensuring supplies of everything from toothpaste to tarpaulins, replacements for casualties, coordination with other units, and so on.
Though Duc Pho was away from the main VC units, it was hardly a garden spot. The first thing I noticed, parked on the edge of the camp, was a "conex" container, the kind used to ship heavy equipment or household effects. This huge crate, I learned, was our backyard mortuary, used to hold Viet Cong dead until we figured out what to do with the bodies. The next thing I noticed was the odor, which almost knocked me out. Excrement was burned all day long in fifty-five gallon drums, and the whole post smelled like a privy. The burning, like laundry, KP, and other menial tasks, was done by Vietnamese whom we hired. The workers' loyalty was supposedly checked by the local vil-lage chiefs, though Lord knows how many people running around inside Duc Pho were moonlighting for the VC, including the chiefs.

We were ambushed regularly and took occasional rounds of mortar and rocket fire. Every morning the roads . . . had to be swept for mines that the VC might have planted during the night. While high-tech warriors back at the Pentagon were dreaming up supersophisticated equipment for this task, our troops used a down-home remedy. The men filled a five-ton dump truck with dirt, the driver put it in reverse and backed down the road. If he hit a mine it would blow off the tires and probably damage the rear end. But the truck could usually be salvaged, and the roads were cleared. We lost an occasional vehicle, but seldom a driver.

Besides getting Duc Pho in shape, I had to go out and make sure that field units were also ready for the annual inspection. We had several FSBs (fire support bases) and LZs (landing zones)—Dragon, Liz, Chevy—located throughout our area. Early in August, I got a helicopter and flew out to LZ Dragon. I had heard that its messing facilities were substandard. Bad chow proved to be the least of Dragon's problems. I had not expected to find stateside spit and polish. Still, what I discovered jolted me. As I stepped out of the helo, I practically stumbled over rusted ammo left lying around the landing site. Sanitation was nil, weapons dirty, equipment neglected, and the troops sloppy in appearance, bearing and behavior . . . deterioration of discipline and morale was obvious. . . .

Our men in the field, trudging through elephant grass under hostile fire, did not have time to be hostile toward each other. But bases like Duc Pho were increasingly divided by the same racial polarization that had begun to plague America during the Sixties. The base contained dozens of new men waiting to be sent out into the field and short-timers waiting to go home. For both groups the unifying force of a shared mission and shared danger did not exist. Racial friction took its place. Young blacks, particularly draftees, saw the war, not surprisingly, as even less their fight than the whites did. They had less to go home to. This generation was more likely to be reached by the fireworks of an H. Rap Brown than the reasonableness of the late Martin Luther King. Both blacks and whites were increasingly resentful of the authority that kept them here for a dangerous and unclear purpose. The number one goal was to do your time and get home alive. I was living in a large tent and I moved my cot every night, partly to thwart Viet Cong informants . . . but also because I did not rule out attacks . . . from within the battalion itself. . . .

Life at Duc Pho took crazy pendulum swings from the trite to the heartbreaking. One afternoon I was getting Coke and beer helicoptered out to the firebases—a daily priority the exec dared not miss—when Colonel Lowder sent word that he had run into a stiff fight at Firebase Liz and needed help. I ordered up a "slick"—had it loaded with 5.56mm rifle and 7.62mm machinegun ammo, and headed out over the treetops. We landed at Liz near dusk. . . . A grim-faced Lowder told me to take back nine of our [*bodies*]. The vulnerability of a helicopter on the ground left little time for niceties. . . . As we took off in the half-light, I slumped to the floor, facing nine recently healthy young American boys, now stacked like cordwood. We landed in darkness at an evac hospital, a MASH unit. The tents were a hive of activity, with wounded being flown in from all directions.

People in combat develop a protective numbness that allows them to go on. That night I saw this shield crack. Eventually the bodies were taken from the slick into the field hospital to be confirmed as dead. Medical staffers unrolled each poncho and examined the bodies with brisk efficiency until the last one. I heard a nurse gasp, "Oh my God, it's . . . " The final casualty was a young medic from their unit who had volunteered to go out to the firebase the day before. Nurses and medics started crying. I turned and left them to their duty.

8

Indian Country

Master Sergeant Billy Waugh
Studies and Observation Group, Command and Control North
Khe Sanh Launch Point, Forward Operations Base One, August 4, 1966
Waugh, who became a legendary special operator, had returned for a second tour. The previous year he had suffered serious wounds on a mission in Binh Dinh Province. Now he was back, not completely healed but so full of piss and vinegar that he talked his way into the Studies and Observation Group (SOG) and then into a field assignment running the launch point at Khe Sanh for SOG's Forward Operations Base One. Sergeant Waugh was at the cutting edge of SOG operations longer than probably anyone else, but the first mission he sent into the field—and one of CCN's early ones as well—was Reconnaissance Team (RT) Montana's patrol near the end of July 1966. After a week the RT was ambushed. Montana's failure to make contact alerted Waugh that something was amiss. The next day RT Montana's remnants staggered into Khe Sanh. Sergeant Major Harry D. Whalen had escaped the encirclement with six indigenous strikers, but the other two Americans—Sergeant Delmer Laws and Specialist Four Donald Sain—had not made it. Whalen described where the ambush had taken place. Waugh initiated aerial searches. Early on August 4 he was in the backseat of a light plane that spotted Sain's body staked out on the ground near Co Roc Mountain in Laos. SOG immediately mounted a recovery expedition led by Major Gerald Killburn and Sergeant Waugh. This was Billy Waugh's first rescue mission. Waugh participated despite the pain from his old wounds. The team

was flown by "Mustachio"—Nguyen Van Hoang, a famed Vietnamese Air Force pilot—using an H-34 helicopter.

We arrived over the vicinity of the body and searched for a landing zone. The five of us looked down from the H-34 at Sain's body as we circled the small clearing where his body was tied and staked. I could feel the anger and disgust as it exuded from each man. Kilburn and I decided to land approximately a hundred meters from Sain's body, and after a quick touchdown [*we sprinted*] toward the body. I moved quickly and forcefully, the pain from the shrapnel in my legs erased by the adrenaline of the moment.

We reached Sain's body and approached carefully. Several hand grenades, with pins pulled, were placed under his body, ready to detonate if we moved [*it*]. Sain had been dead in the jungle heat for more than thirty-six hours. He died of gunshot wounds to the chest, and maggots had filled his wounds like putty. Flies were buzzing in and out of his nose. The maggots were all over his bloated and decomposing body. The stench of rotting flesh was nearly unbearable.

I grabbed a climbing rope and told Kilburn, "Here's what we're going to do. I'm going to tie this around his leg and . . . to the wheel of the H-34. We'll move the body to the LZ and take it from there."

Kilburn and the rest of the team looked at me like I was crazy. To them, it sounded like a wild stunt that would never work. These guys hadn't seen the combat I had, and they weren't accustomed to thinking on the fly, to doing what needed to be done no matter how unusual it might be. There's no manual for this kind of horrid shit. But knowing Mustachio's prowess, I felt this was the fastest and most efficient way to achieve our objectives.

I explained our situation to Mustachio and tied the rope around Sain's leg. I ordered Mustachio to hover over the body as low as possible. He lowered the bird over the body like a man palming a basketball, and I tied the rope to the wheel of the H-34. . . .

"OK, let's move out," I told the team members. Mustachio then lifted the body off the ground while two of the three booby traps exploded harmlessly. Sain was hovering above us while all the fluids and maggots and shit from his body flowed. . . .

Mustachio lifted Sain's body out of the combat area and set his bird down in an open space away from the jungle. With Sain recovered, we began the hunt for Sergeant Laws. I ordered the team to fan out, keeping the man next to them in sight. . . . We fought our way through the jungle, tearing up our arms and faces on "wait-a-minute" bushes. . . . If you didn't keep three paces behind, thorns slashed across your forehead. The damned jungle was a son of a bitch.

Monkeys in the trees and bushes jibber-jabbered at us, their singular focus on our activities a good sign that no NVA platoon was in the vicinity. Mustachio continued to hover away from the area, but within radio range, prepared to move to the landing zone on my signal. We searched and searched, so long that Mustachio left Sain's body in the clearing and returned to Khe Sanh to refuel. We stayed on the hunt, though, and finally, after several hours, Danny Horton called to me from out of the bush.

In seconds he emerged from the cover holding Laws's left leg by the jungle boot.

"Billy," he said quietly, a sick look on his face. "This looks like an American jungle boot."

Tigers prowled this area of Laos, and it appeared they found Laws before we did. I placed the leg in a body bag, and we continued our . . . search. . . . I came upon several more massive bloodstains and numerous trails, but no NVA or bodies were found, and neither was any other portion of Laws. . . . At approximately 5 p.m.—five hours into the rescue mission—the signal was given for the H-34 to exfiltrate the rescue team.

CODE NAME BRIGHT LIGHT

Master Sergeant Richard Meadows
Studies and Observation Group, Command and Control Center, Reconnaissance Team Iowa
near Vinh, North Vietnam, October 16, 1966
Air Force studies showed that nearly half of all failures on search-and-rescue (SAR) missions followed from tardy arrival of SAR helicopters. Air commanders demanded a program for rescue efforts even after initial SAR operations miscarried. In September 1966 this resulted in the creation of an entirely new MACV apparatus, the Joint Personnel Recovery Center, which had a separate identity within SOG. The program code-named Bright Light followed shortly thereafter. The first Bright Light missions were ad hoc and mounted under urgent conditions. Sergeant Dick Meadows led his RT Iowa into North Vietnam seeking a Navy pilot, Lieutenant Dean Woods, whose A-1E aircraft had crashed near Vinh on October 12, and whom SAR had then failed to recover. Meadows was a renowned operator whose RT Iowa had obtained the first hard evidence of North Vietnamese troop presence in South Vietnam. He and RT Iowa, with extra specialists, were pulled off their routine missions out of Kontum and put on a Navy shuttle to the aircraft carrier Intrepid *in the South China Sea. Landing aboard the ship in the middle of the night, Meadows launched for North Vietnam the next morning. This account is by John L. Plaster, a Special Forces officer who served with SOG in 1969 and after.*
The next morning the clouds scattered, and just before dawn a pair of Navy Sea King helicopters lifted from the *Intrepid*'s deck with Meadows and RT

Iowa aboard. As the North Vietnamese coast took shape, there was an uncomfortable realization that ahead was a modern air-defense system whose radars already were tracking their approach and alerting antiaircraft units and ground forces who'd had four days to prepare for them.

When the helicopters crossed the coast, the sky exploded with antiaircraft shell bursts, but the Navy pilots expertly weaved between the worst of it. Minutes later they could see the heavily forested range where that very moment the NVA were converging on the downed flyer. After several false insertions . . . one Sea King [*landed*] RT Iowa about 800 yards from Lieutenant Woods's hiding place. Meadows made a beeline for the ridge.

Lieutenant Woods could hear buzzing planes and helicopters and the booming of antiaircraft guns, but his greatest concerns were more immediate: brush was breaking nearby, and he could hear the shouts of excited soldiers.

Meadows and his men moved fast and had closed to a few hundred yards when they received a sickening radio report: The Navy pilot had been captured. Had they traveled 500 miles only to come up 200 yards short? "A cautious soldier would have taken his men to the nearest extraction point and departed enemy territory," Colonel Singlaub [*the SOG commander at that time*] says. "But Meadows was not overly cautious."

Coming upon a major trail, Meadows decided to set up an ambush and capture a prisoner. A few moments later an NVA officer and three enlisted men walked up, alert, still searching for Woods, apparently unaware he'd been captured.

Perhaps they'd expected a lone, injured pilot with just a pistol. They were astonished when Meadows stepped from the dense foliage and leveled his AK-47, calling a friendly good morning. As one, they went for their guns, but Meadows shot first, killing all four in one blur. While his men searched the bodies, Meadows radioed for an exfil, and soon they were flying away, although their helicopter was sprayed by gunfire and eventually had to ditch near an American destroyer. From this, their first Bright Light mission, every SOG man made it out. Lieutenant Woods returned from captivity in 1973.

HELL AT OSCAR-8

Major Richard E. Romine, USMC
Marine Medium Helicopter Squadron HMM-165
Target Oscar-8, Laos, June 4–6, 1967
A People's Army installation in Laos about ten miles southwest of Khe Sanh, Oscar-8 was certainly a major VPA supply base, or binh tram, *as the Vietnamese called them. It may also have been a command headquarters. The National*

Security Agency identified it as Oscar-8 and decided it was a headquarters on the basis of a high volume of message traffic sent to or emanating from it. MACV decided to destroy Oscar-8 in the summer of 1967, in an operation briefed at the highest level of the U.S. government. The plan was to hit it with a formation of B-52 bombers, following which SOG would land a pair of Hatchet Force platoons—about sixty men—to mop up the dazed enemy and examine the damage. Sergeant Billy Waugh flew in the observation plane that monitored the strike and the Hatchet force insertion. As happened on some other occasions, the Arc Light strike, whatever destruction it inflicted, stirred up the North Vietnamese defenders. The SOG troops immediately came under fire and were quickly in extremis once deposited on their LZ. The Americans' focus became saving their own SOG troopers. Two fighter-bombers, a Vietnamese A-1E and an American F-4 Phantom, were lost early in the fight. Major Richard Romine flew one of the Marine CH-46 helicopters that participated in the landing, the subsequent rescue, and the ground battle. His efforts show why intimate bonds existed between the helicopter community and the elite special units, including LRPs and SOG. Romine won the Navy Cross for this battle.

Gunship helicopters furnished what support they could. It was not long before the lead gunship, piloted by Major G. H. Coffin, sustained several critical hits and limped off, only to crash in dense forest. . . . Major Richard E. Romine, who piloted the lead transport ship . . . disembarked the SOG troopers he was carrying and quickly flew to where another gunship had marked the crash site. Maneuvering along the mountain slope, Romine found the . . . downed chopper, discovering that Coffin had a broken back. With no time to wait, Romine tried the rescue himself, hovering at the treetops while lowering his hoist through a gap in the jungle canopy. Romine stabilized his CH-46 in this precarious position for twenty-five minutes, picking up the . . . crew and dumping fuel to compensate for the weight. . . . When the last airman came aboard, Romine's low-fuel light had already been glowing for several minutes. He set off for Khe Sanh, warning his own crew they would probably have to crash land along the way. Instead Romine made it.

At Khe Sanh, crew chief Corporal Michael S. Bradshaw opened the gas tanks to measure the remaining fuel and found not even enough to wet the dipstick.

Back at the landing zone the American and Nung SOG troops organized a perimeter along the rim of one of the craters left by the B-52 bombing. That night the NVA seemed content to keep the Hatchet men under fire, but by morning the pressure was growing worse. At first light the SOG commander requested fixed wing air support and helicopters to extract his men. Captain Stephen W. Pless, who had covered Romine the previous afternoon and had marked the downed chopper for him, was back with a UH-1E gunship. Bad weather kept away the fixed-wing planes, so Pless and his gunships were what stood between the NVA and the embattled SOG troops. Returning to Khe Sanh for fuel and ammunition, Pless would also brief SOG on the latest developments. [*From Phu Bai an aerial supply expert went to Khe Sanh, where he packed bundles for the Hatchet Force. He and Billy Waugh tried unsuccessfully to deliver them.*]

Major Romine returned to battle that day. He wanted to help extract the SOG troops before nightfall. Told that contact was light, Romine flew into the LZ, where the worst problem seemed to be that everyone wanted to get on board at once. The SOG force was organized into . . . ten-man tactical elements, and the crew chief had instructions to take . . . no more than eight. Corporal Bradshaw had to physically bar the door to Nungs who wanted to escape the battle zone.

Romine's real trouble began when he tried to lift out. . . . As his ship climbed through 200 feet it became the target of intense fire; the entire valley seemed to come alive with muzzle flashes and tracers. Suddenly the number two engine quit and the rotor began to lose speed. Romine realized a crash was imminent and . . . put his ship down . . . broadcasting a Mayday message at the same time. The crash blocked the LZ, with fifty-one men, including Major Romine and his newly-deposited crew.

Meanwhile Captain Jack H. McCracken, Romine's wingman, was also rushed while his ship was on the ground. He got off with an excessive load of nineteen, but the craft was so tightly packed that three strikers fell from the chopper after it became airborne. McCracken believed he was saved by Steve Pless's gunship, which hovered over him to attract NVA fire.

The third ship in Romine's flight was Captain Stephen P. Hanson's CH-46. He got in and out of the LZ with twelve passengers, including the top Nung commander, Mr. Ky, and three American SOG troopers: Sergeants Ronald J. Dexter, Billy R. Laney, and Charles P. Wilklow. Hanson unknowingly turned into the heaviest concentration of NVA forces as he took off; the helicopter sustained fatal damage and several passengers and crew chief Sergeant Timothy R. Bodden were wounded. Bodden got up but then suffered a second bullet wound in his belly. The helicopter crashed in an upright attitude, suspended about four and a half feet above the ground by jungle foliage, with a hut not more than two feet from its left side. [*Passengers and crewmen, many wounded, escaped from the chopper.*]

None of the survivors made it back to Major Romine and the SOG perimeter. Instead [*door gunner Lance Corporal Frank E.*] Cius, Dexter, and ten Nungs spent the night on a hilltop about 200 meters east of the crash site. [T]hey were [*later*] captured. Cius returned from captivity on March 5, 1973.

Sergeants Dexter and Bodden, pilot Hanson, and copilot John G. Gardner are still listed as missing in action.

[*Weather still precluded fixed-wing air support. Captain Pless and his gunships stayed in the fight and kept the People's Army troops from closing in.*] Actually the SOG troops might have been finished already except for Captain Romine and his crew. The crash fortuitously added some extra heavy weapons, ammunition, and a few more men on the ground. Romine himself proved a tower of strength, active everywhere around the perimeter, and when the fixed-wing aircraft finally arrived, the Marine pilot showed himself extraordinarily adept at spotting targets for aircraft and correcting their aim. Through twenty-four straight hours of hell Romine came as close as anyone to being a one-man army. . . .

Romine and the . . . other survivors had to get out of Laos. That happened on June [6], when Major Charles H. Pitman commanded an air armada that included six Marine CH-46s for rescue and recovery, nine Vietnamese H-34s to make the extractions, nine UH-1E gunships for cover, two Vietnamese O-1Es for observation, and two A-1Es for escort. During the final rescue all these aircraft were operating in an airspace of less than two cubic kilometers, in constant danger of midair collision.

Captain Pless set up the gunships so that his division of five operated on the right side of the formation, doing right-hand turns and following an oblong pattern. Another division of four ships took the left and ran a left-hand pattern. In the center the Vietnamese Air Force H-34s landed and picked up Romine and the others. The third ship into the LZ was shot down as it rose, and another was damaged so badly it could not take any passengers. Two more H-34s diverted to pick up the crew and passengers of the downed craft. When the last of the Vietnamese helicopters had cleared the LZ, there remained a dozen men on the ground awaiting a pickup. Captain Byrd did not hesitate—he dove his CH-46 right in and hovered, two wheels touching the lip of the crater, while the last twelve men climbed aboard.

[*Sergeant Wilklow, wounded exiting Hanson's crashing chopper, was left for dead by the VPA. He lay on the ground for four days until he could muster the energy to drag himself away. Wilklow was rescued by Staff Sergeant Lester Pace in a recovery Billy Waugh organized. He would be the only SOG American lost in Laos during the war to escape the enemy. Remains of Billy Ray Laney were discovered at the site decades later. Richard Romine passed away in July 1991. Altogether twenty-three American or Vietnamese airmen or SOG troopers and perhaps double that number of Nung strikers were lost at Oscar-8, along with two fighter-bombers and four choppers. Without direct evidence, Waugh believes that VPA General Vo Nguyen Giap was physically present at Oscar-8. But the detailed record of Hanoi's planning for what became the Tet Offensive, as well as what we know about political purges in North Vietnam at this time, make it exceedingly unlikely that Giap was anywhere other than Hanoi.*]

COMMUNICATIONS

Staff Sergeant Alan F. Farrell
A Company, Exploitation Battalion, Command and Control Central, Studies and Observation Group
Kontum Forward Operations Base, 1968
Sergeant Farrell served as a radio operator with a SOG hatchet force, formally part of an exploitation battalion, mounting forays into the enemy-controlled hinterland, "Indian Country." At the time U.S. soldiers used short-range (8 km) line of sight, push-to-talk FM transceivers for voice communications but more sophisticated (single-side band) radios over longer distances. The latter required the use of Morse code. Since many SOG missions were deep-penetration operations, they frequently relied upon the Morse radios. Morse code used an arrangement of dots ("dih") or dashes ("dah") to represent letters of the alphabet. In addition, certain frequently used texts were condensed by substituting one or a few letters in a given arrangement. Radio operators were schooled in these meanings. Thus QQQ (dahdahdidah, dahdahdidah, dahdahdidah) was colloquial for "kick the birdshit off your antenna." Farrell wrote this poem about SOG communications.

Ditty Dum Dum Ditty

In the days when there were giants in the earth
And men plunged deep into the jungle far beyond
Artillery fan and voice radio range
The keeper of the Runes was the commo man

Any sap can push-to-talk
Call that sit-rep while you walk
But a hundred clicks from transmission source
They only hear when you tap Morse

> Dittydumdumditty dihdah dihdah dahdihdihdit Say all that shit again, slick

The singing letters he flings forth in five-character groups
At random encrypted in the flyconstellation of noontime
Whistle of life from out the endless green
Whine of hunger fear need doubt solitude curiosity shame relief repentance

Any sap can push-to-talk
Call that sit-rep while you walk
But a hundred clicks from transmission source
They only hear when you tap Morse

> *Dahdahdihdah dahdahdihdah dahdahdihdah Kick the birdshit off your antenna*

Black boxes nestled in the rotting leaves
Sweatwrinkled fingers fumble with crystals tickle
That key tune to freq is that antenna cut right
What's the goddam formula again fuck it she'll load

Any sap can push-to-talk
Call that sit-rep while you walk
But a hundred clicks from transmission source
They only hear when you tap Morse

> *Dahdahdihdit dahdit dahdihdihdih Authenticate my shorts*

Crank that generator fill the jungle with the hum of desperation
Do *not* pedal in a counterclockwise direction Gee Enn Four Three generator direct
current man
portable
Lay into that bitch 'cause when I key it
You'll think you're hauling up a goddam Chevy

Any sap can push-to-talk
Call that sit-rep while you walk
But a hundred clicks from transmission source
They only hear when you tap Morse

> *Dahdahdihdah dahdahdihdah dahdahdihdah Send with the other boot*

Radio was pure then tubes crystals keys
Oscillation and silence spoke what we had to say
Music and the deft hand wrote on the air in rhythmic pulses
Halting stubborn itchy staccato key we called Shit Fist

Any sap can push-to-talk
Call that sit-rep while you walk
But a hundred clicks from transmission source
They only hear when you tap Morse

> *Dahdahdihdah dihdahdit dahdihdah Got you two by two . . .*

Plead at a distance no matter what terror
You still translate it into Continuous Wave
Dread of death did it read in the insistent frenetic tremolo of an Echo dih
A nervous India dihdih and funeral spondee of Tango daddah

Any sap can push-to-talk
Call that sit rep while you walk
But a hundred clicks from transmission source
They only hear when you tap Morse

> *Dahdahdihdah dihdihdit dihdah . . . too loud and too often*

No human voice to bring comfort or passion
Only dainty dih and dragging dah for heart's cry
Only these for answer from out of the airwaves
That and the soulchilling silence of ether

Any sap can push-to-talk
Call that sit rep while you walk
But a hundred clicks from transmission source
They only hear when you tap Morse

> *Dahdahdihdah dihdahdit dahdah Can't hear you on account of Manmade Interference*

MISSION PLANNING

Major Alex Lee, USMC
Third Force Reconnaissance Company
Quang Tri, 1969–1970

Intending to patrol throughout the province, where the U.S. and South Vietnamese troops were by then confined mostly to the coastal area and DMZ, Major Lee began by reviewing the many ways missions could be crippled, starting with interference from major ground operations or interdiction by friendly artillery and air, but, quite significantly, also including breached secrecy in planning. To cope with friendly interference he arranged to have sectors made off-limits during the period of a mission, but solutions to the secrecy problem eluded him.

Sadly, we had to face the problem that there was no such thing as a secret in the Republic of Vietnam. The [*area of operations—AO*] provided to a reconnaissance team was deemed to be compromised the moment it was made known to anyone outside the company. Spies and sympathizers for the North Vietnamese were known to be working at every command/political level . . . and we were forced to live with the knowledge that the NVA might be waiting for the Marines when they landed. . . . To counter this . . . we held our messages of notification of assigned AO coordinates until the last possible minute. This was done in the hope that the NVA would not be able to react in time to foil the insertion. Despite that hope, every team landed . . . with an expectation of coming under fire in the first moments after touchdown.

Occasionally in selecting an AO, some nonoperational matters had to be considered, matters one seldom finds in the field manuals. For instance, some wiseacre decided that for a Marine who was new in country—an NIC [*or, more familiarly, an FNG*]—to lose his status as the new guy on the block, he had to dip his toe in the Ben Hai River, which ran directly down the center of the DMZ between the two warring Vietnams, or to walk on ground that was clearly on the Laotian side of the border between Laos and the Republic of Vietnam. Obviously, any NIC who was worth his salt would slip across the artificial boundaries of an assigned AO if he was close enough to either the river . . . or the border. . . .

Of course, I could have loudly issued draconian orders to prohibit this . . . violation of safety and good sense, but [*understanding*] that this tradition was important to the Marines, I never permitted the slightest official notice of the practice, choosing instead to use one AO boundary for the team and one slightly larger—opened in the direction of either the river or the border—for submission to the coordination agencies. Thus if the team slipped outside of its assigned AO to baptize an NIC, the men would have the delicious feeling that they pulled one over on me, and I would be sure that no outside agency would fire on them while this took place.

INTO THE GAME PRESERVE

Staff Sergeant John Luchow
L Company, Seventy-Fifth Infantry (Ranger), 101st Airborne Division
Camp Eagle, August 1969
The A Shau Valley remained a problem despite the 1968 American offensive that had set up Firebase Bastogne and a repeat effort in early 1969, which led to the Battle of Hamburger Hill. The People's Army streamed rockets and mortars into a "rocket belt" west of Hue-Phu Bai and bombarded the allied bases. The foothills of the Annamite Mountains out toward the Laotian border were so deep into Indian Country that lurps knew this area as the "Game Preserve," a place where no scout could go without encountering the enemy. During the last month before the monsoon, divisional lurp commander Captain Robert Guy tried to field as many patrols as he could, in hopes of interdicting the enemy traffic with scout-directed strikes. Guy was so determined that he ordered Sergeant Luchow to assemble a scratch team from other units for a five-day foray into the Game Preserve. The LZ Luchow first selected proved a hotbed of North Vietnamese, so he tried a different insertion point the next day.
The first two aircraft flew west, then were joined near the edge of the mountains by a third Huey carrying Captain Guy. His helicopter was to be the

command and control aircraft during the insertion. The Ranger company commander had departed Camp Eagle earlier that morning to drop off the radio relay team at Fire Support Base Birmingham.

As the three aircraft approached the team's AO, Staff Sergeant Luchow had a sudden unexplainable change of heart and made the decision to attempt a landing in the original LZ. Captain Guy . . . considered the request and quickly okayed the change.

[*Approaching the insertion point, the slick took fire and Luchow opted for a secondary LZ a few minutes farther away, where the lurps landed and successfully got into the trees. The third day, just as they reached their AO, Luchow found fresh footprints, a heavily used trail that must have been a main thoroughfare. Sergeant Luchow set up an observation post to radio targets to U.S. forces. That night they spotted VPA movements and then another North Vietnamese force camped little more than 150 yards from their position. At dawn a People's Army guard sat right outside their laager, within the lethal fan of one of their Claymore mines. Luchow chose to fire the mine to eliminate him. His patrol became a race to escape enemy pursuers.*]

There was no time to question his error in judgment because the NVA were already sweeping the hillside above them, shouting and reconning by fire. And he didn't have to stop and spell out the situation to the rest of his teammates to convince them that there was, at that moment, a very real sense of urgency. . . .

The team began running "balls to the wall" to put as much distance as possible between themselves and their pursuers. Without stopping for a breather they plunged down the . . . slope toward the bottom of the ridge. An hour later they broke out onto the wide floor of the valley and began breaking brush toward the opposite side. Each time Luchow stopped the team to catch a breath and listen for sounds of pursuit, they heard the enemy forces behind them.

The Rangers continued fleeing as the shadows shortened toward midday. Finally, early in the afternoon, they reached . . . the opposite ridge and began climbing. Hesitating for only a moment to catch their breath and listen . . . the Rangers heard the NVA soldiers back in the trees, no longer reconning by fire, but still coming hard less than a hundred meters away.

[*Captain Guy rejected a dangerous proposal to extract the lurps using a ladder rig through trees at night. He ordered them to hide for pickup the next morning. The rescue was confirmed after dawn and the radio relay team told the lurps once choppers were on the way. Luchow moved cautiously toward the pickup point and became quite nervous when the slicks were late. So far the VPA had not put in an appearance.*]

The first slick came in low and hovered right over the team's location. Three weighted sandbags dropped . . . uncoiling umbilical cords of nylon rope behind them as they fell through the jungle canopy. The first part of the extraction went like a dress rehearsal. Just over a hundred feet below . . . the first three Rangers stepped through the nylon loops at the end of their Maguire rigs and attached the D-rings on their harnesses to the ropes.

Suddenly the aircraft commander radioed that he was taking fire. Without waiting for a response . . . the aircraft began to rise, pulling the three men out of the jungle. The enemy fire seemed to be coming from the reverse slope of the ridge they were on. . . . Apparently it was only small-arms fire, but it was enough to force the pilot to take immediate evasive action. Picking up speed, the aircraft commander swung wide out over the open valley to put some distance between his aircraft and the enemy gunners on the ridgeline. . . .

Back on top of the ridgeline, as soon as the first extraction aircraft had cleared . . . the second ship moved in to recover Luchow and Leslie as the Cobra circled desperately, trying to suppress the NVA small-arms fire with rockets and miniguns. Even so, eight to ten enemy weapons were still shooting at the second ship as it carefully pulled the last two Rangers from the jaws of death and departed the AO. The frustrated NVA soldiers continued to fire at the departing helicopter long after it was out of range.

WAR STORY

Sergeant Leigh Wade
Detachment A-242, Fifth Special Forces Group
Kontum, March 1970
This was Sergeant Wade's third tour. A former member of SOG, he stopped at Nha Trang on his way to a new assignment at a Special Forces camp. Wade encountered his friend Sergeant William Martin in from Kontum, the forward operating base of SOG's Command and Control Center. Martin told the story of one of his patrols with RT Texas. Since 1968 the United States had introduced longer-range voice radios, so Morse code was no longer an issue.
His team and another [*were to pull*] off a prisoner snatch. The two . . . infiltrated simultaneously, but at different LZs. The idea was for both teams to sneak over to the Ho Chi Minh Trail and set up ambushes about five kilometers apart. Bill's team would initiate its ambush first, causing a diversion, and shortly afterward the other team would try to snatch the prisoner.

"Both teams got in okay, and my bunch made it to the trail and got into position by the second night without being seen," Bill said. "The other team got compromised before they got there, though, and had to be exfiltrated. Since we were already set up, I decided to go ahead and knock off a truck. We had an AC-130 Blackbird overhead for backup, so I wasn't too worried.

"We were lying on a little high ground right by the trail, and I'd set up two claymores at what I figured was the height of a truck cab. . . .

"Pretty soon we hear this truck chugging along toward us. The bastards drive without lights, so they have to go slow. We were right on top of a hill, and the truck driver had it in low gear. . . . He gets to the top . . . and just as he threw that baby into second gear, I set off the claymores.

"All the guys opened up on full auto, and I put two of those [*M79*] grape-shot rounds through the front windshield. The team covered me, and I ran down to look at the damage and see what was under the canvas in the back. I jumped up on the running board. . . . The driver and his assistant looked like two piles of raw hamburger. I ran around to the back, hoping to see something interesting like secret weapons. . . . The whole fucking truck was full of rice.

"About this time two other trucks come roaring up and stop a hundred meters away at the bottom of the hill. It's their damned reaction force. They're yelling and screaming orders, and when they all get on the ground, it looks like there's at least a platoon. I watched 'em get in a skirmish line . . . then we took off running like hell.

"I still wasn't very worried, because I figured the gunship would cut the bastards to pieces while we made our getaway. I'd just made a commo check with the aircraft an hour before the ambush, and he'd come in loud and clear."

"Let me guess what happens next," I said. "You try to call the aircraft and suddenly there's no answer."

"Yeah," Bill said, "how did you know?"

"Because that's Murphy's Law of Combat Communications," I told him. "In combat, commo is always great until you really need it."

OPERATION TAILWIND

Captain Eugene McCarley
B Company, Exploitation Battalion, Command and Control Center, Studies and Observation Group
Chavane, Laos, September 11–14, 1970
This SOG mission into Laos became one of the most controversial of the war when, in 1998, the television channel Cable News Network (CNN) aired a report alleging that U.S. forces used sarin nerve gas. The reporting was attacked as suspect and the mental acuity of former Joint Chiefs of Staff chairman Admiral Thomas Moorer was called into question. There seems little reason to accept the more lurid claims about this episode. Nevertheless Operation Tailwind stands among the largest SOG missions at this stage. Though it was very costly, Tailwind

is also viewed as one of SOG's greatest accomplishments. Originally conceived as a diversionary attack to distract the enemy from a CIA operation farther north in Laos, Tailwind involved Captain McCarley's full Hatchet Force company, sixteen Americans plus 110 montagnard strikers. They were inserted by an air group that included fifteen big CH-53 transport helicopters and twelve Marine gunship choppers, plus fighters. This account is offered by SOG veteran John L. Plaster.

The fifteen helicopters paralleled the remote border for 50 miles, then turned west into the high mountains of Laos. Almost right away gunners began tracking them, spraying the air with heavy machine guns. Inside the semitrailer-size cargo compartments, bullets cracked through the floors, punctuating the din of whining turbines, hit after hit after hit, sounding like someone shooting a tin can with a BB gun, but the huge choppers just kept lumbering between the jungled hills and limestone cliffs.

[*It was a miracle that just one man, a striker, was wounded. At the LZ, Captain McCarley consolidated his troops. A true anomaly—the sound of telephones ringing in the jungle—alerted him to a People's Army presence, and he investigated, finding a line of bunkers crammed with North Vietnamese rockets up to 140-millimeter size, which the Hatchet Force detonated with explosives. Within a kilometer McCarley began to face increasing opposition, and by nightfall he was brushing off the enemy with interventions from AC-130 Spectre gunships. Rather than hunker down, Captain McCarley kept his men moving west. By morning, without meeting a serious attack, nine SOG Americans and a larger number of strikers were already wounded. Medic Sergeant Gary Rose ministered to these men. The SOG force overwhelmed some North Vietnamese positions early in the morning.*]

By midday the company was walking a ridge half a mile above Highway 165 when the jungle thinned and they could see the road where a long column of hundreds of NVA and a dozen trucks paralleled them. McCarley called in A-1s, destroying the trucks and scattering the infantry. "From the amount of men I saw on that road," [*Sergeant*] Craig Schmidt said, "if they ever really knew where we were at, they could have taken us out."

To keep the enemy guessing, the tactically adroit McCarley kept off roads and main trails, hurrying instead along streambeds, small paths, or thinly vegetated ridges. Each time the NVA blocked the Hatchet Force, he pounded them with Skyraiders or Cobras or Phantoms and bypassed them.

[*Captain McCarley called for a medevac to lift out the worst of the wounded, who slowed his pace. The responding CH-53 was damaged so badly—before loading any wounded—that it should have exploded or crashed. But it managed to limp a few miles before going down. The same happened to another chopper, which came to retrieve the first crew. A third CH-53 managed to rescue both crews. By the end of the day McCarley had to halt, both to rest and to care for his increasing wounded. To avoid any dawn attack, McCarley got his column moving at 4 a.m.*]

They'd marched west another three hours when the point took fire from a few NVA soldiers who fled into a bunker area. McCarley felt it was his to seize so he ordered an attack. After softening the NVA positions . . . the Hatchet Force men advanced. Craig Schmidt and another squad leader, Sergeant Manuel Orozco, got their Yards on line, and assaulted. The enemy [*abandoned*] a battalion-size base camp except for the two bunkers held by cut-off NVA. While fire kept the enemy soldiers' heads down two Yards crept forward and rolled grenades inside.

The base camp was seized, but by now the friendly wounded had risen to forty-nine—nearly 50 percent casualties—and the overworked sole medic, Doc Rose, himself wounded twice, could barely keep up. . . .

While Rose performed miracles, the rest of the Hatchet force searched the base camp's many hootches and bunkers. Fifty-four NVA bodies were discovered but none yielded significant intelligence. The camouflaged bunkers matched the terrain so perfectly they couldn't be seen 50 yards away; noticing the shrubs growing atop them, McCarley concluded the NVA had been there many months, probably several years. Along with four trucks, the [*biggest*] material finds were a 120mm mortar and 9 tons of rice.

Then one search party called Captain McCarley to a large bunker 12 feet below ground; inside were maps covering the walls and hundreds of pounds of documents stored in footlockers and pouches. Clearly this was not just a battalion base camp but a major logistical command center, probably the . . . headquarters that controlled Highway 165.

Pack up all the documents, McCarley ordered, they would carry them out. Less than thirty minutes after seizing the camp, Company B was moving west again; behind them demolitions charges went off, destroying the four trucks.

Already burdened with wounded . . . the Hatchet Force men were unhappy about the additional load of documents. Like any other exhausted soldier, Craig Schmidt thought, "Why in heck do we need all this stuff, it's just going to weigh us down." Given the option of carrying three dead Montagnards or the documents, McCarley chose the documents. By now every American had been wounded, several twice.

[*FAC aircraft could see the People's Army converging on McCarley's unit from at least two directions. There was good reason for extraction. The captain changed tactics, using a road to move quicker, abandoning a first, vulnerable, LZ.*]

Just before the choppers arrived, Company B encircled another LZ while a SOG Covey Rider [*aerial observer*], William "Country" Grimes, brought in A-1s with CBU-19 tear-gas bomblets to blind the antiaircraft gunners.

Then one CH-53 landed and lifted away with the worst wounded and most of the documents. NVA mortars began pounding the LZ, answered by F-4 Phantoms that [*dropped*] a dozen napalm canisters in a single pass.

Rather than get bogged down defending the threatened LZ, McCarley took the two remaining platoons to another . . . where suppressive fire and a sudden landing generated only moderate ground fire. A second platoon climbed into a CH-53 for a clean getaway. NVA by the hundreds were now streaming out of the hills and let loose a nearly constant barrage of gunfire and RPGs.

Down to his last platoon, McCarley boldly repeated his tactic of abandoning one LZ to go secure a new one. Cobras and A-1s hit ahead and behind the last forty Hatchet Force men as they moved. [*They found a field of elephant grass as the last CH-53 was just about into its reserve fuel, and a mad scramble got them into the chopper. Captain McCarley was the last man to board. The documents were the biggest haul of authentic information on the Ho Chi Minh Trail since the National Security Agency broke into Hanoi's messages coordinating Trail traffic.*]

KINGPIN OVER HANOI

Master Sergeant Galen Kittleson
Contingency Joint Task Force, Operation Ivory Coast
Son Tay, North Vietnam, November 21, 1970
Aerial photography of North Vietnam's Red River Delta suggested to U.S. photo interpreters that a certain building complex outside the village of Son Tay, near Hanoi, was occupied by American prisoners. Washington approved a rescue mission conducted from outside the combat theater and carried out directly under the Joint Chiefs of Staff (JCS), eliminating any possibility of leaks from MACV but also cutting out the experts of SOG's Bright Light organization. The principal JCS manager was General Donald D. Blackburn, SOG's first boss, and he assembled a stellar cast. It included Special Forces Colonel Arthur D. "Bull" Simons as ground commander with now Captain Richard Meadows as battle leader. Sergeant Kittleson was one of fifty-six heavily armed Green Berets who participated in the strike, code-named Kingpin. He was a long-serving operator, and as far back as World War II—in the 1944 liberation of Cabanatuan in the Philippines—he had been on a previous prisoner rescue. The strike force flew from Thailand in six large HH-53C and HH-3E helicopters and reached the target area a little after two in the morning. This account is by former Green Beret Charles W. Sasser.

The lights of Hanoi sparkled beautifully toward the northeast. Most cities were beautiful when night covered their scars and scabs and warts. Haiphong Harbor out where the city met the South China Sea was even more spectacular tonight;

U.S. Navy warplanes lit up the sky and harbor gloriously with pyrotechnics, like the greatest Fourth of July fireworks show ever. From the sound and fury it could have been an invasion. The commies wouldn't know right away that no real damage had been done. They certainly had more to think about than a few helicopters attacking a small prison camp.

Kittleson picked out the Song Con River and the scattered lights of Son Tay Citadel, the village, on the other side. Then the chopper banked, cutting off that view. The next thing he saw, startling and confusing him, was the compound looming directly ahead. It lay in darkness except for dim lights shining through the windows of a long barracks-like building. An armed guard glanced up. The chopper flew so low Kittleson looked directly into the sentry's eyes.

He pinned the guard in the sights of his M-60 but held his fire. He swiveled his gun, frantically searching for his target—the southwest guard tower. It was dark, but not dark enough to hide the main features. Not at this low altitude.

Something was wrong. There were no guard towers. The buildings looked different. And where the hell was the river? Barbara [*code name for a terrain model of Son Tay built by the CIA for the mission*] had it looping back . . . and virtually lapping against the compound's west wall.

Jesus! They were crash-landing into the wrong compound!

Up in the cockpit, Lieutenant Colonel Herb Zehnder and Major Herb Kalen, the pilots, realized their mistake. . . . About four hundred yards south of Son Tay compound lay what had been dubbed the "secondary school" during raid . . . preparations. It was almost exactly the size and shape of the target, except it was only partly walled. The rest of it was wire net fencing.

Kalen shot power to the ship. The helicopter bolted into the night, leaving the surprised sentry with only a glimpse of a fragment of reality, like what was left of a nightmare once you awoke.

Kittleson caught his breath in relief.

[*One of the big choppers, modified to act as a gunship, went in ahead of them to knock out the guard towers.*] *Banana One*, the radio sign for Dick Meadows's Compound Assault HH-3, came in hard and close behind. . . . Pilots Zehnder and Kalen pulled its nose down heavily and charged in a fast glide toward the southwest guard tower and the courtyard where it would crash-land. Kittleson saw the bridge over the Song Con sweep underneath and away. The flare illuminated the stone wall, and Kittleson made out each of the buildings. Looking at the compound was almost exactly like looking at Barbara.

He swung the muzzle of his M-60. He stood on the canvas seat and thrust his head and shoulders out the window for a better view. Wind whistled past his goggles.

He found the guard tower in his sights. It was on long pole legs with an open-sided, thatched-roof shelter on top and another hootch built into the base of its legs. Movement inside said it was occupied. Kittleson squeezed his trigger gently and rejoiced in the smooth hydraulic-like recoil.

[*In moments the choppers put down and shock troops spilled out into the very heart of Indian Country. Aboard the ship with Meadows and Kittleson, the men protected themselves by jumping on mattresses. But the target was not a prisoner-of-war camp, and it was not a school either. Some decided the place was a training facility for VPA officers, others that the enemy were not Vietnamese at all but Chinese. Whatever the case, a brief, brutal firefight ensued, where the heavily armed Americans blew away everyone in their way. They tore through the barrack, finding no POWs. Bull Simon's group, meanwhile, had gone for the other complex and had to reembark to conduct a second landing at the real target. By then the battle was in full swing.*]

Kittleson, his CAR-15 at the ready, hesitated a moment to orient himself after the crash. He heard no nearby shooting. Fires burning in the west guard towers sheened dimly off the front of the long, low building in the center of the compound that was his team's first assignment. Captain McKinney shouted something and waved his arms. His team ran to him. Adrenalin pumping, Kittleson and McKinney led the way. . . .

[*While others engaged the enemy, McKinney's troopers made for their building.*] Captain McKinney's building was stucco with a covered walkway along its entire front length. The front door hung slightly ajar. Surprised, Kittleson flattened himself against the wall to one side of the door, rifle prepared, while McKinney took the other side. Both switched on miner's lamps attached to their fighting harnesses.

Ready, Kittleson sprang back and stiff-legged the door wide. It flew open with a bang. . . . St. Clair surged in low to the left, Robbins and Tapley to the right while Pappy and the captain covered for them. Beams from miner's lamps darted in the blackened room like dueling lasers.

Inside, Pappy [*Kittleson*] expected to find a scene like that from Cabanatuan—wide-eyed half-starved skeletons huddling cloaked in rags, terror, and confusion.

Instead, he found one large, open room. He turned in a circle to spray light into every corner. Trash and other debris littered the floor—old boxes, pieces of paper, a broken bunk frame, a Vietnamese sleeping mat. The room emitted a stale, long-unused odor.

Robbins's disappointed voice echoed in the otherwise empty room. "They're gone! They're not fucking here!"

[*The team searched but found no Americans anywhere. At that point the necessities of recovering the force took precedence, and Meadows and Simons began to focus on the extraction. Twenty-eight minutes on the ground outside Hanoi. Though no prisoners were recovered, no Americans were lost.*] Kittleson felt numb, but he had little time to nurse his letdown.

9

Tet I: Saigon and the Countryside

SURPRISE: SURPRISED?

Lieutenant Commander Jack Bolton, USN
Helicopter Light Attack Squadron Three, Coastal Task Force 116
Nha Be, Saigon River, January 30, 1968
Daniel Kelly has contributed a breathless account of the Seawolves (HAL-3), a unique unit, a Navy helicopter attack squadron formed expressly to work with Navy riverine forces (River Rats), special warfare units (SEALs), and the Army's First and Ninth Infantry Divisions in the swamps and rice paddies of the Mekong Delta and the war zones around Saigon. Kelly's account of a command conference illustrates why the National Liberation Front and North Vietnam were able to attain the degree of surprise that they did.
The day before the Vietnamese New Year celebration . . . Lieutenant Commander Jack Bolton called a meeting in the officers' quarters at Nha Be. All the officers were present at the briefing, which Lieutenant Richard Benedict of SEAL Team One was giving. The briefing consisted of a report on the latest intelligence that had been gathered by the teams, with the assistance of the Seawolves and River Rats.

"Gentlemen," Benedict said, "we've come to the conclusion that Charlie has been building up for something really big. . . . All the signs point toward an all-out offensive. . . . I think it's going to happen very soon. It has been reported to the powers that be, and the answer we're getting back is that it won't happen until the 'Tet cease-fire' is over. Even then, they say, it's unlikely to be as big as we're telling them."

"That's correct," Bolton said. "As usual we've been ordered to stand down along with the rest of the U.S. forces in honor of the agreement signed by both sides so as not to disturb the Tet celebration. . . . We're not too surprised that they're taking our warning with a grain of salt."

"How big is this offensive expected to be?" Lieutenant [*Junior Grade*] John Luscher asked.

"Well," Benedict replied, "I'd say every major base and city, including Cam Ranh Bay, Da Nang and Saigon, south of the DMZ, and covering the entire country, is going to get the shit kicked out of 'em."

"Damn, that's going to be nuts!" said Pistol Boswell, who was now back at [*Detachment*] Two.

Bolton went on to say, "We all need to get as much rest as possible during this 'stand down' time, just in case. . . . So don't plan on doing a whole lot of partying. Stay sober, and make sure your men do as well. Remember, the Tet celebration starts at midnight tonight. . . . "

The word was passed, and everyone spent the rest of the day cleaning guns and pulling maintenance inspections on the helicopters.

That night, the entire country went to sleep after spending the day gearing down for the holiday to come. From Binh Thuy to Vinh Long, from Dong Tam to Vung Tau, all was shut down in preparation. . . .

To the south of Saigon there was an outpost manned by the U.S. 9th Infantry. Their call sign was "Digger One." To the north of Saigon another . . . was called "Digger Two." Both were shut down for the night, as was an outpost manned by a Green Beret Mike Force just north of Tan Son Nhut Air Force Base, call sign "Striker King." No patrols being pulled at all that night.

The headquarters of the U.S. 199th Light Infantry Brigade, along with the StarCom-Satellite Communications Center, were tucked in for the coming holiday. The same was true for the Main U.S. PX and Commissary, the National Assembly Building, U.S. [*AID*] Headquarters, the USIS building, the prime minister's office building and compound, the main government office building, and the U.S. Embassy.

Sergeant Garnett Bell
101st Military Intelligence Detachment, 101st Airborne Division
Bien Hoa, January 1968
Bell had just completed Army Intelligence School and Vietnamese language training, though his assignment on this second tour in country was to a "leg" infantry company of the 2/506. Lieutenant Colonel Charlie Beckwith, who ran the divisional intelligence team at this time, knew Bell's reputation from the Central Highlands in 1965 and needed linguists for his work. Beckwith had Bell transferred. Bell recounts a series of discoveries that worried Beckwith. Though they

could convince the CO (commanding officer), however, they had more trouble with MACV's Combined Documents Exploitation Center (CDEC) in Saigon.

As Tet . . . approached . . . we heard vague rumors of an attack in our AO. Then, on January 3, 1968, 101st Airborne troops recovered another important document during an ambush. . . . [*It*] had been found on the body of Major Ut Hiep, commander of the Dong Nai Battalion, which operated as the dedicated reconnaissance element of the Central Office for South Vietnam (COSVN). . . . According to the document, Ut Hiep had been returning from a meeting at COSVN headquarters, where he had been given the mission of conducting a point reconnaissance at "San Bay B H" ("B H Air Base") and "Xa Binh My" ("Binh My Village") between January 7 and 14, 1968. The major had orders to report back to COSVN immediately after completing his mission.

Although the document was handwritten in Vietnamese and difficult to read, what could be translated seemed to me to indicate that COSVN was planning a major attack. . . . Considering the locations mentioned, enemy mortars would probably be positioned in Binh My village, just north of the flight line, in order to prevent tactical aircraft . . . from taking off. . . .

I wrote up my opinion for Beckwith. Two weeks later I was informed by the Order of Battle (OB) shop in 101st Division intelligence that experts of the [*CDEC*] . . . disagreed with my opinion. Per instructions from Beckwith, I went down to Saigon and talked to the experts, who insisted that the document was not associated with Bien Hoa air base. The Americans at the CDEC deferred to their leading expert, a Vietnamese civilian. . . . I returned to Bien Hoa angry and frustrated. A few days later Captain Joe Bolton, the division OB officer, and G-2 [*Sergeant First Class*] Pershka came by. . . . We looked [*the document*] over, referring to the appropriate maps and charts. They were noncommittal, saying the next step would be Beckwith's call.

In late January Beckwith told me his people were receiving numerous reports of enemy troop movements [*in the vicinity*], and he wanted to know what I thought of the Saigon experts' opinion. I told Charlie that, as far as I was concerned, [*the document pointed to*] Bien Hoa air base and nearby Binh My village. I also pointed out that the village was within mortar range of the runway and flight line, and I reminded him that VC cadre from our [*area*] didn't get called back to COSVN headquarters every day. Beckwith professed to have confidence in me, but he also cautioned me not to "put his ass out on a limb."

On the day before Tet began, Beckwith called me in. [*He asked Bell to fly to a 101st unit and speak to a prisoner. The man's accent convinced the intelligence officer that he was actually a People's Army regular, and Bell found more evidence of VPA presence. Very excited at news of Hanoi's troops in the area, and with many 101st GIs away on operations, Beckwith implored the division CO to*] *bolster the defenses.*] The battalion of engineers that arrived took over security of the base perimeter.

Major Michael D. Mahler
Third Squadron, Eleventh Armored Cavalry Regiment
Blackhorse and Long Binh, January 31, 1968
Executive officer of his cavalry squadron, Mahler had a broad perspective on the activities of his unit, which played an important role in smashing Liberation Front attacks at Long Binh and Bien Hoa during Tet.

Over the years since then much has been made of the complete surprise of the Tet attacks, but at the tactical unit level—the battalion level—in the area adjacent to Saigon, we knew that it was coming before we were actually caught up in it. I cannot speak to the strategic surprise or to what the higher echelons had projected in their long-range estimates of enemy capability, but I know that we had two days' warning after the first attacks to the north. What we did not know was the where and the when, and we certainly did not foresee the magnitude of the effort. . . . In part that underestimation was due to the cunning of the enemy and the nature of guerrilla warfare, but in part it was also the result of our own cynicism about the routine intelligence reports that were forever coming to us from "unspecified" sources. These . . . always announced that one hundred or two hundred Viet Cong or North Vietnamese were concentrating at some grid square in the jungle, and we were always sending our troops to find them. After having participated in a number of such futile marches . . . only to find no trace of any human passage, we tended to take all such reports with little more than a grain of salt. And when it came to Tet, it turned out to be our mistake.

For two days we listened to reports of heavy fighting in the northern sections of the country. It was apparent that the series of attacks was moving south—either because of a lack of coordination or according to some plan—and that it was simply a matter of time until our turn came. By the night of 30 January, we were all alert and tense. Our A Troop was located to the north of us on Highway 1, securing an artillery fire support base named Apple, which was midway between Xuan Loc and Bien Hoa. Both our B and C Troops were in base camp at Blackhorse, performing . . . road and local security missions. . . . Then at six o'clock in the morning on 31 January, Tet reached us. Suddenly the division radio channels came alive[:] large attacking forces moving against Tan Son Nhut Air Base, Bien Hoa Air Base, Long Binh, and the city of Saigon itself. We listened particularly closely to the reports being sent in by one of our division's mechanized infantry battalions that had been sent to Long Binh during the night, and we eventually switched to its internal radio channel to get a better idea of the fierce fighting it was involved in. . . . We had been alerted by our division headquarters to have A Troop ready to move to Bien Hoa to protect that air base. . . . At seven in the morning the command came for it to move out.

[*The unit had barely started when it was ambushed near Trang Bom, then had to scoot past defended points in villages down the road. A key bridge blew up once the lead tank crossed it. ACAVs forded the stream, but the tanks were left behind. In Bien Hoa ville the troop sped through NLF infantry, who recovered from their confusion and extracted more losses. When A Troop reached the threatened base, only eight ACAVs and a single tank remained. The unit nevertheless provided a crucial armored element to the Bien Hoa defenses. C Troop later fought at Xuan Loc. Tet cost Mahler's squadron a good 10 percent of its strength.*]

IN SAIGON: UNITED STATES EMBASSY

E. Allen Wendt
night duty officer, U.S. Embassy
Saigon, January 31, 1968
Allen Wendt, a foreign service officer, was four months in country on his first tour in Vietnam. He was an economic analyst, his job tracking the production and prices of rice in South Vietnam. Wendt was senior enough to be detailed as duty officer—in effect the top official of the embassy during its off hours—but too junior to avoid this assignment the night of the holiday. Tet was his first turn in the rotation. Wendt put this account, later declassified, into a February 20 cable.
I was asleep in Room 433, the duty officer's quarters, when the building was shaken by a loud explosion just before 3 a.m. I rolled out of bed and reached for the telephone. Automatic weapons fire broke out. I called Mr. [*John A.*] Calhoun [*the political officer*] at his home and told him the embassy was under attack. As I was speaking, another explosion tore into the building. Recalling the need for shelter from falling debris . . . I crawled in under the bed while talking to Mr. Calhoun.

I emerged from under the bed just as [*James A.*] Griffin, who was on duty in communications, came in and asked what was happening. I said I was not sure but I presumed the embassy was being attacked. I quickly dressed, gathered up my few personal possessions, and withdrew into the communications room next door, which was safer than the duty room and had more telephones. Neither of us could know the extent of the attack or whether the Viet Cong were already in the building. One of our first reactions, therefore, was to close the vault door to the communications room.

I called Mr. Calhoun's residence and by that time Mr. Carpenter of the political section and Mr. [*Gilbert H.*] Sheinbaum, the ambassador's aide, had reached the residence and set up a command post. I reported that we had moved into the communications room and should be called on extension 321 or 322. I told them I would pass information to them as soon as I obtained it. I understood they would undertake to alert others, both in Saigon and elsewhere. It is worth noting that I had left the duty officer's manual in Ambassador [*Ellsworth*] Bunker's outer office on the third floor. I was not in the habit of taking it with me to the duty officer's quarters, for I knew that much of the information in it was out of date. Even had this not been so, it contained little that would have helped in the crisis that had suddenly burst upon us.

Automatic weapons fire continued, interspersed with periodic louder explosions that we took to be rockets or mortars. All of the shooting and explosions seemed to be very near, so much so that we feared not only that penetration of the embassy was inevitable, but that our lives were in imminent danger. Indeed, we thought our only hope lay in securing the vault door to the code room and simply staying inside. We knew it would take a very heavy charge to blow that door, but we did not exclude the possibility that the Viet Cong were capable of doing it.

We next called the extension of the Marine guard on the ground floor. . . . I personally thought he must be dead. To my surprise he answered, and although he was obviously very harassed, he was quite coherent. This was to be the first of many conversations with [*Sergeant Ronald W.*] Harper, who, despite his predicament, remained virtually our only source of information on what was happening. . . .

Harper told us that the VC were inside the compound but not in the embassy building itself. He said he could hear them talking outside. . . . He did not know how many of them there were. A few minutes later Harper told us he had a wounded Marine. . . . He asked us to come and get him.

With trepidation, I went downstairs in the elevator and stepped out onto the ground floor. With the aid of [*Sergeant*] Harper, I picked up the wounded Marine [*Corporal George B. Zahuranic*] and put him on the elevator. Griffin then came down and helped me assist him to the fourth floor. (Then, and always thereafter, we locked the elevators in place so that they could not be called down to the ground floor had the VC gotten into the building.) A hurried and fearful glance at the ground floor revealed that considerable damage had already been done. The situation of the one remaining Marine looked bleak. We carried the wounded man to the fourth floor duty room and placed him on the bed I had been sleeping in. He was covered in blood but did not appear to be critically wounded. His leg seemed broken and he was obviously suffering from shock. Unfortunately none of us had any usable knowledge of first aid.

[*Wendt gave Zahuranic some water and a couple of Bufferin tablets and took his .38 pistol. Within the embassy, in addition to those named, were a CIA duty officer with two communications men and an Army signals specialist. The embassy had had extraordinary good fortune. Though South Vietnamese police at the outer gate and along the exterior wall had vanished before the attack, the Liberation Armed Forces commandos, from its C-10 Sapper Battalion, stopped to spray the gate with gunfire before moving in and then set their explosive charge against a side wall rather than at the gate. Inside the compound they were delayed by two MPs, Specialist Four Charles L. Daniel and Private First Class William E. Sebast. The men died but held up the sappers, and Sebast radioed an alert that brought two more MPs, who also perished but again distracted the enemy. The delays gave Harper and Zahuranic time to slam shut the front door before the NLF sappers charged it. There were only seventeen commandos. A tense stalemate ensued. The enemy sappers shot into the building—the second explosion Wendt had heard was their attempt to blow out the door with a B-40 rocket. Harper returned fire from his interior guard post.*]

About 4 a.m. [*Major*] Hudson called. We gave him an account of the situation as we saw it. He had already heard about the wounded Marine and said a Medevac helicopter would arrive shortly to evacuate him. We were to take him to the roof and wait for the chopper. Only the Marine guard on the ground floor, however, had the keys to the two doors through which one must pass to get from the sixth floor, where the elevators end, to the roof. We called Harper and told him we needed the keys. He said someone should ride the elevator downstairs, stay in the corner of it so as not to be directly in the line of fire, and he would throw the keys in. [*The Army communications man, Private Charles M. Fisher, did this*] and was back in a few minutes.

[*Wendt and the CIA duty officer accomplished the delicate task of getting the wounded marine to the roof, with Fisher opening doors and acting as armed guard. Told the medevac would arrive in fifteen minutes, Wendt checked after half an hour and learned the chopper had been driven off, perhaps hit by enemy fire. Soon afterward, the MACV operations center informed Wendt that two choppers were now en route, one the medevac, the other bearing ammunition. The pilots had trouble finding the embassy in the dark. The wounded Zahuranic spent an hour awaiting evacuation on the top floor and another hour and a quarter on the roof before the first helicopter arrived, piloted by Chief Warrant Officer Richard Inskeep of the 191st Assault Helicopter Company. He brought ammunition and took the wounded marine away. But the ammo in the middle of the helipad obstructed it for other choppers until Griffin, by his account, and the CIA communications man crawled out and retrieved it. (Inskeep maintains that his own crew chief and gunner pushed the ammunition across the roof and dropped it down a hole they found.)*]

At this point I should mention some of the many calls we received. They are not in sequence, and I do not remember exactly when they came in. They were handled by Griffin and by me. Frequently we were both talking at the same time on extensions 321 and 322.

[*Deputy Assistant Secretary of State*] Philip Habib called twice from the White House Situation Room. The first time, I gave him a full account of what was happening as we saw it. I recall having told him, among other things, that the VC had surrounded the building inside the compound, which was in turn surrounded by U.S. MPs and Vietnamese police, none of whom, however, had broken into the compound. (The VC were thus protected from the outside by the wall around the compound.) I said we had been promised a reaction force but none had arrived. . . . This was about 5 a.m. [*Around 6:30 the MACV operations center informed Wendt that the reaction force could not land before daylight due to poor visibility, and later called back to say the plan was to land troops on the roof while other choppers gassed the sappers inside the compound.*] We immediately called [*Sergeant*] Harper and told him of this plan. He pleaded with us to stop the use of gas, since by this time (about 7:30), the U.S. MPs had fought their way into the compound. We would be gassing our own men.

Major Hillel Schwartz
C Company, First Battalion, 502nd Infantry (Parachute), 101st Airborne Division
U.S. Embassy, Saigon, January 31, 1968

The reaction force dispatched to the embassy was drawn from the paratroopers at Bien Hoa, who had little more than a month in country. Their newly arrived brigade had been held for base security and to acclimate them to Vietnam. Some had thought this a boondoggle; now they were thrown into the breach. Charlie Company had been listening in on the action—at Bien Hoa, at Long Binh, and inside Saigon—on their radio net. With the alert order, slicks arrived to transport the heavily armed troopers. Though only two platoons went to the embassy, they were led by a senior officer, Major Schwartz. The wait until after dawn, however, meant that when paratroops arrived, the 716th Military Police Battalion was already on the embassy grounds, mopping up the NLF sappers. A couple of the commandos who tried to take position in an adjoining villa were shot by its occupants, Colonel George Jacobsen and Robert L. Josephson, another Bunker aide, whom the MPs supplied with pistols. As for the airborne, Jack Speedy, one of the 101st paratroopers, supplies this account of the reaction force's arrival.

Once over the city the picture changed. Something was radically wrong. Streets that should have been teeming with people were deserted. Grunts quickly concluded that things must be really "screwed" up—the reserve mission boondoggle had ceased to be a chance to "get over."

The flight came in parallel to the front of the embassy and the troopers strained to see all they could that would help them once they were on the ground. The choppers turned in a wide circle to the left . . . so that they could make the final landing approach over the embassy compound and into the rear of the helipad. . . . No useful information came from the pass, and the enemy became aware of an airmobile force in the vicinity.

Tension mounted as they went into the final approach and the helipad loomed larger and larger. Sounds of the rushing air and the laboring helicopter filled their ears with a rhythm they all knew too well. Familiar vibrations from the aircraft. . . . They tried to think about what they would do when they dismounted. . . . The tension was like a burning fuse that disappeared in the flash of an explosion. . . . Automatic weapons fire punched through the right side of the C&C (Command and Control) ship with a terrifying popping sound. Blood from the wounded right door gunner splattered on the passenger compartment ceiling, and the occupants . . . were pinned to their seats as the pilot instinctively turned from the fire and accelerated. M-16s and the remaining door gun pointed toward the sound of the incoming fire, but exact target identification was impossible, and there were friendly forces in the area. Not a round of return fire went out. The following aircraft broke off their approach and maintained formation at a prudent distance from the mauling of the lead ship. [*The chopper made the embassy roof, where Allen Wendt met Major Hillel and four of his men. Only one airborne platoon actually landed. The U.S. Embassy was declared secure at 9:15 a.m. Until that day, there had never been an air assault on an American embassy. Many things about Tet were extraordinary.*]

IN THE CITY

Brenda Rosen
Agency for International Development public health advisor
Saigon, January 31, 1968
A former Peace Corps volunteer in Brazil, Brenda Rosen had ten months in country and was working on a project to fluoridate the Saigon water supply. She lived in one of two hotels filled with AID employees. Rosen slept at home the night of Tet, conscious of the imminent ringing of the alarm clock that would summon her to work. This is an excerpt from her diary.

January 31, 1968, Saigon, Vietnam
I'd thought I'd heard excuses for calling off work, but this one was new. At 6:16 this morning, as I rolled over for the third time, my little clock radio

alerted me to morning. Instead of the usual pop tune of the week blaring the arrival of another day, there was a special announcement: "All American civilian personnel employed by the embassy, CORDS (Civil Operations and Rural Development Support), or AID are to remain inside their billet until further notice over Armed Forces Radio." Now I didn't even know what "billet" meant, but if it meant more sleep, I was for that.

It took about 30 seconds for the announcement to register, and then I jumped out of bed so fast you'd think I'd found myself in someone else's. There was a stillness. The usual sounds of traffic outside the front window of my hotel were gone, leaving an eerie feeling of evil in the air. Nothing could be seen or heard stirring.

January 31, 1968, 10 a.m.

Four hours later I am still in my "billet" waiting for further notice. Armed Forces Radio keeps us well-informed—" . . . at 2:55 a.m. there were several terrorist attacks by infiltrating VC . . . " Radio Washington is quoted as saying, "We feel this is a pretty serious attack." Yes, there is nothing like being well-informed. My fear is we'll be stuck here through lunch. I don't mind skipping breakfast, but lunch too? I wish I hadn't eaten my last can of spam.

This town has been unbelievable for the last week. Yesterday was the first day of Tet. I've recorded the sounds that ushered in the holiday. I hear tell all those firecrackers are to scare away evil spirits. Tradition says the more noise there is, the better the expression of happiness. Saigon must have been hysterical with happiness. Perhaps I could have enjoyed Tet's entrance if there wasn't a war, but all it did was make me a nervous wreck. . . .

January 31, 1968, 3:15 p.m.

It's no joke. The sky is buzzing with choppers. The rooftops are covered with crazy American civilian sightseers and military guards. Every now and then there is a round of fire or a mortar shell. A couple must have hit, because there are two visible fires underway.

The only thing that really worries me is the reports my folks must be getting. I fear they are scaring the hell out of them. It is not fair to worry them when the only thing worrying me is my stomach. I know one thing: I'd rather skip food altogether than to venture unauthorized over to the Officer's Club across the street.

January 31, 1968, 5 p.m.

Latest report—I'm starving. Oh, it's a strange war. There are American GIs outside patrolling the street. Along with them are the Vietnamese kids. Believe it or not, one youngster must have gotten a toy pistol for Tet. He, too, is out patrolling. This place has got to be the place to end all places.

[*It was three days before Rosen heard the Saigon traffic again—and that standard annoyance delighted. On February 1 she could return to work and eat, and a few days on the job convinced Rosen that she was finally earning the extra pay AID distributed for work in a hazardous area. Tet changed her perspective.*]

AROUND SOUTH VIETNAM: AT BAN ME THUOT

Gerald Hickey
RAND Corporation anthropologist
Ban Me Thuot, January 30, 1968
The California think tank RAND Corporation consulted on every aspect of activity from military strategy and intelligence to pacification. Gerald Hickey was a key figure in the latter area, having compiled some of the first studies of social structure in Vietnamese villages. Hickey had special interest in the montagnard tribes. In fact, he had participated in the battle when one of the upland Special Forces camps, Nam Dong, was attacked in 1964 (p. 85). The U.S. government had actually sent RAND a commendation for Hickey's heroic service there. Political differences with the tribes had been a thorny problem for the Saigon government for years. The latest effort at accommodation had been creation of a ministry for tribal affairs, plus an ethnic minorities council with montagnard participation. Hickey worked with tribal leaders on a list of approved candidates for members and had been negotiating this with Saigon officials. He felt necessary a new round of conversations with montagnards and on January 27 flew to Ban Me Thuot, a tribal center, by Air America. The next day he met with Y Bham, a prominent montagnard leader, and was warmly welcomed. On the twenty-ninth Hickey returned to the village.

Upon entering . . . it was immediately clear that the atmosphere had changed. There was no gong music and villagers wore anxious looks as we made our way to Y Bham's longhouse. He emerged looking harried and explained that the night before, the Communists had savagely attacked the post at Lac Thien to the south, leaving many of the defenders and villagers dead [*among them some from Y Bham's village*]. Y Bham was organizing a dog sacrifice, an offering for those killed in battle. "Don't go farther south on Route 21B," he warned, adding, "All the villages are filled with North Vietnamese troops, and they're taking the villagers' rice and killing all their animals for food." [*Montagnard*] troopers . . . said the Communist troops were well armed with

AK-47s and had many rockets and mortars. [*Some of Y Bham's men disguised as ordinary villagers*] heard the North Vietnamese discussing a planned attack on Ban Me Thuot the following day, 30 January 1968.

I greeted the news with a sense of dread similar to what I had experienced before the Nam Dong attack. Having survived one violent battle I had no taste for another, but it was too late to leave. At this point all I could do was hope against hope that the Communist attack somehow would not take place.

[*At Ban Me Thuot the North Vietnamese attacked prematurely, a day early, imperiling their ability to achieve surprise in the main offensive. Hickey thus witnessed one of the first Tet battles.*] Around 1:30, in a jarring reminder of Nam Dong, the still, black night was shattered by a rapid succession of explosions as mortar rounds and rockets began to rain down. . . . Quickly there was small arms fire and then machine guns began to sound. . . . Tracers zoomed and flares lit the sky. Automatic weapons fire burst from the Darlac Hotel and the nearby CIA compound. Flames shot up from buildings in the . . . market area and the crowded Vietnamese quarters. Clutching our weapons we huddled behind the sandbags on the balcony as the house shook from explosions all around. South Vietnamese tanks positioned themselves in front of the gate, and we could hear the high-pitched voices of the soldiers shouting on their radios. Armored personnel carriers moved into the traffic circle in front of the cathedral and began opening fire. Helicopter gunships swept from the American 155th Assault Helicopter unit at the nearby city airstrip to fire rockets in the vicinity. . . .

Ban Me Thuot was fast becoming a battle ground, but unlike the tiny Nam Dong camp which became immediately inundated, the unrestrained violence was coming in waves that seemed to be getting closer. The clatter and staccato of automatic weapons mixed with the explosions in a strange counterpoint steadily mounting to a staggering crescendo that fell and then rose again. To the west an enormous explosion sent shock waves over the roof tops as a fuel dump went up. Then, around 3:30, there was an unusually resounding blast from . . . the south. Mike miraculously reached the nurses by telephone and they assured him they were alright.

Suddenly the house was engulfed in violence (we found out later that a Communist unit was coming up the road behind us). Explosions all around, and tanks began to spray gunfire in every direction. Windows splintered when some of the tanks' 50-caliber rounds came crashing into the living room of the house. Tracer bullets streaked overhead. In an instant, gunships began swooping over the roof, firing rockets that spewed sparks before exploding.

[*With dawn came a lull, and some people opened their shutters to see what was happening. Refugees streamed into town to shelter at the cathedral. Bombing in the area increased. Toward afternoon, battle could be heard in the distance.*

That night, as Tet attacks engulfed South Vietnam, Ban Me Thuot was again a battleground, and Hickey helped man defenses at the compound of Special Forces Detachment B-23. But fighting was sporadic and no attacks were aimed at the Green Beret base.]

With sunrise, fighting subsided, but mortar rounds continued to fall near Bao Dai's lodge and the province chief's house. Finally, when quiet descended, there was movement around the B-Team compound. We took turns going to the mess for some breakfast. I went to one of the latrines to wash and shave, and then fell into one of the empty bunks for some badly needed sleep. At Colonel Reed's office the news came in that there had been attacks on urban areas throughout South Vietnam and that fighting in Saigon was very intense.

[Hickey made his way to the airfield, but there were no flights to Saigon. Instead he hitched a ride to Nha Trang, where battle was also in progress but there were better air links to the capital. Still it was February 3 before the RAND analyst was able to get a seat aboard an aircraft. He landed at Tan Son Nhut— which had itself been subjected to fierce attack—and found it eerily quiet. The Air America terminal, teeming when he left, was deserted. A single plane stood before the usually busy commercial terminal. Saigon streets were empty too—except where they were blocked by South Vietnamese troops.]

AROUND SOUTH VIETNAM: AT VINH LONG

Brigadier General Lam Quang Thi
ARVN Ninth Infantry Division
Sa Dec, January 31, 1968
Informed a day earlier that the Liberation Front and North Vietnamese had already attacked in some places in II Corps, General Thi cancelled holiday leaves for his division. This was different from before. The previous year Thi had used the holiday to take his eldest son to Dalat for vacation. Now he spent the New Year making the circuit of his regimental commands.

My wife had suggested that I stay home because it was a popular belief that anything you do on the first day of the Tet would impact your activities for the rest of the year. Thus, if I went out to inspect my units that day in combat uniform, I would have to fight the VC all year long. I disregarded my wife's advice because I did not believe in superstitions. Now that the enemy had attacked all over my tactical area, I painfully realized the relevance of certain popular beliefs.

When I arrived at the division [*tactical operations center—TOC*], the atmosphere was gloomy. The city of Vinh Long was completely isolated. Except for the military installations and the province chief's residence, the city was practically under VC control. [*Lieutenant Colonel*] Huynh Ngoc Diep, the province chief, who was lightly wounded in an ambush on January 6 . . . appeared to have lost control of the situation. At the airport, the enemy occupied part of the runway. All access routes to the city were blocked by VC units.

I was especially concerned about the fate of the Vinh Long archbishop and thousands of residents who had taken refuge in the historic Vinh Long Cathedral [*located at the junction of key roads*]. . . . [*It*] was now occupied by a VC unit, which practically controlled all access to the city. Any effort to bring in reinforcements and supplies . . . would require that the cathedral be retaken. I was faced with a dilemma because any attack would inevitably cause substantial loss of life among the refugees and heavy damage to the Cathedral. . . .

While I was following the tactical situation [*in*] the provinces under attack, I heard the sounds of gunfire in the direction of my residence. Then, one of the TOC telephones rang and an agitated [*Colonel*] Tran Ba Di, my deputy, handed the phone to me. "Help! Help! Come back!" I heard the voice of my wife yelling in the phone, "the Viet Cong are attacking our house!"

I dashed outside and grabbed a light machine gun positioned in the bunker at the division Headquarters' main gate. Leaving my security detail behind, I rushed to my residence while bullets were flying around me. "Halt!" yelled the guard at the front gate of my residence. "It is the General!" my aide yelled back. I hastily put the machine gun in position at the side yard directly in front of the rear gate, ready to beat back any new assaults. At the same time the two armored vehicles I had earlier sent out to patrol in the city of Sa Dec . . . took up position behind my residence. I ordered my aide and security detail to man the machine gun, then I dashed inside my house. Fortunately no one was hurt. By that time, the gunfire had died down. . . .

I sometimes wondered why these VC didn't shoot the division commander they were sent out to kill and to make good on Radio Hanoi's announcement the next day that I was killed with a few other division commanders. According to astrologers my wife had consulted, 1968 was supposed to be a bad year for me, because I was also born in the Year of the Monkey. Somehow, my family and I survived unscathed from a raid on our home. But it was a close call.

[*Thi's wife converted her orphanage into a makeshift field hospital, where hundreds of wounded were treated. Losses would have been worse but for that. She was helped by the wives of other ARVN officers. General Thi directed a series of counterattacks in Vinh Long that ejected the Liberation Front forces from the airport, though heavy fighting continued in the commercial district. The cathedral remained in enemy hands. Gunships were summoned to support assaults by the ARVN Sixteenth Infantry Regiment. Thi replaced Colonel Diep and sent his own deputy to supervise the operations. By February 2, with the situation*] *still critical, Thi felt confident it would be restored. A regiment surrounded the cathedral but deliberately left a retreat corridor open to the enemy, and the NLF quietly decamped. Before the end of the month troops had cleared all threatened places in the division sector.*]

Georgeanne Duffy Andreason
Special Services
Vinh Long, January 31, 1968

Special Services concerns itself with troop morale. It does everything from running recreation centers and organizing intramural basketball or volleyball leagues, to escorting visiting celebrities, to anything management asks. Georgeanne Andreason was an expert. She had done special services for the Red Cross and for large military hospitals at Camp Pendleton and in Hawaii. She applied for a post in Vietnam to direct a club and its programs, got the job, and arrived in Saigon in December 1967. At the time there were fewer than fifty persons in the entire Special Services cadre in South Vietnam. Ms. Andreason was to open clubs through the Mekong Delta area, working out of the airfield complex at Vinh Long.

Just adjacent to the airfield was a Catholic convent run by ten delightful nuns from Ireland and one from Singapore. We were dependent on them to do the laundry for the base, and our transportation unit flew them to Saigon often. Everyone considered it a treat to be aboard with the "Flying Nuns." The convent had been there since the French occupation of the 1950s. They had a lovely chapel, an old brick tennis court, and a swimming pool with a helicopter rotor blade for a diving board. Despite such makeshift facilities, visiting them was like entering another, more civilized world. They welcomed me with open arms and were always so hospitable. They were very courageous ladies. . . .

I had been in Vietnam two months when the Tet offensive occurred. We received word from General Westmoreland's office to go on red alert, in other words, to guard our perimeter heavily. At 2:45 a.m. the Viet Cong began to mortar the compound and airfield. I immediately dove under my bed, as I felt I didn't have time to get to my bunker. Within five minutes Lieutenant Colonel Thompson, the airfield commander, was there to insist I go to the bunker. He saw I was safely [*there*] and continued on to his . . . bunker at the perimeter. An hour later word filtered back that he had been found in his jeep, killed by a VC suicide squad before he reached his bunker. I've wondered many times if this tragedy would have happened had he not taken the time to look after my welfare. I truly believe he gave his life for me.

The other girl with whom I worked was in Vung Tau at the time. . . . So the morning after Tet I opened the club alone. It was undoubtedly one of the most memorable days of my tour. We had suffered so many casualties but the morale continued to be high. Three days later the temporary commanding officer came running into the club and announced that I had to be evacuated because the VC were burning the town of Vinh Long and were approaching the airfield. I resisted . . . as I believed I was performing a fairly important role. Regardless, he said I had to grab my toothbrush and that was all. He raced me out to the waiting Chinook, which had detoured from Saigon to get me. I later learned from the pilot . . . that because of the detour we were flying on fumes. As we [*lifted out of*] Vinh Long I could see out of the open end of the Chinook. The city was in flames and they were definitely headed toward the convent and the base. I'll never forget that sight.

The convent was badly destroyed during the battle between the suicide squads and the allied troops. While I was in Vung Tau the nuns [*back in Vinh Long*] occupied our two rooms and the children slept in the chapel. For two weeks we remained in Vung Tau. Finally they allowed us to return during the day, but at night we were still being heavily mortared so we returned to our temporary trailer in Vung Tau. Each morning we were picked up at 7:00 a.m. for the forty-five minute flight to Vinh Long. . . . I can recall many nights when we would just be airborne and the VC would be "walking" the mortars across the airfield.

AROUND SOUTH VIETNAM: AT MY THO

Lieutenant Richard Taylor
assistant senior advisor, Second Battalion, Eleventh Infantry, ARVN Seventh
Infantry Division
My Tho, January 31, 1968
Having just recovered from accidental wounds inflicted by a South Vietnamese officer examining captured weapons, Lieutenant Taylor returned to his advisory team billet in My Tho a few days before Tet. He was to resume full duties after a little more recuperation. Instead Tet threw him into the maelstrom. Taylor's ARVN unit left its own base after first light and headed for My Tho. The battalion senior advisor was visiting friends up-country for the holiday. For a day or two Lieutenant Taylor was the top advisor to the Second Battalion. He learned that South Vietnamese president Nguyen Van Thieu had been at his wife's family home in My Tho for the holiday. Whether or not the National Liberation Front knew this and used the knowledge in its calculations, it made a major play for My Tho. The People's Liberation Armed Forces' Ninth Division infiltrated right into the city. Though the adversary had previously deployed division-size formations out toward the Cambodian border, in the delta Taylor and his cohorts had never even heard of an NLF division. Several NLF battalions the Seventh ARVN had

been accustomed to fighting were suddenly part of this formation in the city. The
fight for My Tho was fierce.

The ARVN soldiers knew they should clear houses from the top down, but
they had no way to go up, except from the bottom. As they tried to go up,
the Viet Cong dropped grenades on them from above. [*Captain*] Xuan kept
me informed of the details of the skirmishes. I didn't like what I heard with
my own ears nor the reports he gave me. I grew more concerned with each
passing hour.

Each residential block we cleared, each building we took were major vic-
tories, but new obstacles stretched endlessly before us. As we approached the
city, enemy fire grew more intense and we took more casualties. Initially a
large open field protected our right flank, but it quickly merged into an urban
wilderness . . . and it became perfect for snipers. We constantly ducked because the fighting was so close that we never knew who was firing at whom—
shots erupted all around us. I detested our situation more by the minute but
felt powerless to do anything. I was just being swept along by events.

Shadows grew longer as the protracted day sagged into afternoon. Large
concentrations of VC were positioned in front and across the road to our left.
Captain Xuan identified a single two-story dwelling . . . as a CP and established defenses around it. Hedges fifty meters from the house bordered it on
two sides, and a shallow ditch with stagnant water cut across the other side.
As we approached the house we passed an apartment building to our rear; it
dominated our position across 100 meters of wide-open field. I didn't like the
. . . building that overlooked us, but any position we took in the urban jungle
presented inherent problems. This house appeared to be where we would
make our stand—our Alamo.

[*Sure enough, NLF troops were in that building. Snipers hit more men, including an ARVN lieutenant who was wounded so badly he took his own life. In
other parts of My Tho an ARVN artillery unit leveled its guns over open sights
to defend its position. A soccer pitch just a block from ARVN Seventh Division
headquarters was hotly contested. The ARVN's armored cavalry squadron was
blockaded and heavily hit. About forty ARVNs of the Second Battalion turned up
late on the second day. Once Tet became a major battle, they had returned from
leave, picked up their weapons, and rejoined. These troops made up for losses,
but the Second Battalion remained very weak, no more than about 150 soldiers.
Fighting continued.*]

By the middle of the afternoon the sun had baked us. I kept thinking of
hamburgers on a grill. The house, transformed from an aid station into a
morgue, was filled with the smell of death. I went inside once to see about
the wounded, but the smell made me dry-heave from my empty stomach.
The sight was as awful as the smell. [*The Liberation Front division had its*

headquarters at the My Tho bus station, not far from the U.S. advisory com-
pound and also close to the ARVN Second Battalion position. The NLF controlled
the bridge over the Rach Bao Dinh, the wharf on the river, the helipad, and the
cemetery. A firefight at the cemetery, and the appearance of American aircraft,
induced them to pull back. There were no U.S. troops available until a battalion
of the Ninth Infantry Division arrived.]

We had not eaten for three days and were in desperate need of ammunition, water, and medical supplies. We were so hungry and thirsty that I
doubted our effectiveness. . . . I became dizzy when I moved suddenly. At
this point our hunger was beyond growling stomachs and hunger pangs—we
were losing touch with reality, and maybe that was not a bad thing under the
circumstances. Reality was too terrible to contemplate.

[*Air strikes, and then U.S. artillery support, encouraged the ARVNs into the*
fourth day.] We held our position until noon, when a company from the U.S.
9th Division linked up with us. I shook hands with Captain Matz, feeling relief
at seeing Americans again. While we had to count each bullet, the Americans
were armed to the hilt. As we stood and chatted casually with our fellows, the
sniper in the apartment complex saw a target of opportunity and fired a round
harmlessly into the ground at our feet. It was the greatest mistake of his life. [*A*
grunt with an M79 grenade launcher put a round into the sniper's window and
blew him to kingdom come. The GIs gave the South Vietnamese ammunition and
fresh radio batteries, then moved on to sweep the rest of their sector. ARVN soldiers
executed the enemy prisoners that the Americans left with them. Then the unit
began to sweep the western edge of the city.] I was astounded by the devastation.
The city had been bombed, shelled, shot, and burned into a ruin. Burned-out
buses and cars were scattered in the road, and sometimes the passengers were
still in them. One burned-out Lambretta taxi was still manned by a driver with
the back of his head blown off and his body charred from the fire. In a macabre
gesture, someone had placed sunglasses on him and stuck a cigarette in his
mouth. [*Fighting around My Tho continued until February 7.*]

AROUND SOUTH VIETNAM: AT BIEN HOA

Corporal Richard R. Burns
Pathfinder Detachment, 101st Airborne Division
January 31, 1968
A full brigade of the 101st Airborne Division had been flown out to Vietnam
almost six weeks before. Landing at Bien Hoa, they took over well-constructed
quarters vacated by another Army unit. Corporal Burns's small detachment of
pathfinders were surprised to find such nice digs. Their cushy duty came to an end
at Tet. Not long after, the division would be sent to I Corps.

At three in the morning . . . mortar and rocket fire began pouring into our compound. It sounded like the Fourth of July, except louder. The Communist 122mm rocket was particularly menacing. It weighed 112 pounds and had a range of ten miles. Carrying an immense warhead of forty-two pounds, each one sounded like a low jet fighter ripping through the sky overhead. It made a thunderous explosion, which shook the ground. Although extremely inaccurate, it scattered huge chunks of jagged metal, which tore through anyone and anything in its kill radius.

Rushing to the bunkers, we stumbled and fell on top of one another like the Keystone Kops. Explosions continued, jolting the ground around us. The bunker was a four-foot deep, four-foot wide trench, protected by a steel culvert and a few layers of sandbags. It probably would not have withstood a direct hit, especially from one of the rockets.

[*The GIs were ordered to protect helicopters in their revetments, and presently some began to blow up. Burns thought the enemy were shelling the flight line until he saw a man running from a chopper, which promptly exploded.*] Our primary concern was a possible assault by enemy sappers.

Sappers were elite enemy soldiers highly skilled at the art of infiltration. They could penetrate just about any perimeter given the right circumstances and a little luck. . . . Normally, sappers toted explosives attached to their bodies, usually a satchel charge that they could easily throw into a bunker or building, or beneath an aircraft. Since they were not expected to survive, or to return from an attack, it was not uncommon for them to blow themselves up along with the intended target, if necessary, to ensure its destruction. [*Actually the Vietnam People's Army never aimed to use these units as suicide attackers; rather, the sapper units were engaging heavily protected targets with quite small groups of fighters, consequently suffering very high casualty rates.*] The probability of their successful penetration increased when they were assaulting under the protection of a mortar or rocket attack.

[*The 101st pathfinders protected the helicopters long enough for most aircrews to get their choppers off the ground—and these ships were the ones that carried reinforcements to the U.S. embassy. Meanwhile, fighting broke out along the perimeter of Bien Hoa base. For a time the pathfinders were looking toward the perimeter and over their shoulders at the flight line as well. Come morning the focus shifted to Bien Hoa town, where U.S. and South Vietnamese troops moved in to clear out the enemy. At the base occasional sniper fire still threatened. About 8 a.m., an awesome detonation took place at some distance—everyone at Bien Hoa was awestruck and thought of an atomic bomb—and the pathfinders eventually learned that guerrillas had blown up the huge ammunition dump at Long Binh. Sapper attacks occasionally did succeed.*]

Watching the shock wave move toward us was one of the most fascinating occurrences I have ever witnessed. A huge spherical ring was actually distorting

the sky as it rippled toward us. Ironically, none of us sought cover; we just remained stationary, in awe. I was wondering how many people get to see something like this in their lifetime. What a sight! It passed over with a thunderous
boom, and for a moment it felt as if the earth had quivered on its axis. After the
shock wave [*passed*], we returned once more to fighting.

[*As the battle line moved away, Burns figured the fighting was about a kilometer away. Air strikes were supporting GIs who had now gone on the offensive.*]
I noticed a plane pull up. . . . At around five hundred feet its engine sputtered
and it started losing altitude. The aircraft banked a hard right, turning in our
direction. As it neared, I recognized it as an A-1 Skyraider, a large fixed-wing
aircraft with a propeller and a piston engine. . . . [I]t was slower than the newly
designed jet fighters, therefore more susceptible to ground fire.

The plane was trailing smoke, the pilot obviously in trouble. It continued
losing altitude, and as I watched, began descending right toward us. I decided
to warn the others.

"Hey, guys! There's a plane in trouble, and it looks like it's heading right
for us."

Locked in some debate about who did what, none of them really bothered
to take me seriously. Larry was his usual humorous self. "Oh sure, where's it
going to land, on top of the hootch?"

My voice grew louder and I pointed at the aircraft. "No! . . . I think it's
going to crash right into us." [*Consternation followed.*]

By now the plane was a hundred meters away and closing fast. I felt like I
was part of a World War II movie, watching a plane plunging head-on at me,
trailing smoke. I picked up [*the mascot dog*] Torch and began to run for it.

Luckily, at only thirty meters away, the plane overshot us, but not by
much. It flew right above our heads about the height of a telephone pole,
still sputtering and smoking. I could actually see the pilot, a Vietnamese. The
expression on his face was one of terror mixed with determination. [*The pilot
regained control of his Skyraider at the very last second, scrabbled for a few feet of
altitude, and made for the runway. The GIs were immensely relieved.*]

AROUND SOUTH VIETNAM: AT DAU TIENG

Corporal Herb Mock
**Second Battalion, Twenty-Second Infantry (Mechanized), Twenty-Fifth In-
fantry Division**
Fire Base Burt, January 30, 1968
*The Twenty-Fifth Infantry Division, "Tropical Lightning," based in Hawaii,
had long been the Army's main combat force oriented toward the Pacific Basin*

countries. It had arrived in Vietnam in March 1966. Though based at Cu Chi, the Twenty-Fifth was responsible for a large area west and northwest of Saigon, a sector that included Dau Tieng. Liberation Front rocket and mortar attacks on the Cu Chi base frequently involved troops who passed through the Dau Tieng area, and it was also important to battles in the Michelin Plantation and Boi Loi Woods sectors. Dau Tieng was considered a high-risk sector. Corporal Mock had two months in country.

The night of January 30 I was having a fantastic night in this crap game in the track [*armored personnel carrier*], won sixty-five bucks, and they were mortaring us. I didn't think nothing about it. It was just standard operating procedure to be mortared. 'Cause I was hot-streaking, boy, rollin' them sevens. I crawled out into my bunker as they started mortaring us again. It got real, real heavy. I knew nothing but shit was going to hit the fan.

What it was is [*the enemy*] give all their men mortar rounds and line them up . . . and as each man goes into battle he dropped his round into the tube and charged, so that by the time he gets there all the mortars have hit and he's right on top of you. We lost one track on the road, hit by an RPG, and another track on the perimeter got hit with one too.

Well, they come on us, and Don and all of them got in the bunker with me. Lieutenant Kelly got in the bunker because it was about the only one left. They were firing at us from the woods, trying to RPG our tracks. So [*Second Squad, Second Platoon*] ended up the only squad left to hold this side of the perimeter. And this whole area was no man's land. A duster [*quad .50-caliber mount on a vehicle*] tried to pull up and hell, it never even got to the perimeter. They blew that son of a bitch up. The first squad had to abandon their bunker because it was filling with hot metal from a destroyed track. It melted, killed one or two guys. . . . It looked like a smelter or something.

[*The firefight went on from about midnight to dawn. Helicopters lifted in ammunition. With his own .50-caliber machine gun, Mock fired so long he burned out two barrels, and he had to run across the field to lug back more ammo. The enemy threw satchel charges and kept coming. Mock and his buddy Don both made ammo runs and at one point set up a new gun.*]

Anyway, me and Don made five or six trips over there. Finally ended up setting up a .50-caliber. We couldn't get it working right and we had been fighting for so goddamn long, got so irritated, ended up in a goddamn fistfight. Man, we were surrounded by these motherfuckers and me and Don were fighting over who was going to shoot the .50.

Sergeant Alexander came over and cussed us out: "Goddamn it, what the fuck are you doing?" We got up. "Aw, I'm sorry," I said, and started shooting. . . . [*Battle raged through the night.*] We got three hundred fifty or sixty of them. The next day you just found their bodies laying all over. General

Westmoreland flew in. All the news outfits and everything. It was the most hilarious thing. As these sons of bitches came over here, the GIs started lying. The newsmen would walk up to just anybody and say, "What did you do?" "I singlehandedly killed three hundred thousand with my Bowie knife." And man, they'd write it up.

AROUND SOUTH VIETNAM: AT CHU LAI

Warrant Officer Chuck Carlock
Seventy-First Assault Helicopter Company, Fourteenth Aviation Battalion,
Task Force Oregon
Chu Lai, central coast
The Tet Offensive started on January 30 in our area by accident. Eight locations in South Vietnam were attacked a day before the offensive was actually supposed to begin. Hoi An, between Tam Ky and Da Nang, was one of the towns that was attacked on January 30. I guess the NVA and VC military was like ours in that there was always someone who never received the correct word. . . .

Flying back on the morning of January 31, I saw an incredible sight. It looked like Chu Lai had been hit by a nuke, and we were flying straight toward the inferno. An NVA 122mm rocket had hit the ammunition dump and also blew up thirteen aircraft. The initial explosion was huge, and the ammo continued exploding for hours. Everything was blown up or under attack. LZ Baldy, LZ Ross, Hill 35, Tam Ky, and Chu Lai were all being hit by rockets or mortars. The time was somewhere around two or three o'clock in the morning.

Since we still had ammo and fuel, we were directed to Tam Ky, and flew into the war without even landing. Latimer's flight helmet was acting up, so Taylor had to talk to the American commander on the ground at Tam Ky. The grunt told him they would fire a string of .50 cal. Tracer rounds, and we were to attack several hundred meters from this location. I was aircraft commander of the wing gunship and listened to the directions.

Shortly, Taylor saw a string of orange tracers. The grunt commander started screaming, "Don't fire! Don't fire!" The enemy had been monitoring the transmission on the radio and had fired tracers at the Americans. . . .

At daylight the NVA started their retreat. They were pulling back to the north-northwest out in the open, pulling their dead and wounded along with them. Over the radio, there was the most confused and madhouse atmosphere I ever heard in Vietnam. Marine jets, air force jets, South Vietnamese A-1Es (propeller-driven bombers), a C-130 Spectre (large plane with miniguns on it), plus all kinds of artillery units were trying to get permission to shoot at the same instant. An Air Force FAC (forward air controller) was attempting to control the bedlam. One problem he encountered was that McCall and I were already on the deck chasing after the NVA like ducks going after June bugs. . . . The NVA survivors made it to a tree line next to a creek, and apparently an officer rallied the troops . . . the gunfire that immediately came out was amazing. . . . We once again engaged in our "look back" tactics. (We looked back at them while we got the hell out of the area!). . . . The 196th Light Infantry [*Brigade*] credited the helicopter gunships and the Spectre with six hundred NVA and VC killed at Tam Ky on January 31, 1968. That was our personal initiation to the start of the Tet Offensive. . . . I truly did not believe we killed that many.

10

Tet II: Hue and Khe Sanh

THE FIRE OF BATTLE

First Lieutenant Tran Ngoc Hue
Hac Bao Company, ARVN First Infantry Division
Hue, January 31, 1968

Hue, a trained Ranger, had been aide to a general, attended a prestigious British jungle warfare school, and had a growing reputation as a tough fighter. He was a veteran in the A Shau Valley. Assigned to the First Division, regarded as ARVN's finest regular unit, Hue took command of its elite scout company in the summer of 1967, when General Ngo Quang Truong decided to replace the leader. To Lieutenant Hue, the Black Panthers (Hac Bao) command represented opportunity to act independently. Truong, one of ARVN's finest generals, suspected trouble at Tet, but the situation forced him to keep his units in motion. The best Truong could do was alert his troops, canceling leaves for those who had not already left. A new threat, a VPA effort to cut the Hai Van Pass, just north of Hue City, came during the first week of January. When Truong committed the Black Panthers there, Lieutenant Hue dared to land his force right in the middle of an embattled post. Later, on January 28, Hue's scouts observed a large enemy formation—estimated at three battalions—leave the mountains for the coastal plain. The next day U.S. communications intelligence at Phu Bai, about ten miles southeast of Hue, intercepted disturbing North Vietnamese message traffic. But there were few troops available in the city. The Hac Bao company, returned after their operation, were resting in Hue. They were posted at Tay Loc airfield near the First Division headquarters, and were the only ARVN regular unit present. This account is by American historian Andrew Wiest.

The initial salvos of incoming artillery and rocket fire awakened Tran Ngoc Hue at his home in the northwest portion of the Citadel. It only slowly dawned on Hue that the fire was not the usual explosions of myriad fireworks in celebration of Tet but something much more sinister. Hue bundled his parents, wife, and daughter into the family bunker and prepared to rejoin his unit. . . . Without a jeep for transportation, Hue commandeered his father's bicycle and pedaled toward the Hac Bao perimeter. Hue soon noticed hundreds of NVA soldiers moving in the direction of 1st ARVN Division [*Headquarters*]. As it became apparent the entire city was under attack, Hue's thoughts shifted to his family; he was the father of an infant daughter, he was the senior son of elderly parents. Hue hesitated and wondered if he should return home and care for his loved ones in their time of greatest need. Hue decided . . . that his duty was with his ARVN brethren. . . . Galvanized, Hue brazenly joined the marching NVA, hoping that darkness would cover his identity. After a harrowing journey, Hue finally regained the Hac Bao lines just in time to face a frontal assault by the 800th NVA Battalion.

As the NVA surged forward . . . what amounted to a reinforced Hac Bao platoon stood firm in its defensive bunkers, firing light anti-tank weapons (LAWs) into the massed enemy ranks with devastating effect. In fighting so difficult that even the NVA grudgingly admitted the fierceness of the Hac Bao resistance, Hue and his men . . . diverted the strength of the 800th Battalion from the airfield. During the confused battle, the Hac Bao rescued two dazed American soldiers . . . caught in the crossfire. . . . Tragically, as the battle raged around him, Hue learned that the platoon he had detached to defend the provincial jail was being overrun and destroyed south of the Perfume River. The last communication . . . received from the doomed platoon leader, as he instructed his men to fix bayonets, was a request for Hue to look after his wife and seven children.

[*While Lieutenant Hue's men held out, People's Army sappers broke into General Truong's headquarters, where a scratch force of a couple of hundred clerks that GIs knew as REMFs mounted a desperate defense. Lieutenant Hue answered Truong's order for every available ARVN soldier to help defend the command post. The Hac Bao infiltrated past enemies who were unfamiliar with the city and rescued the position. Still, the next day, Hanoi's men held practically all of Hue on both banks of the Perfume, except for General Truong's hard kernel of resistance. VPA troops and political officers began circulating through the city arresting civilians, using lists they had prepared in advance. Somewhere between 2,300 and 3,500 persons were massacred during the battle of Hue. The North*]

Vietnamese manhunt threatened every American and South Vietnamese soldier or official caught in the city.]

PRELUDE AND ENGAGEMENT

Gunnery Sergeant Bruce D. Trevathan et al., USMC
First Force Reconnaissance Company
Hue, January–February 1968

The Marines had a special warfare organization that was a sort of a cross between a theater-wide unit like SOG and the Army's formation-based lurps. This was Force Reconnaissance. The First Company was in the vicinity of Hue just before Tet. Its teams detected indications of North Vietnamese activity but had trouble being taken seriously. The following account is drawn from a history of Force Reconnaissance rather than a personal reminiscence.

Bruce D. Trevathan remembers that many NVA were observed by the recon teams but that the reports were generally disregarded. One of the company's platoon leaders, [*First Lieutenant*] Russell L. Johnson, recalls that he frequently talked with officers from the infantry battalions assigned to Task Force X-RAY, who told him that none of the patrol's findings ever made it down to their level. According to Johnson, the failure of other units to react to the patrols' findings caused a morale problem. . . . "There'd be two or more times a month, troopers would come up and ask, 'What good are we? We're going out there and getting all this information, but we never get any readback on it. We never get any word that an operation has been planned because of it.' The information we provided simply wasn't getting out to the units that could use it to improve their own operations."

The Tet attack on Hue might not have come as such a surprise if anyone had been paying attention to the patrol reports of the First Company. These reports, forwarded to Task Force X-RAY, with copies to III MAF and MACV headquarters, were quite revealing. . . . The written comments by the debriefer in Patrol Report 46-68 state,

> In view of the great number of sightings made by this [*observation patrol*] it could be assumed that Route 647 is being used by the NVA as an infiltration route into Hue City. A number of NVA were guided by local VC. On numerous occasions NVA were observed talking to the local populace and then being led away. Some NVA were spotted arriving from the North, changing into civilian clothes, and then moving south. It is recommended that a sweep-and-destroy operation be held in the vicinity and that all civilian homes be searched for caches.

Oddly, the first major contact during Tet by the First Company was not via a patrol but during bridge security, an unusual mission for recon. On 5 February the First Company was directed to provide support for engineers of the 1st Marine Division, who were to repair a damaged bridge within the city of Hue. A provisional platoon under . . . [*Second Lieutenant*] Howard W. Langdon, Jr., was assigned the mission.

The platoon, along with the engineers, was transported by truck to the objective. Just short of the bridge, the convoy found the road blocked. As the recon Marines dismounted . . . they were ambushed by the front and left flank by NVA concealed in the surrounding buildings. The NVA were firing small arms, automatic weapons, mortars, and recoilless rifles. In the initial bursts, [*Lance Corporal*] J. E. Prideaux was killed and [*Private First Class*] J. A. McIntosh was mortally wounded. . . . Seven other recon Marines were wounded.

Langdon ordered his men to pull back. [*Private First Class*] Ronald S. Miller, despite having taken a bullet in the back, managed to drag another wounded Marine more than 20 meters until they were out of the kill zone. Another casualty was rescued by [*Lance Corporal*] Andrew Q. Ventura. After reaching a relatively safe position with his injured comrade, Ventura again exposed himself to the hostile fire to retrieve another downed recon man. On the return he received a painful wound to the ankle but was still able to drag the injured Marine to safety. Miller and Ventura later received Bronze Stars. . . .

The recon platoon was . . . able to break contact only after air strikes using 500-pound bombs leveled the built-up area protecting the NVA. Over two city blocks were destroyed in the fight.

AMERICAN ARRANGEMENTS

Corporal Mike McCain, USMC
Communications Company, Headquarters Battalion, First Marine Division
Phu Bai, January 30–31, 1968
The U.S. command was in a certain disarray, not least due to the ongoing battle at Khe Sanh, where a combined force consisting primarily of Marines under Colonel David E. Lownds had already been fighting for ten days what looked like a full-scale battle. To cope with that, General Robert Cushman's III Marine Amphibious Force had begun revising its command arrangements, concentrating the entire Third Marine Division in Quang Tri while extending the First Marine Division sector to include Hue. A radioman with the First, Corporal McCain served as a sort of utility infielder for the division command net, which sent him on operations, on road convoys, wherever commanders felt the need to

be in better touch. McCain estimates he spent about half his time in combat and the other half making trouble. On the night of Tet, McCain had seven months in country and was at the Phu Bai headquarters of Task Force X-Ray, the First Division group formed to cover Hue. McCain became a bodyguard for its boss, General LaHue.

X-Ray . . . was the unit that [*went into*] Hue City. It was Brigadier General Foster Carr LaHue, a graduate of VMI, straight, traditional, Old Corps. I couldn't leave the boy's side. I was like connected with an umbilical cord with this guy.

We moved up to Phu Bai . . . a combined Army and Marine Corps [*base*]. . . . We were the ones who had to go into Hue . . . when Tet started.

On the first night of Tet, when I was in Phu Bai, [*a*] CIA officer in Hue City came through the lines and walked into the command center totally unannounced. He and his Vietnamese radioman got through our lines and just walked into the commanding general's bunker to make their report. These guys were tripped out to the fucking nines. They're dressed in solid black. They got weapons I'd never seen before. They had the highest-quality, most brand-new radios that existed—weighed half as much as I had, twice the battery life. They had stuff I would have given my eyeteeth to have.

He came in and he just gave the list of names of thousands of people that the CIA thought were sympathetic to the North. [*As a result of witnessing this exchange, McCain later doubted the charge that the North Vietnamese were responsible for the murders that occurred in Hue during and after Tet, believing the United States responsible. He stopped carrying ammunition. Whatever the truth about the Hue massacres, the North Vietnamese were not the only ones who had lists.*]

INTO THE CITY

Captain Ronald Christmas, USMC
H Company, Second Battalion, Fifth Marines
Hue, January 31, 1968
American units were shuffled and reshuffled everywhere. The First Division's ad hoc team, Task Force X-Ray, had less than three rifle battalions. The First Battalion, First Marines General LaHue sent immediately. Though ambushed along the way, 1/1 was the unit that saved the MACV compound at Hue. The Second Battalion, Fifth Marines, dispatched soon after, was an example of the confusion created by the Marine redeployment. Hotel Company's leader Ron Christmas, incidentally, was married to David Lownds's daughter. This excerpt is by historian Keith Nolan.

The North Vietnamese attacked the bridge on Highway 1 that his men were guarding. The shooting went on for hours. By daylight the enemy had been driven down the river bed.

Captain Christmas was getting ready to lead the counterattack against them, when one of his radiomen said word had come to cease fire.

"What!" Christmas yelled. "You must be kidding me!"

"No Sir. The CO wants us to withdraw to Route 1 and await further orders."

The grunts trudged up the road and Christmas made contact with the commander of 2nd Battalion, 5th Marines, [*Lieutenant Colonel*] Ernest Cheatham. The colonel filled him in. . . . Hue had been attacked and Chuck Meadows's Golf Company was going in with elements of 1/1, and Mike Downs's Fox Company was on its way to Phu Bai for transport to Hue.

"You will probably be next," Cheatham told Christmas. "In fact, we'll probably all end up in Hue." Then the colonel muttered, "Why must they always piecemeal us into a battle?" [*The complaint was quite accurate: when Ron Christmas actually set off for Hue, his column contained part of the 1/1, which had been left behind at Quang Tri a couple of days earlier and was only now catching up to the battalion.*]

TRAPPED

James R. Bullington
Civil Operations and Rural Development Support coordinator, Quang Tri Province
January 31, 1968

Bullington—"J.R." as he liked to style himself—was a U.S. Foreign Service officer on his third tour in South Vietnam. He had previously served at Hue, at the Saigon embassy, and as a field representative in the Central Highlands. He volunteered for another tour in 1967, primarily to be close to his girlfriend, a young Vietnamese who worked as an interpreter at the consulate. By the end of 1967 they were engaged, their wedding planned for March, and Bullington spent every spare moment in the Imperial City. Intelligence at Quang Tri suggested a VPA attack at that place, but battle already raged at Khe Sanh, and it was not clear the enemy would have capability to spare for Quang Tri City. So Bullington flew to Hue to spend the holiday with his fiancée's family, arriving aboard Air America on January 30. He checked with U.S. officials, who had attack predictions similar to those at Quang Tri, but no one took them very seriously. Bullington had no qualms celebrating what would be his future wife's last Tet at home. The American stayed in a guesthouse at the Hue power plant. A pair of Foreign Service friends also attended the Tet dinner.

During the dinner, one of [*Bullington's fiancée*] Tuy-Cam's elderly uncles warned that he had heard the enemy was planning to attack the city that night, but the rest of us were either unconcerned or fatalistic. Most were veterans of other attacks—raids, really—which involved fighting and danger to be sure, but were over by dawn. The enemy would retreat to hide-outs in the countryside to avoid the overwhelming firepower that American and South Vietnamese forces could bring to bear on troops in fixed positions during daylight.

[*Bullington left before midnight. About three in the morning the sound of mortars woke him up, but the fighting seemed remote so he went back to bed. In the morning there was no noise of battle. Bullington was about to step outside when his host frantically motioned him to stay invisible, but by 10:30 a.m. Bullington was overcome by curiosity and emerged. The plant director, his host, stopped him, explaining that the enemy seemed to have taken over the city—which they had, except for General Truong's headquarters and the MACV compound. He told the American to stay in his room. The director said he would try to arrange a hideaway for the American. Bullington complied, but worried that his vehicle outside, which bore U.S. Agency for International Development markings, would give him away. His host returned as promised.*]

Promptly at 6, the four knocks came again. I eased open the door and watched Albert [*Istivie, the host*] move across the courtyard. When he reached the power plant, he looked back at one of the buildings where . . . NVA soldiers were located, then moved away without signaling me to follow. Something had gone wrong.

Albert returned in half an hour. He explained that one of the NVA had been looking out the window, but now they appeared to be busy cooking and eating dinner, so we could make another attempt. This time, after Albert crossed the courtyard, he signaled me to come ahead. The NVA could easily see me if they looked, but I fervently hoped they would assume I was a Frenchman who worked at the power plant rather than the owner of the American-marked vehicle parked nearby. So I tried to walk deliberately, as if I belonged there. . . .

[*The two men exited and made their way, through backyards, to the home of Father Cressonier, a French priest who had been in Vietnam since World War II. The priest sheltered Bullington, who pretended to be an acolyte, for days. They had not understood the strength of the North Vietnamese, and their hopes that U.S. and ARVN troops would quickly regain control eventually faded. Bullington maintained his disguise of being a French priest.*]

By the third day, as we realized liberation was not imminent, our spirits fell. Our anticipation was replaced by anxiety and boredom. We could sometimes see NVA soldiers and groups of refugees moving along the streets, but we never left the house, both to avoid being noticed and to avoid the bullets and occasional mortar and artillery rounds that fell in the neighborhood.

Sometimes, when the shelling became intense, we would move to the relative safety of a closet under the stairwell. . . . Fortunately, that is where we were when a large shell hit the house. The roof and walls of the second floor were largely blown away. . . . We were shaken but unhurt.

My greatest fear was not artillery but a knock on the door by Communist cadre . . . who I guessed (correctly) would be out organizing the city's inhabitants and looking for enemies. That knock never came. Subsequently, it was discovered that in the initial stages of the occupation the cadres were instructed to leave French residents alone. . . .

Albert Istivie and the French priests . . . had no way of knowing this, of course; and, in any case, this benign attitude . . . would have changed had the Communists known that they were hiding an American. It was extraordinarily brave and generous for them to take me in.

[*Bullington worried about other Americans in the city, especially his friends, and about Tuy-Cam and her family. Those fears were justified. Both friends who had been at Tet dinner were lost—one executed, the other never seen again. Similarly, Phillip W. Manhard, his opposite number as CORDS senior advisor for Thua Thien Province, was captured and held prisoner until the end of the war. The same happened to Eugene A. Weaver, the CIA base chief, and two of his counterintelligence agents. A couple of others were killed by mortar fire. The deputy chief disappeared, and the Army's spy boss was killed by rifle fire. An ARVN officer who was mayor disguised himself as a hospital patient. Tuy-Cam and her family survived, hiding her two brothers who were with the South Vietnamese military—in the attic—and giving food to People's Army troops when they demanded it.*]

Finally, on the morning of February 8, liberation was at hand. I heard American voices coming from a couple of blocks away. I climbed to the rubble of the . . . second floor and saw them—honest-to-God U.S. Marines cautiously moving our way.

They reached the house in a quarter of an hour. When I introduced myself, the sergeant said, "Oh, yeah! They told us there might be some sort of VIP hiding around here. I'd better call the captain."

Soon the company commander, Captain Ron Christmas, arrived. (Captain Christmas, one of the heroes of the Battle of Hue, went on to a distinguished Marine Corps career, retiring as a lieutenant general.) After giving him all the information the Frenchmen and I had about the situation in the immediate area, we had some of the Marines wrap me in a blanket and carry me out as if I were a wounded Marine. This was so the neighbors would not see that the priests had been hiding me.

Major Robert Annenberg
A Company, 149th Military Intelligence Group
Hue, January 31, 1968

Until his promotion to major, Annenberg had led the detachment of the 149th in Hue. At that point he moved to Da Nang as company commander, with responsibility throughout the northern provinces. The 149th Group ran unilateral (U.S.-controlled) agents, collecting "human intelligence." He returned to Hue on January 30, escorting a senior officer on an informal inspection. They were to stay one day, then go on to Quang Tri. Flying into Tay Loc, General Truong's little airfield, the two officers bunked at a villa in the new city, south of the Perfume River, that housed the Joint Technical Advisory Detachment (JTAD), a combined American–South Vietnamese spy unit. Unlike the 149th's spies, JTAD agents were run jointly. Security at the JTAD villa, though not much, was better than at the 149th's own team house.

On the ride over to the JTAD villa from the airport I noted that Hue seemed much more subdued than the madhouse we had left behind at Da Nang. There, Tet celebrators were milling about on the streets and shooting off firecrackers, balloons were flying, decorations were abundant and everyone had a carefree, holiday air. Such was not the case at Hue that afternoon. . . .

We were briefed by various teams, after which [*Lieutenant Colonel James*] Erskes wanted me to show him around the town. As we drove around . . . Hue looked almost like a ghost town. There was virtually no traffic on the street, no one walking around, no evidence of celebrations or fireworks. The shops and open-air restaurants were closed. Finding that even the Cercle Sportif was closed, I became quite concerned and drove Erskes back to the JTAD villa.

After dropping the colonel off around dusk, I did some more checking. . . . If there was one place where information could be obtained quickly, it was at the whorehouse just off Tran Hung Dao Street on the north side of the river. I drove over there and found it was closed, too.

You did not have to be much of an intelligence officer to see that something was happening—or going to happen—in Hue. Someone at the ARVN compound at the Citadel told me they were on alert status. As I drove to the MACV compound over those dark and eerie streets, I had the feeling that a thousand eyes were staring at me and wondering, "Who is he, why is he there, and what is he doing?"

When I reached the MACV compound, I was told that the staff was on alert, but it did not seem like [*that*] to me. I went into the bar and saw many of the usual drunks hanging on the rail. When I tried to tell people that something bad was probably going to happen soon, I was derided for dampening their "Tet celebration." [*Annenberg was at least able to connect with the area counterintelligence chief, who had a defensible villa, and get permission to move the JTAD people over there. Before that could be done, the battle began.*]

The attack started at about 3:30 a.m. From the intensity of the incoming mortar shells and rockets, it was clear . . . that this was more than the usual aerial barrage that was often aimed at Hue during the night. Fire from the direction of the Citadel and the MACV compound indicated that ground attacks were being mounted by enemy troops.

At first light, we saw a Communist flag waving above the Citadel. Communist troops—including some women—were moving individually and in groups . . . right in front of the JTAD house, most of them wearing olive-colored uniforms with small red armbands hiked up on one arm. Some carried AK-47s, others carried M-16s. Clearly the enemy had taken the town.

There were a few American helicopter gunships flying overhead . . . strafing the ground but not doing much damage that I could see. One of them pinned me down near the wall of our villa with machine-gun fire. At the time, I was wearing civilian clothes and had a rifle in my hands. To the gunship pilot, I was just another VC. None of the rounds hit me, but they came close enough to gouge big holes in the concrete . . . right beside me.

When I got back, I traded . . . for some Army fatigue trousers I found in a pile of dirty clothes and tried desperately to find a flak jacket and steel pot, but they were all in use. . . . The electricity and water supplies had been cut off. . . . But we had C rations to eat, and JTAD had 20 or more cases of canned beer—which could take the place of drinking water—stacked in the pantry. I don't know if it was my powers of persuasion or the colonel's innate good sense, but we decided we should stay where we were. . . .

About that time I heard heavy machine-gun fire coming from the house just to the north of ours. There was a wall connecting that villa to ours, with a small passageway on one side that was covered by rocks and mold. I carefully removed the rocks and took a peek inside the passage. To my surprise and relief, I found a fairly large group of U.S. Air Force and Army troopers, part of an aerial reconnaissance team, who . . . were trapped like us. We combined forces under the command of Colonel Erskes. [*The half dozen men who had been present turned into twenty, later twenty-five, and the place became known as "House 8" to U.S. commanders at Phu Bai, whom they contacted using the scouts' jeep-mounted radio. Close-in artillery fire protected House 8 for several days, but Annenberg had to use his pistol to stop a trigger-happy GI from firing their machine-gun, which threatened to draw unwanted attention. On the sixth day the men discussed attempting a breakout after dark, but that became unnecessary.*]

Later the same morning, a Marine tank unit came rumbling down the street to our position. Our rescuers had arrived. We ran as fast as we could behind the tank toward the MACV compound. We had been lucky, unlike many of the other Americans on the south side.

THE COUNTEROFFENSIVE

Lieutenant Colonel Pham Van Son, ARVN
Historical Section, Joint General Staff, Republic of Vietnam Armed Forces
Saigon, 1970
South Vietnamese were proud of their fighting efforts during Tet, and their Joint General Staff assigned personnel from its Historical Office to assemble an official campaign account, edited by Pham Van Son. This excerpt picks up the South Vietnamese overview of the actions that began to clear the city. It was published in Saigon while the war continued.

The actual counterattack by friendly forces did not begin until the fifth day of Tet.

The combined Vietnamese-Allied operation was conducted as follows:

- The American forces, consisting of the 2/5 Marine Battalion with three companies and an armor battalion, started out from the MACV compound while the [X-]RAY Battle Group, consisting of two companies, set out from the An Cuu bridge. Their mission was to clear the right bank of the Perfume River.
- The Vietnamese forces, consisting of the First Airborne Battle Group with three battalions and one armor squadron initiated their action from north of the Citadel. The 9th Airborne Battalion, helilifted from Quang Tri . . . on the afternoon of the fourth day of Tet, also maneuvered into the Citadel. The First Airborne Battle Group, reinforced by elements of the First Infantry Division, was to clear the left bank of the Perfume River.

Another friendly force took position northwest and southwest of Hue. This was the First U.S. Air Cavalry Division which had moved from An Khe in the pre-Tet days in order to assist with the military situation at Khe Sanh.

THE BLOCKING POSITION

Major General John J. Tolson
commander, First Cavalry Division (Airmobile)
Outside Hue, Camp Evans, February 1968
General Westmoreland had put Tolson on notice to move the Cav to III Marine Amphibious Force/I Corps. This was not a complete redeployment, as Tolson left a brigade in Binh Dinh to fight in the Bong Son valley and he concentrated other troops in Quang Tri, with division headquarters at Camp Evans, formerly a Marine regimental base. As a result of the fighting at Hue, Tolson received new

orders to interdict enemy supply lines into the city and destroy the VPA west of it. The mission at first absorbed two Cav battalions.

The 2nd Battalion, 12th Cavalry began to seal off the city from the west and the north with its right flank on the Perfume River on 2 February. The weather was miserable . . . with ceilings being at most 150 to 200 feet. Nevertheless, helicopters kept flying and placed the troops close to the assault positions even if they could not make an actual air assault. I think it was at this time that General Creighton Abrams said that any previous doubts that he had had about the ability of the helicopter to fly in marginal weather were removed.

The 1st Cavalry was spread particularly thin at this time. The 1st Brigade with four battalions was completely occupied at Quang Tri. The base at Camp Evans with approximately 200 helicopters had to be secured and the main land supply line from Dong Ha down to Camp Evans had to be reinforced.

The logisticians had more than their share of problems. . . . The road from Hue-Phu Bai to Da Nang was cut and we actually backtracked some supplies from the north at Cua Viet. The Air Force did a tremendous job in flying parachute resupply missions to Camp Evans. At times they were dropping supplies from the air with the ceiling around 300 feet using our pathfinders and Ground Control Approach radar. It was eerie to see the parachutes come floating out of the clouds minutes after the C-130s had passed. During this same period, our flying cranes and Chinooks flew out to sea and landed on the [*transport vessels*], picked up supplies, and flew them back to Camp Evans. To the best of my knowledge, this was the first example of ship-to-shore resupply in combat [*a statement that perhaps might raise Marine eyebrows*].

Two Cavalry battalions were initially committed to the mission at Hue and eventually four battalions were involved in some of the most furious combat that had taken place in Vietnam since the beginning of the war. Air strikes were very difficult to call in because of the bad weather and low ceilings. Most of our helicopter operations were at an altitude of about 25 feet. The Cavalry had cut off one of the enemy's main supply lines and had taken a heavily fortified tactical headquarters at [*Thon*] La Chu on the outskirts of the city of Hue.

CAVALRY BATTLE

Captain Charles A. Krohn
intelligence staff officer, Second Battalion, Twelfth Cavalry, First Cavalry Division (Airmobile)
Thon La Chu, February 2–5, 1968
Krohn's battalion was one of those the Cav moved up from Bong Son and committed almost literally on the fly once Tolson was ordered to isolate the city. Thon

La Chu was picked off a map as a suitable blocking position. Krohn, the battalion S-2, or intelligence officer, had no information and figured out only during the battle that they had actually struck the People's Army command center for the Hue City fight. Knowing nothing, the Second Battalion, Twelfth Cavalry had left much of its gear behind and went into combat with little more than what the men carried, further hampered by the fact the Cav had yet to organize a supply line. Everything went wrong. Artillery was delayed for nine hours and arrived with no ammunition. Air support was occupied elsewhere. Reinforcing units were not available. The troopers landed away from their objective rather than chop-pering into the enemy position. They were up against a tough VPA headquarters guard, attacking across open terrain with no cover. At one point in the ensuing fight the cavalrymen were virtually surrounded and out of supplies. The toll was enormous. One company was reduced from its standard strength of 171 GIs to just forty men. Fully half the grunts who died during the battalion's entire Hue campaign were killed in this action. It began with a brave advance. Krohn likened it to the Charge of the Light Brigade during the Crimean War of 1856, immortal-ized in Alfred Lord Tennyson's poem by that name.

I was hiding behind a palm tree at the forward edge of the treeline. I couldn't help thinking about the trench warfare during World War I. Just before the order was given. . . . I checked again to make sure I chambered a round of ammunition in both my rifle and my pistol. I repressed an urge to empty my bladder, and clicked the weapons' safety catches off so they'd fire if I pulled the trigger. Despite the temperature my hands were sweaty, and my glasses were beginning to fog.

"Move out," [*battalion commander Lieutenant Colonel Richard S.*] Sweet ordered.

Some four hundred of us got up to charge. A few never made it past the first step. By the time we got to the other side of the clearing, nine of us were dead and forty-eight wounded, cut down by accurately aimed interlocking fields of grazing fire. ("Grazing fire" is a military term for weapons fire that never rises above the height of a man. Every shot has the efficient potential to kill or disable.) An estimated fifty additional soldiers received wounds that they deemed too slight to report; they did not want to interfere with the medics, who were busy treating far more serious cases.

Under the circumstances, I thought we had done rather well. The com-parison with the Light Brigade didn't escape me. I was tired but unhurt, and I felt good about it. But the facts were uncomfortable to contemplate. Fifty-seven casualties after we started the attack, and we were stopped cold—we only got two hundred yards closer to Hue. . . . We made the NVA pay a price for stopping us, but not a high price: we killed only eight NVA (at best) and took four prisoners. We didn't know how many NVA wounded there were.

We reported higher figures to brigade, based on wishful thinking that made us feel better, but privately we knew the enemy had scarcely been scratched. Regardless of their casualties, enough remained to fix us in place.

By the time we realized where everyone was, we knew that we weren't even at the center of the hamlet—we hadn't got much past the treeline at the edge of the built-up area when our forward momentum ground to a halt.

Our attack into Thon La Chu was not the American Army at its best. Certainly, it didn't have anything to do with air mobility, the 1st Air Cav Division's forte. The fact is, we were sent on a semi-suicide mission. There might be nothing wrong with this, if the decision were calculated. In our case, the decision was based on erroneous assumptions.

[*The grunts immediately tried to dig in and prepare themselves for the inevitable enemy counterattack.*] Our strongest defense was to move into the treeline as far as we could get. The enemy anticipated our plans, and . . . moved in behind us. We finished improving our defense just in time to realize we were surrounded. That meant we'd have to fight our way out. We did our best to show that we still had the firepower to exert our will by firing our M-16s at every visible target, but as the hours passed, it was obvious they were stronger than us. [*The enemy commander, protecting the battle headquarters, simply encircled the GIs and kept them under fire. A few days later the cavalrymen broke out. Shaken, they never forgot the experience.*]

FLAG ABOVE THE IMPERIAL CITY

Major Pham Van Dinh
Second Battalion, Third Regiment, ARVN First Infantry Division
Hue, February 24, 1968
While some American troops fought to seal the enemy in Hue off from the outside, other GIs and South Vietnamese struggled to drive them out of the city. This was a fierce battle that continued for weeks. The ARVN committed Airborne troops, and once those battalions were down to an average strength of only about 160 men, switched them for Marines. General Truong summoned his Third Infantry Regiment. The U.S. Marines brought in Major Robert Thompson's First Battalion, Fifth Marines, and its fight to cross the Perfume River and breach the Citadel's walls attracted huge media attention. But right next to them in line were Major Pham Van Dinh's ARVN infantry, the South Vietnamese Marines, and Tran Ngoc Hue's Hac Bao scouts. As the combined forces pressed in, on February 22 the North Vietnamese attempted a desperate counterattack. Hue's scouts arrived at a key moment and drove the enemy back. The next day General

Truong issued orders for the final assault. He gave Major Dinh's Second Battalion, Third Infantry the mission of capturing the last stronghold, at the flag tower. This account is by historian Andrew Wiest.

Dinh realized that the attack would likely be very difficult. Throughout the battle, the NVA had proved very adept at transforming the towers of the Citadel walls into deadly defensive emplacements, and Dinh believed that the NVA would defend the massive three-story flag tower complex to the last. Making matters worse, the men of 2/3 would have to cross hundreds of yards of open ground . . . before reaching the outer ring of enemy defenses. Facing such a difficult task, Dinh and [*his American chief advisor, Joseph*] Bolt opted for a daring night raid, and, in the predawn hours of February 24, select volunteers of 2/3 rushed the tower, with one company dedicated to its seizure while the remainder surrounded the structure. Announcing their advance with a fusillade of gas grenades, 2/3 stunned the NVA with the audacity of its attack. Routed, some . . . defenders fought to the end in the upper level of the tower, while others leapt to their deaths. At [*5 a.m.*], the men of 2/3 lowered the NLF banner and informed an elated General Truong of their success. Later, after sunrise, a volunteer from 2/3 climbed the battered flagpole to put the flag of South Vietnam in its place and was shot in the leg during the process. As the flag unfurled in the breeze, a cheer went up from the weary soldiers across the Citadel, who realized that the month of agony in the city of Hue was at an end.

KHE SANH: HELL ON THE COMBAT BASE

Private First Class John Corbett, USMC
Headquarters and Service Company, First Battalion, Twenty-Sixth Marines, Third Marine Division
Khe Sanh Combat Base, January 21, 1968
A recent arrival sent to Khe Sanh, Private Corbett was a gunner with the 81-millimeter mortar section that was a key fire support for the First Battalion, Twenty-Sixth Marines on the eastern face of the combat base. John Corbett had just a few weeks in country when the siege began, with an early-morning bombardment by North Vietnamese mortars and rockets. By the standards of Con Thien, this shelling—a hundred mortars of roughly the same caliber (82-millimeter) as Corbett's own (81-millimeter), plus sixty rockets—was about a day's ration. But Khe Sanh Combat Base had not previously been targeted like this, and some facilities were not well protected against bombardment. This was true of the main ammunition dump, just a few dozen yards from Corbett's position, which sustained a direct

hit. The first explosion started fires and destroyed some of the shells, while the heat and successive explosions ignited even more rounds. Private Corbett writes in the present tense.

Even with our base's main . . . dump exploding, with fires burning all around us, with our mortar's barrel still glowing and overheating, with an unexploded enemy mortar round sticking out of the dirt several feet away, the men in my squad are singing. Though I am undoubtedly the most scared Marine in Khe Sanh at that moment, I am also the proudest because of the song we are singing: the "Marine Corps Hymn." "From the halls of Montezuma to the shores of Tripoli, we will fight our country's battles on land or on the sea." I join in. This singing together, under these circumstances, keeps our courage up. I am very proud to be here with these Marines.

[*The ammo dump fire was a huge disaster at the very outset of the siege. The previous night Marine medium artillery (105-millimeter) had expended almost a third of its shells firing in support of a nearby position, Hill 861, that was under attack. Fortuitously, a few days earlier some of the ammunition had been moved to another dump. Brave Marines rushed into the maelstrom of exploding shells to move—and save—the munitions. But the combination of expenditure and the fires deprived Khe Sanh of 80 percent of its 105-millimeter ammunition.*]

It is believed that the enemy rockets being fired into our base's ammo dump come from Hill 881N. Our ammo dump continues to blow up in explosions of varying sizes, depending on the amount of ammunition cooking off. . . . The lesser explosions tell me that a few boxes just blew up. The larger blasts . . . a pallet or two of ammo. . . . Each . . . is spectacular and frightening to watch and illuminates our positions in the predawn darkness. I am sure the explosions can be seen by the Marines on the hilltop[s]. From our mortar emplacements we have the most spectacular view because Khe Sanh's ammunition dump is our neighbor.

[*The People's Army shifted target to Khe Sanh village, about three miles away, where VPA troops opened a ground assault. Marine commander Colonel Lownds, thinking it too dangerous to send reinforcements, restricted help to fire support. Corbett describes shelling on behalf of the defenders—one of those Marine combined action companies.*] We fire for the Marines at Khe Sanh village with our mortar. We drop the bombs where they tell us. We use our remaining ammo in an attempt to help them. Hopefully, the Marines . . . can hold. When we are out of mortar rounds, an order is given from our fire direction center, via our radio headset: "Stand down. Take cover!" It's about time. Our mortars have been returning fire since the attack first started. I believe we are the last to leave our guns.

KHE SANH: ASSAULT ON HILL 861-A

Captain Earle Breeding, USMC
Echo Company, Second Battalion, Twenty-Sixth Marines, Third Marine Division
February 5, 1968

Breeding's company was detailed to set up an outpost on this hill after the People's Army tried and failed to attack nearby Hill 861. The height dominated other important positions and was thus a key to the defenses. Breeding led his men in overland to establish the 861-A strongpoint. It was Khe Sanh's last bastion. After a few days of digging in, the North Vietnamese hit 861-A with a heavy attack, as if they wanted to eject the Marines before their defenses were perfected. By now Breeding's men had trenches and some bunkers, with a few strands of barbed wire around the post. This excerpt is drawn from the account by 1/26 chaplain Ray W. Stubbe and me.

The sole indication of anything untoward was a pungent smell that the Marines . . . detected from about midnight on. Some likened it to marijuana, others to unwashed troops. Shortly after four o'clock . . . of February 5 came a tremendous volley of 82mm mortar fire simultaneously with a battalion-size assault. The wire barriers were professionally blown. North Vietnamese troops quickly closed with Lieutenant Edmund R. Shanley's 1st Platoon. They seemed to know the locations of weapons pits and other support positions and fired into them. Echo Company was in trouble immediately.

Earle Breeding told debriefers later that most of his casualties occurred during the initial mortar barrage, primarily because Echo had not been in place long enough to have really good fortifications. Typical of this phase . . . was the experience of Corporal Eugene J. Franklin, with the mortar squad of Shanley's platoon:

> All I heard was one shot go off, and I thought that was just somebody, like they thought they saw something in the wire and they just fired. All of a sudden mortar rounds . . . dropped all around the gun pit and around my hootch. And I had one man that got trapped inside his hootch when they busted the lines. And myself, I was still inside my hootch.

[Franklin eventually got to his mortar and Marines fired it until the enemy were so close that shrapnel was flying right back into Marine entrenchments. By then he could actually see People's Army soldiers. Mortar section leader Corporal Billy E. Drexel, distressed at the screams of his buddies and told that all Marines in the trenches before them had been wiped out, tried to get a second weapon into action.]

Then there was Tom Eichler, a machine gunner moving toward Shanley's platoon positions to provide more help:

Making my way down the trench line I found three of my machine gun crew lying severely wounded. Thinking they had been hit by a mortar shell, I took off my ammunition belt, laid down my rifle, and placed one . . . on my back. [*Making*] my way back through the trench line I suddenly came face to face with an NVA soldier. Instinctively I turned and began running down the trench. . . . The NVA soldier opened fire and I could hear the bullets striking me in the back, but they were not penetrating. The wounded Marine was absorbing the rounds in his flak jacket. I ran into another NVA soldier who was firing a rocket down the trench line. With the wounded Marine on my back I strangled the NVA soldier with the strap from his rocket pouch. During this incident the young Marine on my back who was now close to death was whispering directions in my ear. Funny, I had started out saving his life, now he had saved mine. Then and only then did I realize we had been overrun.

[*There were many harrowing moments, but fire support from Khe Sanh's main position, from Hill 881 South, and even long-range 175-millimeter Army guns from Cam Lo soon began to tell. The North Vietnamese lost momentum inside the strongpoint. Some were caught looting, even sitting down in Marines' hootches to ogle the women in copies of* Playboy. *Captain Breeding organized an immediate counterattack. He recalls:*]

The M-16 didn't come into play too much because of the hill we were on. There were really no fields of fire to speak of, and it turned out to be a hand grenade war. And then when Charlie got inside the wire it was just like a World War II movie with . . . knife fighting, bayonet fighting, hitting people on the nose with your fist and all the rest of that, and Charlie didn't know how to cope with it all. We just walked all over him once we were able to close. . . .

Five Navy Crosses and many other awards were given for actions on 861-A that night. Lieutenant Don Shanley, who rallied his platoon despite a painful head wound, received a Bronze Star. The company lost seven Marines with another thirty-five wounded seriously enough to be evacuated.

KHE SANH: TANKS IN THE WIRE

Lieutenant Paul R. Longgrear
Twelfth Mobile Strike Force Company, I Field Force Mobile Strike Force Battalion
Lang Vei, February 7, 1968

On a few occasions Americans had caught glimpses of VPA tanks, either through observations by recon teams in Indian Country or in aerial photography. But the enemy's first significant employment of tanks came during the siege, when they attacked the outlying Lang Vei position, a Special Forces camp that barred Route 9 between the Laotian border and Khe Sanh. A reinforced border camp, Lang Vei had been moved and reconstructed after an attack in the spring of 1967. It now boasted four outlying bastions, each defended by a Civilian Irregular Defense Group (CIDG) company; a central position, with several platoons of Nung strikers plus heavy mortars and recoilless rifles; and Special Forces Detachment A-101, commanded by Captain Frank A. Willoughby. The camp was further augmented by Lieutenant Longgrear's company from the Mike Force battalion at Kontum. For days they had known the enemy was on the move. Not only had there been the attacks on Khe Sanh village and some of the Marine strongpoints, nearby Laotian troops had been attacked, and one of their own patrols had been overrun a week earlier, with American Specialist Four John Young captured. People's Army interrogators showed Young close-up photos of the Lang Vei positions—they knew all about the base and had made detailed preparations to assault it, including the tanks. The CIA later made an extensive aerial survey of the area and were able to identify where the armor had crossed the Sepon River. These were the Third and Ninth companies of the VPA 198th Armored Battalion. Ground troops included two battalions of Le Cong Phe's Twenty-Fourth Regiment, the Third Battalion of the 101D Regiment, and elements of the Fourth and Fortieth sapper companies. The equivalent of a battalion of 122-millimeter artillery fired in direct support. Heavier 152-millimeter guns also shelled Lang Vei from positions on Co Roc Mountain. All this against the five hundred or so Americans, South Vietnamese, and tribesmen in the camp. Paul Longgrear, a product of Officer Candidate School and a trained pathfinder, arrived in Vietnam in November 1967, had been posted to the Mike Force at Lang Vei a couple days later, and took command soon after Christmas. On the night of February 6–7, Longgrear had had some experience, but he had never seen anything like this. The North Vietnamese began desultory artillery fire that afternoon and went to final bombardment at 11:15 p.m. Vietnamese sources recount that sappers breached the barbed-wire barriers on Lang Vei's western face at 11:50. This excerpt is by William Phillips, a 1965–1966 Vietnam veteran.

Lieutenant Longgrear had had a bad start to his evening on 6 February, when his MIKE Force platoon had initially refused to return to its [*observation post outside the camp*]. He had come back to his sleeping bunker below the 81mm mortar pit about fifty meters southeast of the TOC, to try to relax just before dark.

With him was one of his platoon commanders, [*Sergeant*] John Early, who was sharing his bunker while his own was being built. They were just about asleep when the radio crackled as the battle began, less than an hour into [*the new day*].

[*Unknown station to Sergeant Early:*] "We've got enemy tanks in the wire!"

"We've got what? Where?"

Longgrear and Early dashed up the bunker steps to their assigned fighting position, the 81mm mortar right above. . . . Since there were no visible targets, they pumped out a number of illumination rounds. The radio request had been urgent. Several hundred NVA accompanied five tanks, and 104 [*CIDG*] Company needed illumination. Sergeant Thompson soon joined them to form a fire-support team that dropped illumination and [*high explosive antitank—HEAT*] along the wire to the south. Almost thirty minutes passed before the team finally saw the first tank. Two more rolled into view. Surprisingly, the tanks did not appear to have the infantry that would normally be present to protect the armor from the camp's defenders. Longgrear remembers thinking, "Good. The indigenous troops and the mortars were doing their job."

Lieutenant Longgrear sent his two men down into the bunker . . . to retrieve the fifteen [*light antitank weapons—LAWS*] stashed there. Meanwhile he attempted to drop some HEAT right on the tank turrets. Thompson and Early returned with the LAWs. Longgrear saw a tank amid the reddish-orange and green tracers burning through the dark and fog. It was heading directly toward the inner perimeter and his mortar pit. He armed a LAW and aimed at the tank. The LAW failed to fire when he squeezed the rubber triggering mechanism. Early passed him another LAW. Again it failed to fire. This time Thompson handed him one, with the same result. Longgrear rearmed it and tried again. Now it fired, but when it struck the armor of the tank, which it should have penetrated easily, it simply glanced off at an upward angle. None of the three tank killers could believe the result.

The three split up as the tank approached their mortar pit, firing its 76mm main gun. Longgrear dispatched Sergeant Early to his platoon area to help the others. He sent Sergeant Thompson to assist Sergeant First Class Brande and his platoon, heavily engaged with the enemy. Lieutenant Longgrear decided to try his luck . . . from its more vulnerable flank, and the move proved successful, as he knocked out his first tank.

[*Longgrear joined Lieutenant Colonel Daniel F. Schungel of the Fifth Special Forces group, who happened to be visiting the camp. Shungel's radio handle was "Crossbow."*] NVA infantry and tanks penetrated 104 Company, and the CIDG there were in deep trouble. The tanks were decimating the CIDG on the southern perimeter with close-range firepower and infantry assault by some five hundred NVA. [*Sergeant*] Holt was successful in knocking out two of the tanks while they were still in the wire. Willoughby had left the TOC momentarily and saw Holt blow the turret completely off the second tank. Two other tanks clanked around the knocked-out, burning hulks . . . penetrated the defensive wire, and were heading directly at Crossbow and Longgrear. It took at least five hits from LAWs to disable the one most directly threatening them. A shower of orange sparks indicated each had been hit . . . but it was almost as if the LAW round was traveling at half speed and therefore not delivering its normal lethal blow.

When the LAWs had finally destroyed the tank, the three crewmen grabbed their AK-47s and crawled out to avoid being burned to death. Crossbow and Lieutenant Quy [*the ARVN Special Forces team commander*] killed all three with small arms fire and grenades. The second tank maneuvered its way . . . to continue the attack and help exploit the penetration of the camp's inner perimeter. It was firing at Schungel's anti-tank team with both the main gun and the 7.62mm machine gun from a distance of about thirty meters. Crossbow had set up his team behind some rock-filled fifty-five gallon drums just outside the TOC. Lieutenant Longgrear engaged and killed four sappers before Schungel dispatched him down the stairs to the TOC to bring back more LAWs and hand grenades. Lieutenant Wilkins . . . joined them.

Crossbow was throwing grenades at the oncoming tank. "I can't seem to get it," he yelled to Wilkins. Wilkins then threw a grenade that got under the front track of the tank, but it kept coming, closing to within twenty meters. The 76mm main gun of the NVA tank concentrated fire on the drums, destroying the . . . team's cover and at the same time blasting the TOC entrance and destroying the stairs.

Lieutenant Longgrear saw the blast. . . . Convinced that Crossbow had been killed, Longgrear reported the demise of their brave commanding officer to Captain Willoughby. Schungel had repeatedly exposed himself to deadly fire in trying to knock out the tanks.

Of the four men who had been with Schungel at the time of the blast, only Lieutenant Quy had escaped a wound. Schungel later said that Lieutenant Quy's continuous stream of small-arms fire was the only thing that saved his team from certain death from the NVA infantry trying to outflank them. [*Wounded, Longgrear retreated into the command post, by now crowded with many other wounded men. The North Vietnamese tried everything to destroy the TOC, solidly built by U.S. Seabees. They drove tanks on top of it to crush the structure, exploded demolition charges and gas, used flamethrowers and direct fire. Nothing worked. Though Lang Vei had lost radio contact with the outside, an hours-long stalemate ensued, during which the enemy could not get into the bunker, but the Americans could not get out. Finally People's Army sappers blew out a six-foot section of the TOC's side wall. They called for surrender. Most of the indigenous troops and Vietnamese filed out, but the Americans did not.*]

Knowing air power would be out in force with first light, the enemy withdrew before dawn. In daylight the Americans made a break for freedom, and they met a relief expedition cobbled together by SOG's Forward Operating Base Three at Khe Sanh.]

For Longgrear, the escape will always be like something that happened yesterday. "I had the point. As soon as I got to ground level, I ducked behind the barrels to cover the others. [*As they emerged, they huddled beside him.*] It was too crowded to stay behind the barrels, so I hopped over them. I was exposed then. Fragos was helping Willoughby and came out last, as I recall." . . .

Longgrear could not believe the sight as he emerged. . . . The familiar landmarks no longer existed. . . . Only a few destroyed Russian-made tanks were still upright. The plan called for the men to move out [*toward*] supply bunker number 2 in the northeastern corner of the camp. Longgrear, still the point man, without landmarks, and in a weakened condition, became disoriented momentarily.

Seeing something out of the corner of his eye, he turned quickly to see two NVA armed with a machine gun. They were calmly counting a large quantity of money looted from several of his dead MIKE Force troops. Longgrear had paid his men in cash just two days before. Realizing that the NVA machine gun crew could wipe out all seven of the escaping Green Berets, Longgrear fired what he wanted to be a six-round burst. He had loaded an eighteen-round magazine just before leaving the TOC. Four bullets cut down the . . . machine gunners just as his rifle stopped firing and his bad ankle gave way. He went down in a heap, rolled automatically, and thought this was the end for him.

At this moment, Lieutenant Longgrear's outlook on life changed permanently. Everything seemed to stop—the jets in the sky, the noise around him—almost as if the world, or perhaps his destiny, was waiting for him. "God, please don't let me die! I don't want to die, not now I want to live!" Longgrear remembers praying, recognizing just how mortal he was. A peace came over him like a warm blanket, and suddenly reality returned. The jets were zooming and Longgrear struggled to his feet, using his disabled weapon as a crutch. For some reason the enemy did not fire on him, and he hobbled as quickly as possible to rejoin the TOC survivors, not moving at full speed themselves. The little group had traversed only about seventy-five yards.

True to form, Lieutenant Quy of the Vietnamese Special Forces was waiting for them at the front gate with a jeep. They piled in and Lieutenant Quy sped off to Old Lang Vei.

[*There were more trials before the survivors boarded relief force helicopters, but by 4 p.m. of February 7 the main action had ended. The North Vietnamese moved on to other Khe Sanh positions. Every man at Lang Vei was a hero. Wil-*]

liam Phillips titles his study of the battle Night of the Silver Stars. *Sergeant Eugene Ashley Jr. was awarded the Medal of Honor. Paul Longgrear was taken to a hospital in Japan. Later he convalesced at Fort Benning and became an instructor there. The siege of Khe Sanh went on for another six weeks.*]

KHE SANH: BUNKERS AND BASE

Lieutenant Bernard D. Cole, USN
naval gunfire liaison officer, Headquarters, Twenty-Sixth Marine Regiment
Khe Sanh, January–March 1968
Lieutenant Cole arrived in January, halfway through his tour, having previously been naval gunnery liaison officer—or "NoGlow"—with a Marine battalion serving as special landing force. At Khe Sanh he worked with the fire support control center (FSCC), the unit that managed artillery fire distribution throughout the area. While the whole issue of fire support is important—artillery would be critical in holding Khe Sanh—Cole's comments here describe conditions in the entrenched camp.

The Marine helicopter crews who supplied the hill outposts in the face of difficult terrain, frequent fog, and lousy weather in general, were awesome. New tactics were devised on the spot, and Marines flew their helicopters in ways not imagined by their designers.

Marine CH-53 "Super Stallion" helicopters were also used to ferry personnel and supplies to Khe Sanh. Often, these aircraft did not land, but discharged and onloaded cargo while flying slowly and just above the runway. It was exciting, to say the least, to fly into Khe Sanh this way, leaping off the lowered rear ramp of a CH-53 and running for the trenches as enemy gunners marched mortar shells down the strip towards the bird. The Marine and Air Force personnel [*who performed similar feats with larger fixed-wing aircraft like the C-123 and C-130*] led very dangerous lives, and suffered a high rate of casualties.

Airlift is inherently limited, however, and ammunition and medical supplies had priority on inbound flights. Building materials for troop fortifications at Khe Sanh were in short supply; personnel protection along the fighting lines at the main combat base was mostly ramshackle and inadequate. The only first-rate bunkers at the place were the two medical bunkers built by Navy Seabees, the bunker built by Marine engineers for 1/13 [*Marine Artillery Battalion's*] fire control computer, and a couple of French-built bunkers left over from an earlier war. At one point the bunker housing the FSCC personnel took a hit from a North Vietnamese rocket that collapsed part of the roof and reduced the available living space by about a third.

Living in that bunker was a thought-provoking affair, both because of the partially collapsed roof and the numerous, brazen rats who shared our quarters. We were unable to make much of a dent in their population. Ordinary rat traps were routinely robbed of their bait. We tried poisoning them, but the rats apparently thrived on trichloroethylene tablets ("heat tabs") coated with C-ration peanut butter. On another occasion, some of the troops tried using partially loaded .45 caliber rounds to shoot the rats, but they were seemingly "faster than a speeding bullet."

We sometimes made the trip to the FSCC in a "Mighty Mite," a sort of under-powered miniature "jeep," driven by Kent Steen. He naturally drove the thing as fast as it would go, to minimize our exposure to incoming artillery. When on foot we walked around Khe Sanh rapidly but very quietly; the North Vietnamese were so close that we could hear the "pop" of their mortars as they fired, which allowed more time to take cover from the incoming round than if the first indication were the scream of a round "on final."

I later moved to the bunker used by Charlie Med's four Navy doctors. This medical "firm" of Finnegan, Magiligan, Feldman, and Wolfe saved a great many lives under conditions far harsher than television's *MASH*. My invitation to move into their bunker came from the 3rd Marine Division surgeon, who was delighted to have someone with an M-16 and a .45 living with his doctors. I was equally delighted to have such sturdy living quarters. Since sleeping bags were unavailable, we slept in "body bags."

Khe Sanh Combat Base looked like an ill-kept Third World city dump. Trash and metal fragments littered the place. Noise was a constant, from exploding artillery rounds and bombs, and from helicopters and strafing jets, as was smoke from detonating explosives and burning garbage. Most pervasive was the smell of burning shit, as the waste from the "heads" (latrines) mixed with kerosene was constantly burned in 55-gallon oil drums. Even using the "head" nearest the FSCC was an experience: the wooden building was riddled with shrapnel holes and the cry of "incoming" or "arty, arty, arty," warning that North Vietnamese rounds were inbound, would bring folks tumbling from the "head" without hesitation or thoughts for personal dignity.

Food was scarce, with one C-ration meal per day not unusual (at least for us headquarters pukes), the ammunition depot was unprotected, and clothing was difficult to come by. The situation at Khe Sanh emphasized the strain placed on American logistical lift during the Tet offensive. The priority of allocating available airlift for casualty evacuation and ammunition resupply and the poor weather conditions characteristic of this corner of Vietnam during the winter months stressed available airlift. It also showed that the Marine Corps was not prepared to fight a long-term battle in situ. The Corps had neither the resources nor the organization to keep Khe Sanh properly supplied.

KHE SANH: WELCOME TO THE WAR, MACHO MAN

First Lieutenant Ernest E. Spencer, USMC
D Company, First Battalion, Twenty-Sixth Marines
Khe Sanh Combat Base, February 1968
Lieutenant Spencer returned from R&R in Hawaii just after the battle of Lang Vei. He had eight months in country and was a veteran of patrol actions, hill fights, and holding two of Khe Sanh's strongpoints. Due to his tactical sense and dynamism and the long siege, Spencer had the distinction of leading a rifle company during his entire tour. His own battalion commander favored Delta for the hairiest assignments, and Colonel Lownds made the company his tactical reserve at the combat base. The missions remained tough ones.

Charlie has moved onto a small plateau near our water point, which lies just outside our wire. . . . We pump our water from an undefended pond beyond our wire. I always wait for someone else to drink it first.

If I were Charlie, I'd fuck with the water. If I were given a shot at Charlie's water, I'd make every guy who had just been on R&R soak his dick in it. I'd poison the drinks if I had a chance. Give me this morality shit? It's being taken out that's the morality. How doesn't count a rat's ass. I've seen guys die, die so hard, so bad, they would have taken a nuke if given a choice. You're missing the point if you think that the morality is in the how. It's irrelevant how you do it or get it done to you.

Regiment [*Colonel Lownds*] orders a platoon-sized search-and-destroy mission on the plateau. They choose Delta Company, and I pick 2nd Platoon. . . . I wait in my bunker, in radio contact with the lieutenant. . . .

Only minutes after starting, the platoon gets hit. RPG—a rocket-propelled grenade—a B-40. The lieutenant's first report is brief: "Contact, point!" As usual, the assistant S-3 from battalion requests a report almost instantly. I sit and say nothing.

The lieutenant of 2nd Platoon is new. A real cocky, macho, South Boston kid. Right from the beginning he calls me Skip. He's fresh out of Basic School and hotter than a popcorn fart.

Again the lieutenant speaks. He's freaked. His voice is three octaves up. . . . I ask him, "You still taking?"

"We got something going with the one who hit us," he says. I hear grenades exploding and rifle fire over the radio as he speaks. "I need a dustoff, now!" More explosions. "Right now, goddamn it! Do you hear me?" He is screaming at me. "My guy's real, real bad."

As soon as the hiss of the open mike comes on, I press the button on the side of the handset. Speaking deliberately and slowly I say, "OK . . . listen to me . . . listen to me. I don't care what else happens, you hang on. You hang on. You have got to hold together. Hear me?"

A brief hiss from his open mike. Then: "Roger, 6" [*the number being a radio identifier for the company commander; "2" would denote the platoon leader*].

"OK," I'm saying, "you carry him in. You're right outside the wire. It's faster than a chopper."

Behind me I hear . . . battalion . . . telling the hospital to send an ambulance to the wire. . . . A short time passes. The lieutenant calls again. He's got a couple of others slightly wounded. . . . They've killed two gooks and the one who fired the RPG is critically wounded by a grenade. Pressing the green rubber-covered button again, I say, "Delta 2, this is 6. They want anyone who is alive to be brought in, copy?"

"The gook ain't going to make it, 6. He ate most of a grenade."

"If he's alive, you bring him in, copy?"

"Roger, 6."

. . . .

"6, this is 2."

"Go ahead."

"We're coming in. The gook is a flunk. Over."

I tell one of my radio operators to check on the wounded. When he returns he tells me that the two wounded aren't so bad. I ask him how the point died. He doesn't say a word. He just contorts himself while standing in front of me. . . . A whole play, a 2-second death. No words necessary.

After a man's been in a fire fight, his eyes light up. Then they slowly darken and sink back. . . . By the time the lieutenant and I meet, he is fast sinking into his sockets. His jowls seem heavy . . . his eyes . . . glazed. With minimum details he recounts the ambush. Charlie was dug in and popped him first. His guys moved well . . . really unloaded, just like in training. "I didn't even have to tell 'em," he said. "They just went at 'em." We are alone near the entrance to my bunker.

He starts to leave, then pauses. He says in a hushed tone, "Skip, I did the gook myself. I did him right between his eyes with my pistol. He never would have made it, Skip. . . . " The lieutenant's eyes are so sad.

Good sign, I'm thinking, not the type to lay bad shit off on somebody else. Welcome to the war, macho man. With that blank look of mine, I say, "You did what you had to do, is all."

KHE SANH: MAGGIE'S DRAWERS

Captain William H. Dabney, USMC
I Company, Third Battalion, Twenty-Sixth Marines
Hill 881 South, February–March 1968

The Khe Sanh area had originally become a concern to U.S. commanders, and the Khe Sanh Combat Base had been established, after Marine units maneuvering among the nearby hills in the spring of 1967 had run into the VPA. One of those encounters took place on Hill 881 South, and after grunts fought the enemy off the hill, a strongpoint had been built there. Like the other hilltop positions around Khe Sanh, the Marine presence ensured the People's Army could not dominate the main position, as the Viet Minh had in the battle with the French at Dien Bien Phu. Captain Bill Dabney's India Company of 3/26 replaced Spencer's D/1/26 on the hill around the turn of the year. At the time of the siege Dabney's India Company still garrisoned 881 South. Theirs was a constant duel with death.

There were as many expressions of defiance of the North Vietnamese as there were Americans at Khe Sanh. One of the best known and most obviously defiant gestures was one Captain Dabney's men made atop Hill 881 South. Early during the siege the Marines began to raise an American flag over their position every morning and night. The gesture may have been patterned after the battle of Iwo Jima, at which it had also been the 26th Marines who raised the American flag atop Mount Suribachi . . . creating an icon of heroism in the Pacific war and indeed an enduring symbol for the Marine Corps. In any case, on top of 881 South, this flag-raising ceremony occurred twice a day, at first using a small flag that belonged to one of the men and a radio aerial. The raising of the colors always followed the prescribed ceremonial procedures, but the time was varied to fool the NVA.

One day Dabney found one of his platoon leaders crouched in a foxhole sobbing. The young lieutenant had arrived only three days earlier and already twenty-nine of the thirty-three men in his platoon had become casualties. While commiserating Dabney discovered that the man could play the bugle, a skill for which he had long been searching. After that, the young officer would run to a knoll on 881 South at each ceremony. In the morning he would play "To the Colors," in the evening "Retreat." Two Marines would run with the flag and raise it while everyone else stood in their positions and saluted or presented arms. Marines rotated the flag detail so that every man could have a chance to participate.

It was a fine piece of calculation. The NVA replied to the flag ceremonies with mortar fire, and Marines could hear the shells inserted into the tubes an instant before firing. India Company worked out its ceremony . . . so that precisely twenty-nine seconds elapsed, after which every man dived for cover. The North Vietnamese shells took thirty-one seconds to arrive on target. [*One day early in the siege, the Marines saw one of the People's Army mortars responding to their flag raising and took it out with a howitzer.*]

Another flag that flew on 881 South was "Maggie's Drawers," the signal traditionally used on the firing range to denote a complete miss of the target.

This was for a North Vietnamese sniper . . . who seemed unable ever to hit anyone. Every morning Marines' heads appeared above the trench line as they had their flag ceremony, and never was anyone hit. Finally, one day Privates First Class James Schmelia and Charles Reed turned to each other and said, "We'll fix 'em!" They thought of Maggie's Drawers. Schmelia and Reed got a section of tent pole and Schmelia came up with a pair of 3rd Marine Division swim trunks the men had been issued at Khe Sanh but had never used. They nailed the trunks to the pole. After that, each morning the sniper missed, the Marines would raise Maggie's Drawers.

[*The strongpoint was bombarded often, including by 122-millimeter guns and weapons suspected to be self-propelled. Dabney's observers were usually able to provide the combat base with at least ten seconds extra warning. Dabney was also convinced, in the face of all contrary opinions, that the main VPA artillery positions were west of 881, not atop Co Roc Mountain as others believed. Vietnamese sources confirm that some of their guns worked from this area.*]

Toward the end of February, Captain Dabney recalls, one night the NVA themselves fired illumination rounds, a string of parachute flares ignited on a line north of 881. . . . Fearing assault, Dabney called an immediate artillery mission into that area and then had the eleven mortars on his own hill fire in all directions at different ranges. The North Vietnamese used more. . . . It was extraordinary for the NVA to give up the advantages of darkness. Once the illumination stopped,

It was quiet, just like a church mouse. About a minute after everything stopped and the last flare burned out we heard what I could best describe as what sounded like standing in a New York subway station when an express train . . . goes by . . . coming out from around Co Roc. The noise got louder until it sounded as if what was making it had passed right over the hill from south to north, and then, about a thousand meters to the north of us, there was a horrendous explosion. And that was it.

[*Americans speculated this could have been a battlefield tactical missile of a kind never seen in Vietnam, but there is no evidence available to resolve this matter.*]

KHE SANH: KHE SANH 207 RED

Captain Walter A. Gunn Jr.
senior advisor, ARVN Thirty-Seventh Ranger Battalion
Khe Sanh, January–April 1968

Captain Gunn trained at Fort Bragg to be an advisor to a Vietnamese militia unit. When he arrived at Saigon, however, after a few days he was sent to Da Nang and asked if he would be prepared to work with ARVN Rangers. This entry is combined from Gunn's account to Ray Stubbe and Stubbe's separate reconstruction of the final battle—for it would be the Thirty-Seventh Ranger Battalion who faced the last ground assault the North Vietnamese threw at Khe Sanh.

I remember the following morning being awakened by the detachment 1st [*sergeant*] and being told that I had to get my gear together and board a helicopter for transport to Quang Tri Province to join the 1st Ranger Group. I asked . . . about what the [*colonel*] had said; I thought I had a choice. He told me I was the only Ranger-qualified Officer replacement for an officer killed in the past few days. After a week or two in Quang Tri Province, the Ranger Group returned to Da Nang to recuperate and conduct small unit operations around their base camp. I was then assigned to the position of Senior Advisor to the 37th Ranger [*Battalion*].

On or about the 25th of January 1968, I was informed that I and the 37th . . . commander were to take a trip to the Khe Sanh Combat Base and make coordination for our move to the base. Grabbing a map of the area of Khe Sanh and locating where it was . . . made me aware for the first time of its isolated position in Vietnam. I recall my helicopter flight to the base and talking to my counterpart en route about the area. He was not excited about the place nor about deploying there, which in turn gave me thoughts . . . concerning the place we were going. I remember upon the approach to Khe Sanh the pilot told us the base was receiving incoming artillery and rockets and, as soon as he touched down, that we were to get off quickly.

[*Captain Gunn was not enthusiastic, but that had no effect on the move, which took place on January 27. In the first two days several ARVN Rangers were killed or wounded in the bombardments, and on the day of Tet another was evacuated to Phu Bai with a snake bite. The ARVN sent no replacements to the Thirty-Seventh Rangers, already understrength, until early March. Meanwhile, the battalion CO, unable to get the attention of one of his company leaders on the field telephone, fired a machine-gun burst at the man's CP and killed him in error. When the CO refused to take orders from U.S. commander Colonel Lownds—and then from ARVN chiefs as well—he was relieved, but the executive officer took over and Gunn stayed at Khe Sanh. Another Ranger died of heart attack following an enemy bombardment. The Rangers fought several patrol actions against the VPA before late February, when intelligence indicated a major North Vietnamese attack in the offing. The Khe Sanh fire control center, and Colonel Lownds, sought emergency diversion of B-52s to strike the suspected assembly area and called on tactical air, artillery using beehive rounds, and 175-millimeter artillery to level the enemy. The strike aimed at the target box "207 Red." Judging from the actual attack, these efforts had considerable results. Stubbe writes:*]

The main attack—by those remnants of the assaulting regiment that did manage to close—was against positions of the 37th ARVN Ranger Battalion. Three probes were made by the NVA. . . . By [*4:30 a.m.*] the Ranger's front was secured. Results of the attack included at least 71 NVA killed and one ARVN Ranger wounded. Included among the materiel captured by the Rangers was a large number of enemy devices to be used to breach the wire . . . indicating that a major effort . . . had been planned. The dead were still huddled in trenches, many in the kneeling position, in three successive platoon lines, as if they had been caught in the assault position.

11

Life on the Line

OFFICERS AND COMMANDERS

Corporal Roger Hayes
First Battalion, Fifth Infantry (Mechanized), Twenty-Fifth Infantry Division
Cu Chi, fall 1967

There were a number of reasons, excepting certain special operations forces, why American unit commanders changed so frequently in South Vietnam. For one thing the National Liberation Front and Vietnam People's Army put a premium on inflicting officer casualties, so there were numerous losses. For another, officers put themselves in harm's way as they set examples for their men. Meanwhile, within the military, with only a certain number of formations engaged in combat, there was a desire to endow as many officers as possible with combat experience, and so the military set high rotation rates. Roger Hayes's observations are compelling.

Another factor that made life in the company uncertain, and resulted in decreased safety for us infantrymen, was the rotation of officers in combat assignments. Vietnam was the first war the United States had engaged in since 1953, and the majority of officers did not have combat experience, upon which the army—and I suspect the other branches of the military—places high value. In order to remedy that . . . it was decided that each officer would serve a maximum of six months in a field assignment as a platoon or company commander. After that, each would be reassigned to a staff position at the battalion or brigade level and be replaced by an inexperienced new officer, usually one fresh In Country. Even battalion commanders rotated.

For example, the Bobcats, 1/5 (Mech) Infantry, had six battalion commanders during the year I served. . . . Lieutenant Colonel Chandler Goodnow commanded from May to October 1967, which was considered a full tour for a command position. Lieutenant Colonel Fremont Hodson commanded the battalion from October to December. Major Ralph Hook held the reins from December to January 1968. He was followed by [*Lieutenant Colonel*] Henry Murphy, who served as commander from January to February. Lieutenant Colonel Thomas Lodge was in command from February to June. Finally, [*Lieutenant Colonel*] Andy Anderson took the lead in June . . . for the remainder of my tour. He was medically evacuated after his [*vehicle*] was struck by an RPG in October, the month I left Vietnam.

My platoon had seven platoon leaders, a lieutenant position, during my tour. This isn't a good example of rotation . . . , however, because most of them became casualties. Three captains commanded my company during my tour.

In the long run, perhaps this action plan of rotating officers to optimize the number of men with combat experience resulted in improvements to the military. In the short run, however, life in the platoons and companies was more complex and dangerous. Often, by the time an officer learned the nuances of combat in Vietnam, which differed significantly from those of previous engagements, he was rotated out and was replaced by someone who, regardless of rank or time in the military, knew less than many of our privates about the war and our enemy. These officers . . . made daily decisions affecting . . . lives. . . . The smallest mistakes could lead to the death of an infantryman. Some of these poor decisions resulted in the deaths of some of my fellow soldiers.

Some of the officers, but certainly not all, seized the opportunity to make a name for themselves. These men took aggressive action that led to increased danger for those under their command. The platoon watched new officers for signs of trustworthiness. Officers, as with all new arrivals, were tested before they were accepted. Once [*they*] were accepted . . . the platoon's trust was earned, and the combat troops would follow them almost anywhere.

WHO IS THE ENEMY?

Sergeant W. D. Ehrhart, USMC
First Battalion, First Marines, Third Marine Division
Quang Tri, fall 1967
Promoted to sergeant and battalion assistant intelligence chief, during this period Ehrhart's element included the scout platoon. As a result of his enlisted status, and to get a better feel for the operating area, Sergeant Ehrhart frequently pa-

trolled with the Marine scouts. The contradictions of the war began to hit him then. W. D. Ehrhart has become one of the foremost poets of the war, and expressed the ambiguities of combat in this composition, among others.

Guerrilla War

It's practically impossible
to tell civilians
from the Vietcong.

Nobody wears uniforms.
They all talk
The same language,
(and you couldn't understand them
even if they didn't).

They tape grenades
inside their clothes,
and carry satchel charges
in their market baskets.

Even their women fight;
and young boys,
and girls.

It's practically impossible
to tell civilians
from the Vietcong;

after a while,
you quit trying.

FIREBASES FROM THE SKY

Major James E. Shelton
staff operations officer, Second Battalion, Twenty-Eighth Infantry, First Infantry Division
Saigon Region, spring–fall 1967
The thirty-two-year-old major had seen soldiers all his life. As a young boy the streets of his northern New Jersey town were full of the uniformed soldiers, sailors, and airmen of World War II. In high school it was the men of Korea. ROTC was mandatory at his college, and he needed little convincing to switch from the reserves to the regular forces. Shelton's first Vietnam tour began in the summer of 1967. Though two waves of Tet took place on his watch, the event that dominates his memory is the battle of Ông Thanh, in which his battalion, 2/28, the "Black

*Lions," was chopped up in a messy fight that cost more than 130 GIs. Memorial-
izing the Black Lions, Shelton created a fine oral history of the Ông Thanh battle,
but his general observations on tactical methods are more valuable here. This
recollection begins in August 1967, when the Black Lions were sent to set up a
new firebase northeast of Bien Hoa.*

Because there were no trees in the vicinity, we could not build overhead cover
for our bunkers. To solve this problem, division provided us with steel pickets
that were normally used for erecting a barbed wire fence. We used these . . .
in lieu of logs, and they worked out quite well. The only problem came later
when we tried to collect the pickets [*when*] we were [*closing*] the firebase. The
word had been passed that we were to evacuate everything, and burn any refuse that we didn't want to evacuate. The Vietnamese marines somehow got
the wrong word. When we went to get the pickets, we found that the marines
were burning them in a huge bonfire! Obviously the pickets were not going to
burn. Nor could we place them in a sling load to be carried out, as they were
white hot. To salvage our metal posts, we had to wet them down with water,
using our steel helmets as buckets. We never figured out why the Vietnamese
marines had tried to burn these posts, and the incident did make us worry
about marines in general.

[*Major Shelton discovered that much of his life revolved around firebases—
creating them, protecting them, taking them down. The Black Lions soon had
fresh orders.*] Finally, we extracted from that remote firebase and headed back
to Lai Khe. Once we arrived there we were immediately alerted for another
operation. Plans called for . . . a two-battalion search of an area only about
five miles north and slightly west of Lai Khe. Our job was to secure a position
for a two-battery firebase. The placement of the firebase . . . would allow the
1/18 Infantry . . . to conduct search operations beyond the 105mm fan (ten
thousand meters) provided by the artillery batteries in Lai Khe.

The 105mm fan requires some explanation. Ordinarily, no units of the Big
Red One were allowed to operate on the ground unless that ground could be
hit by 105mm artillery fire. That meant that on an operations map a plan-
ner would draw a circle around any 105mm battery in firing position. The
radius of the circle was ten thousand meters, and thus troops [*could*] operate
within that circle. Consequently the position of the 105mm artillery batteries
controlled the area in which any unit of the Big Red One could maneuver.
Artillery and firebases were like solid gold. An infantry unit had to have them.
. . . If an infantry battalion or brigade commander wanted to conduct an
operation somewhere, then he had to ensure that he had 105mm coverage.
The only man with authority to move 105mm batteries was the division commander. . . . On occasion . . . commanders would try to conduct maneuvers
outside the 105mm fan, only to incur his wrath.

The maneuver plan was relatively simple. Our battalion, the 2/28 Infantry . . . would conduct an airmobile assault into the area selected for the firebase and secure it. The CH-47 Chinooks would bring in the 105mm tubes and ammo. As soon as the batteries were ready to fire, the 1/18 Infantry . . . would conduct an airmobile assault into the new ten thousand meter fan created by the positioning of the new batteries.

I am still in awe of the precision and perfection with which these operations were conducted. Many of my memories of Vietnam are ugly, involving waste of materiel, lives, and effort. However, the precision with which we conducted airmobile assaults, particularly when a firebase was being established, was phenomenal. I marveled at the split-second timing involved in coordinating a prep (air strikes and artillery), with the maneuver of the lift ships, the speed with which security and communications were established, and then the efficiency with which our artillery units were able to mount their tubes. It was only a matter of minutes from the time the CH-47 brought in the sling-loaded 105mm tubes with piggybacked ammunition until the tube was firing.

DETACHMENTS

Major Alex Lee, USMC
Third Force Reconnaissance Company
Quang Tri Combat Base, 1969
Returning to Vietnam on his second tour and now a major, Lee's operational role became one of conducting deep penetration scouting missions into Indian Country. But ensconced solidly within the Third Marine Division, Major Lee could not help observing the tactical practices of conventional troops, which brought back memories of poor methods. Lee had seen them leading a rifle company in 1965–1966, and in 1969 he found practices unchanged. Major Lee refers to both periods here. It should be added that the Army used this practice as much as the Marine Corps.
Within the mission statement for the . . . operations [*in December 1965*] was a requirement for one platoon of 2/7 infantrymen to be left at Tam Ky to provide security for the supporting artillery. . . . Later, that unit was to move to Thang Binh where the artillerymen would be co-located with the support Marines of the logistical support area (LSA), and the 2/7 Marines assigned for the security force would be released for return to [*the field*]. That security decision was typical for most major operations. Always, at the outset of extended combat, there would be an early bleeding-off of assets from the lead elements for security assignments of all sorts. The effect of that reduction in combat power was to ensure that the unit sent to fight during the opening

stages of a battle was often growing more and more short-handed—just when the heavy fighting began. In simple terms, this use of the lead elements as a source of security troops tended to arbitrarily strip combat power from the hands of the commanders on the ground. [*In this case the officer appealed the decision and—typically—was overruled.*]

That same secondary-mission assignment concept, effectively an ill-considered reduction in the ability of the lead element to maneuver and engage the enemy, continued in use in the Vietnam war for years. Identical actions were still being used, to my personal knowledge, as late as the summer of 1969 when I observed a maneuvering battalion being bested in a brutal battle by elements of the North Vietnamese Army (NVA) in the Demilitarized Zone (DMZ). That Marine battalion was fighting for its life with four platoons of its infantry—25 percent of its riflemen—assigned away from the control of the battalion commander. They were sent elsewhere to provide security detachments for other units. Had not air power tipped the balance in favor of the infantry Marines on the ground, that battered, understrength . . . battalion would eventually have been surrounded, defeated, and destroyed.

ROAD CLEARING

Major Michael D. Mahler
Headquarters Company, First Brigade, First Infantry Division
Phuoc Vinh, fall 1967
Major Mahler was Regular Army all the way—so much so that writing nearly two decades after the war, he still felt it appropriate to conceal his unit assignments. South Vietnam was Mahler's destination after a tour in West Germany. An armor officer by combat arm, Mahler had an atypical reversed progression, assigned first as staff officer to a brigade and later as executive officer in a squadron of the Eleventh Armored Cavalry Regiment. Usually officers served first in line units and later in staff positions. In any case, the road clearing he recounts here was a norm for just about every soldier in the war. Even in the late-war period, when the NLF had been considerably weakened and roads were considered open more often than not, guerrillas used mines to harass U.S. and South Vietnamese movements. Mahler's observations suggest why GIs were so often leery of the constant and obligatory road-clearing operation.
After three days, the clearing operation reached the gate of Phuoc Vinh and the road was declared open. Then our convoys of supply trucks began to run. Despite the clearing and outposting of the road, however, there were still mines that had not been detected and there was always the chance of an ambush from the jungle undergrowth on both sides of the road. Each morn-

ing before the convoys moved, a quick sweep . . . was made to make sure that [*it*] was still clear. On the first day . . . the morning clearing sweeps cost us two tanks and a recovery vehicle, two soldiers were killed, and another ten were wounded. Then the convoy rolled, and the trip to Phuoc Vinh was made without further incident. The next morning the pre-opening sweep of the northernmost section of the road started at Phuoc Vinh. Just outside our front gate the first mine-sweeping team was hit by a command-detonated claymore mine, no doubt captured from us, which spewed fragments all across the road. One soldier was killed and four others wounded. The stunned security squad . . . spotted two figures in black running away across the fields as the smoke cleared and fired *warning* shots over their heads!

Before the last empty convoy made its . . . return run five days later, our troops had discovered and destroyed 136 land mines in one twenty-mile stretch of road. That did not include the undetected mines that claimed [*the tanks, the recovery vehicle*], and an engineer bulldozer. The Viet Cong had been laying mines in the soft dirt of that road for so many years that it was literally seeded with them. Some went off the first time pressure was placed on them, and some malfunctioned and did not [*detonate*] until the third or fourth time. . . . Many were constructed of plastic explosives and wood triggering mechanisms with only the tiniest metal contact points, which our mine-detecting equipment could not pick up. In addition there were the command-detonated mines, which were buried in the road and had no triggering devices. They were set off by a person hiding in the jungle who waited until he had a target on top of it before sending an electric spark along a wire. . . . The mines ranged from the small plastic and wooden ones to the converted five-hundred pound bombs, which could turn over a medium tank with the force of their explosions.

LURPS AND FRIENDS

Specialist Four James W. Walker
Long-Range Reconnaissance Patrol Unit, First Brigade, 101st Airborne Division
Chu Lai, summer 1967
Of British extraction, James Walker—naturally—was nicknamed Limey. Stuck without transport, he hitched a ride to his base with a helicopter whose pilot admired the 101st Airborne.
There was always a special bond between chopper pilots and recon people. We made sure to let them know how much we valued their risking their butts to pull us out of the tight ones, and they always took care of us in return. We

were both in high-risk occupations. That common bond between us was simply understood, and words were rarely necessary—or sufficient—to affirm it. We had often aborted missions to go after downed chopper crews, and they had reciprocated by aborting milk runs to come to our aid, many times flying at night or in bad weather to pull out teams that had been surrounded by overwhelming enemy forces.

The flight to Chu Lai was uneventful, but looking down I thought about how beautiful the landscape of Vietnam really was. The green and brown checkerboard rice paddies, interrupted by the occasional village and dark patches of dense jungle, provided a panorama of the finest artwork of man or nature. Even the forest-covered mountains, with their promise of ever-present danger, seemed to beckon one in for a closer look.

The flight . . . was over too quickly for me. We landed at a rather ugly, unimpressive American base camp. Besides serving as the new home for the 1st Brigade of the 101st Airborne Division, Chu Lai was also the home of the U.S. Marines' Mess Kit Repair regiment (even the rugged Corps had its share of REMFs). . . .

Squad-size tents were set out in long, perfect, military rows and already heavily sandbagged for protection against rockets and mortars. A few tents were still without blast walls, but a large pile of white sand and bales of sandbags sat in the center of the compound, promising that the problem would soon be corrected. What made the situation even worse was that a detail of shirtless, sweating Lurps was already at work filling them. Welcome to Chu Lai, Spec Four Limey! Your low-ranking young ass is soon going to be on that very same work detail.

VICTUALS

Major William I. Scudder
Second Battalion, Twelfth Cavalry, First Cavalry Division (Airmobile)
Camp Evans, February 1968
The Second of the Twelfth played a crucial role at Tet by blocking one of the principal People's Army approaches to Hue, preventing the enemy from further reinforcing their battle force in the city. Battalion staff officer Charles A. Krohn tells the story of firefights that were central to this. In at least one, his unit almost ran out of ammunition and would have been destroyed but for the efforts of Major Scudder, its executive officer. In addition to other obstacles, Scudder's difficulties were magnified because the Cav had just redeployed from farther south, where most of its stores remained. Krohn acknowledges Scudder's energy in a reflection

that illustrates the enterprise of all those scroungers and supply REMFs whose feats kept GIs in the field.

After the medevacs arrived and departed, a few supply helicopters started coming in, bringing us fresh . . . rations and small arms ammunition. We had run out of both. One of the supply ships also brought Major Scudder. Although he could only stay for a few moments before returning to Camp Evans . . . he thought it necessary to appraise our situation. He wanted to hear . . . directly what our priorities were, regardless of the risk to himself. It was an act typical of Scudder.

In wartime, many acts of heroism are performed on the battlefield; some are recognized and awarded and some are not. That's how life is. The work performed behind the battle lines is rarely recognized and almost never rewarded, although the efforts performed there are often of heroic proportions. Scudder is one such unsung hero.

Scudder did not deploy with maneuver units of the battalion on the march toward Hue. He stayed behind at Camp Evans to ensure that the combat elements . . . received the support needed to sustain themselves in battle: food, ammunition, replacements, and so forth. Normally, arranging for supplies is not a very exciting job for a former company commander.

During routine times, the executive officer does little more than monitor the work of the battalion staff operating in the rear area, ensuring from time to time that food and clothing reach the forward operating units; that the battalion's administrative functions proceed as they're supposed to, so that people leave, and depart as scheduled with the proper rank and decorations; and that there is a battalion representative at all the brigade staff meetings, however irrelevant to the needs of his own organization. Normally, this is very prosaic work. But Tet was not a normal time. Established systems that were functional in the past suddenly ground to an abrupt halt. Few officers knew what to do.

Scudder . . . was a dazzling wartime officer, whose body chemistry thrived in war. When the Tet Offensive caused the division's support mechanism to collapse, Scudder seized the responsibility for taking care of his unit and shouldered the battalion's support burden. Without him we wouldn't have made it.

When we pleaded for ammunition through routine sources, we were told that there was none available, that the division's stocks hadn't arrived yet, regardless of what conditions were at [*the point of battle*]. Scudder instinctively recognized that without ammunition the battalion would die, and sensed that he was the only one who could save it. He was right. We might have made it through half the night, until one outpost after another ran out of ammunition. We would have tried to distribute the grenades fairly, but they wouldn't have lasted very long either. First one position would be overrun, then another, until the few remaining soldiers fell from wounds or exhaustion. What remained of the battalion would have to surrender.

With the hours before dark ticking off and the weather nearly unflyable already, Scudder saw that complaining wouldn't do any good. Even if he won the argument, the battalion was about to die unless ammunition could be moved forward immediately. Not in five hours or tomorrow, but IMMEDI-ATELY. With no one to turn to, Scudder took on the challenge alone.

Scudder searched high and low until he found what he was looking for: grenades and small arms ammunition piled up at the ordnance disposal site to be destroyed when the experts got around to it. The munitions had been left by the Marines and declared unserviceable. There were probably too many duds in the discarded lots to justify using the ammunition in combat. Scudder snatched the stuff before the experts could stop him and got it out on the next helicopter out. It must have made the purists nervous as hell, but it saved the life of the battalion.

It may sound frivolous to make a big deal over socks, but later we needed dry socks to prevent trench foot and immersion foot—painful diseases than can incapacitate soldiers. Scudder scrounged some old socks somewhere, but they needed to be laundered. At least they needed to be dried. Scudder went to the division laundry for help. He was told there was no gasoline to run the dryer, but if he furnished the gas, they'd dry whatever he brought in until the gas ran out.

A West Point graduate and normally an officer inclined to follow the book, Scudder set out to find gas so we could get dry socks. The fuel came from the commanding general's personal kitchen or mess—Scudder didn't ask for it, he stole it. It was only sufficient to operate the dryer for an hour, barely enough time to dry 250 pairs of Army-issue socks. It was also the only change of socks the battalion received during the entire month of February, and even then it was not enough to go around.

Scudder decided he needed a landing pad in the battalion area of Camp Evans so he could get materials to the field faster by not having to move everything twice. It was muddy at Evans, and the helicopters bogged down in mud. At the time, road graders and other engineer equipment were tied up building an air strip to handle Air Force cargo planes. Scudder knew that soldiers are susceptible to liquor, although he didn't drink himself. With bribes of whiskey, offers of new boots, and vulgar intimidation when it seemed to be effective, Scudder "borrowed" some of the men and equipment from the airfield long enough to get a helicopter pad built.

MEDICS

Ronald J. Glasser, MD
military hospital
Camp Zama, Japan, September 1968
Glasser discusses the dedication of the "docs" who gave everything of themselves,
in an excerpt written while the war still raged.
All medics talk the same and they all act the same, whether they come from
the ghetto or the suburbs. No one planned it this way. It was the kids themselves, caught between their skeptical seventeen or eighteen years, and the
war, the politicians, and the regular Army officers. Growing up in a hypocriti-
cal adult world and placed in the middle of a war that even the dullest of them
find difficult to believe in, much less die for, very young and vulnerable, they
are suddenly tapped not for their selfishness or greed but for their grace and
wisdom, not for their brutality but for their love and concern.

The Army psychiatrists describe it as a matter of roles. The adolescent who
becomes a medic begins after a very short time to think of himself as a doctor,
not any doctor in particular, but the generalized family doctor, the idealized
physician he's always heard about.

The excellent training the medics receive makes the . . . thing possible, and
the fact that units return the corpsman's concern and competence with their
own wholehearted respect and affection makes the whole thing happen.

Medics in the 101st [*Airborne Division*] carried M&M candies in their
medical kits long before the psychiatrists found it necessary to explain away
their actions. They offered them as placebos for their wounded who were too
broken for morphine, slipping the sweets between their lips as they whispered
to them over the noise of the fighting that it was for the pain. In a world of
suffering and death, Vietnam is like a Walt Disney true-life adventure, where
the young are suddenly left alone to take care of the young.

A tour of Nam is twelve months; it is like a law of nature. The medics, though,
stay on line only seven months. It is not due to the good will of the Army, but to
their discovery that seven months is about all these kids can take. After that they
start getting freaky, cutting down on their own water or food so they can carry
more medical supplies; stealing plasma bottles and walking around on patrol
with five or six pounds of glass in their rucksacks; writing parents and friends
for medical catalogues so they can buy their own endotracheal tube; or quite
simply refusing to leave their units when their time in Nam is over.

And so it goes, and the gooks know it. They will drop the point [*lead man*
of a patrol], trying not to kill him but to wound him, to get him screaming so
they can get the medic too. He'll come. They know he will.

PREMONITION

Captain Lewis H. Burruss
First Battalion, Fifth Mobile Strike Force Command
Nha Trang, June 1970
The counterpoint to fine medics, helicopter medical evacuation, and field hospitals, which transformed the treatment of injuries and wounds, was premonition. Many soldiers in Vietnam experienced such premonitions, and numerous examples exist in personal narratives. One exemplar is Captain Burruss, returned for a second tour in the spring of 1970. He had been with the Special Forces' Mike Force in 1967–1968 and had helped defeat the Tet attacks at Nha Trang. Though he put in for an infantry or airborne assignment, "Bucky" Burruss was told Special Forces needed him, and he was happy to return to the Mike Force, where he took command of one of the two MSF battalions that served as reaction forces for operations throughout South Vietnam. In June, when the MSF battalion dedicated to I Corps was recovering from losses, Burruss's unit would be sent to substitute. Bucky Burruss's observation shows that premonition affected everyone, not only Americans, in the war.

The night before we left, I was in the shower room with Llewellyn and Otis Parker, who was now fully recovered from the wounds he had suffered . . . and back in command of his company. As we lingered in the luxury of the last hot shower we would have for at least a month, Parker looked over . . . and said, "You know, one of us isn't going to make it back from this operation." Such a prediction was totally out of character for the hard-fighting little sergeant first-class, whose attitude was always so positive.

"Screw *you!*" my team sergeant and I responded. "If someone isn't coming back, it's going to be *you*, you crazy son of a bitch!" But his premonition turned out to be an accurate one.

Such premonitions were frightening to me, because I had heard them before, and all too often they came true. I had once had one myself, just before we conducted an airmobile assault from Nha Trang . . . during my previous tour. We were . . . beside the airfield waiting for the choppers to arrive . . . when I turned to the others and said, "You know, I must have dreamed it last night or something, but we were standing here like this, looking across the airfield, and a C-130 crashed right in front of us." The others gave me a weird look and changed to some more meaningful conversation. Not five minutes later an Air Vietnam aircraft landed in front of us, but continued past the end of the airstrip, through the perimeter fence, and across the road. It crashed . . . into an orphanage, burning and killed a large number of civilians, many of them orphan children. Stunned, the others looked at me in fearful awe. "For God's sake," one of them said, "if you ever have a dream about me getting killed, please don't tell me!"

The Chams [*a tribal group from the central coast area*] had the most aston-
ishing record of such psychic incidents, though. Khoe, [*a*] courageous platoon
leader, seemed always to know when he could stand in a hail of enemy fire and
not be hit, and when he needed to avoid doing so. His company commander
had predicted the hot LZ when they were attached to Project Delta for [*an*]
operation. Many were the times the Chams had stopped, sensing imminent
contact, to put on their religious amulets or prayer vests, only to make contact with the unseen enemy moments later. But there was one episode which,
beyond all others, defies explanation.

The Chams had been in a battle in II Corps, and their wounded were
evacuated to the CIDG hospital in Pleiku. Shortly after . . . the old Cham high
priest from Phan Rang showed up at our headquarters, saying he was there to
pick up the body of one of the men who had been wounded. . . . We checked
with the Americans in the company; [*his platoon leader*] said that the young
Cham had been evacuated with a minor wound in the arm. . . . The priest
would not be deterred, though, he had had a vision of the soldier's death, and
was convinced the man lay dead in Pleiku. To keep [*him*] from being alienated, we dispatched him to Pleiku—where he had never been before in his
life—and sent Sergeant Roberson to accompany him. At the CIDG hospital,
Roberson learned that there was a record of his admission, but [*none*] of the
man's release. The medics and Roberson assumed that . . . the striker . . . had
simply left when he felt well enough to do so. . . . The old priest was adamant,
now claiming he could visualize the soldier's grave somewhere within the unfamiliar city. To humor him, Roberson borrowed a jeep, and with the Cham
priest giving him directions, traveled around Pleiku until the old man stopped
him and pointed to a fresh mass grave. . . . After some difficulty, the skeptical
Roberson got permission to have the grave opened. There . . . was the body of
the dead Cham striker. Roberson, and many of the rest of us, never [*ignored*]
Cham premonitions . . . after that.

[*Several weeks into their deployment in I Corps, Sergeant Parker was wounded
by fragments of a B-40 rocket grenade and died from blood lost before he could
be evacuated.*]

ATROCITIES

Lieutenant Joseph W. Callaway Jr.
C Company, Second Battalion, Sixtieth Infantry, Ninth Infantry Division
Long An Province, spring 1967
*By far the greatest attention has focused on such atrocities as the My Lai Massa-
cre, or the unacknowledged but real atrocity potential of "body counts," as raised
by the Ninth Infantry Division's operation "Speedy Express" in 1969. But it is a*

fair bet that the majority of horrific incidents, hardly documented and largely ig-
nored, took place in the field during routine operations and resulted from casual
contempt for Vietnamese people. In this forthright example, coincidentally from
the same Ninth Infantry Division, Lieutenant Callaway reveals the dilemma that
faced American leaders in these circumstances.

I was once ordered to kill a VC prisoner we captured hiding in a spider hole,
a one-man camouflaged enemy fighting position. We reported the prisoner,
who was already wounded, and the M-2 carbine rifle we captured. I asked
my RTO . . . to call the CO . . . for direction. . . . [*He*] turned to me and said,
"Shoot him." Even though we were in a high-risk situation in the rat's nest
around Doi Mai Creek, we had time to stop and evac the prisoner, and I saw
no justification for the order.

The responsibility was mine if it had to be done. I had always hoped to
avoid a situation like this, but here it was. . . . I could not delegate it to anyone
else. I wanted to make it difficult for myself, so I decided I had to look right
at the victim and not do it from some detached distance. This was personal,
and I felt extremely uncomfortable. . . .

I took my medic's .45-caliber pistol and put it to the VC's forehead, right
between his eyes, but I couldn't pull the trigger. This was no Alabama steer; he
was a human being. . . . I could not find enough hatred within myself to kill
this man. . . . He was on his knees, at my feet, pitifully begging for his life. . . .

One of my men, a private, came over and said, "If you can't kill him, then I
will." He saw the situation as a failure of courage on my part rather than a moral
issue. I told him very clearly to wait until I had talked to the CO directly. . . . As
I walked to my radio, the blast of an automatic M-16 ripped behind me. The
private said the prisoner tried to run. . . . [*The GI*] had put his [*rifle's*] selector
switch on automatic and, in the troops' jargon, rocked 'n' rolled. I will never
forget the Vietnamese victim's grotesquely distorted face. . . .

The CO had not given an order to execute the prisoner [*after all*]. I learned
that the execution directive was issued by the first sergeant, who is not in the
chain of command and cannot give me any order. It was just deadly confusion
and mean hatred on the battlefield. . . .

In another incident, I learned that two of my soldiers had raped a young
Vietnamese girl. I remember seeing the girl during a combat search-and-
destroy operation. She was a pretty nursing mother. I told the soldiers to leave
her alone, then had to leave the area on an emergency. My point squad was
hung up in a mined area, and we stopped our movement for awhile to work
out a safe route. About a week later [*my radioman*] told me the troops were
talking about how two of my men had raped the defenseless Vietnamese girl
in a hootch bomb shelter after I left, so I started asking questions and learned
that the reports were true.

I was responsible for the actions of my men, so these beastly murder and rape incidents really bothered me. Even though I was too young and naïve to anticipate the events, I still agonized over the heinous crimes and considered them to be my personal failure. I did not see them occur and therefore could not prove anything. My predicament was complicated. If I brought the three men who participated in these two incidents up on charges, it would tear my platoon apart. It would require soldiers from my platoon to testify against one another, and it would destroy the . . . fabric that made us strong and helped us survive.

As the weeks passed, my anger and bitterness grew. Every time I looked at these three men, it disgusted me. I began to hate them for what they had done. I looked for a solution to the horrific situation. The law here was hard to determine and enforce. The difference between murder and everyday work was not always clear. There was no concept of justice. In the worst situations only power and violence were respected. . . .

In my darkest moment I considered taking the three men out on patrol and killing them myself.

Ironically, the only people I ever thought about wanting to kill in Vietnam were three of my own men.

MY LAI

Warrant Officer First Class Hugh Thompson Jr.
161st Assault Helicopter Company, 123rd Aviation Battalion, Twenty-Third (Americal) Infantry Division
Quang Ngai, March 16, 1968
A Georgian from Atlanta, Hugh Thompson enlisted in the Army so that he could fly. It was his second military commitment—Thompson had previously served three years as a Navy Seabee. He flew an OH-23 Raven scout helicopter in support of the Americal Division. Debate rages to this day about how prevalent were war crimes by Americans in Vietnam, but unquestionably the incident at My Lai, involving Lieutenant William Calley and Charlie Company of the First Battalion, Twentieth Infantry, in which 504 Vietnamese civilians were massacred by U.S. troops, was the largest acknowledged atrocity. Warrant Officer Thompson flew reconnaissance for the maneuver, with the 161st Assault operating out of LZ Dottie. His Raven had cover from a pair of gunship helicopters. Thompson intervened when he saw what was happening around My Lai Four, which grunts knew as "Pinkville." He had slightly less than three months in country at the time. This is his own account of that day.
My job was to recon out in front of the friendly forces and draw fire; tell them where the enemy was; and let them take care of it. The village was prepped

with artillery fire prior to the assault. We went in right in front of the "slicks."
. . . We started making our passes, and I thought it was going to be real hot
that day because the first thing we saw was a draft-age male running . . . out
of the village with a weapon. I told my gunner to get him. He tried, but he
was a new gunner and missed him. That was the only enemy person I saw
that whole day.

We kept flying back and forth, reconning in front and in the rear, and it
didn't take very long until we started noticing the large number of bodies
everywhere. Everywhere we looked, we saw bodies. These were infants; two-,
three-, four-, five-year olds; women; very old men; but no draft-age people
whatsoever. What you look for is draft-age people. . . .

We were flying around and saw wounded people. There was one lady on
the side of the road, and we knew something was going wrong by then. Larry
Colburn, my gunner, motioned for her to stay down. She was kneeling on
the side of the road. We hovered around, looking everywhere, and couldn't
understand what was going on. We flew back over her a few minutes later. . . .
It wasn't pretty. We saw another lady who was wounded. We got on the radio,
called for some help, and marked her with smoke. A few minutes later up
walks a captain. He nudges her with his foot, steps back, and blows her away.

We came across a ditch that had a lot of bodies . . . and a lot of movement
in it. I landed and asked a sergeant there if he could help them out. There were
some wounded people there who needed help. He said the only way he could
help them was to help them out of their misery, I believe. I was shocked. . . .
I thought he was joking. . . . As we took off . . . my crew chief, I guess it was,
said, "My God, he's firing into the ditch!" We had asked for help twice, actually three times by then. Every time the people had been killed. We were not
helping out these people by asking for help.

Sometime later, we saw some people huddled in a bunker-type deal . . . a
woman, an old man, and a couple of kids standing next to her. We looked
over and saw them and looked over there and saw the friendly forces, so I
landed the helicopter again. I didn't want there to be any confusion or anything. I really don't know what was going on in my mind then. I walked over
to the ground units and said, "Hey, there's some civilians over here in this
bunker. Can you get them out?" One said, "Well, we can get them out with a
hand grenade." I said, "Just hold your people right here please, I think I can
do better." So I walked over to the bunker and motioned for them to come
out and that everything was okay.

At that time I didn't know what I was going to do, because there was more
than three or four there. There were a lot more . . . nine or ten or something
like that. . . . How was I going to get these people out of this area? They would
be dead if I didn't. The Americans just kind of stayed at bay. They didn't

interfere. They didn't challenge me or anything. My crew and I were by that time very mad and upset. I don't remember the exact words, but I had told my crew what to do if the Americans started shooting. That didn't happen, so we were okay there. . . . I walked back over to the aircraft and kept the people around me. I called a buddy of mine that was flying the low gunship and asked him to do me a favor. I said, "Hey, I got these people down here on the ground. How about landing?". . . . "I can't haul them. You all land and get them out of here." He agreed, which I think was the first time a gunship was ever used for that. He asked, "Where do you want me to take them?" "Away from this place," I said. He could only get about half of them in the first load, so he had to make two different trips. He picked them up and took them about ten miles or so behind the lines and dropped them off. I was sitting on the ground and had only one gunship covering me. That was not the best thing to do, I guess, but I couldn't leave these people there. After he came back and got the rest of them, we took off.

A short while later we went back and made another pass by the ditch. There was still some movement in there. We got out of the aircraft, and Glenn Andreotta, my crew chief, went down into the ditch. He disappeared for a while . . . [then] came back carrying a little kid, who was covered with blood. We didn't know what we were going to do with this one either, but we all got back in the aircraft and figured we would take him . . . to the orphanage or hospital in Quang Ngai. . . . Taking the child to the hospital that day was something I'll never forget. It was a very sad day; it was a very mad day. . . . We flew over and dropped the boy off. I told the nun that I didn't know what you are going to do, but I don't think he has any family left.

[*Back at LZ Dottie, Thompson protested what happened at My Lai, first to his platoon leader then the company commander. He refused any more ops like this one. Within a couple of days there was a more formal inquiry where a full colonel took statements and made notes. Nothing happened. Rumors of My Lai circulated through the Americal. A month later Specialist Ron Ridenhour, a chopper door gunner who worked with the division's lurps, began hearing about Pinkville. Ridenhour transferred into the lurps himself, and several he knew supplied details. More than a year later, with the Army still having done nothing about the massacre and Ridenhour back from Vietnam, he put what he had discovered into a letter sent to thirty congressmen. Efforts to suppress the allegations failed, and the Army's official inquiry resulted in charges against fourteen officers and the courts-martial of five, of whom Lieutenant Calley was convicted. Calley's sentence to life in the stockade was reduced to house arrest, and he was paroled in 1974 on grounds that prejudicial publicity had compromised the proceeding. Hugh Thompson was awarded the Distinguished Flying Cross (under a citation that falsified the events of My Lai). He went on flying. Thompson survived four shoot-downs during his tour and his choppers were damaged that many times again. He was commissioned and left the Army as a captain. In 1998 Thompson and his crew were awarded the Soldier's Medal for their My Lai intervention. Troubled by his Vietnam experience, Thompson committed suicide in 2006. Ron Ridenhour died of heart attack in 1998.]*

FRAGGING

Captain Claude D. Newby
First Cavalry Division (Airmobile)
Tay Ninh, June 1969
Americans at war in Vietnam were ably served by their military chaplains. Captain Newby, a Mormon chaplain, had returned to the Army after early service as an MP and with Special Forces in the National Guard. Chaplains upheld moral values and the morale of the soldiers. Together with officers, chaplains were keys to keeping units together. They also often heard things the men would never tell officers, and Newby had unusual perspective here as a former enlisted GI as well as a combat-experienced chaplain with a pair of Vietnam tours. In fact, Newby was one of only two Army chaplains who earned the Combat Infantryman Badge. He participated in more than fifty air assaults and held three Bronze Stars as well as the Vietnamese Cross of Gallantry. When he worried about GIs' morale, it was for good reasons.

Though I saw more combat action with the companies of the 1/5 Cav than with the 2/12, I provided about the same number of worship services for each battalion. Early in June, during a visit to Alpha [*Company*] 2/12, I learned of threats to frag a company commander. Several troopers confided to me that most of the men . . . believed Captain James Robert Daniel of Atlanta, Georgia, cared very little for what he put them through. "Plans are afoot to 'frag' Captain Daniel the next time the company's in a fight," I was told.

The phrase "fragging" came into use early in the war and described the rare practice of troops killing unpopular leaders, by tossing a hand grenade in their hooch or whatever. I knew personally of no fragging incidents during my first tour . . . but I heard of two or three—all involving rear-area personnel. The closest I came to a fragging, or anything like it, during my first tour was when troopers allegedly tried to kill a fellow grunt for reporting an atrocity. . . .

But this was a different war in a different time, and we heard of fraggings almost weekly, some quite close. By 1969 fragging meant killing friendlies by any means, including shooting leaders and others in the back. This evolution of definition made sick sense considering the different conditions between the rear and the field.

In the rear, the grenade was often the weapon of choice because small arms were more carefully controlled. . . . Usually, with patience, an unpopular individual could be found alone and blown away without anyone else being hurt. And hand grenades left no tell-tale fingerprints and rifling marks to lead the Criminal Investigation [*Division*] back to the guilty parties.

In the field, on the other hand, small arms were weapons of choice for fragging. This made morbid sense. First, in the field it was difficult to isolate an individual from his RTO and others for a grenade attack. Second, it was extremely easy to shoot backward or sideways at the targeted individual during . . . a firefight. Finally, even if a fragging were suspected, an adequate investigation . . . was very difficult, and successful prosecution was unlikely. Rifling marks on full-metal jacket M-16 bullets and markings on shell casings didn't carry the same evident[*iary*] weight in the field as these would in rear areas.

Knowing all this, I alerted Captain Daniel and Lieutenant Colonel Boone [*the battalion commander*] about the fragging threats, and assured them the threats were serious, based on my confidence in my sources. Captain Daniel reacted with, "Chaplain, there is nothing I can do about that, and worrying won't change it. I'm doing my job the best I can." Another tragedy intervened before we could find out how these fragging threats might have turned out.

Warrant Officer Ezell Ware Jr.
Sixty-First Assault Helicopter Company, 101st Airborne Division
Landing Zone English, summer 1968
A chopper pilot, Warrant Officer Ware had seen the horror of Tet operating out of Kontum in the Central Highlands and from a South Korean base. Most of this time, his unit had been detached from its parent airborne brigade. They were brought together again in mid-1968 in the coastal plain to work in Binh Dinh Province. It was then that the fragging phenomenon worsened.

Whenever there was fragging—soldier slang for killing officers—or race fights, boredom was probably the instigator. To a young man whose sex hormones were already raging and whose kill-or-be-killed instinct was on a hair trigger, idle hours weren't just the devil's playground, they were hell itself. It was in the quiet and stillness that dark thoughts would snatch his mind.

Me, I tried never to be idle. In that, I had company. Most of us volunteered for every mission we could, but the rules kept you out of the cockpit if you'd flown 140 hours in a given thirty-day period. Then you had to stand down for at least five days. Most guys went on R&R to the Philippines or Thailand or whatever exotic place the postings board listed quick flights for. I did that, too; after all, our [*military pay*] bought an awful lot of fun.

IDLE TIME

Private First Class Ches Schneider
D Company, Second Battalion, Sixteenth Infantry, First Infantry Division
Di An, February 1970
Private Schneider faced a problem that became increasingly common in the Army late in the war: only a few months in country, Vietnamization sent home his First Division at a moment when Schneider still had long to go in his tour. He recorded typical GI behavior for this period. Schneider would be reassigned to the Cav, but what he saw applied across the board.

The lift arrived and took us back to Firebase Rhode Island. The fire support base was alive with excitement; the First Infantry Division was really going home and the REMFs [*rear-echelon motherfuckers*] were as busy as ants. They had a million and one chores to do as they prepared to transfer men and materiel to other divisions.

Each of the 11Bravo20 [*the Army's occupational designation for infantrymen*] grunts hoped to be part of the packing . . . and thus stay in the rear. . . . Maybe, we reasoned, we could even snooker a rear area job with a new unit. At best, we each hoped that we could get lost somewhere in the confusion. . . . Many grunts demanded to see a doctor, dentist, or chaplain. Some demanded to see not only those but everyone or anyone they thought might help them secure a safer position. . . . Every grunt in our company wanted out of the field. I kept telling anyone who would listen that I could type.

We pulled perimeter on Firebase Rhode Island for two days and then hit the bush again. Our instructions were to make one more big push for the good ol' Red One. Send the colors home in glory with more enemy kills. Bullshit! We hid most of the time and contemplated our impending separation from the Big Red One. I was surprised. Everyone seemed to detach from one another. We turned inside ourselves and pursued individual thoughts and dreams of the future. . . .

I noticed that once we hit the rear area, our close-knit platoon broke up into factions. The blacks all formed brother groups, and the heavy boozers started to buddy up. A few potheads emerged, and they sought out REMF dopers and were soon zonked. I can truly say that until that time, I hadn't seen any of our guys do any dope in the field or on a fire support base.

I was sort of the odd man out. I didn't short-time, get drunk, blow smoke, or take part in any other form of self-abusive recreation. For that reason, I was one of the suckers who was lying on a bunk reading a paperback when a REMF captain came to our barracks and recruited volunteers to be in the ceremony retiring the 1st Infantry Division colors. [*Schneider participated in the stand down. The division battle flag was cased for the journey home, and the First*

Cavalry Division took charge of its area of operations. After his reassignment to the First Battalion, Eighth Cavalry came more combat, right through the April 1970 Cambodian invasion. Eventually Schneider benefited from his typing skills and found himself detailed to the office of the company clerk. Note that Schneider was among those veterans who felt the enemy had been effectively beaten at Tet, which gives additional punch to his observations of the Army in 1970.]

My military education was to be of two kinds. One part would be the formal way that the army demanded things be done. The other part was the informal way that things really got accomplished. In addition to the Cambodian incursion, the army and the war were going through a dramatic transformation. First, because everyone, even the lifers, understood that the war was useless, no one was committed to it. Everyone fought to get a safe job and then go home. "One year and out" was the goal. Second, racial problems were developing. Black soldiers had gotten the idea that Vietnam was a white man's war. Third, dope had grabbed the attention of many of the younger troops. Lifers were generally more into alcohol. Fourth, the army was about to change from an army of draftees to an all-volunteer army.

How to effect such a change in the middle of an unpopular war would create myriad problems. Among them . . . the troops felt they had democratic powers and, at times, should be allowed to vote as to what military actions should be taken in the field and in the rear areas. One way the troops got the attention of the brass and expanded their role in the decision-making process was through the fragging . . . of officers. Furthermore, the antiwar movement at home and the bias of the strongly antiwar media had influenced recruits in Nam.

CONSEQUENCES

Special Agent Douglass H. Hubbard Jr.
Naval Investigative Service
Saigon, fall 1970
Special Agent Hubbard served in South Vietnam for three years, longer than any other Naval Investigative Service (NIS) agent. He worked at regional offices in both Saigon and Da Nang. NIS agents tracked black militant groups, ad hoc conspirators who attempted to import a case of hand grenades from the United States, individuals who bought grenades from Vietnamese for fragging, and many other kinds of illegality. The case here took place while Hubbard was in Saigon and shows how difficult it was to distinguish fragging from simple assault. Saigon had its share of mayhem, but it was not of the scale that the I Corps agents in Da Nang had been conditioned to. Fraggings [were not] a problem

in Saigon, perhaps because commands had taken measures to limit ready access to offensive ordnance. There were shootings and serious assaults, but no fraggings until late 1970. One evening after work several of us had gathered . . . for a few beers when a call came through for the duty agent; that was me. I took [*it*] and was told that a frag had just been thrown into a small room occupied by two enlisted Navy advisers at a downtown [*bachelor enlisted quarters—BEQ*]. Both men were seriously injured and were being rushed to Third Field Hospital. . . . I requested that U.S. Army military police establish a cordon around the BEQ and that all personnel be confined to their rooms; then I rushed across the street to the office, where I hastily assembled crime scene equipment. All available agents turned out to help.

[*The investigators arrived at the scene forty minutes after the incident, spoke to the MP first responders and guests, and examined the crime scene. Hubbard decided that a grenade must have been thrown into the room and rolled against a wall before detonating. Witnesses disclosed that the two occupants had been drinking with a third man before the apparent fragging, and NIS searched for him. He appeared of his own accord at the agency's Cholon office.*]

Clayton Spradley and I interrogated the suspect. A first-class petty officer in the Seabees, he was interviewed . . . after waiving his right to remain silent. He admitted he had been with the victims when it became apparent we had confirmed these details. . . . Becoming uncomfortable, he nevertheless did not terminate the interview, and we continued to go over . . . his story.

Spradley and I were an effective interrogation team. We had several successful confessions behind us and had developed a close rapport and ability to read each other. . . . Some may have thought that [*Spradley*] might be duped; he, however, had a voluminous memory for minute facts and could call these up effortlessly when the time was right. I worked as an opposite to keep the interview flowing.

After two hours the suspect was very aware that a comprehensive investigation into his activities on the evening of the fragging had been carried out. His alibis had been systematically disproven. Spradley and I were already at the stage of illustrating the inconsistencies. . . . "Why don't you just tell us and get all of this behind you," Spradley finally said. After a long pause, the suspect nodded his head and said, "OK, I threw it." He then related how he had been drinking with the two victims late in the afternoon after coming in from the field. He was ready to relax after the "bush time" and joined them in a friendly spirit. The victims were engine room petty officers, while the suspect was a SeaBee, a part of the Civil Engineer Corps. There was some gentle banter about SeaBees in comparison to fleet sailors. They had been drinking for several hours before the victims suggested they all go to their room to continue the party there.

The suspect said that once in their room, the victims' mood had turned surly with drunkenness. The banter had become vicious, culminating in the victims' assaulting and ejecting the suspect . . . after he had accidentally disturbed cards in a poker game. Angry and bleeding . . . he had gone to the room where his field gear was stowed, removed a fragmentation grenade, and returned. . . . He pulled the pin and threw the grenade through the open window.

[*The perpetrator received a felony conviction, was dishonorably discharged with forfeiture of pay and allowances, and was sent back to the United States. Hubbard does not record whether the man was sentenced to the brig. During this period the NIS dealt with a continuing stream of similar cases.*]

COFFEE SHOP R AND R

Lieutenant Colonel J. M. Moriarty, USMC
Marine Observation Squadron (VMO) Two
Da Nang, early 1970
As a Marine pilot, Colonel Moriarty took a chance and qualified on the OV-10 observation aircraft, figuring that this way he might make squadron commander more surely than flying the F-4 Phantom, which many others of his rank piloted. The gambit paid off and Moriarty took over VMO Two in January 1970.
A squadron coffee mess is about as dangerous an enterprise as a squadron commander has ever tried to avoid. It was illegal, and every squadron has one. It couldn't be avoided, so you learned to live with it.

Making money was not the problem. Getting rid of it was.

The coffee mess began innocently enough. People working on airplanes needed a coffee break, and so a small corner of the hangar was sectioned off, and a counter was constructed. A coffee urn was set up, and coffee was brought down from the mess hall.

But before long the troops wanted something cold.

Simple enough. The sergeant major found a refrigerator, the officers each chipped in a few dollars, and cases of soft drinks were purchased from the PX.

As I recall, a can of Coca-Cola cost us eleven cents, and we sold it for fifteen in order to be able to buy more.

Two or three cents profit didn't seem like much, but there was absolutely no overhead. We weren't even paying the kid who stood there, pouring and selling. He was the squadron driver, by the way. We wouldn't have wasted a valuable mechanic on the coffee mess.

Pretty soon the troops wanted pretzels and potato chips, and they were purchased and sold at similar bargain prices.

And after a few short months, there were hundreds of dollars in the coffee-mess fund. As I recall we had about three thousand dollars when I left.

Now here's where it got really dangerous.

The fleshpots of Thailand were only a few hours away from Da Nang, even in an airplane as slow as the OV-10, and we ran our own R&R program in the city of Udorn, in the northeastern part of the country.

Every three days a pilot and either an aerial observer or a staff NCO left Da Nang for the U.S. Air Force base there, and that afternoon the plane returned, piloted by a crew that had already spent three days at the Sharon Hotel in downtown Udorn.

This was not totally illegal, but it was highly improper, and presented two problems which required covert measures.

We could not purchase fuel at Udorn, for that would have left a paper trail of gas chits, and sooner or later someone would wonder why VMO-2 was always buying gas a couple of hundred miles away from the war.

We solved this with long-range fuel tanks. Jet squadrons had their own subterfuge. Pilots would be scheduled for late-afternoon training flights, and after a respectable amount of time, would decide that the weather at home base was too poor for landing and divert to Udorn or Korat, where they would spend the night. It was legal, but marginally so.

But the second problem was the dangerous one. In Vietnam the only legal tender was MPC, military pay certificates, and it was illegal to have American green money. In Thailand there was no requirement for a controlled currency, and so the MPC was worthless.

When an American serviceman left Vietnam, all he had to do was show a copy of his orders to the disbursing office and they would convert his MPC into green dollars. Our trips out of country, however, were clandestine, and we had no orders. Therefore, we had to run our own money exchange.

Before long the coffee mess fund included hundreds of dollars in green money, which we had collected from people coming into Vietnam legally.

What does one do with the money? It depends on how brave he is.

We found that floor shows in the hangar were nice.

The day crew secured at [6 *p.m.*] when they were relieved by the night crew, and that seemed to be a good time for a party. About five-thirty, we'd set up the charcoal grills, and the lieutenants would come rolling in with about a ton of cold beer in jeep trailers. And at six, some floor show would get up on the stage and start performing.

The stage was a flatbed truck-trailer that always appeared mysteriously, sometimes with bunting, sometimes without, and the floor show was purchased through the local booking agents, just like USO shows.

The sergeant major ordered me to be ignorant as to the details of these questionable booking transactions, but I doubt if that lack of knowledge would have helped at my court-martial. Someone would have been bound to ask how we paid for them.

Inevitably the night crew started to complain. They could eat the steaks, but they couldn't drink the beer. The lieutenants had the perfect solution, and soon we began champagne breakfasts for them at [*6 a.m.*] when they were going off duty. Couldn't get a floor show at that hour, though.

12

The Abrams Era

SAPPER ATTACK

Master Sergeant Nguyen Van Mo
Fortieth Sapper Battalion, Vietnam People's Army
Duc Pho, June 1969
Sergeant Mo infiltrated down the Ho Chi Minh Trail from North Vietnam and was sent to the central coast area, which the VPA called Interzone V. There he was assigned to a sapper unit of the sort the People's Army increasingly relied upon during the late-war period.
The training was elaborate. We learned how to crouch while walking, how to crawl, how to move silently through mud and water, how to walk through dry leaves. We practiced different ways of stooping while we walked. In teams of seven men, we practiced moving in rhythm to avoid being spotted under searchlights, synchronizing our motions, stepping with toes first, then gradually lowering heels to the ground, very slowly, step by step. . . .

In an actual sapper attack we would prepare the battlefield beforehand. That meant getting as close to the objective as possible—say a fortified post or a fire base—so that we could observe the enemy . . . positions we were going to hit. To do this we would first have to crawl through the barbed wire, but without cutting [*it*] or removing mines—we couldn't leave any traces. We were supposed to tie the wire up with string and mark the mines on the route we were following.

After penetrating into the post and observing, we'd return to our base and make a sand table model for the assault troops to study. During the attack we'd come in as slowly as we could, following the route we had marked. . . . To avoid making noise, we couldn't clip the barbed wire, only cut it two-thirds of the way through, then break it with our hands, holding the wire firmly so the fence wouldn't move. To detect mines we used our hands, feeling the ground ahead of us. . . .

The worst part was reaching the inner fence around a position. I was always scared to death at that point. Even after I was a veteran . . . I would still start trembling. If the Americans discovered you at that point, you were certain to be killed. There was no chance of getting away back through the fences under machine gun fire. . . .

In June 1969 my unit was engaged in a battle in the Duc Pho district of Quang Ngai. Our objective was the Go Hoi airstrip, defended by the 11th Brigade of the Americal. . . . There were American technicians quartered in the area, and the facility was lit by floodlights all night long. . . .

Halfway through the fences the assistant company commander pulled out. He told us he had to go back to deploy the B-40 gunners and that we should [move] ahead according to the plan. The fact was that he was afraid for his life and didn't have the guts . . . himself.

But the rest of us managed to get in without being spotted. We got all the way to the barracks and the vehicle park. According to the plan, I was supposed to make the deepest penetration and fire a signal for the attack. Everything went off exactly on schedule. As soon as I fired the signal cracker, the others began to [assault] the blockhouses with explosives and grenades. A couple of the blockhouses were destroyed in the first minutes, which eliminated a lot of the Americans' firepower, so they weren't able to get a counterattack going. Then we attacked the technicians' barracks. Most of the Americans were running into the trenches. It seemed to me they must have thought they were under mortar attack.

I found the generators and fixed the explosives. When they blew, all the lights went off. I kept on, setting charges to trucks and more buildings. Meanwhile the sappers deployed in the outer area had been successful in silencing the American machine guns. While we were getting out, one of our people was killed. But the other six made it.

Lieutenant Colonel H. Norman Schwarzkopf
First Battalion, Sixth Infantry, Twenty-Third (Americal) Infantry Division
near Chu Lai, November 1969

Colonel Schwarzkopf returned in 1969 and led a battalion in Quang Ngai. He found the unit in poor condition: men without helmets, some positions with la-trines located outside the perimeters, machine guns flecked with rust. A recent pa-trol had been ambushed and lost six GIs without reply. Schwarzkopf determined to whip his men into shape—and he did. His determination would be stoked on his second day in command.

I was awakened with the news that a dawn patrol had shot a Vietcong sneaking through the wire along our perimeter. On his body they'd found detailed sketches of LZ Bayonet—the sort of reconnaissance needed for one of the Vietcong's most devastating tactics, called a sapper attack. . . . Finding those sketches of our base made everybody's pucker factor increase considerably, mine included—not least because the drawings clearly indicated the locations of the operations center and my hooch.

Ten minutes later, as I finished dressing, there was a knock on my cabin door. It was my brigade commander—a legendary combat infantryman named Joe Clemons, who had become a national hero and won the Distinguished Service Cross in the battle of Pork Chop Hill during the Korean War. . . . He'd heard about the Vietcong in our wire and wanted to make sure I knew how to protect my base.

I saluted, and he asked me to brief him on the dead Vietcong. Then he said, "Let's go inspect your perimeter."

I hadn't seen the LZ Bayonet perimeter the night before, but I had no illusions. . . . Clemons was furious within fifteen minutes. The bunkers had long since caved in. All along the barbed wire were yawning gaps where anyone could enter. The Claymore mines, which had originally been positioned to cut down enemy soldiers charging the wire, had mostly rusted away from their detonating wires, so they'd have been useless during an attack. Worse, some had been turned around so that if we had set them off, their shrapnel would have blown back into the camp. Joe Clemons chewed me out. I was furious too, but all I could say was, "Sir, I'll take care of it." . . .

"This is a disgrace! I've never seen anything this bad in all my years in the Army!" We walked the whole perimeter, and the colonel berated me the entire way. I knew he was right: if there had been a sapper attack the night before, a great many of my men would have died.

As soon as he left, I rounded up the officers and NCOs and we spent the entire day making sure sandbags got filled, foxholes dug, and Claymores replaced. . . . We extended the perimeter to take in the operations center and my cabin, although I had decided that eventually both would be moved down into the base. Clemons's reproaches kept echoing in my mind. . . . I called and asked if we could meet. He received me at his headquarters that evening but did not offer me a seat.

"Sir, you had every reason to be angry at what you found at my unit today," I said. "But I want you to know that I was angry too. I was as shocked as you at the state of that perimeter. And I recognize I was at fault not to have inspected it as soon as I took command."

Clemons locked eyes with me as I spoke and didn't say a word. I took a breath and continued, "I don't know what you know about my unit. But on the basis of two days' experience, I can tell you I've probably inherited the worst battalion in the United States Army. I know what's wrong and I will fix it, but that can't happen overnight. And it won't do any good for you to chew out my ass every time you come around. You'll just slow me down."

He didn't say anything, just kept staring at me with his icy blue eyes. Finally he said, "Colonel Schwarzkopf, I want to tell you that *I've* inherited the worst *brigade* in the United States Army. I'm willing to believe you know what needs to be done. Now let's do it together." There was no smiling or backslapping— we were both under the gun.

TIME ON TARGET

Sergeant W. Charles Truitt, USMC
First Radio Battalion
Fire Base Fuller, November 1969
An enthusiastic radioman with the First Battalion, the Marine Corps' unique signals intelligence (SigInt) unit, Sergeant Truitt specialized in high-frequency direction finding (HFDF), which located enemy troop units by taking bearings on their radio transmissions. On a peak a little bit south of the DMZ, Fire Base Fuller was ideally located for this, since certain radio frequencies depended on line of sight. In most cases, once a North Vietnamese unit was located, artillery and air strikes targeted its position.

There were a lot of different aspects to SigInt, but I felt so very fortunate to work HFDF which was what I wanted to do more than anything else in the world at that time.

Once, after locating a nearby enemy unit . . . an artillery fire mission was called. After the "splash," a patrol of some strength was sent out to investigate. We ended up with a captured ChiCom radio. It was that "puke green" Chinese army color (every piece of Chinese gear I ever saw was that same yucky color), and the radio had two [*bullet*] holes . . . near the top. Interestingly, both rounds passed right through . . . without hitting anything of importance inside before they took the operator's head off. The radio still worked perfectly. It was voice capable, and had a BFO which made it useful for Morse code operations as well. Not only that, it had an integral Morse key built in, right on the side. What a neat piece of gear! The gook was wearing it strapped on his back when he died, and there was blood all over the thing and the headset had blood and chunks, but it still worked, and we used it. . . .

During the day of November 17, our own . . . SigInt efforts produced an incident very reminiscent of . . . the American victory at the Battle of Midway in World War II. In this particular event we found that a [*North Vietnamese*] regiment was in comms with an [*enemy*] arty unit—a combination that always spelled t-r-o-u-b-l-e for someone. Whenever any part of the 304th [*VPA Division*] was on the move, somebody was going to die. And, amazingly it was "them" that always got hit way harder than us, but they'd just *didi mau* back across the DMZ or into Laos. There they just regrouped, resupplied, rebuilt, and retrained with immunity . . . while awaiting another time to create hate and discontent. . . .

Every American unit in the whole northern "I" Corps area was alerted that something was up. Everyone was on standby to assist the "chosen somebodies." Every arty unit that could push out a round far enough with maximum charge was ready to participate. Every air unit was standing by to render assistance, even though the cloud cover was heavy and no aircraft could drop bombs without possibly hitting the good guys.

Early in the evening, up in my pig pen, the speaker crackled, "*All stations, this is Florida Vacation Alpha with a message on Bravo Zulu; stand by to receive traffic.*" Net control at Dong Ha had a target. . . . In just a short minute's time I was sending my own [*message*] back which was a really good shot/bearing on the enemy . . . whom I believed was [*an*] artillery battalion. It seemed that they were to provide artillery support for the . . . infantry [*as it*] made its assault. . . .

We were all in the bunker as Camp Carroll's 175s were doing their fly-by. Those of us who were not actually on the radio . . . were playing back alley. . . . [*At 9:30 p.m.*] we were all actively discussing who was going to get hit. All of a sudden I remembered that all my [*combat*] gear was in our sleeping bunker next door. That required my leaving the entrance to our bunker, traversing the ledge and going into the other bunker to retrieve my flak jacket and junk. I recall standing at the entrance and saying, "Who's it gonna be." "Not us," came the consensus. . . . One step along towards the other bunker, just one step, and all of a sudden a great big KA-WAAAM. An RPG impacted on the other side of the bunker entrance where I was headed. . . . I yelled back into the Ops bunker, "It's us!"—as if they hadn't already figured that out.

Fortunately for Truitt and his buddies, American fire really had knocked out the VPA artillery. Only mortars and infantry heavy weapons shot at Fuller. The threatened assault never occurred.

HELL IN THE HIGHLANDS

Sergeant Leigh Wade
Detachment A-242, Fifth Special Forces Group
Dak Pek Camp, April 12, 1970
Sergeant Wade, back in South Vietnam for the first time since 1967, finds conditions much changed. Strict rules, enforced by nonjudicial punishments, now

apply to wandering outside Army posts; General Abrams has cracked down on the Special Forces' freewheeling methods. A colleague told him the United States had been defeated: "that phrase 'the war's over; we lost,' pretty much sums up the attitude in the Fifth Group during that last year the unit spent in Vietnam." This is the complete opposite of what U.S. authorities were putting out for public consumption. Wade was assigned to Dak Pek Special Forces Camp. There, with the war far from being over, Wade found himself in the thick of a major battle. The assault reached inside the compound, where the enemy held some positions for a few days, but then fell back and besieged the CIDG camp. This Central Highlands siege went through a couple of rounds over a period of weeks.

Although Dak Pek was once one of Special Forces' showplace camps in Vietnam, after the battle of April 12, we no longer got a lot of visitors. That was actually okay with me, because I'd long before gotten tired of conducting dog-and-pony shows for touring dignitaries. Some of the guys . . . spoke a little wistfully about the good old days before the battle, however, when the big shots used to drop in to be impressed by the new Montagnard school, the team club room—its wall adorned with captured flags and weapons—the "impregnable" American [*command post bunker*], and all of that.

Around the first of June, however, I received a message that we would be getting a couple of visitors of a different type. Two Air Force F-4 pilots who had flown strikes for us during the battle had decided to spend their one week of R&R out at our camp. They just wanted to see what the area looked like from the ground, they'd told our higher[-*ups*], and wanted to get a better idea of what damage their bombing and strafing had done.

Hell, I decided, they were our kind of guys. Anyone can go on R&R to some sissy place like Australia or Bangkok; it took a couple of real nutcases to want to spend their limited rest and relaxation time in a place like Dak Pek.

They arrived one morning via helicopter, and jumped out carrying parachute kit bags full of whiskey, cigarettes, and skin magazines—the bare necessities for a week at a Special Forces A-team camp—somebody had briefed them well. They had flown numerous strikes against the 203 Company hill, and wanted to go up there first. From the air, they told us, the target had looked small, the friendly forces very close. From ground level it seemed worse. "Good thing we didn't fuck up," one of them said.

That evening, with Hull manning the radios, I grabbed a bottle of scotch that one of the pilots offered and retired to our newly reconstructed mess hall. . . . Getting drunk while at an A-camp in Vietnam was a very dangerous and stupid thing to do, but by that stage in the war my morale was such that I just didn't give a good shit anymore. Besides, it was the first alcohol we'd had in camp since being overrun.

A TOUCH OF CAMBODIA

Sergeant Kregg P. J. Jorgenson
First Squadron, Ninth Cavalry, First Cavalry Division (Airmobile)
north of Saigon, April 1970
Arriving in Bien Hoa in the fall of 1969, Sergeant Jorgenson had volunteered for
Hotel Company of the Seventy-Fifth Rangers, the long-range reconnaissance unit
of the Cav. After the special training and some service with the lurps, in which
Jorgenson won the Silver Star, he contracted malaria, a constant danger for GIs
in Vietnam.

I came to Vietnam not really knowing a thing about war; with only four months In Country, I now had a working knowledge of what it entailed. I was also painfully aware that soldiers don't write their own lines . . . for all the importance we put into our roles, we could easily be replaced or omitted, written out of the script with a quick stroke. . . . We didn't fucking matter.

Two weeks before Christmas of 1969, if there was a "light at the end of the tunnel" as they said, then from our point of view it was the light of an oncoming train.

[*Recovering from malaria and with valuable ranger training, Sergeant Jorgenson transferred to First Squadron, Ninth Cavalry, the "Blues," who specialized in finding and fixing the enemy and often extracted threatened patrols, rescued wounded grunts, or brought back the dead. There he faced a classic Vietnam dilemma—how much risk to accept as a "short-timer" near the end of his tour of duty.*]

The Tay Ninh base camp was filling with soldiers and equipment for the push into Cambodia. We knew it was coming, as did the Vietnamese. You couldn't have that many soldiers, let alone new tanks, armored personnel carriers, and helicopters flying in every day without something being in the wind. We knew Cambodia had to be the target. . . . The Fish Hook, Parrot's Beak, and Angel's Wing [*regions of Cambodia*] were major infiltration routes into South Vietnam, and we were certain they'd be targeted in the push. Since we were under nightly enemy rocket and mortar attacks from those areas, it didn't bother us that they would be [*hit*]. When the push finally did come, taking US forces twenty-four miles into Cambodia, the relief from the nightly attacks was well-received. "Rocket City" became Tay Ninh base camp once more. . . .

In the initial drive into Cambodia, we'd lost several scout helicopters, the first getting shot down but able to land safely, where the Blues could pick up the crew. The second proved more costly; the scout helicopter took a direct hit from an RPG and fell in flames into the large bunker complex it had uncovered. The pilot and crew were killed instantly. Another scout doorgunner had died when he was dropping grenades on another bunker complex, when [a] white phosphorous . . . blew up as he released it. The Blues hadn't encountered much contact, which made me feel better about staying behind.

Less than a week later Lieutenant Hugele, Blue, was knocking at my door. "Sergeant Jorgenson?"

I opened the door and found Blue looking troubled.

"A Ranger team from your old company is MIA, and we're looking for volunteers for a rescue mission. You interested?"

"Damn right, sir!" . . .

A short time later we were ready to go. The Vietnamese evening was muggy and the dusk was hiding patches of ground fog. We'd managed to put together an eighteen-man force. Since the platoon usually operated with twenty-one men, eighteen was close enough to satisfy the lieutenant, who was coordinating his plans. . . . Once that was done, he briefed the rest of us.

"A LRRP team was hit last night in Cambodia. One of the five Rangers managed to make it back to Fire Base David, saying that the team leader had decided to move after he called in their last night position. Nobody had any good reason to worry about them until this morning, when they couldn't be reached by radio. When the lone survivor got into David, he informed them that two Rangers are dead and the other two are still out there, somewhere. . . . "

[*The rescue team stopped to question the escaped lurp and used his information to find the search area. Jorgenson discovered that not only was the beleaguered team from his old unit, but its leader and some members were friends. He was desperate to succeed. They found the location and one of the missing team members and called in artillery to back the enemy off. Bigger reaction forces of Rangers and troopers from the firebase landed to reinforce the rescue.*]

On the long flight back to Tay Ninh, I was proud . . . of being in the Blues. We hadn't been able to find the two dead LRRPs but we had the two missing in action and yes, damn it! That did count for something!. . . . I felt good, too, knowing that I didn't always have to be the hero and that there were enough heroics to go around. The burden was no longer as heavy as it had been. . . .

Yeah, we were the good guys all right, and riding back . . . the only thing missing was the proverbial sunset. I didn't complain. Some days you take what you can get.

GUMSHOE INTELLIGENCE

Officer Orrin DeForest
Central Intelligence Agency
Bien Hoa, 1969–1970

Orrin DeForest, a former military special investigator, had served a previous tour during 1966–1967 with the Army's Criminal Investigation Division. The CIA recruited him to help identify members of the National Liberation Front infrastructure as part of the pacification program. DeForest was assigned to head the interrogation center of the agency's Military Region Three unit. There he interviewed "hoi chanh" defectors and captured enemy personnel, using methods learned in Japan to fashion a new system of recording details, then conducting friendly, not hostile, interrogations. DeForest's card index became the envy of other staffs, and his techniques—building on the detailed intelligence collected already—yielded a sea of fresh data. The North Vietnamese and NLF apparatus in Cambodia was naturally a prime CIA target.

Information we were able to provide . . . included targeting data for the B-52 Arc Light bombing of enemy base areas in Military Region Three and across the border in Cambodia. Many of our sources had been in Cambodia with their units or in hospitals, and from our debriefings we were able to specify coordinates, especially in Mimot, the site of Hanoi's Central Office for South Vietnam, COSVN. . . . By the spring of 1970 we had become quite good at this; we were able to identify enemy units, approximate numbers . . . and quite exact coordinates. Our sources would come in from one of these areas and they would draw us maps. (Vietnamese, especially those who had been guerrillas for any length of time, tended to be excellent map readers and map drawers.) Sources could (and did), for example, point out precisely where COSVN was located; they would draw it, indicating trees and streams and other specific features. And they could tell us precise distances—from this point here it is twelve klicks [*kilometers*] due north to the COSVN alternate headquarters . . . or five klicks west to a trail terminus . . . or twelve klicks southeast to a certain supply dump.

Often they knew the region intimately. They had been chased from one side of the border to the other by American actions and they had had a bellyful of experience moving around frantically in an attempt to avoid bombing raids. We were able to take the maps they drew, transpose their drawings onto our own detailed maps, and come up with precisely located targets, which were then sent in by cable, providing a "box" of coordinates for the bombers. These included the Ho Bo Woods, the Straight Edge Woods near Go Dau Ha (which the B-52s just blew away), and Mimot, as well as other . . . bases on both sides of the border, from Parrot's Beak up to Fishhook. Despite the domestic furor over the "secret bombings," that sector of Cambodia was exactly as the United States government said it was. . . .

We were . . . able to report the consequences of Arc Light strikes as well as provide targets for them. Within weeks of a significant series of strikes, we would be interrogating a new batch of defectors for whom those . . . had proved the last straw. One interesting fact was that most often they knew when the bombers were on their way and they knew the general direction of the attack, although not the exact target. . . . [W]e were aware that Russian radar trawlers located in the Pacific beyond the Philippines tracked the bombers, checking speed, altitude, and headings, and relayed the information to the North. Commonly the targeted base areas would receive word an hour or so ahead of time. But still the VC and NVA units couldn't run fast enough. And we learned too about their evasive procedures; if, for example, they thought a strike was heading for Mimot, they would take off to the northwest, toward the secondary complexes. Of course we included that in the targeting information.

LIFE IN THE MAQUIS

Truong Nhu Tang
member, Central Committee, National Front for the Liberation of South Vietnam
Ta Not, 1969–1970
A founding member of the Liberation Front, Tang maintained his NLF affiliation secretly while openly pursuing a career as a businessman, heading South Vietnam's national sugar company and later serving as a Saigon government economics official. Tang became an advocate for nonpolitical "third force" approaches. Quietly he helped Party cadres, including sheltering senior organizer Vo Van Kiet. As a member of the self-determination movement, Tang was detained and interrogated, and in 1967 his NLF role was revealed by a captured cadre. He was imprisoned and tortured. Eight months later, as part of a political feeler launched by the CIA, Tang was freed and joined the NLF leadership at Ta Not (and later Ben Ra), about twenty-five miles from COSVN headquarters but inside the boundary of South Vietnam. When the Front established its Provisional Revolutionary Government in 1969, Tang became minister for justice. The hardships of the bush were great.

Infiltrating into areas under secure government control to see wives and children who had often been marked as Vietcong dependents was a chancy business. To get around this, from time to time we would be able to bring families out to the jungle, something that was done for soldiers as well as cadres. But such meetings were brief and necessarily dangerous themselves. (Vo Van Kiet's wife and children were killed on their way to one such rendezvous, when they were caught in a B-52 raid.) More often than not these men went for extended periods without any contact at all with their families.

But for all the privations and hardships, nothing the guerrillas had to endure compared with the stark terrorization of the B-52 bombardments. During its involvement, the United States dropped on Vietnam more than three times the tonnage of explosives that were dropped during all of World War II in military theaters that spanned the world. Much of it came from the high altitude B-52s, bombs of all sizes and types being disgorged by those invisible predators. . . . From [*our*] perspective . . . these figures translated into . . . undiluted psychological terror, into which we were plunged, day in, day out, for years on end.

From a kilometer away, the sonic roar of the B-52 explosions tore eardrums, leaving many of the jungle dwellers permanently deaf. From a kilometer, the shock waves knocked their victims senseless. Any hit within half a kilometer would collapse the walls of an unreinforced bunker, burying alive the people cowering inside. Seen up close, the bomb craters were gigantic—thirty feet across and nearly as deep. In the rainy seasons they would fill up with water and often saw service as duck or fishponds, playing their role in the guerrillas' never-ending quest to broaden their diet. But they were treacherous then too. For as the swamps and lowland areas flooded under half a foot of standing water, the craters [*became*] invisible. Not infrequently some surprised guerrilla, wading along . . . a familiar route, was suddenly swallowed up.

It was something of a miracle that from 1968 through 1970 the attacks, though they caused significant casualties generally, did not kill a single one of the military or civilian leaders in the headquarters complexes. This luck, though, had a lot to do with advance warning of the raids, which allowed us to move out of the way or take refuge . . . before the bombs began to rain down. . . . COSVN headquarters . . . would then order NLF or Northern elements in the anticipated target area to move away perpendicularly to the attack trajectory. Flights originating from the Thai bases were monitored both on radar and visually by our intelligence nets there. . . .

Often the warnings [*gave*] us enough time to grab some rice and escape by foot or bike down one of the emergency routes. Hours later we would return to find, as happened on several occasions, that there was nothing left. It was as if an enormous scythe had swept through the jungle. . . . It was not just that things were destroyed; in some awesome way they had ceased to exist. You would come back to where your lean-to and bunker had been, your home, and there would simply be nothing there, just an unrecognizable landscape gouged by immense craters.

Equally often, however, we were not so fortunate and had time only to take cover as best we could. The first few times I experienced a B-52 attack it seemed, as I strained to press myself into the bunker floor, that I had been caught in the Apocalypse. The terror was complete. One lost control of body functions as the mind screamed incomprehensible orders to get out. On one occasion a Soviet delegation was visiting our ministry when a particularly short-notice warning came through. When [*the attack*] was over, no one had been hurt, but the entire delegation had sustained considerable damage to its dignity—uncontrollable trembling and wet pants the all-too obvious signs of inner convulsions. The visitors could have spared themselves their feelings of embarrassment; each of their hosts was a veteran of the same symptoms. [*The Front and the North Vietnamese eventually found a method of constructing shelters that made them proof against B-52 bombs falling as close as a hundred meters away.*]

ARC LIGHT ON COSVN

Sergeant First Class Jerry Shriver
MACV Studies and Observation Group, Command and Control South
Cambodia, April 24, 1969
The B-52 attacks to which Truong Nhu Tang refers began in the spring of 1969 as part of Operation Menu, the secret bombing of Cambodia carried out by the Nixon administration, officially at peace with that country, recognizing it as neutral. Tang's recollections leave the impression that nothing was left after a B-52 strike. This was not uniformly true. In fact, Studies and Observation Group reconnaissance teams sent to evaluate bomb damage following two early Menu attacks were chewed up pretty badly. When the Nixon administration decided on a huge new Menu strike against COSVN—ninety-eight B-52 bombers (each typically carrying fifteen tons of ordnance)—MACV decided to follow that with a much larger SOG unit. This was Captain William O'Rourke's Hatchet Force company, a powerful weapon in SOG's arsenal. The key figure in the operation would be Sergeant Jerry "Mad Dog" Shriver, a renowned warrior in the special warfare fraternity. "The enemy was stirred up like ants coming out of the wood-work," writes Ranger Bill Goshen, who had been wounded in an LRP mission nearby a couple of months earlier. "The Hatchet Force was eaten up by large numbers of NVA troops." This account is by Captain John L. Plaster, who fought in SOG and has become its major chronicler.
At CCS the . . . mission fell upon its most accomplished man, that living legend . . . Sergeant First Class Jerry "Mad Dog" Shriver. *Mad Dog!* At Fort Bragg no one mentioned SOG but everyone had heard of Jerry Shriver, dubbed a "mad dog" by Radio Hanoi. Now into his third year in SOG, Mad Dog Shriver had practically gone native, preferring the company of his Montagnards and his German shepherd, Klaus. . . . He cared not one whit about medals, though

he'd been awarded a Silver Star, five Bronze Stars, and the Soldier's Medal. And he was phenomenally adept in the jungle. "He was like having a dog you could talk to," Captain Bill O'Rourke, the Hatchet Force commander, explained. "He could hear and sense things; he was more alive in the woods than [*anyone else*] I've ever met."

Among the dozen Americans accompanying Shriver on the COSVN mission was an old Boy Scout friend from Minneapolis, Lieutenant Greg Harrigan. . . .

A half hour after the last of the . . . B-52s dumped their loads on COSVN, the Hatchet Force company launched from Quan Loi. Twenty minutes later, descending into incredible devastation, the choppers dropped off the seventy men and climbed away.

Again, an instant killing zone.

From everywhere, automatic weapons and RPGs pounded the SOG men, pinning them in craters right on the LZ. Sergeant Ernest Johnson dashed out to retrieve a wounded man; heavy fire cut him down, killing him on the spot. On the far side of the LZ, Jerry Shriver radioed that a machine gun bunker had his men pinned down and asked if anyone could fire at it.

No one could. It was up to Mad Dog. Shriver and several Yards rushed into the jungle, and Mad Dog was never seen or heard from again. He vanished.

Forty-five minutes later, while calling gunship fire around his position, Greg Harrigan was shot to death.

Trapped on that LZ most of the day, a majority of the men were wounded. Finally [*command*] looked the other way and allowed fighters to bomb the encircling enemy, which enabled choppers to extract the survivors. In addition to Shriver, a number of Yards were missing.

"That really shook them up at MACV, to realize anybody survived that strike," Chief SOG Colonel Steve Cavanaugh reported.

NOT AS BAD, BUT THEY GOT AWAY!

Sergeant Al Sever
116th Assault Helicopter Company
Tay Ninh, February 1969
Chopper crews were amazed at what Arc Light wrought. Most poststrike scouts found little in the way of bodies, equipment, or enemy documents. But traces of the adversary's presence—and sometimes disturbing signs of resilience—were evident.
Following an air strike by B-52 bombers, we went on an assault of an NVA base camp near Dau Tieng. Our company was airborne with ten slicks . . . and

three gunships minutes away from the landing zone as . . . bombs tore apart the jungle near a rubber tree plantation. As the last bombs exploded, we flew into an impenetrable dust cloud and quickly turned around. It would have been suicide to continue . . . we couldn't see a damn thing and might have flown into each other. Every [*chopper*] except the C&C ship flew to Tay Ninh to . . . wait for the dust to settle.

After an hour of loafing along the . . . flight line, the call came . . . for us to saddle up and get our rotor blades turning. The crew chiefs quickly untied the rotor blades on their ships and the pilots started the turbine engines whirring. Our three gunships dragged their skids down the runway, passing the infantry as they started [*to*] climb back on the slicks. . . . In minutes we were on our way and headed for the impact area. We were going straight in without first reconning the LZ, as we didn't expect any opposition. This LZ was going to be an easy mission for the guns, but difficult for the slicks. They had to land in the fine ankle-deep powder of pulverized earth, vegetation and people. As the slicks were on their final descent . . . their pilots were cautioned not to fly into each other in the expected dust cloud. Ten ships flared to land and we momentarily lost sight of them as each slick churned up its own separate tornado of dirt and debris, which screened the troops jumping out better than any smokeship could do. It was a cold LZ; there was no opposition as the infantry jumped. . . . As the empty ships departed to pick up another load of infantry, our gunships flew quick figure eights over infantry and over the hundreds of bomb craters to determine what damage the B-52s had done. Our first loads of infantry wandered beneath us through a barren moonscape . . . searching for signs of the enemy . . . shredded and torn by bombers who never saw the destruction they caused. . . . I suppose they rationalized everything by assuming that only trees and shrubs were vaporized in the dust clouds beneath them. As we circled the devastation, our pilot mentioned that the Air Force was also using B-52 strikes on population centers in North Viet Nam [*not true until 1972*]. Dale and I didn't believe him. As hard and callous as we were, we could not believe anybody could be found to fly such missions.

A quick look showed the bombers had obviously hit in the right place. Concrete slabs of bunker roofs could be seen twisted on the edge of bomb craters. Our first impression was that hundreds of men must have died here. Then we noticed that the fallen dust covering the impact area was churned with the footprints of separate individuals, which then converged into trails, all heading into the rubber plantation. The infantry found no dead or anything of value. We flying overhead [*saw*] no signs of men within or around the bomb craters. A lot of North Vietnamese had survived the bombing and disappeared into another sanctuary, a Michelin rubber plantation.

These plantations owned by the French were normally large swaths of trees, planted in straight rows, with few signs of battle damage. We were limited when taking offensive action in the rubber plantations because our government paid for every individual tree damaged by our weapons. While our government condoned the wholesale destruction of farms, villages, and families without compensation, the assets of a multinational business could not be harmed. It was pure capitalism in action and we were on a crusade for Capitalism.

ARC LIGHT AGAIN

Sergeant Kregg P. J. Jorgenson
First Squadron, Ninth Cavalry, First Cavalry Division (Airmobile)
Tay Ninh, early 1970
Like the chopper crewmen, trooper Jorgenson of the Cav's aerial scout unit, saw the B-52 strikes from the American side. His Arc Light follow-up also took place inside South Vietnam. It would be Jorgenson's first mission since a bloody encounter with the Vietnam People's Army.
Division intelligence wanted us to check out the results of an Arc Light, the code name for a B-52 bombing mission.

When we were just a few minutes out of the target area, we could see the effects of the blanket-bombing strategy. In the midst of the lime greens and fading browns of the rain forest, blue water pockets lay ringed with orange-brown rims where five-hundred pound bombs had ripped large chunks of earth out of the jungle and scattered them the way a farmer might scatter seed over a field. From our height of a few thousand feet, the pockets and pools seemed to go on for miles. As we descended we saw the going would be difficult. It always was after an Arc Light because nothing was where it should have been. Trees were uprooted and splintered, sometimes hanging in other trees. Fire ants once housed in three-foot high mounds were blown into the vegetation where they clung to leaves, stinging anyone or thing that brushed past them. Small animals and birds lay on the ground dazed, too stunned to move. If there had been any North Vietnamese Army units in the immediate area when the bombs fell, then they would be in much the same condition.

We would have to move through the bombed-out area, going around the deep craters, getting stung by the angered ants while trying to find survivors or bodies.

13

The Final Act

AMERICA'S LAST BIG BATTLE

Colonel Benjamin L. Harrison
Third Brigade, 101st Airborne Division (Airmobile)
Camp Evans, Thua Thien, spring–summer 1970

Almost the last major offensive operation undertaken by purely U.S. forces was another push into the A Shau Valley, beginning early in 1970. This started with the creation of a firebase and soon encompassed efforts to protect it. Here is a brief introduction by the late Keith W. Nolan, among the best Vietnam combat historians, for his book on this campaign.

Firebase Ripcord was originally established by the 2nd of the 506th, a line infantry battalion commanded by [*Lieutenant Colonel*] Andre C. Lucas, to support an offensive into an enemy base area overlooking the A Shau Valley. . . . Occupying the denuded crest of a ridge, the firebase was a whitish brown lump amid jungle-covered mountains. East of the firebase, the mountains descend to foothills, beyond which, barely visible from Ripcord, sandy plains meet the South China Sea. To the west the green peaks push suggestively skyward; along the far horizon stretch the great mountain ranges that originate in central China and dominate the entire frontier between Vietnam and Laos.

Dependent on helicopters for logistical support, Ripcord was less than twenty-five kilometers, a fifteen-minute flight, southwest of Camp Evans, the rear area of Lucas's battalion and its parent command, the 3rd Brigade, 101st Airborne. . . . Ripcord was nevertheless deep enough in the mountains, closer to Laos than its own support base, that the heavier of the two howitzer batteries on site could fire southwest into the A Shau Valley. More to the point, both batteries could range on the supply installations on Co Pung Mountain, a major terrain feature . . . nine kilometers south of Ripcord. Those supply installations and the two North Vietnamese regiments that protected them were the objective. . . . Fighter-bombers utilized a navigational beacon positioned on the firebase to further soften up the area with air strikes, as did—flying too high to be seen or heard—B-52 Stratofortresses of the U.S. Air Force's Strategic Air Command.

No more than a bare hilltop when first established, Ripcord was two and a half months later a heavily bunkered bastion standing ready to provide artillery coverage for the opening of three firebases directly in the objective area. It was at that time, on the eve of the allied offensive, that the enemy struck. . . .

Thus began the battle for Firebase Ripcord. Colonel Benjamin L. Harrison, the brigade commander, was given operational control of the division reserve, a full battalion, but it was not enough. The enemy had prepared the battlefield too well.

LETTER HOME

Specialist Five Thomas Pellaton
101st Aviation Group, 101st Airborne Division
Phu Bai, July 1970
An intelligence staffer, Specialist Pellaton wrote this shortly after U.S. troops, threatened with major attack near the mouth of the A Shau, pulled back from Firebase Ripcord. In this disaster, units sustained crippling losses, including several large helicopters and all their artillery. Pellaton has some details wrong, but his emotions were common among GIs of this period.
You may have read about Fire Support Base Ripcord, southwest of Hue. The 101st, true to its reputation, had another defeat like Hamburger Hill and Khe Sanh. You will get the whitewashed version of what happened, I'm sure. But let me tell you, we were driven off that hill after overwhelming casualties. We lost over 80 men in KIAs in less than two weeks and over 420 wounded. A full battalion of men. And for what? There is absolutely nothing out there in the jungle but mountains and triple canopy. Nothing but [North Vietnamese] who have built roads and who outnumber us in the province by two or three to one.

Yes, it is no longer a case of the big imperialistic American aggressor killing the pure VC patriots. Instead, the VC are almost completely out of the picture. Instead we [are fighting] highly trained, well-equipped [VPA] regiments and divisions. The South Vietnamese are doing very well militarily here. The 1st

ARVN Division does as well, if not better than, the 101st Airborne Division. The popular and regional forces keep the VC pretty much under control, but the fact remains that we are very much outnumbered and our best weapon cannot be used for political reasons. Napalm is almost out of the picture.

You may be surprised at my seemingly changed position. Talking of napalm, etc. When you see people, Americans, dying for lack of protection, for phony Vietnamization (it's not working because there are not enough ARVN troops—they lose about a regiment a month in AWOLs and desertion) and for lack of good leadership. . . . My position has not really changed. There is no reason to be here—and there is even less reason to see Americans dying here.

MEDAL OF HONOR AT RIPCORD

Lieutenant Colonel Andre C. Lucas
Second Battalion, 506th Infantry, 101st Airborne Division
Fire Support Base Ripcord, Thua Thien Province, July 1–23, 1970
Congressional Medal of Honor Citation
Lt. Col. Lucas distinguished himself by extraordinary heroism while serving as the commanding officer of the 2nd Battalion. Although the firebase was constantly subjected to heavy attacks by a numerically superior enemy force throughout this period, Lt. Col. Lucas, forsaking his own safety, performed numerous acts of extraordinary valor in directing the defense of the allied position. On one occasion he flew in a helicopter at treetop level above an entrenched enemy directing the fire of one of his companies for over 3 hours. Even though his helicopter was heavily damaged by enemy fire, he remained in an exposed position until the company expended its supply of grenades. He then transferred to another helicopter, dropped critically-needed grenades to the troops, and resumed his perilous mission of directing fire on the enemy. These courageous actions by Lt. Col. Lucas prevented the company from being encircled and destroyed by a larger enemy force. On another occasion Lt. Col. Lucas attempted to rescue a crewman trapped in a burning helicopter. As the flames in the aircraft spread, and enemy fire became intense, Lt. Col. Lucas ordered all members of the rescue party to safety. Then, at great personal risk, he continued the rescue effort amid concentrated enemy mortar fire, intense heat, and exploding ammunition until the aircraft was completely engulfed in flames. Lt. Col. Lucas was mortally wounded while directing the successful withdrawal of his battalion from the fire base. His actions throughout this extended period inspired his men to heroic efforts and were instrumental in saving the lives of many of his fellow soldiers while inflicting heavy casualties

on the enemy. Lt. Col. Lucas's conspicuous gallantry and intrepidity in action, at the cost of his own life, were in keeping with the highest traditions of the military service and reflect great credit on him, his unit, and the U.S. Army.

PERNICIOUS PROBLEMS

Sergeant Yusef Komunyakaa
Headquarters and Headquarters Company, Twenty-Third (Americal) Division
Chu Lai, 1969–1970
An African-American with a literary bent, at twenty-one a bit older than the typical GI, Yusef Komunyakaa (his later name) landed an assignment as a reporter for, and later editor of, Southern Cross, *the Americal division newspaper. Between reporting on such events as the fighting in the A Shau Valley, Komunyakaa followed the grunts closely enough to earn a Bronze Star—and later make them the centerpieces of his powerful poetry. This poem shows that the hell of the tunnel war extended throughout South Vietnam.*

Tunnels

Crawling down headfirst into the hole,
he kicks the air and disappears.
I feel like I'm down there
with him, moving ahead, pushed
by a river of darkness, feeling
blessed for each inch of the unknown.
Our tunnel rat is the smallest man
in the platoon, in an echo chamber
that makes his ears bleed
when he pulls the trigger.
He moves as if trying to outdo
blind fish easing toward imagined blue,
pulled by something greater than life's
ambitions. He can't think about
spiders and scorpions mending the air,
or care about bats upside down
like gods in the mole's blackness.
The damp smell goes deeper
than the stench of honey buckets.
A web of booby traps waits, ready
to spring into broken stars.
Forced onward by some need,
some urge, he knows the pulse
of mysteries and diversions

like thoughts trapped in the ground.
He questions each root.
Every cornered shadow has a life
to bargain with. Like an angel
pushed up against what hurts,
his globe-shaped helmet
follows the gold ring his flashlight
casts into the void. Through silver
lice, shit, maggots, & vapor of pestilence,
he goes, the good soldier,
on hands and knees, tunneling past
death sacked into a blind corner,
loving the weight of the shotgun
that will someday dig his grave.

RESCUE IN LAOS

Warrant Officer Tom Marshall
158th Aviation Battalion, 101st Airborne Division
Laos, March 1971
Tom Marshall flew helicopters in I Corps during of the last fierce months of the American war, August 1970 through August 1971, in fact starting with Firebase Ripcord and including the intense invasion of Laos, Operation Lam Son 719. For the helicopter force, Lam Son proved to be a meatgrinder. Carrying the ARVN into heavily defended terrain, ships were shot out of the sky with depressing regularity. The ARVN made an initial incursion, then sat down. Further advances were made only by means of air assaults emplacing new firebases, each of which became a magnet for enemy attacks. Soon the ARVN were reeling on the edge of rout. After six weeks of hell, the retreat began.
Attempts to lift out ARVNs continued, but the panicked soldiers swamped any aircraft that approached the pickup zone, packing twenty to thirty men into a Huey designed to carry no more than ten. This horrified the pilots and crew members, who knew the load limits of the aircraft.

The enemy fire continued to take a toll. On the afternoon of March 21 Major Bunting, commanding officer of the 48th Assault Helicopter Company, knew his men were physically exhausted, emotionally shot. All the remaining aircraft were battle damaged. But the withdrawal was a trial of resolve and honor of the kind few ever experience. . . . Major Bunting didn't climb up to altitude like some . . . but flew the lead helicopter, down in the dirt, leading the army's charge. His leadership by example, with disregard for his own personal safety, had already gotten him shot down [*twice*]. . . .

During the evening briefing the night before, Bunting had told [*us*] of the mission. Warning them it would likely be a repeat of the disastrous one of March 20, he informed the men he needed ten aircrews, all volunteers.

In the morning . . . Major Bunting led his flight of ten Blue Stars as the final string behind thirty other Hueys. When they entered Laos, the antiaircraft fire [*exacted its price*]. As Bunting listened to those ahead of him, he heard horrifying commentaries of hits taken, wounded crewmen, and constant calls of "Going down!" *Every* aircraft in the first three flights of ten Hueys each was either shot down or damaged so badly it wouldn't fly again.

The debacle of panicked, unarmed ARVNs swamping hovering Hueys while the NVA took target practice was lunacy. Bunting realized that the pickup zone had to be moved. He called Lieutenant Colonel Peachey and asked . . . to call it off until the PZ could be moved a short distance. Peachey was adamant. The extraction would continue.

For Major Bunting, combat risk had observable, carefully measured limits. Sanity had to be set a limit. A month earlier Bunting had been told by General Sutherland that a lift company was an acceptable sacrifice to maintain the diplomacy of the army support of the ARVN effort.

But Bunting had reached a rational limit. There would be no senseless sacrifice of his Blue Stars. He radioed Peachey, telling him they would not go until the pickup zone was moved. Infuriated, Peachey ordered him to proceed. Again, Bunting requested that he move the PZ. A general of the 101st Airborne Division circling above, call sign Right Guard, overheard the conversation. He ordered [*both officers*] to meet him at the . . . pad at Khe Sanh.

Bunting ordered his Blue Stars back to Khe Sanh and headed for the log pad. Was he going to be relieved of command or worse? Bunting was hoping the general would back him up . . . but thought that was highly unlikely. . . . Then, in a moment of divine intervention or poetic justice, Lieutenant Colonel Peachey was shot down in Laos!

VIETNAM PEOPLE'S ARMY ON THE MARCH

Lieutenant Colonel Robert E. Stoffey, USMC
staff, Seventh Fleet
off the Quang Tri coast, April 2, 1972
Lieutenant Colonel Stoffey was a Marine aviator assigned as assistant amphibious warfare officer on the staff of Seventh Fleet commander Vice-Admiral William P. Mack. Stoffey was on his second Vietnam tour, having flown out of Da Nang in 1965. Now he was aboard the fleet flagship, light cruiser Oklahoma City, *which steamed close inshore because the vessel's six-inch guns could furnish fire support. Hanoi's offensive that began at the end of March overwhelmed ARVN positions below the DMZ within a few days and closed in on the key obstacle of the Cua Viet*

River. If VPA tanks and infantry could get across that river, nothing would stop them from reaching Quang Tri or, beyond that, Hue. The admiral and his staff witnessed something that American sailors in Vietnam had never seen before.

On April 2, Easter Sunday, I stood next to Admiral Mack and his chief of staff, [*Captain*] Earl Godfrey, on the bridge. . . . There were about ten other officers out on the bridge observing as well. We all watched in awe as hundreds of NVA tanks continued crossing the Cua Viet River, heading south for Dong Ha and Quang Tri City. Every now and then staff members would run back into the war room . . . to read our message traffic, hoping that Admiral Mack would, after repeated requests, be authorized to execute swift retaliation raids into the DMZ as well as [*the DRV*]. After all, it was from North Vietnam that the enemy continually came, visiting all this bloodshed upon their southern neighbors. His requests were not answered by . . . Washington.

As we floated in the Gulf of Tonkin, very close to shore and off the [*Cua*] Viet River, the *Oklahoma City*'s 5- and 6-inch guns fired heavy volumes at NVA Soviet-built T-54 tanks and amphibious [*P*]T-76 tanks on both sides of the . . . river. I saw six NVA tanks destroyed by the *Oklahoma City*'s guns in just a few minutes, before I had to get back to my staff desk to monitor the big picture.

The [*warship's*] executive officer, [*Commander*] Joe Fairchild, was down in the . . . combat information center (CIC)—the combat brain of the ship responsible for operating [*its*] air- and surface-search radar and for maintaining voice communications with other ships and aircraft. During these heavy shore bombardments, particularly those aimed at the enemy tanks and troops crossing . . . well south of the DMZ, CIC was the active focal point for naval gunfire support. . . . CIC also coordinated antiair warfare by . . . collecting, processing, displaying, evaluating, and disseminating tactical information throughout the ship. Joe Fairchild stayed very busy in CIC . . . managing and coordinating weapons firing with navigation and engine room crews.

Commander Fairchild called up to the ship's bridge, "Captain Tice, this is Commander Fairchild in CIC. Our radar screens indicate we are making many hits on what appear to be fast-moving vehicles heading south."

"You sure as hell are, Joe! We . . . can easily see it from up here. Your hits . . . are fantastic. Tell your personnel they are doing one helluva job! Tell them the captain is most impressed."

A SOUTH VIETNAMESE SURRENDER

Lieutenant Colonel Pham Van Dinh
Fifty-Sixth Infantry Regiment, ARVN Third Division
Camp Carroll, April 2, 1972
American gunfire support and aerial attacks inflicted heavy losses on the Vietnam People's Army, but they did not blunt its offensive. Hanoi's troops pressed

hard against the Vietnamese Marine and ARVN positions below the DMZ and took them one by one. Only four days into the offensive, a couple of Marine strongpoints and the fire support base at Camp Carroll were virtually all that remained of the defenses. Camp Carroll was held by the ARVN Fifty-Sixth Regiment under Colonel Pham Van Dinh, the famed fighter who had led the assault to recapture the flag tower in Hue's Citadel at Tet. Colonel Dinh's troops fought hard, but they were no match for the enemy. Units he sent to other strongpoints were surrounded and wiped out, his main position eventually being held by survivors of the rifle battalions. Orders to defend at all costs clued Dinh there would be no reinforcements. He was forced into an agonizing decision controversial among Vietnamese ever since. This account is by historian Andrew Wiest.

Dinh contacted 3rd ARVN Division [*headquarters*] and reported on events to [*Brigadier General Vu Van*] Giai's executive officer [*XO*], Lieutenant Colonel Cuong. Dinh then asked how he could be expected to continue the battle without support, supplies, or reinforcements. The XO had no real answer . . . and General Giai was unavailable, dealing with the crisis at Dong Ha. The lack of any news, coupled with the fact that General Giai was devoting his time to a regiment that was fleeing from battle, only served to solidify Dinh's belief that "nobody was looking after my regiment any more. We were alone."

At [*2 p.m.*] a second NVA human wave assault struck the defenses of Camp Carroll from the west near the main gate. Though again repulsed, the attackers had come so close that their bodies festooned the perimeter wire. . . . As the fighting raged, Dinh received a call from the NVA. The caller said he was near and knew all about both Dinh and his men and was aware of their danger. The caller then went on to make an offer; if Dinh surrendered, he and his men would be welcomed by the NVA. If they did not, they would die. [*No one but Dinh knew of this exchange. His American senior advisor, Lieutenant Colonel William Camper, spoke to him of a possible resupply by U.S. helicopters. Dinh also heard from the purported commander of the surrounding People's Army troops, repeating their surrender offer. Colonel Dinh got the enemy to stop shooting while he convened his officers.*]

Just before [*3 p.m.*], the battalion commanders and regimental staff present at Camp Carroll, some thirteen men, met in the [*command post*]. Dinh informed his . . . subordinates that the situation was bad and that they did not have the strength to hold out long against the constant enemy assaults. He then bared his soul and said, "If we continue to fight, many people will be killed. Even if we die or are wounded and win a victory, nobody will take care of us. Now we must take care of ourselves." Dinh then told the group of the NVA offer . . . and asked for their ideas . . . [*indicating*] he would accede to their wishes. Only Major Ton That Man of 1/56 spoke in favor of continuing the resistance. The remaining staff sat silently; they had no answers. . . .

If nobody had any other options, Dinh counseled surrender. The vote was unanimous. Dinh informed the NVA of the decision and arranged for a longer ceasefire while his staff prepared for the surrender. [*The North Vietnamese wanted Dinh's American advisors, but he reported them long gone—and then went to Colonel Camper to tell him to flee or suicide. To his American counterparts Dinh seemed a broken man. They made their escape with a handful of ARVN soldiers who refused to capitulate. Colonel Dinh and about six hundred men went to North Vietnam as prisoners. Ironically, Dinh was put in a prison camp at Son Tay, where the Americans had once staged a spectacular raid to free U.S. POWs.*]

BEDLAM AT ARVN THIRD DIVISION

Lieutenant Colonel Gerald H. Turley, USMC
senior advisor, Vietnamese Marine Corps
Ai Tu Combat Base, April 2, 1972
Coincidence put "Gerry" Turley at the center of the action. Lieutenant Colonel Turley had arrived recently—he had less than one month in country—to take up the reins as senior American advisor to the Vietnamese Marine Corps. He was making familiarization visits to Vietnamese marine units when Hanoi attacked, and he happened to be at the DMZ because Marines were holding part of the defenses. On a courtesy visit to the headquarters of the ARVN Third Division, which was controlling the DMZ defenses, Gerry Turley became caught up in a helter-skelter rush to shore up disintegrating forces. Turley was pressed into service as a coordinator. When South Vietnamese General Giai pulled his main headquarters out of Ai Tu Combat Base—and his U.S. advisory team with it—Gerry Turley suddenly found himself the senior advisor to the ARVN's entire remaining defense line. Colonel Donald Metcalf, the Third Division's senior advisor, essentially put a marine in charge of an Army advisory function. Over four days the situation became progressively more desperate.

The fog of war seemed to be thickest within the [*division command post*] bunker itself. I walked to the side of a destroyed jeep and relieved myself. Alone, I began to wonder just how and where my casually planned "orientation visit" was eventually going to end, since it had turned into a personal dilemma I had neither anticipated nor sought out. As a visiting . . . officer, I was far more involved in assisting a unit of another service than tradition or the structure of military command allowed. Fate had put me and a number of other Americans together under dire circumstances.

[*Turley was resolved on one thing: so long as Vietnamese marine units remained in the DMZ sector, their Marine advisors would stay on too. That left*

him to be used the way he was. When Colonel Dinh's regiment surrendered and
the defense evaporated, survival seemed to depend upon destroying the bridge
that spanned the Cua Viet at Dong Ha.]

Ahead of the larger NVA tank column on Highway 1, terrorized civilians surged onto the roadway in their flight south to cross the Dong Ha Bridge. Most refugees were forced to walk; a few families rode atop trucks, while others jammed into small three-wheeled trucks and clung tightly to their perilous positions. Prized water buffalo were being urged along the shoulders of the roadway.

Meanwhile, back in the TOC several important events happened in quick succession. First, the South Vietnamese Air Force (VNAF) liaison officer and his tactical air control party . . . suddenly picked up . . . and left. As an omen of this . . . earlier in the morning, Major Brookbank had attempted to process an air request with his VNAF counterpart who refused to clear the air strike with the comment, "What's the use?" Now, without notice or authority to leave, the captain and his vital air control party had fled the bunker because they were afraid of the enemy's incoming artillery.

Next, a radio transmission to the senior adviser of the 57th Regiment confirmed that none of the . . . battalions of the regiment had any capability to blow the Dong Ha Bridge. While he had heard that some ARVN engineers were supposed to be [*there*], he was not sure if that was true.

Finally, based on my own evaluation of the critical tactical situation confronting the 3rd ARVN Division, I decided that the Dong Ha Bridge must be destroyed. I personally telephoned the FRAC headquarters in Danang and informed them of our desperate situation and my plan to halt the NVA's advancing tank column by blowing the bridge.

Within minutes a telephone call [*ordered*] me not to destroy the bridge. The reason given was, "We have to save it for our counterattack north." Under the circumstances such an unrealistic statement could only have been made by a staff officer isolated from [*reality*]. I vehemently disagreed with the Army lieutenant colonel who made the call and told him it was our only hope of stopping the North Vietnamese offensive.

He remained adamant. . . . In spite of my efforts to describe how tenuous our whole defensive posture was and that we were barely holding the lines . . . the telephone voice from Danang was crystal clear. "Don't destroy the bridge. This is an order, Colonel Turley."

"This is ironic," I thought. "I've been coordinating the advisory team's efforts for three days now and have made seemingly endless decisions involving tactical situations and supporting arms employment which have affected the lives of thousands of ARVN soldiers and several Americans and until this very moment have received absolutely no command guidance. . . . [*Moreover,* top *ARVN and U.S. officers had visited the TOC and recognized Turley as the senior advisor, with the authority that entailed, and also without providing any instructions.*] Now, when I disagree with a lieutenant colonel staff officer on the most critical and time sensitive of tactical decisions he gives me my first order, an order not to act."

I acknowledged the order and again repeated my decision to destroy the Dong Ha Bridge, if there was no other means to halt the enemy's attack. It was our last option. [*South Vietnamese sources insist that it was their decision to blow the Dong Ha Bridge.*]

THE BRIDGE AT DONG HA

Captain John W. Ripley, USMC
U.S. advisor to Third Battalion, Vietnamese Marine Corps
Dong Ha, April 2, 1972

A ten-year Marine Corps veteran from West Virginia, Captain Ripley had led a U.S. Marine rifle company along the DMZ in 1967. In 1972 Ripley was back as senior advisor to Major Le Ba Binh of the Third VNMC Battalion. When the South Vietnamese defenses began to collapse, the Third Battalion moved up to hold the Cua Viet and its key bridge. The Vietnamese Marines teamed up with an armored unit to reach Dong Ha and had to fight enemy tanks to get there. The scale of the disaster was becoming more apparent every minute. This account of the bridge is by Ripley's Marine colleague John Grider Miller.

Half an hour later, they were nearing the intersection of the perimeter road and Highway 1. [*Ripley's*] radio had been silent . . . but fragmentary reports of fighting continued to arrive on Binh's tactical nets, plugged into Vietnamese Marine and ARVN chains of command. Binh seemed to be calm as he translated the reports for Ripley, though the radio chatter sounded intermittently high-pitched and excited.

"South Vietnamese units are falling back behind the river," Binh said. "Some ARVN soldiers are throwing away their weapons and helmets."

"Helmets! With all this incoming? They've got to be crazy to do that."

Presently they reached the intersection . . . and he could see them, a second wave of deserters who had removed badges and insignia to blend in with the refugees. They must be from the Fifty-seventh Regiment, he thought. The ones from the Fifty-sixth couldn't have made it through Dong Ha during the last attack. These men looked scared but not terrorized. Unlike the civilians, they knew where they were heading. And they were going to survive no matter what. They'd worry about the rest later, after better men had died to protect them.

Binh's radio continued to pour out bad news. "Tanks are crossing the Dong Ha bridge unopposed," he said to Ripley, speaking as he listened. "They are being followed by [*People's Army*] infantry. . . . The enemy is in Dong Ha. . . . Dong Ha has fallen." Binh took the radio handset and held it at arm's length as though he wanted to choke the life out of it. He cursed it. . . .

[*Initial reports were exaggerated. The Vietnamese Marines and ARVN tanks did make it to the river, where they engaged the enemy across it. But the pressures on them were tremendous. At one point Major Binh even executed one of the deserters without that having any impact on the others. At length it seemed the only available course was to destroy the highway bridge. That proved much more difficult than anyone imagined. Ripley and Major James E. Smock, advisor to the ARVN Twentieth Tank Battalion, had to run onto the bridge in search of explosives, then cord, then detonators; Ripley had to get past the antisabotage barriers Seabees had built into the bridge, place the explosives, and wire them. Later, when it seemed the detonators were not functioning, Ripley found a battery in a blown-up jeep to use for a power source. Smock helped find the materials and dragged some of them to the older French bridge nearby. All of this was under enemy fire, with the South Vietnamese Marines trying to keep the other side down as best as they could. Ripley couldn't figure out why the explosives had not fired properly.*]

Then a mortar round hit the road behind [*a Vietnamese child who had suddenly appeared*] and he was up and running, realizing she would never make it on her own. At the last instant she looked up. . . . Her wailing stopped and her eyes widened in terror; she was screaming silently. He scooped her up from the front and her small legs flopped like a Raggedy Ann doll's. His momentum carried them a few steps, then he pivoted and broke into a full run for the crossroad. Seconds later he rounded the corner onto Highway 1.

He had almost reached the little girl's mother when the bridge blew.

It was the shock wave that came first, not the noise. The two of them went flying as if a powerful hand had slapped them from behind. His body was moving through the air faster than his legs could have taken it, faster than he ever could have run.

Then the noise arrived, growing louder and louder in a series of explosions that soon merged into a steady roar and branded itself into him. He clung to the girl and grunted as his shoulder slammed against the stony roadside. They tumbled into a ditch, their fall cushioned by the bodies of the dead.

The girl had landed on top of him. For an instant she lay there, stunned. Then without a sound she scrambled to her bare feet and ran away.

Large irregular chunks of debris hurtled through the air. Smaller pieces spun upward, rising hundreds of feet before falling back to earth in random patterns like handfuls of flying jacks. They thudded into the streets and clattered into the gnarled sheets of tin roofing. . . . The time fuses had done their job after all. The near span had dropped into the river, leaving a hundred foot gap. . . . The force of the explosion had gouged out a large section of the bank and a pressure wave was rising and expanding, upstream and downstream. . . . The bridge's thick timbers were on fire, and a cloud of gray smoke mushroomed from them, intensifying the pall over Dong Ha.

The old French bridge was cut too. Whatever Smock had dragged over there had packed enough explosive force.

[*Stymied by the destruction of the bridges, People's Army tanks milled around long enough to be attacked by aircraft and naval guns. But the lead plane was destroyed by a shoulder-fired anti-aircraft missile—the VPA here unveiled another new weapon. In any case their surviving armor had to recoil, move west, and reenter South Vietnam from the Laotian side. Their momentum dissipated. The Dong Ha Bridge cost Hanoi about a week. But its infantry were already spilling down from the hills, and soon enough they began crossing the river too. The Marines and ARVN armor were encircled and had to cut their way out. When they regrouped at Hue, the armored unit had no combat-ready tanks, and there were fifty-two men left of the seven-hundred-strong Marine battalion. No marine of the two companies that had covered Ripley at the Dong Ha Bridge stood in that formation.*]

ONE MORE CONTRADICTION

Lieutenant Michael Jackson, USAF
Twentieth Tactical Air Support Squadron, 504th Tactical Air Support Wing
Quang Tri, April 1972
Lieutenant Jackson piloted an O-2A for 210 combat missions during his tour. Radio call sign "Covey," the forward air controllers (FACs) were trained to spot targets on the ground and guide strike aircraft to hit them. Shortly before the Easter Offensive, acting as a squadron staff officer, Jackson had visited Quang Tri on routine assignment. Then came the attack, and he was sent back in his plane on a combat support sortie. As it happened, Jackson was furious at that moment because personnel officers were proposing that his next assignment be with the Strategic Air Command rather than having him, as he wanted, transition to fighter jets.

On the heels of my SAC scheming came my orders to return to Quang Tri and blow the hell out of it.

[*This*] was a strange assignment. I had just been there . . . during my abbreviated stint as duty officer. Now, suddenly, as the North Vietnamese forces mounted a full-scale assault, the ARVN troops defending the city were beating a hasty and none-too-subtle retreat. Quang Tri sat on the edge of the DMZ a scant ten miles shy of North Vietnam, and the whole province was clearly a major jumping-off point for Charlie's grand plan.

[*People's Army*] forces were shelling the hell out of the place and showing no indication of slowing their assault. With the ARVN troops heading southward at a record pace, the first order of business was to extract the American advisers . . . now being overrun by the advancing enemy. Once they were out of the line of fire, we turned our attention to the multitude of tanks and weapons that were sitting exposed and abandoned, just waiting for Charlie's loving caress. The last thing we needed was to have the dinks use our weapons against us; they were doing just fine with their own arsenal.

So I was ordered to head north and blow up anything that might hurt us if it was pointed in our direction.

It felt odd to direct air strikes against American equipment, especially because it signaled a defeat. They were the biggest air strikes I'd ever lead—lots of secondary explosions, all kinds of pyrotechnics. The irony did not escape me. I imagined taking my children on my knee many years hence and hearing them ask, "What was your biggest air strike of the war, Daddy?" *Ah yes, kids, I remember it well, blowing the crap out of your tax dollars.*

We were being pushed back even farther, and it left me with the uncomfortable but accurate impression that we were being caught with our pants down, despite the best efforts of every FAC in I Corps to convey the growing urgency of the situation.

Charlie hosed us down good. . . . He knew full well what we were doing, and it was in his best interest to prevent it. FACs throughout Vietnam, and especially in I Corps, were being knocked out of the sky. . . . There was no question that the North Vietnamese were rapidly gaining the upper hand. There was also no question in my mind that it didn't have to be that way. The military had the power and the resolve; if only we had been turned loose to run an actual military campaign, it could have been over in a matter of weeks—if not in 1972, then certainly a few years prior. But like everything else in this comedy of errors, it was a case of too little, too late.

THE REINFORCEMENT PLOT

Lieutenant Colonel Robert E. Stoffey, USMC
staff, Seventh Fleet
off the Vietnamese coast, April 1972

Admiral Mack's surface gunnery ships were busier than ever. The Oklahoma City and her consorts engaged the enemy in Quang Tri, then sped south to oppose the enemy spilling out of the Central Highlands, from firing positions off Qui Nhon. Then it was back to Quang Tri as Hanoi's legions threatened Hue. Colonel Stoffey was acutely aware that aircraft withdrawals under Vietnamization had reduced air power in the theater. He insists that Washington did not respond to appeals to reinforce the air units, and he recalls plotting with the Seventh Fleet commander to restore Marine squadrons. (Unknown to Stoffey, apparently, is that for weeks the White House, the secretary of defense, and the Joint Chiefs had already been earmarking aerial reinforcements. Documents clearly show that as early as February 2 the National Security Council had considered augmentations, that an additional aircraft carrier had been ordered to the South China Sea on February 4 [and arrived on Yankee Station a month later—before the offensive—bringing the number of carriers to four], that B-52 and Thailand air assets had also been built up, and that further increases were considered in early March, still three weeks before the North Vietnamese attacked.)

The NVA invasion forces near Quang Tri were continuing their attacks. I felt it was time to bring some of our Marine jet squadrons back . . . before Hue City and Phu Bai fell. [*If they did*] the NVA would quickly move south and attack Da Nang. Our Marine jet squadrons had been [*withdrawn*] to Iwakuni, Japan, a year ago in 1971. . . . I initially discussed my desire to bring the Marine squadrons back . . . with my immediate boss, [*Commander*] Jim Froid. We both then discussed it with our N-3, operations officer, [*Captain*] Bob McKenzie. They agreed that I should direct Marine aircraft . . . back into South Vietnam. . . . I then discussed it with the chief of staff, [*Captain*] Earl F. Godfrey, and finally, with Admiral Mack.

I explained to Admiral Mack: "We must get more attack air into the Quang Tri and Hue areas, or they may fall to the NVA. The enemy still has extensive momentum. I can get our Marine fighter/attack bombers back into Da Nang quickly. If JCS doesn't want them back In Country, they can stop them on their way before they get to Vietnam. By the time the Marine squadrons mount-out from Iwakuni . . . after receipt of my execute message, the entire chain of command will have copies of it." . . .

Admiral Mack listened intently, sipped some coffee, and said, "We have the assets. We're still committed to assist South Vietnam. We'd be remiss in our duties in not responding with forces on hand, within the restrictions and rules of engagement dictated to us by Washington. Yes, go ahead . . . draft a message. Let me personally see it." . . .

[*Washington did nothing to obstruct the reinforcements. The first squadrons arrived on April 6, followed by a stream of Navy, Marine, and Air Force aircraft. By the summer of 1972 U.S. airpower had more than doubled, to 1,400 aircraft.*]

ONE IF BY LAND . . .

Major Van Nguyen Duong
intelligence staff officer, ARVN Fifth Infantry Division
Lai Khe, February–March 1972
Major Duong had no doubt that a coming enemy offensive would strike the Saigon area as well as the north. The Fifth Division, where Duong led the G-2 staff, was responsible for Binh Long Province, where the city of An Loc became the locale for ARVN's greatest victory, with AVRN beating out enemy assaults and then a siege. Like Duong, the III Corps intelligence chief, responsible for the larger sector, had no doubts. Major Duong sketches the intelligence background for the An Loc battle.

From early February 1972, intelligence had gathered information from contacts between ARVN units and regular NVA reconnaissance force elements in III Corps and Region concerning a huge new communist offensive campaign. Captured documents revealed that all NVA units under . . . COSVN were studying the option of a "combined attack of tank[s], artillery and infantry" into cities and towns. Lieutenant Colonel Tran van Binh, III Corps . . . G-2, briefed the III Corps commander and all ARVN regional [*leaders*] regarding this intelligence. . . . [*It*] suggested the communists would conduct a massive attack into Tay Ninh or Binh Long . . . to seize one of these provinces for the presentation of their Southern Regional Provisional Revolutionary Government. Binh Long could possibly be the NVA main target. . . .

Contrary to the general opinion . . . that General [*Nguyen Van*] Minh, III Corps commander, neglected the defense of Binh Long, he believed in the estimate of his staff intelligence and perceived the COSVN intention to attack Binh Long instead of Tay Ninh. First, he sent Colonel Ly Nguyen Vy, his operational assistant, to Binh Long to prepare to shift his field . . . headquarters from Tay Ninh to An Loc, and then reinforced the 5th Division with the 52nd Task Force of the 18th Division. . . . He also requested Saigon to reinforce the 5th Division with an Airborne brigade. In mid-March the 1st Airborne Brigade was dispatched to Chon Thanh . . . 18 miles south of An Loc. The defense of Binh Long was almost completed.

As . . . G-2 of the 5th Infantry Division, during February and March, I sent continuous long-range reconnaissance teams and covert intelligence agents across the . . . borders into Cambodia . . . to collect any evidence of NVA tanks in the region. Air observations were also used but in vain. No traces of NVA tanks were found. Later, during the fighting at An Loc, a captured NVA officer from the 203rd Tank Regiment confessed that 60 tanks, including PT-76 and T-54, were carried into [*III Corps*]. This shifting of NVA tanks . . . must be regarded as an incredible feat. However, when these tanks came into the fighting, they became the prey for the An Loc defenders.

[*South Vietnamese General Lam Quang Thi, who published his own account of the An Loc battle, provides a different account of the enemy armor. He notes reports of VPA tanks in at least three places in Cambodia as early as October 1971 and adds that in December the Cambodian military confirmed a specific number of enemy tanks—thirty—in a People's Army base area not far from Binh Long and An Loc. According to Thi, these reports were discounted.*]

AN LOC BESIEGED

Colonel Tran Van Nhut
Binh Long Province chief
Vung Tau, April 5, 1972
Colonel Nhut had been the province chief of Binh Long, which included An Loc, since 1970. He reports that the ARVN expected attacks but remained unaware of targets or timing. His own concern was with the pacification program, which was also being emphasized by the Saigon government. That was what he was about when the offensive began.

As these attacks unfolded, the South Vietnamese province chiefs and ARVN corps commanders were attending a conference in Vung Tau on pacification and rural development, organized by [*Lieutenant General*] Cao Hao Hon and presided over by President Thieu and Prime Minister Khiem. The province chiefs from Military Regions One and Two [*I and II Corps*] were ordered to leave the conference and return immediately to their provinces.

The province chiefs of Military Regions Three and Four were directed to remain in Vung Tau. On April 5, 1972, at eleven o'clock, Lieutenant General Hon summoned me to his office and said, "Nhut, the president has ordered you to return to Binh Long immediately. The military situation in your province is extremely serious." . . .

Although I was away from my province, I had been telephoning [*Lieutenant Colonel*] Nguyen Phong Thanh, my deputy sector commander, every day. . . . I had been informed of a number of scattered [*firefights*] between communist troops and RF and PF units along Highway 13 north of Can Le bridge. . . . Sector intelligence was monitoring the situation and had noted an increase in enemy traffic along the road . . . so Thanh had ordered the district . . . to intensify ambush operations. . . . These ambushes had resulted in a number of armed clashes during the nights of April 3 and 4. . . . Of particular interest was the fact that the communist dead, based on their uniforms and equipment, were main force regulars, not the local force VC troops usually encountered. This fact caused me a great deal of concern.

To make matters worse, Mr. E. Gaudeul, director of the Cexso Rubber Plantation at Loc Ninh [*the district of Binh Long closest to Cambodia*], informed us that many field telephone wires had been set up in the northwestern part of Loc Ninh. The military commanders in Loc Ninh had not paid attention to this report, though, and had not sent out reconnaissance troops to verify the report and . . . destroy the enemy's communications network. . . .

As my jeep drove past the helicopter refueling station along Highway 13 inside the Lai Khe base, I saw someone motioning us to stop. As we slowed down I recognized Thanh and [*Lieutenant Colonel*] Robert E. Corley, senior advisor to sector headquarters. They had recognized my jeep because of the small green flag flying from my radio antenna (it was a Vietnamese Marine Corps flag, even though I had been out of the marines since 1966). I got out and shook hands with Thanh and Corley. Before I could ask a single question, Thanh gave me a quick briefing. . . . He said 122mm rockets had shelled the sector headquarters and one of our barracks was on fire; Loc Ninh district military headquarters was under siege; and the communists had set up a fortified roadblock on Highway 13 . . . south of An Loc, cutting off all vehicular traffic into the city.

[*In quick succession, the enemy overran Loc Ninh, forced the surrender of an ARVN armored cavalry unit, and closed in on An Loc. Colonel Nhut helicoptered around but fought his battle mostly from within An Loc. The commander of the ARVN Fifth Division and many of his officers were also at the ninety-four-day siege.*]

CRITICAL DANGER AT AN LOC

Brigadier General Le Van Hung
commander, ARVN Fifth Infantry Division
An Loc, May 11, 1972
South Vietnamese consider An Loc to be ARVN's greatest victory, on a par with Russia's World War II triumph at Stalingrad. Part of the troops of General Hung's division, along with Colonel Nhut's local forces, eventually reinforced by paratroopers and airborne rangers, stood off the best the VPA and NLF could throw at them over a lengthy interval, during which they were cut off and supplied by air. The People's Army made repeated assaults during the early weeks of the siege. The most dangerous came on May 11, when the enemy fought to split the ARVN defenders in two, culminating in a battle at General Hung's own command bunker. One of the great heroes of An Loc, Hung was among the "Mekong

Mafia" of ARVN officers who had spent much of their careers in the Delta. In his case he had been a province chief and regiment commander and received promotion to brigadier general in the midst of the siege. Soon afterward he would be elevated to deputy commander of the III Corps. This account is by Lam Quang Thi, then a general posted to the north as a senior commander in I Corps.

On the north side, the column of [enemy] tanks continued to move slowly toward the city. On each side of the road, one reinforced infantry battalion progressed alongside the tank column. When the tanks reached the area that was previously targeted by ARVN artillery, just north of the defense perimeter, [Major] Hoang Trung Liem, the artillery liaison officer . . . ordered a "fire for effect." At the same time the 81mm mortars of the [Eighth] regiment started to fire on the accompanying infantry. The latter, taken by surprise, ran in all directions; the tanks in the rear . . . were stopped by artillery fire while the tanks in . . . front, unable to back up, continued. . . .

However, the enemy tanks were able to regroup after the cessation of ARVN artillery interdiction fire, and a column of about fifteen [T]-54s started to move south on Ngo Quyen Street, which was the section of Route 13 that traversed the city. . . . When the tanks were about to reach Nguyen Trung Truc Street, the soldiers from the 8th Regiment began to fire their M-72s and machineguns from the . . . windows, killing or wounding many tankers, and causing the remaining enemy machine gunners to abandon their weapons, close the hatches and hide inside their tanks. When the lead tank reached Hoang Hon Boulevard, the third tank . . . was hit by an M-72 rocket fired by a soldier of the regiment. The tank exploded and burst into flames; the burned tankers jumped out . . . and rolled back and forth on the sidewalks in pain; they were finished off by a volley of M-16 bullets. While the lead tanks continued to roll down toward the center of the city, the tanks in the middle . . . had to stop and the soldiers of the 8th Regiment took this opportunity to kill three more. The tanks at the end . . . backed up and turned left and right; three . . . were destroyed by the soldiers of the 3rd Ranger Group and two by the 7th Regiment.

The two lead tanks, which had escaped . . . the ambush, accelerated and rushed southward. The first . . . approaching Phan Boi Chau Street, was closing in on the 5th Division's headquarters. The soldiers guarding the gate . . . panicked and ran for cover because this was the first time they had faced an enemy tank and also because they didn't believe in the effectiveness of the M-72 weapon. General Hung grabbed a hand grenade and was ready to hurl it at the enemy in case they ventured into the bunker. As the tank was turning around in an effort to identify the location of General Hung's command post, [Colonel] Le Nguyen Vy, deputy division commander, emerged from the . . . bunker, aimed his LAW at the tank and set it ablaze just in front of the division headquarters. The tank was finished off at the junction of Phan Boi Chau and Hoang Hoa Tham Streets. . . .

Nguyen Cau, a TV reporter who stayed in An Loc during the entire siege, recalled that, when the enemy tanks were closing in on his command post, General Hung told his staff that he would not be captured alive and that in case he had to commit suicide, they must destroy the division's signal code immediately.

[*Meanwhile the People's Army infantry reorganized and attacked from two directions, driving Saigon's troops toward the tank action. And a fresh VPA tank unit drove into An Loc. Some ARVN soldiers heard the vehicles and assumed a South Vietnamese relief force was arriving. By the afternoon, fighting again approached Hung's headquarters. An Loc was declared to be an "extreme tactical emergency." Troops of the enemy's 271st Regiment then made a wrong turn and occupied the public works building, a useless objective. They did, however, capture the office that handled "chieu hoi" enemy deserters.*]

The mission to retake the building fell to a company of the 52nd Battalion. As the Chieu Hoi building was . . . on high ground with good fields of fire, the attackers had to cross an open area to assault [*it*]. [*Lieutenant*] Nguyen Van Hieu, the company commander, personally led his men in the attack; he was shot in the head and fell dead right in front of the building. His company was pinned down by all kinds of weapons, including heavy machine guns and also M-79 grenade launchers that the enemy had captured from dead ARVN soldiers. By late afternoon the 52nd Battalion was still unable to retake the Chieu Hoi building. . . .

[*Air strikes finally suppressed the enemy fire enough so that late that night the building could be recaptured. The fighting died down until another assault two days later. That too was beaten off. Subsequent People's Army attacks never came so close to capturing An Loc.*]

VISIONS OF THE FUTURE

Lieutenant General Lam Quang Thi
I Corps deputy commander
Da Nang, April 21, 1972
Until the military disaster in Quang Tri, Lam Quang Thi had headed the South Vietnamese military academy at Dalat. When President Thieu shook up the command structure in I Corps, he sent General Thi as deputy commander. Thi arrived at headquarters on April 14 and quickly began to see things for himself. A few days later Thieu and other officials attended a conference where the leaders of the South Vietnamese Marine and Airborne divisions denounced the corps com-

mander, who resigned. Thieu appointed the redoubtable First Division leader, General Ngo Quang Truong, to head I Corps, with Thi as deputy. The two generals infused the Saigon troops with new spirit, supervised the breakout of remnants still in Quang Tri, and began a series of counterattacks that returned the ARVN to that shattered city after a long battle rivaling that at An Loc. In the meantime General Thi had had an experience which proved prescient.

One week after I reported to I Corps, Navy Captain Ho van Ky Thoai, the commandant of Navy [forces] in MR I, invited me to visit the naval installations in Tien Sa on the east side of Danang Bay. I was struck by the strategic value of this area. I knew that ultimately, we had to fight a last ditch battle to defend the important enclave of Danang and Tien Sa would be an ideal place from which I Corps could conduct its defense. . . . During my visit to the United States in 1970, I observed firsthand the growing antiwar movement in the country that, in my opinion, would eventually cause the United States to disengage from Viet Nam. I knew that President Nixon's "Vietnamization Program" would not work because it was too little and too late. I was certain that we had to fight alone to defend that last enclave of MR I. Tien Sa would be the fateful place where we would fight the last battle.

The Tien Sa-Son Tra area reminded me of Bataan in the Philippines where American and Philippine troops fought their last battle before surrendering to the Japanese in World War II. A small peninsula surrounded on the north side by Danang Bay and along the west side by the Da River, which constituted a natural barrier to infantry attack, Tien Sa was also protected from direct fire by a small hill located behind the Navy headquarters building. On the other hand, due to its location on the ocean front, the Tien Sa-Son Tra peninsula could be resupplied by sea.

Thus, I directed I Corps Engineer units to excavate under the hill behind Captain Thoai's headquarters and to construct an underground [command post] from which we could direct our last battle that I was sure was coming.

[After the strenuous campaign of 1972 the United States was in fact compelled to leave the Vietnam War, by means of a cease-fire agreement signed in Paris in January 1973. The uneasy truce quickly gave way to renewed hostilities between Hanoi and Saigon, which still enjoyed American military and economic aid plus technical assistance. But Saigon's position gradually deteriorated until the final battle in the spring of 1975. Generals Truong and Thi, who remained in command of I Corps, did their best to marshal the troops, but the defenses collapsed. The enclave at Da Nang indeed became the last bastion in the northern region. Surviving troops and any civilian refugees who could escape were evacuated by sea until the North Vietnamese captured Da Nang on March 30, 1975. General Thi and many others struggled to organize a desperate defense of South Vietnam, but Saigon itself fell almost exactly one month later.]

14

Air War

FIRST AIR FORCE PRISONER

Major Fred V. Cherry, USAF
Thirty-Fifth Tactical Fighter Squadron
Takhli Air Base, Thailand, October 1965

Major Cherry was among the early air warriors, in Thailand to carry the war to the enemy and defeat North Vietnam. He was also a quintessential pilot, loving the plane he flew. In this excerpt Cherry makes a distinction between 1964, when the adversary had no surface-to-air missiles (SAMs), and late 1965. By then the Soviet Union had sent the first SAM batteries to the North—and the initial air strikes against SAM sites occurred at this exact time. The low-altitude penetration tactics Cherry describes were specifically designed to avoid SAMs. Unfortunately they left planes vulnerable to simple rifle fire.

I'm flying a[n] F-105 by now. It was fast. Mach 2.5. Had good range. Dependable. Comfortable. Good weapons. Good navigational systems. But it was primarily a tactical bomber.

We could carry up to 16 750-pound bombs. On a normal flight we'd have 10, and then 2.5-inch rockets, and a 20-mm cannon, which was a real jewel. It was a far cry from what I could load on an F-84 or F-100.

The F-4 Phantom was certainly a better aircraft for air-to-air combat. And sometimes they would give us coverage. But the F-105 could carry a bigger load, faster and farther. I really loved that airplane.

In 1964 we mainly hit the supplies headed down the Ho Chi Minh Trail in Laos. But in 1965 it was sort of open bombing against the North. The initial targets were radar installations. Then we went after military barracks, and some bridges and roads. At the time they didn't have the SAMs, just plain old 57-[*mm*] antiaircraft weapons with radar control. But they were pretty accurate.

I was leading the squadron that day, the twenty-fifth of October '65. The weather was bad. But they sent my wingman up and said you got a mission. The Ironhand. That's the codename for the [*antiaircraft*] missile installations. So I rushed down and got briefed and picked up my maps. We had "snake eyes," 500-pound target bombs. And CUBs [*sic—CBUs*]. Cluster bomb [*units*]. A pellet bomb. This would be my fiftieth mission of the war.

We refueled over Laos, the 19th Parallel. Then just east of Dien Bien Phu, we cut down to low altitude. I mean low. We call it the deck—50 to 100 feet. Just clearing the trees and sometimes below 'em to get under the radar net. I had to keep the wingman and everyone else higher. . . . You gotta watch what's going to be in the way of the wingman, 'cause he's not. . . . He's watching the lead, and everybody's watching him. You're flying for all four other guys.

We were on the deck 34 minutes at 500 knots when we reached the IP [*initial point—a term of art in the mathematics for accuracy in bomb delivery*], the predetermined point, after which you don't make any deviations and just head for the target. And the maximum [*bomb*] release altitude for the reference scan was 100 feet. To get the maximum effect. . . . Any higher, half of 'em be blowin' themselves up before they got to the ground.

About three minutes from the target, I could see 'em shooting at me. Just rifle fire. Everybody carried a rifle down there. They just fired up into the air, and you run into it. Then I heard a thump. And I turned off the electrical stuff and hydraulics. I thought they hit something electrical.

I went right to the target, released my weapons, and started headin' out to the Tonkin Gulf, where the Navy could pick me up. The last thing I said to the flight was, "Let's get the F out of here."

Then smoke started to boil up from behind the instrument panel. Electrical smoke. I reached over to turn off the battery and the two generators. And before my hand got to the panel, the airplane exploded. Just blew up. The smoke was so dense, I couldn't see outside the cockpit. I got a real jolt. Nothing like that thump. I couldn't see whether I was upright, upside down, or what. I just pulled the nose up a few degrees to give me the best ejection altitude. I ejected instantly. At 400 feet. And I prayed.

[*Major Cherry did not make the coast—he was two minutes away—but he survived the ejection. Cherry landed next to a dozen North Vietnamese militiamen and was taken prisoner, the first African-American pilot in captivity, released in 1973.*]

RADAR INTERCEPT OFFICER

Lieutenant James B. Souder, USN
Fighter Squadron VF-154
Aircraft Carrier *Ranger*, Yankee Station, March–August 1966
During the early period of Rolling Thunder, *the U.S. Navy was transitioning to a new-generation tactical aircraft, the F-4 Phantom, which introduced a two-man crew—pilot and radar intercept officer (RIO)—the latter being responsible for navigation, detecting the enemy, and managing radar-directed missiles. The RIOs were not pilots, so were the butt of discrimination from a community that celebrated fliers. Until late in the war non-pilot-rated flying officers were not even permitted to command air units. Many RIOs wondered why they bothered. Lieutenant Souder was one. This account is by Navy official historian John Darrell Sherwood.*

After about ten easy missions in the South, J. B.'s first . . . in North Vietnam occurred early in May. The target . . . was a truck refueling station on a little side road near Vinh—a city notorious for its antiaircraft artillery. As the [*RIO*], Souder needed to monitor airspeed, altitude, and dive angle and prompt the pilot on when to drop his bombs. "I remember we were making our roll-in. The AAA was going off all over the place and I caught myself reflexively ducking my head as all these big explosions went off all around me. Hell, I completely messed up the bomb run." After that mission [*pilot Terry*] Born told Souder he had to do his job no matter what . . . and Souder vowed to keep his eyes on the instruments . . . from then onward. Souder, however, continued to make mistakes, and Born began to "slowly boil" inside.

A few nights later, Born and Souder launched from *Ranger* to intercept two unidentified surface contacts. While Born flew the F-4 500 feet off the Gulf of Tonkin at 300 knots, Souder searched for the targets and tracked his leader's position (Souder and Born were flying as the wingman that night) on the F-4's radar. Souder also stayed in contact with a controller whose calls seemed inconsistent with their known position. At one point, he told Born, "something doesn't make sense . . . one of those guys is totally fucked-up." Souder then began questioning the controller about the calls and navigation plots. Born, thinking that his RIO was "fucking up again," got impatient and started scolding. . . . Ignoring the barrage of criticism . . . Souder continued to concentrate on the problem . . . and soon figured out that the lead plane . . . was using an incorrect tactical air navigation (TACAN) station. . . . Souder tried to inform . . . but [*the latter*] immediately dismissed the notion and told Souder to "get your head out of your ass and get it right back there." Souder then informed the lead RIO and the controller of his theory, and they confirmed he was right. The [*unidentified targets*], though, ended up being false radar signals (gremlins)—a factor that only increased [*Born's*] resentment . . . toward Souder. When the two men returned to the carrier, they did not speak . . . except for essential communications. After three days, the two sat down and rehashed the flight so they could both understand exactly what had happened, and then apologized to each other. They next formulated a plan to eliminate future disagreements or mistakes from the time their "feet hit the plane's boarding ladder until we got back out of it." The plan called for the person who made a mistake, no matter how small, to buy a beer for the other. . . . "Eighty-three beers later," Souder recalled, "I finally figured out what I was doing in the back seat of an F-4."

One of the high points of that first tour was a fighter patrol in June 1966 in support of an A-4 strike against the massive petroleum storage tank farm in Haiphong. This was the first U.S. attack of the war against this major facility. "We were watching the A-4s go in there and drop their bombs and fire their rockets when all of a sudden, kaboom, there goes a big tank. I remember saying, 'Terry, we were there. We were there! 29 June 1966. We stopped the war,' and I remember looking in my rearview mirrors . . . on the way back to the ship and still seeing smoke coming up from those tanks." At this point . . . the young Souder naively believed that one well-placed air strike was the beginning of a major air campaign that would end the war. By the time his second tour concluded in 1967, he had begun to lose his optimism and take a more jaundiced view. . . . By his last tour in 1972, his only goal was to help . . . win the release of his friends and comrades—the POWs held by the North Vietnamese.

[*On his third tour in April 1972, in desperate efforts to blunt Hanoi's Easter Offensive, by then Lieutenant Commander Souder logged forty-nine sorties in less than a month, three on April 26. The next day his F-4 sustained a crippling hit from an air-to-air missile fired by the MIG-21 piloted by Hoang Quoc Dung of the North Vietnamese 921st Fighter Regiment. Souder spent the last nine months of the war as a POW with the friends he had been fighting to free.*]

HUNTING GROUNDS

Colonel Jack Broughton, USAF
355th Tactical Fighter Wing
Takli, Thailand, 1965–1966
Colonel Broughton commanded this air wing and helped establish it at the Thai base.

Everyone who flies a combat tour in fighters finds a favorite area to work in. You find places you detest and have no desire to fly into, and [*others*] where you feel more relaxed, more competent, more aggressive. The index is not necessarily the severity of the defenses, in fact a flier's favorite section may be very heavily defended. It is just a case of feeling that you can master all the challenges in one spot and adopting that section as your personal hunting grounds. When you make that identification, it is amazing how well you can manipulate both the schedule and the conduct of the mission to allow you to comb your hunting grounds regularly.

I despised the northeast [*Hanoi-China border*] railroad. I didn't like the long haul that we had . . . to get there and I didn't like the approaches to the targets, even though it was easy enough . . . and the landmarks made navigation no problem. While there were plenty of people shooting at you on the way in and the way out, the gunfire was not an overriding factor until you got to the target itself. The targets were blah targets, and they were all heavily defended. We smashed most of the worthwhile ones early on, and after we had knocked out the better targets in other complexes to the west of the railroad and toward Hanoi, the North Vietnamese loaded the railroad with guns from these other areas and then moved them up and down the rail line as needed. Our plan of hitting the same places again and again helped them . . . and there were not too many places where they couldn't hammer you pretty hard from all sides. Nobody wants to bust his rear end, but I abhorred the thought of doing it for some crummy beat-up piece of railroad track or a couple of used railroad cars.

I didn't like the egress route either, because once you got past the guns that chased you to the coast, you would have to look at all of those ships lined up waiting to get into the port at Haiphong with the flags of many nations we had knocked ourselves out to help flapping in the North Vietnamese breeze. It was rough to watch some kid blow up in your face and moments later watch your supposed allies unloading more equipment to be transported to the gunners so they could either work you over the next day or ship it down south to clobber some poor grunt crawling around in the mud. I didn't like the refueling on the way out because everyone was always hunting for fuel, and the rat race to find your tanker and hook up . . . was always more confused out there. And I didn't like the long haul home. As far as I am concerned, all single-engine fighters still have an automatic rough running engine once you pass the shoreline and look out at all that water.

My favorite bombing and hunting areas started around Viet Tri [*some thirty miles west-northwest of Hanoi*] and then went south straight past Hoa Binh, then west along Route 6 up to Son La [*on the Vietnamese supply line to northern Laos*]. I never went into that area that I didn't find a good target . . . and I always managed to find excellent armed reconnaissance targets after I had dropped the bombs. When you pick an area you get to know it quite well, and you know where to look for the elusive targets. It thus becomes easier to generate a good mission. I have found as many as fifty trucks in convoy in there, I have played games with the MiGs . . . and I have hammered countless buildings and supply caches and a goodly portion of them have gone boom. This has not been completely one-sided, and I hasten to add that I have been hit three times . . . and there have been several moments of doubt as to my chances of getting out.

It was a murky gray Sunday afternoon when SAM hit me just to the east of Hoa Binh. I am very pleased to be a member of that exclusive club of aviators who have been hit by a SAM and lived to tell about it, and I have to admit that it is quite a sensation.

COMING BACK

Lieutenant Richard Wyman, USN
Fighter Squadron VF-162
Aircraft Carrier *Oriskany*, Yankee Station, July 1966
On July 12, 1966, I flew my first strike over the beach. Jesus, what a day! There were twenty-four planes in the strike group. Four of us were from Squadron 162—Bellinger, me, Butch Verich and Rick Adams. I was flying Bellinger's wing. We went north and cut back down to Haiphong. Like I say, this was my first hop and I got permanent wrinkles around my eyes from widening them so much. I was expecting and not seeing. My head was on a swivel. The theory was, in those days, that if they shot missiles, you got as low as possible, in order to defeat them. That was the theory. You tried to grab the dirt. Somebody called, "SAMs!" and we all dove for the deck. There were twenty-four airplanes trying to fit into a small valley at five hundred knots apiece, fifty feet off the ground. Talk about wild—that was all the wildness a person could stand. You had the probability of a midair collision, of hitting the ground, or of getting shot down.

When we got to the far side of the valley, Rick took a hit. That's why the following year the theory changed completely on how to fight the missiles. If you went down low to evade the SAMs, then the antiaircraft fire got you. Anyway, Rick took a hit and Butch Verich, who was always polite, was saying, "You gotta jump, Rick, you gotta jump. Your whole wing's on fire."

Rick was saying, "Negative, I'm not getting out of this thing until it quits flying." And he didn't. I saw him as he cleared a ridge. His plane was a ball of flames. Suddenly out he went. . . . I saw his parachute hanging on a tree. Bellinger didn't know where Rick was, and Butch Verich was having trouble directing the [*propeller-driven A-1E*] Spads that came to fly cover for the rescue helicopter. . . . I took them to where he was. "Dip your wing and Rick is right below you." I was so busy trying to help Rick that I forgot to check my gas gauge. I looked up and saw I was about to run out. I . . . went up to plug into the tanker, then returned to the ship. The squadron crowded around Rick on the flight deck when he returned. It was like a family reunion. He was the first pilot to be shot down twice over the beach and rescued.

THE DEFENDERS

Lieutenant Nguyen Van Thanh
Vietnam People's Army Air Defense Forces
August 19, 1968
[*This was*] the worst day for my unit. . . . I was commanding a battery that was providing air defense to a supply area. We had fifty-two men on duty. At [*9 a.m.*] we were attacked by F-4Hs and F-105s. By the time it was over forty of my battery personnel were dead, including two platoon leaders and the company executive officer. The political officer and I were both wounded and three of our four guns were knocked out.

My battery had been deployed right at the center of the attack and we had taken all the fire. The 26th Battery, which was one of my flanks, had seven killed. The 38th Battery was at my rear. They had one killed and three wounded. The 27th off to the east took five wounded.

The guys commanding these batteries had been playing tricks. In principle, the moment battalion gave orders, we were all supposed to open fire. . . . But the other companies had withheld their fire for a couple of seconds. With that kind of delay, the target might have been out of sight. If you delayed just one or two seconds, you could conceal your position. The unit that opened fire first would be pinpointed. Of course the other units would be identified as well, but they wouldn't be considered the main objectives. . . .

I complained about this to the battalion officers, but all I got out of it was a reprimand for "lack of vigilance in leadership." I was lucky I wasn't subjected to disciplinary action. Battalion didn't realize what was going on. From then on I used the same tricks myself.

THE UNFORGIVING SKY

Major Walter McDonald, USAF
unit unknown
Vietnam [Cam Ranh Bay?], 1969–1970

The thirty-five-year-old McDonald had been teaching at the Air Force Academy for some time when he took his turn in Vietnam. With more than a decade in the cockpit, the major knew his trade—and he had taken time on the side to earn a doctorate in English, which led him to become a poet. His poem "Flight Orders" reminds us that a host of realities determined survival in the air war. Major McDonald went back to the Air Force Academy following his Vietnam service and went on to teach at Texas Tech University. He was Poet Laureate of Texas in 2001.

Flight Orders

It
has come, the
pledge
of all uniforms,
the
flat spin no
jet
can rudder out
of, suction down with
no
operative ejection seat.
War.

A FIGHTER PILOT REMEMBERS

Major Edward Rasimus, USAF
469th Tactical Fighter Squadron, 388th Tactical Fighter Wing
Korat, Thailand, 1966 and 1972
Ed Rasimus did his first combat tour in 1966, flying an F-105 out of Thailand at the height of the Rolling Thunder campaign. After completing a hundred missions, he went home and worked in Air Force training and staff jobs. Rasimus volunteered for a second Southeast Asia tour and went on a waiting list. Rolling Thunder had ended in November 1968, and though the air war over Laos accelerated, budgetary constraints steadily reduced the flights (sorties) permitted, hence the number of pilots required. Rasimus here reflects on the air war as a whole.

When the air war started, no one thought it would last indefinitely. Certainly no one could have overlaid a series of starts and stops linking American political campaigns to the application of tactical air power. In 1965, '66, and '67, we went to North Vietnam delivering good capitalist iron on the evil communists and suffering incredible losses. It was bearable because we knew our leadership sought victory and the American people supported us. But by 1968, it had become apparent that election victory . . . on the home front was more important than victory in the war in Southeast Asia. That's when President Lyndon Johnson added one more stop to the sequence and announced an indefinite cessation of the air campaign. . . .

From 1968 until the spring of 1972, we entered a period that Robert E. Lee couldn't have begun to comprehend. We weren't there to win and we didn't seem to want to lose. Fighter pilots went because it was the thing to do. It had become a career move, absolutely required for promotion and conferring the authority to swagger and pontificate to others who either had not yet been to the war or had been earlier. A culture of combat grew that leaned much more toward the fondness for war than the need to aggressively pursue victory. We fought to fight, and with the most deadly targets suspended, it became simply a routine excursion expected of those who wore wings. . . . [T]he fighter pilots in Thailand built a fantasized reality around the machismo of it.

Thailand became a place for those who hadn't made the cut as fighter pilots when they graduated from pilot training to get quickly credentialed. Bomber drivers and trash-haulers, training commandoes and desk jockeys went through the pipeline that turned them into instant heroes. The catch was that the war had become institutionalized. It simply droned on, and, with any real objectives gone, the daily pattern became finding a use for the sorties, with the rest of the day dedicated to designing new ways to demonstrate that somehow those assigned to fly fighters were special.

THE NAVY INTEGRATES

Lieutenant Commander William S. Norman, USN
Carrier Division Three combat warfare officer
Yankee Station, September 1969–June 1970
It was one of those long nights on watch. In the combat operations room. Carrier Division 3. The command ship. On Yankee Station. In the South China Sea. In 1970. In the middle of the war.

I was directing aircraft. Giving orders. Whatever you are supposed to do militarily. I was doing . . . and doing it well. But at that point I decided to get out of the Navy.

I was not frustrated by the war as much as I was . . . by the role of blacks in the Navy. . . . I wasn't really certain by then that our best vital interests were being served by the war effort. Yet the Navy was asking black people to take part in a war while subjecting them to institutional racism—institutional racism intentionally.

You could go aboard a carrier with 5,000 people, and you would find the overwhelming majority of the blacks in the lowest level in jobs, in the dirtiest jobs, down in the laundry room, down in the bowels of the ship. You walk into the areas where I work with all the sophisticated computers, and it would look as if there were no blacks on the entire ship.

The commander of the carrier division felt that I was very good, that I had been promoted to lieutenant commander early, that I had a good career, and that I, therefore, ought not to be getting out. He felt that I was being affected by a lot of the other things that were going on in Vietnam. But Vietnam was secondary to my feelings of what was happening to blacks who were a part of the war. And I didn't have the kind of disaffection . . . that would cause me to refuse to do certain things. When I gave directions I made sure they were effectively executed. . . .

Everybody knew how I felt about equal opportunity. I pushed actions on board ships. I used to write people back here and make suggestions on . . . equal opportunity. I felt that the system was set up in such a way as to per-petuate racism, and that we were not doing anything about it. Other than symbolic things like trying to recruit blacks or work with a civil rights group. But the substance was not being done.

I didn't just write an ordinary letter of resignation. Most of it had to do with improving conditions for minorities in the Navy. I felt I had an obliga-tion. My letter went through channels, and when it reached Washington, they wanted to know who it was that had written it. Of course it was embarrassing that it was done by someone who was getting out. . . .

It was perhaps fate that when I was writing the letter, we got a new Chief of Naval Operations, Admiral Elmo Zumwalt. Because of my letter we would meet and I would go to work for him. Most of the admirals opposed the changes we would make. They would call Zumwalt a nigger lover. And they would call me Zumwalt's Rasputin.

SEARCH AND RESCUE: BAT 21

Lieutenant Colonel Iceal Hambleton, USAF
Forty-Second Tactical Electronic Warfare Squadron
over the demilitarized zone, April 2–12, 1972
Efforts to recover pilots and aircrew forced to bail out of damaged aircraft, and to find and rescue those whose planes were downed, were a major aspect of aerial activity throughout the Vietnam War. Search and rescue—or SAR as it was called—helped maintain crew morale. SAR saved significant numbers of men to fight another day. Whole groups of squadrons were devoted to the

mission, and ground alert or even airborne orbiting of SAR helicopters were regularly programmed into strike planning. Specialized techniques evolved in the search-and-rescue effort, in which the extraction choppers were supported by flights of fighter-bombers, forward air controllers (FACs), gunship helicopters, and other assets.

One of the best-known rescue missions of the war occurred when Colonel Hambleton's plane, radio call sign Bat 21, was lost. Hambleton was flying an EB-66 "Destroyer" electronic countermeasures aircraft to help prevent enemy radars from tracking B-52 bombers striking the DMZ. Hambleton and his wingman, Bat 22, neutralized ten North Vietnamese SAMs before one of a flight of three missiles damaged Bat 21. Of his six-man crew, only Hambleton could eject before the aircraft exploded. The Bat 21 SAR was unusual in incorporating both ground and aerial operations, and because it took place in the midst of the considerable VPA force engaged in their offensive across the DMZ. This account is condensed from a comprehensive history of SAR by Navy air veterans George Galdorisi and Tom Phillips. The story illustrates the length to which American commanders would go to rescue airmen.

An O-2 FAC, [*First Lieutenant*] Bill Jankowski, who had seen the crash and the chute, quickly diverted a flight of A-1s who were coming off an aborted mission nearby. Within minutes they were able to blast back enemy forces closing in on Hambleton's position, while Jankowski broadcast for emergency support. None of the participants was fully aware of the strength of the invasion, and rescue forces at first operated as if it was another "normal" SAR.

The call was monitored by the operations officer of the U.S. Army's 8th Cavalry, Troop F, [*Captain*] Thomas White, who quickly organized already-airborne assets to respond. . . . White assigned [*Captain*] Mike Rosebeary, in Blueghost 28, to take his fire team and escort Blueghost 39, a UH-1H Huey "slick," to the scene of the SAR. He then assigned Blueghost 30, another slick, to join the group. Rosebeary peeled off his Cobra wingman, Warrant Officer George Ezell, to . . . escort the straggling Huey while he and Blueghost 39, piloted by [*First Lieutenant*] Byron Kulland and Warrant Officer John Frink, continued.

They approached the area as it began to get dark, with Kulland down on the deck at fifty feet and Rosebeary behind and, at three hundred feet, in position for top cover. . . . Both helicopters began to take heavy fire, and the Cobra responded with rickets and 40mm. . . . Rosebeary was unable to suppress [*the enemy fire*] and both birds immediately began to take hits. He called for Blueghost to . . . leave the area. His canopy was stitched and shattered, and other vital components were damaged. Equipment began to fail, and he turned away, still taking hits as he watched Blueghost 39 go down in a controlled crash-landing, remaining right side up. Rosebeary ordered the other two helicopters to stay south of the river, and limped his failing helicopter away.

[*Captain Rosebeary also crash-landed, but was recovered by an HH-53 "Jolly Green Giant." Kulland's crew, most wounded, were immediately assailed by enemy troops, who fired until the slick exploded. One American, the door gunner, was captured; the others went missing. FACs plotted Hambleton's location, and at first light strike planes came to keep the enemy at bay.*]

With full daylight next morning, a break in the cloud cover allowed two Jollys from the 37th [*Air Rescue and Recovery Squadron*] to attempt an approach for pick-up. The first, an HH-53, Jolly Green 65, was commanded by an exchange officer, [*Lieutenant Commander*] Joseph Crowe, U.S. Coast Guard. He and his crew started in low and fast. They found themselves racing . . . over columns of men, trucks, and tanks, and [*encountered a*] blizzard of hostile fire, more intense than anything Crowe had ever seen. His helicopter shredded with hits and severely damaged, Crowe pulled away. . . . Jolly Green 66 then tried it, breaking through the clouds right over the top of ten North Vietnamese tanks. He took a savage crossfire as he cleared the area, with his gunners engaging targets on all sides.

[*The pilot had to break off a bare hundred yards from the downed Hambleton. Meanwhile Crowe barely managed to nurse his chopper to a safe landing at Phu Bai—with damaged tail rotor controls, a wrecked gyrocompass, busted instruments, and rapidly failing hydraulics. Later that day the FAC orbiting Hambleton was engaged by a SAM—possibly the first time a U.S. tactical aircraft over South Vietnam had faced an SA-2. Two more aircrew went down, though only Lieutenant Mark Clark survived. The air over the DMZ proved extremely hazardous. That day eight of ten A-1 fighter-bombers trying to drop the Cam Lo River bridge were damaged. Colonel Hambleton actually directed those strikes. Then weather closed in and made rescue efforts completely impossible for two days.*]

The morning of . . . April 6 dawned bright and clear, and strikes resumed, with another forty-two sorties flown delivering ordnance around Hambleton and Clark [*the downed FAC copilot*]. By mid-afternoon another rescue task force had assembled, consisting of four Jollys, six Sandys [*A-1 fighter-bombers*], two FACs, and other support aircraft. The . . . forward air controllers, [*Captains*] Harold Icke (Bilk 11) and Gary Ferentchak (Nail 59) had just completed planned strikes when Sandy 1, [*Captain*] Fred Boli, established the Jollys in holding while he went trolling for hostile fire. He spent thirty minutes flying the ingress route for the helicopters, strafing anything that looked suspicious, and getting no reaction. . . . Once Boli had relocated the two downed men, he . . . went out to holding orbit to brief the plan. But the meeting was scattered by a SAM call, which sent all their aircraft diving for the deck. Ominously, there was no accompanying AAA. Something was fishy; SAMs were *never* left unprotected.

[*Jolly 67 tried the recovery run and was smashed by a hail of North Vietnamese fire. The tail rotor broke up, debris wrecked the front one, and the ship crashed in flames near Hambleton and Clark. All six aboard were lost. Hambleton wept for the brave airmen who had tried to reach him. Aerial operations were called off. Yet another FAC was downed on April 7, leaving another American survivor, Bruce Walker. Three men were now trapped behind enemy lines. The area had to be considered too dangerous for choppers. Meanwhile, an exclusion circle of seventeen miles in radius, created to prevent bombs from killing the Americans, became extremely controversial, since it restricted air support for desperate ARVN troops. General Abrams ordered termination of aerial SAR attempts.*]

The Joint Personnel Recovery Center (JPRC) enlisted the support of a U.S. Navy SEAL, [*Lieutenant*] Tom Norris, who had been working for the Naval Advisory Group and with South Vietnamese LDNN, the [*Vietnamese*] version of SEALs. He organized a team of five LDNN to go with him. Their plan was to go up the Song Cam Lo and meet the three Americans . . . who would float down the river.

Norris and his team arrived at an ARVN outpost on the Song Cam Lo on April 10, 1972, and patrolled two kilometers up the river bank that night, passing enemy troops, tanks, and trucks. Clark, who had been in hiding next to the river, entered the stream and floated right past the SEAL team, but was not noticed until he had gone by. Norris slipped into the chilly river and worked to overtake Clark, finally catching up with him at dawn the next morning. They were able to get Clark to safety without further incident. Getting Hambleton would not be so easy. First, the airman would have to reach the river through a jungle alive with the enemy.

The attempt to rescue Hambleton was to be the next night, April 11, but two of the LDNN were wounded in an artillery attack . . . while the team was awaiting darkness. Norris went ahead with just the three remaining men, but their departure was delayed a day. . . . The array of enemy soldiers and equipment so unnerved two of the Vietnamese with Norris that he had to discontinue the patrol.

The next night, Norris and one Vietnamese, Petty Officer Nguyen Van Kiet, set out. . . . They discovered a sampan . . . and used it to [*paddle*] up the river to the Cam Lo Bridge and then worked their way back . . . searching for Hambleton. Finally finding him, they placed the near delirious man in the bottom of the boat and silently stole down the river through the heart of an enemy army. Radioing that they had Hambleton, Norris arranged to have aircraft to stand by to assist as daylight exposed them. . . . Suddenly, the shouts of North Vietnamese soldiers announced that their disguise was no longer effective, and the two men paddled furiously, assisted by the strong current in a race for their lives. Calling for help, a providential smoke screen, laid by a Johnny-on-the-spot aircraft, shielded them from view, and they used it to continue on, finally nearing the friendly outpost. In broad daylight now, North Vietnamese lined the north bank of the river, firing at the boat, while South Vietnamese on the south bank returned . . . fire. Beaching the sampan . . . Norris and Kiet carried Hambleton, who was no longer able to walk, up the slope to the outpost bunkers, assisted by willing ARVN hands. [*Lieutenant Walker tried to reach the coast for a pickup there, but on April 18 he died in a shoot-out with North Vietnamese troops.*]

LINEBACKER I

Major Edward Rasimus, USAF
469th Tactical Fighter Squadron, 388th Tactical Fighter Wing
Korat, Thailand, April 1972
Returning in the spring of 1972, Major Rasimus found the Korat base much the same as when he left it. But some things were different. Among them was his aircraft—Rasimus now flew the F-4E Phantom in place of the F-105s of his earlier tour. The F-105s themselves, now styled "Wild Weasels," functioned as electronic warfare platforms rather than as the fighter interceptors and bombers they had been when Rasimus flew them on his 1966 tour. The F-4E itself had on-board computers far superior to anything in the old F-105. Most important, bombing North Vietnam had resumed in Operation Linebacker, a Nixon administration response to the Easter Offensive.
My reintroduction to combat . . . was a good, old-fashioned two-ship [*mission*] loaded with Mk-82, 500-pound dumb bombs, assigned to attack a "suspected truck park" about five miles from the long-destroyed runway at Dong Hoi in the . . . panhandle of North Vietnam. Six years and two months earlier, I flew my first combat mission to virtually the same place. Maybe technology wasn't winning the war all that fast.

[*As an experienced pilot, though with no combat flight time in the E-model F-4, Rasimus got experienced colleagues as flight leader—"Oak"—and for his weapons system officer. They left Korat, refueled in the air, and made for the target.*] In a matter of minutes we're within sight of the coast. The deep blue water of the gulf, the white sand of the beaches, and the vibrant green of the jungle paint a beautiful picture of an Asian tropical paradise disrupted by the bomb craters that pockmark the coastal plains. The runway at Dong Hoi is clearly visible, a mile of decrepit asphalt that's been bombed and repaired repeatedly since the French occupation. . . . [*Oak*] begins walking me through the switch setup to drop our first pair of bombs. He reminds me that I've agreed to try dive toss, and he explains once more that all I have to do is let him lock the radar onto the ground return when we roll in, then put the pipper [*indicator*] on the ground target and hold the [*release*] button down as I make a wings-level pulloff. The bombs will come off when the computer decides that the time is right.

Oak lead repeats the briefing we went through at Korat: "Okay, Oak, the target area is about two miles inland from the north end of the runway. Take spacing for left hand roll-ins and we'll make multiple passes. I'll be rolling in from the north in about twenty seconds." I ease up on the left turn we've been in and allow the lead aircraft to drift away from me. If I've got to do this dive-toss business, I'm going to give the system a challenge. It won't be easy to make me a believer. [*Rasimus makes what he expects is a poor "dive-bombing" pass, never descending below fifteen thousand feet.*] I look back at the smoke from lead's bombs and then watch as my pair impacts precisely on the southern edge of the smoke. It's exactly where I had the pipper. The bombs aren't short, they aren't blown by the wind, they're on target. It's like magic!

BACK TO HAIPHONG

Commander Richard A. Bordone, USN
Carrier Air Group Three
Aircraft Carrier *Saratoga*, Yankee Station, July 31, 1972
The Seventh Fleet, reinforced with additional aircraft carriers, fought hard in Linebacker. There is actually no good account of this, for there are few Vietnam naval aviation memoirs. The Navy completed its official war history, which hardly extends past the first retaliatory bombings of 1965, much less takes in Rolling Thunder, *the bombing of Laos, or the 1972 fighting. Fortunately there are some excellent works by journalists or historians, among them this one by Carol Reardon, who set out to detail the efforts of a single naval air squadron, specifically in the 1972 climax. Naval Attack Squadron Seventy-Five (VA-75) flew from the carrier* Saratoga. *It began a second deployment "on the line" at Yankee Station in July, and soon there were plans for alpha strikes, major aerial assaults in fulfillment of Linebacker objectives.*
The alpha strikes of 30 July served as a warm-up for a so-called "super alpha" scheduled for 31 July. The target, Haiphong Shipyard Number 3, now appeared on the target list for the first time since the Joint Chiefs of Staff had declared it off limits in 1967. The reasons for the boatworks' previously protected status seemed clear enough. Even though a legitimate military target, the shipyard lay near the population center of the city of Haiphong, close to

civilian hospitals, a temple, and, possibly, a POW camp. Thus, even in mid-1972, planners viewed this as a "point target" only, one that demanded great skill and precision to hit. They evaluated many targets within the shipyard that might be attacked by individual aircraft or a section of three or four planes, but they focused on a sawmill, three graving docks, a marine railway with cradle, four floating piers, and a floating drydock.

[*Commander*] Robert R. Cowles of VF-103 led the planning group for this strike, Ultimately, the final design called for forty aircraft, including five A-6As [*all-weather attack aircraft*] and both of VA-75's A-6Bs. Three A-6As led by [*Commander*] Earnest and [*Lieutenant Commander*] Pieno headed up one of the two elements that composed the main strike force. Redshirts hung five Mk84s—2,000-pound bombs—on each of these three A-6As.

VA-75's two other A-6As received a special tasking. Since the Haiphong shipyard enjoyed strong protection . . . the planners decided to use the two aircraft to surprise the enemy. . . . About thirty nautical miles from the target, [*air group commander*] Bordone and [*Lieutenant Commander*] Jackson in one plane, along with [*Lieutenant Commander*] Graustein and [*Lieutenant*] Mullins in the other, planned to ingress at very low altitude—fifty feet or lower. A few minutes before the rest of the strike force rolled in on their targets . . . these two aircraft [*would*] press their low-level attack, each dropping eighteen specially-fused Mk82 [*delayed-action*] bombs. If all went as designed, these two aircraft would fly a south-to-north path, release . . . and egress quickly. Then, in the chaos caused by the initial run, the two main attack elements would begin their runs from 15,000 feet, one from east-to-west, the other from west-northwest to the east. The planners hoped that the three-pronged, high-low, multiple roll-in, coordinated attack would so completely confuse the air defenders that all crews could drop their ordnance on target and egress safely. The plan required precision in both targeting and timing.

On 31 July the strike group—reduced from forty planes to twenty-six, partly due to aircraft availability problems—launched and rendezvoused as planned. The two A-6As assigned to make the low-level run . . . detached from the main group as scheduled, going feet dry at fifty feet and 420 knots. Then, Murphy's Law took over. As [*Lieutenant Commander*] Jackson navigated to the target, he discovered that his planning map and the visual clues from the ground did not match up. He was unable to get a navigational update from his computer, using heading and time and distance to navigate. He gave Bordone a heading change based on "where I thought we were." Jackson's course change took them away from their target.

By the time Bordone and Jackson discovered the error and got back to the correct heading, the two high-altitude strike groups had arrived. . . . Indeed, as Jackson recalled, "they could see us quite clearly down there on the ground and saw that we were well left of the target." The high flyers could not continue to orbit at 12,000 to 14,000 feet in the SAM envelope until the two low-altitude planes arrived and made their . . . run. Radar-guided AAA fire already probed the airspace around them. And [*Lieutenant, Junior Grade*] Swigart, flying with [*Lieutenant*] Cook, watched a series of black puffs rapidly closing in on their aircraft. A few SAMs now streaked through the skies too, one cutting through the narrow airspace separating [*Commander*] Earnest's aircraft from [*Lieutenant*] John Miller and [*Lieutenant, Junior Grade*] Sanford on his wing. The missile did not detonate. The two attack elements waited no longer. The sudden release from the pylons of five 2,000-pound bombs, and the absence of . . . drag, created three "slick" A-6As, and Swigart recalled the egress from Haiphong as "near supersonic."

Once the high-altitude elements began their bombing runs, [*air group commander*] Bordone's low element had no choice but to stay out of the way. They made a wide turn west of town and circled back . . . watching the action. When Bordone and Graustein finally began their own runs, dust, smoke, and fire so completely obscured the area that the two A-6As abandoned their original plan to drop their ordnance at fifty feet and [*released*] instead at a more reasonable two hundred feet. As they pulled off the target, Bordone and Jackson discovered that five of their eighteen Mk82s had not released.

Officially, of course, the strike was declared a major success. The airwing's annual command history noted that the strike on Haiphong Shipyard Number 3 "marked the first attempt at a strike tactic that was to prove highly effective during the remainder of combat operations."

LINEBACKER II: ON THE DEFENSE

Captain Dinh Huu Than
Forty-Fifth Company, 291st Radar Regiment, Vietnam People's Army Air Defense Corps
Nghe An, North Vietnam, December 18, 1972
The Americans' Linebacker raids went on through the summer and into the fall. In October and November there was a pause when it seemed as if Washington and Hanoi were about to sign a cease-fire agreement. But the Saigon government, which had been cut out of the secret negotiations, objected to a number of provisions in the draft, and then the Nixon administration failed to obtain Hanoi's approval of revisions. In an effort both to reassure Saigon and to compel Hanoi, the Nixon administration ordered Linebacker II, a bombing specifically aimed at the Hanoi-Haiphong sector, using the huge B-52 bombers plus other aircraft. Captain Than led a radar unit as some of the American B-52s flew through the

night toward Hanoi. Than's was one of thirty-six early-warning radars in the
first layer of North Vietnam's defensive system.

His crew were hunched over the scope of their Soviet-made P-12 radar watching as the line of radar returns came into view, returns that had first been detected an hour earlier by Company 16 of the same regiment and had been passed on to [*Than*]. The radar images were proceeding north in a stately procession up the Mekong River . . . surrounded by heavy electronic jamming. From the jamming patterns Dinh knew that the returns . . . were B-52s. The 45th's radar operators had seen B-52 radar returns many times before but never in this number, and they watched transfixed as [*the incoming strike*] moved up to Point 300, the point where the B-52s normally turned west to bomb targets in Laos' Plain of Jars or east [*for*] targets in the North Vietnamese panhandle.

But tonight the B-52s moved past Point 300 and continued north and [*Than*] suddenly realized they were following a course that many U.S. aircraft used when they were attacking Hanoi. He watched the returns for a few seconds longer, then, at 7:15 in the evening, Hanoi time, he sent a message. . . . "Large numbers of B-52s have flown past Point 300. B-52s appear to be on a course for Hanoi."

The regiment quickly forwarded the message to the Air Defense Command Headquarters in Hanoi. There was a delay of a few moments then a response, almost unbelieving. "Are you certain? Comrade, do you maintain that the B-52s are striking Hanoi?"

Dinh repeated the message.

The word of the incoming raid was passed to the General Staff, who proceeded to their bunkers. The [*defense minister*], General Vo Nguyen Giap, told the Air Defense Headquarters to inform him every five minutes of the progress of the raid.

ABOARD LILAC 01

Major Billy Lyons, USAF
Forty-Third Strategic Wing
Anderson Air Force Base, Guam, December 18, 1972
The B-52 strikes at and around Hanoi would go on for eleven days, with a
twenty-four-hour pause at Christmas, and they have become known as the
"Christmas Bombing." The big bombers, familiarly known as "Buffs"—for big
ugly fat fuckers—flew partly from the island of Guam in the Pacific and partly
from the Royal Thai Air Base at Utapao. Major Lyons's plane was a B-52D air-
craft of Colonel James R. McCarthy's Forty-Third Wing from Guam. The wing

had been reconstituted in 1970 for the Arc Light mission after a decade during which crews set a number of aeronautical records flying supersonic B-58s for the Strategic Air Command. Many B-52Ds had been modified to maximize bomb capacity. On this night the Utapao B-52 leader, Colonel Bill Brown, headed the initial wave from the copilot's seat in the first "serial," or group of bombers. Major Lyons, call sign "Lilac 01," was flight leader of the second serial. One of his B-52s would be among the first Buffs damaged in the Christmas Bombing.

At the aircraft, the survival gear, radios, and weapons were checked and double-checked. Our crew chiefs and ground-support specialists knew that something big was in the air. . . . After take-off there was time to think about the mission—we were flying the first B-52 raid on Hanoi. Although we would penetrate far more known SAM sites than our crew did at Vinh, and be exposed to more MIG fighters, I had a great feeling of confidence that we would successfully accomplish our mission. . . . [W]e flew across the northern part of South Vietnam and rendezvoused with the wave from Utapao exactly on schedule. From this point we turned northwest and flew up the eastern portion of Laos before heading into North Vietnam. . . . It was night by this time. . . .

The sight as we turned over the [*initial point*] inbound to our target is one I'll never forget. The red rotating beacons of the three-ship cell . . . ahead of us stood out vividly against the dark night. We were entering the area of known SAM sites, and we started [*to see*] SAMs being fired at our wave. The F-111s were hitting the airfields, and our radar sites were picking up and informing us of the MIGs as they launched to engage. . . . The calls of visual SAM site guidance-radar lock-ons from our electronic warfare officer were almost constant now. The weather . . . was overcast with low clouds, and we could see the bright glow through the clouds of SAMs being launched on either side of our bomb run track. After the bright glow of the launch, the SAM would punch through the clouds and could be detected as a small, bright, pencil point of light as it approached. . . . Closer to the target area, a break in the clouds afforded us a view of the intense [*AAA*] fire that was being thrown up . . . over Hanoi. If you could take the largest Fourth of July fireworks display, and multiply it one million times, you would have an idea of the scene. . . .

ENGAGING THE ENEMY

Captain Nguyen Van Phiet
Fifty-Seventh Battalion, 261st Anti-Aircraft Regiment, Vietnam People's
Army Air Defense Forces
Hanoi, December 18, 1972

Captain Phiet had been fighting American airplanes since 1967 and had risen to command his SAM battalion. In all his years of combat, he had never seen anything like this.

All the radar screens were buried in a jamming curtain of bright, white fog. The screen of the guidance officer and the tracking operators showed many dark green stripes slanted together, changing at abnormal speeds, one strobe overriding and mixing with another, this stripe joining that one and splitting away. After that hundreds and thousands of bright dots specked the screens like bunches of target blips moving sluggishly. With all that mass confusion coupled with constantly blinking signals like a downpour of rain, how were we expected to distinguish between fighter jamming and bomber jamming, or which was EB-66 jamming and which was the passive type metallic chaff strewn across the sky by F-4s?

Major Billy Lyons

The SAM firings, although numerous, and in many cases in salvos of four at a time, had not presented a direct threat to our aircraft until about two minutes before bomb release. Suddenly my copilot yelled, "Break left!". . . . I knew he had a real reason for wanting me to break left. I rolled into a tight fifty-degree left bank and was able to move the aircraft just enough so that two SAMs headed directly at us . . . missed. . . . After the SAMs passed by and exploded harmlessly some four or five thousand feet above our aircraft, I quickly returned . . . to our original heading while asking the radar navigator how our position was for release. The navigator and radar navigator downstairs seemed remarkably calm. . . . Things were hectic after release as we broke to the west to head back to Laos. During the turn we were fired upon by several salvos of four SAMs at a time. Just as we would break in one direction to avoid a salvo, another firing . . . would come from the other side. The gunner who rides in the tail of the D-model was invaluable in directing our evasive action. . . . He also reported that our number three aircraft in the cell didn't make the post target turn to the west . . . but had continued south. [*Lyons learned later that* Lilac 03 *had been damaged and went for an emergency landing at Utapao. The other planes reached Guam after fifteen and a half hours in the air.*]

THE ADVERSARY

Brigadier General Nguyen Quang Bich
Air Defense Headquarters, Vietnam People's Army Air Defense Forces
Hanoi, December 19, 1972

General Giap supervised the defense quite closely. Not only did he demand frequent reports, the Combat Operations Department of the General Staff reached out for information and to convey orders. General Bich of the defense forces was the focal point of these contacts. But as the bombing began to extend over days, the North Vietnamese made changes. General Van Tien Dung, chief of the General Staff, issued orders to concentrate the available assets and placed his deputy, Phung The Tai, in charge of the air force, the parent service of the air defense troops. The practice of inserting a high command representative to supervise field officers is something Hanoi often did during the war

The hub of the Air Defense Headquarters was an amphitheater dominated by a large transparent plastic map with an overlay of grid squares where information about the incoming strikes was posted. On one side of this transparent map sat the air defense staff with telephones to the various units. On the other side . . . were plotters. As the raid moved the changing position was called out . . . and they marked progress . . . on the map, writing the information backwards so it could be read by the air defense staff. . . . [W]hile the system was well-organized and covered the country, it was a manual system that had difficulty coping with multiple raids or a changing situation, and the radars were very susceptible to jamming, further complicating the problems.

The Hanoi region was the responsibility of the 361st Air Defense Division. The division had numerous radars and five antiaircraft regiments, but its heart was the three SA-2 Guideline regiments. The 261st Regiment was responsible for the area north and east of the city, while the 257th and 274th Regiments covered the south and west. The 261st and 257th had four battalions, but the newly arrived 274th had only two battalions ready for combat. The U.S. forces considered Hanoi the most heavily defended target in the world, but when Linebacker II began, the General Staff's decision to redeploy many of its missile battalions to the south earlier in the month meant there were far fewer . . . around Hanoi than there had been in 1967.

The Air Defense Headquarters alerted their missile crews that the B-52s were inbound, and the trucks that carried the missile control vans started up their noisy diesel engines to provide power to the units. In the command vans for each battalion, the commander moved his radar switch to the "power on" position and sent [*electricity*] to all parts of the system, waiting for four minutes until the system was fully powered. The Fan Song tracking radar was now in "standby," ready to go to full power in four seconds but not giving off electronic emissions that might be picked by a prowling Wild Weasel.

[*The system swung into action against the bombers. Captain Phiet's Fifty-Seventh Battalion achieved a success the first night, downing a B-52. Two others were destroyed and two damaged. On the third night, December 20–21, the air defense troops took advantage of the Americans' repeating their flight paths* and tactical formulas to score major gains, no fewer than six B-52s shot down plus another damaged (Vietnamese sources maintain seven B-52s were destroyed that night). American commanders modified their tactics to minimize time over target, vary approaches, and reduce aircraft exposure to the defenses. During the rest of the Christmas campaign, only a half dozen additional Buffs were lost, one of them to a North Vietnamese pilot's deliberate aerial collision. The bombing ended on New Year's Eve. North Vietnam returned to the negotiating table. A Vietnam cease-fire was signed at Paris on January 27, 1973. The rest is history.]

Sources

We are grateful for permission to excerpt material from the following sources, listed in order of first appearance:

Year of the Horse–Vietnam: 1st Air Cav in the Highlands by Kenneth D. Mertel, copyright © 1989 by Kenneth D. Mertel. Used by permission of Bantam Books, a division of Random House, Inc.

Delta Force by Col. Charlie A. Beckwith (Ret.) and Donald Knox. Copyright © 1983 by Charles A. Beckwith. Epilogue © 2000 by C.A. Mobley. Reprinted by permission of HarperCollins Publishers.

We Were Soldiers Once . . . And Young by Lt. General H.G. Moore and Joseph L. Galloway, copyright © 1992 by Lt. General H.G. Moore and Joseph L. Galloway. Used by permission of Random House, Inc.

Chickenhawk by Robert Mason, copyright © 1983 by Robert Mason. Used by permission of Viking Penguin, a division of Penguin Group (USA) Inc.

Ron Steinman, *The Soldier's Story: Vietnam in Their Own Words.* New York: TV Books, 2000.

Reprinted with permission of Simon & Schuster, Inc., from *About Face: The Odyssey of an American Warrior* by Colonel David H. Hackworth and Julie Sherman. Copyright © 1989 by David Hackworth and Julie Sherman. All rights reserved.

Baptism by Larry Gwin, copyright © 1999 by Larry Gwin. Used by permission of Ballantine Books, a division of Random House, Inc.

S. L. A. Marshall, *West to Cambodia.* Nashville: Battery Press, 1984. Reprinted with permission of the publisher.

Battle for the Central Highlands by George E. Dooley, copyright © 2000 by George E. Dooley. Used by permission of Ballantine Books, a division of Random House, Inc.

John Ketwig, *. . . and a hard rain fell.* New York: Macmillan, 1985. Reprinted with permission from the author.

William C. Haponski, *One Hell of a Ride: Inside an Armored Cavalry Task Force in Vietnam.* Copyright © 2009. Reprinted with permission of the author.

Robert Tonsetic, *Forsaken Warriors: The Story of an American Advisor with the South Vietnamese Rangers and Airborne.* Havertown: Casemate Publishing, 2009. Reprinted with permission of the publisher.

Capt. Roger H.C. Donlon, *Beyond Nam Dong.* Leavenworth: R and N Publishers, 1998.

A Rumor of War by Philip Caputo. Copyright © 1977, 1996 by Philip Caputo. Reprinted by permission of Henry Holt and Company, LLC.

Otto Lehrack, *The First Battle: Operation Starlight and the Beginning of the Blood Debt in Vietnam.* New York: Ballantine Books, 2006.

Utter's Battalion by Alex Lee, Lt. Col. USMC, copyright © 2000 by Alex Lee. Used by permission of Ballantine Books, a division of Random House, Inc.

William Van Zanten, *Don't Bunch Up: One Marine's Story.* New York: Presidio Press, 2007. Reprinted with permission of the author.

William Broyles, Jr., *Brothers in Arms: A Journey from War to Peace.* New York: Knopf, 1986.

Reprinted with the permission of Simon & Schuster, Inc. from *The Village* by Bing West. Copyright © 1972 F.J. West, Jr.; copyright renewed 200 F.J. West, Jr.

William R. Corson, *The Betrayal.* New York: W. W. Norton & Company, 1968.

Bronson P. Clark, *Not By Might: A Viet Nam Memoir.* Chapel Rock Publishing, 1997.

Not Going Home Alone by James J. Kirschke, copyright © 2001 by James J. Kirschke. Used by permission of Ivy Books, a division of Random House, Inc.

Never Without Heroes by Lawrence C. Vetter, Jr., copyright © 1996 by Lawrence C. Vetter, Jr. Used by permission of Ivy Books, a division of Random House Inc.

Jim Brown, *Impact Zone: The Battle of the DMZ in Viet Nam.* Tuscaloosa: The University of Alabama Press, 2004. Reprinted with permission of the publisher.

James P. Coan, *Con Thien: The Hill of Angels.* Tuscaloosa: The University of Alabama Press, 2004. Reprinted with permission of the publisher.

Pathfinder: First In, Last Out by Richard R. Burns, copyright © 2002 by Cathy Burns. Used by permission of Ballantine Books, a division of Random House, Inc.

Bruce Davies, selection from *The Battle of Ngok Tavak: Allied Valor and Defeat in Vietnam.* Copyright © 2009 Texas Tech University Press. Reprinted by permission of Texas Tech University Press.

Masters of the Art by Ronald E. Winter, copyright © 1989, 2005 by Ronald E. Winter. Used by permission of The Ballantine Publishing Group, a division of Random House, Inc.

My American Journey by Colin Powell with Joseph E. Perisco, copyright © 1995 by Colin L. Powell. Used by permission of Random House, Inc.

Roger S. Hayes, *On Point: A Rifleman's Year in the Boonies: Vietnam 1967–1968.* New York: Presidio Press, 2000.

David Fitz-Eng, *Why A Soldier? A Signal Corpsman's Tour from Vietnam to the Moscow Hotline.* New York: Ballantine Books, 1995.

Claude D. Newby, *It Took Heroes: A Cavalry Chaplain's Memoir of Vietnam.* New York: Ballantine, 2003. Reprinted with permission of the author.

Papa Bravo Romeo by Wynn Goldsmith, copyright © 2001 by Wynn Goldsmith. Used by permission of Ballantine Books, a division of Random House, Inc.

Lynda Van Devanter, *Home Before Morning: The Story of an Army Nurse in Vietnam*. Amherst: University of Massachusetts Press, 2001.

From Classrooms to Claymores by Ches Schneider, copyright © 1999 by Ches Schneider. Used by permission of Ivy Books, a division of Random House, Inc.

Mike Jackson and Tara Dixon-Engel, *Naked in Da Nang: A Forward Air Controller in Vietnam*. Minneapolis: Zenith Press, 2004.

My Detachment: A Memoir by Tracy Kidder, copyright © 2005 by John Tracy Kidder. Used by permission of Random House, Inc.

By Duty Bound by Ezell Ware, Jr. and Joel Engel, copyright © 2005 by Ezell Ware, Jr. & Joel Engel. Used by permission of Dutton, a division of Penguin Group (USA) Inc.

Larry Rottman, Jan Barry and Basil T. Paquet, eds., *Winning Hearts and Minds: War Poems by Vietnam Veterans*. New York: McGraw-Hill, 1972.

W. D. Ehrhart, *Passing Time: Memoir of a Vietnam Veteran Against the War*. Amherst: University of Massachusetts Press, 1995.

War Paint by Bill Goshen, copyright © 2001 by Bill Goshen. Used by permission of Ballantine Books, a division of Random House, Inc.

Richard Stacewicz, *Winter Soldiers: An Oral History of the Vietnam Veterans Against the War*. Chicago: Haymarket Books, copyright © 2008 by Richard Stacewicz. Reprinted with permission of the author.

13 Cent Killers by John J. Culbertson, Foreword by Ronald J. Brown, copyright © 2003 by John J. Culbertson. Used by permission of Presidio Press, an imprint of The Ballantine Publishing Group, a division of Random House, Inc.

First Recon—Second to None by Paul R Young, copyright © 1992 by Paul R Young. Used by permission of Ballantine Books, a division of Random House, Inc.

Gone Native by Alan G. Cornett, copyright © 2000 by Alan G. Cornett. Used by permission of Ballantine Books, a division of Random House, Inc.

James W. Walker, *Fortune Favors the Bold: A British LRRP with the 101st*. New York: Ballantine Books, 1998.

The Killing Zone: My Life in the Vietnam War by Frederick Downs. Copyright © 1978 by Frederick Downs. Used by permission of W. W. Norton & Company, Inc.

Tom A. Johnson, *To the Limit: An Air Cav Huey Pilot in Vietnam*. New York: NAL Trade, 2007. Reprinted with permission of the publisher.

Chuck Carlock, *Firebirds: The Best First Person Account of Helicopter Combat in Vietnam Ever Written*. New York: Bantam Dell, 1997. Reprinted with permission of the author.

Hunting the Jackal by Billy Waugh and with Tim Keown. Copyright © 2004 by Billy Waugh. Reprinted by permission of HarperCollins Publishers.

John Prados and Ray W. Stubbe, *Valley of Decision: The Siege of Khe Sanh*. New York: Dell Publishing, a division of Random House, Inc., 1992. Reprinted with permission of the authors.

"Ditty Dum Dum Ditty" by Alan F. Farrell. Reprinted courtesy of the author.

Phantom Warriors: Book II by Gary A. Linderer, copyright © 2001 by Gary A. Linderer. Used by permission of Ballantine Books, a division of Random House, Inc.

Charles W. Sasser, *Raider: The True Story of the Legendary Soldier Who Performed More POW Raids than Any Other American in History.* New York: St. Martin's Paperbacks, 2002.

U.S. Navy Seawolves: The Elite HAL-3 Helicopter Squadron in Vietnam by Daniel E. Kelly, copyright © 2002 by Belle R. Kelly. Used by permission of Ballantine Books, a division of Random House, Inc.

Garnett Bell, "Predicting Test: Chargin' Charlie Beckwith at Bien Hoa." *Vietnam Magazine 12*, no. 5, February 2000, pp. 50–51. Reprinted with permission from Weider History Group.

Michael D. Mahler, *Ringed in Steel: Armored Cavalry, Vietnam 1967–68.* New York: Jove Books, 1998.

State Department, Saigon Embassy Cable, February 20, 1968. Printed in the *Wall Street Journal,* November 3, 1981, and November 4, 1981.

Jack Speedy, "Charlie Company to the Rescue," in *Vietnam Magazine 3*, no. 1, June 1990, p. 25.

Brenda Rosen Rodgers, "A Civilian in Tet '68." *Vietnam Magazine 9*, no. 5, February 1997, pp. 43–44. Reprinted with permission of Weider History Group.

Gerald C. Hickey, selection from *Window on a War: An Anthropologist in the Vietnam Conflict.* Copyright © 2002 Texas Tech University Press. Reprinted by permission of Texas Tech University Press.

Lam Quang Thi, *The Twenty-Five Year Century: A South Vietnamese General Remembers the Indochina War to the Fall of Saigon.* Denton: University of North Texas Press, 2000. Reprinted with permission of the publisher.

Everything We Had by Al Santoli, copyright © 1981 by Albert Santoli and Vietnam Veterans of America. Used by permission of Random House, Inc.

Andrew Wiest, with a Foreword by Jim Webb, *Vietnam's Forgotten Army: Heroism and Betrayal in the ARVN.* New York: NYU Press, 2007. Reprinted with permission of the publisher.

Inside Force Recon: Recon Marines in Vietnam by Michael Lee Lanning and Ray William Stubbe, copyright © 1989 by Michael Lee Lanning and Ray William Stubbe. Used by permission of Ivy Books, a division of Random House, Inc.

Keith Nolan, *Battle for Hue: Tet, 1968.* New York: Dell Publishing, 1985, p. 59.

J. R. Bullington, "Trapped Behind Enemy Lines." *Vietnam Magazine 11*, no. 5, February 1999, pp. 21, 22–23. Reprinted with permission from Weider History Group.

Robert Annenberg, "Firsthand Account: Intelligence Team Under Siege." *Vietnam Magazine 13*, no. 5, February 2001, pp. 38–39, 41. Reprinted with permission of Weider History Group.

Pham Van Son, ed., *The Viet Cong "Tet" Offensive (1968).* Saigon: Printing and Publications Center/Joint General Staff, RVNAF.

John J. Tolson, *Vietnam Studies: Airmobility 1961–1971.* Washington: Department of the Army, 1973.

Charles A. Krohn, *The Lost Battalion of Tet: Breakout of the 2/1 2 Cavalry at Hue.* Annapolis: Naval Institute Press, 2008. Reprinted with permission of the publisher.

John Corbett, *West Dickens Avenue: A Marine at Khe Sanh.* New York: Presidio Press, 2004.

William R. Phillips, *Night of the Silver Stars: The Battle of Khe Sanh*. New York: St. Martin's Paperbacks, 2004.

Bernard L. Cole, "A Noglow in Vietnam, 1968: Air Power at the Battle of Khe Sanh." *Journal of Military History 64*, no. 1, January 2000, pp. 154–155.

Ernest Spencer, *Welcome to Vietnam, Macho Man: Reflections of a Khe Sanh Vet*. New York: Presidio Press, 1987.

"37th Rangers," in *Red Clay*, no. 41 and from Ray William Stubbe, *Battalion of Kings*. Chicago: Khe Sanh Veterans Association, Inc. Reprinted with permission of the publisher.

W. D. Ehrhart, *Carrying the Darkness: The Poetry of the Vietnam War*. Lubbock: Texas Tech University Press, 1989.

Brig. Gen. James E. Shelton, USA (Ret.), *The Beast Was Out There: The 28th Infantry Black Lions and the Battle of Ong Thanh, Vietnam, October 1967*. Chicago: Cantigny First Division Foundation, 2002. Reprinted with permission from the publisher.

Ronald J. Glasser, *365 Days*. New York: George Braziller, Inc., 1971. Reprinted with permission of the publisher.

L. H. "Bucky" Burruss, *Mike Force*. Lincoln: iUniverse, 2001.

David L. Anderson, *Facing My Lai: Moving Beyond the Massacre*. Lawrence: University Press of Kansas, 1998. Reprinted with permission of the publisher.

Douglass H. Hubbard, *Special Agent, Vietnam: A Naval Intelligence Memoir*. New York: Potomac Books, Inc., 2006.

Ground Attack Vietnam: The Marines Who Controlled the Skies by J. M. Moriarty, copyright © 1993 by J. M. Moriarty. Used by permission of Ivy Books, a division of Random House, Inc.

Portrait of the Enemy by David Chanoff and Doan Van Toai, copyright © 1986 by David Chanoff and Doan Can Toai. Used by permission of Random House, Inc.

W. Charles Truitt, *Pop a Yellow Smoke and Other Memories! From a Combat Veteran Marine, Vietnam 1969–1970*. Copyright W. Charles Truitt, 2005. Reprinted with permission of the author.

Kregg P. Jorgenson, *Acceptable Loss: An Infantry Soldier's Perspective*. New York: Ivy Books, 1991, pp. 75, 207–216.

Orrin DeForest and David Chanoff, *Slow Burn*. New York: Pocket Books, 1991. Reprint with permission of the author.

Truong Nhu Tang with David Chanoff and Doan Van Toai, *A Viet Cong Memoir*. New York: Vintage Books, 1986.

Reprinted with the permission of Simon & Schuster, Inc. from *Secret Commandos: Behind Enemy Lines with the Elite Warriors of SOG* by John L. Plaster. Copyright © 2004 John L. Plaster.

Keith Nolan, *Ripcord: Screaming Eagles Under Siege, Vietnam, 1970*. New York: Presidio Press, 2003.

Yusef Komunyakaa, "Tunnels" from *Dien Cai Du*. Copyright © 1988 by Yusef Komunyakaa. Reprinted by permission of Wesleyan University Press.

The Price of Exit by Tom Marshall, copyright © 1998 by Tom Marshall. Used by permission of Ivy Books, a division of Random House, Inc.

Col. Robert E. Stoffey, USMC (Ret.), *Fighting to Leave: The Final Years of America's War in Vietnam, 1972–1973.* Minneapolis: Zenith Press, 2008.

Col. G. H. Turley, USMCR (Ret.), *The Easter Offensive: The Last American Advisers in Vietnam,1972.* New York: Presidio Press, 1995.

John Grider Miller, *The Bridge at Dong Ha.* Naval Institute Press, 1996.

Van Nguyen Duong, *The Tragedy of the Vietnam War: A South Vienamese Officer's Analysis.* Jefferson: McFarland & Co., Inc., 2008.

Tran Van Nhut, with Christian L. Arevian, selection from *An Loc: The Unfinished War.* Copyright © 2009 Texas Tech University Press. Reprinted by permission of Texas Tech University Press.

Lam Quang Thi, *Hell in An Loc: The 1972 Easter Invasion and the Battle that Saved South Viet Nam.* Denton: University of North Texas Press, 2011. Reprinted with permission of the publisher.

Bloods: An Oral History of the Vietnam War By Black Veterans by Wallace Terry, copyright © 1984 by Wallace Terry. Used by permission of Random House, Inc.

John Darrell Sherwood, *Afterburner: Naval Aviators and the Vietnam War.* New York: NYU Press, 2004.

Jack Broughton and Hanson Baldwin, *Thud Ridge: F-105 Thunderchief Missions over Vietnam.* Manchester, U.K.: Crécy Publishing Ltd., 2006. Reprinted with permission of the publisher.

Zalin Grant, *Over the Beach: The Air War in Vietnam.* New York: Pocket Books, 2005.

Walt McDonald, "Flight Orders" from *Caliban in Blue.* Copyright © 1976 Texas Tech University Press. Reprinted by permission of Texas Tech University Press.

Ed Rasimus, *Palace Cobra: A Fighter Pilot in the Vietnam Air War.* New York: St. Martin's Paperbacks, 2006.

George Galvorisi and Thomas Phillips, *Leave No Man Behind: The Saga of Combat Search and Rescue.* Minneapolis: Zenith Press, 2009.

Carol Reardon, *Launch the Intruders: A Naval Attack Squadron in the Vietnam War, 1972.* Lawrence: University Press of Kansas, 2005. Reprinted with permission of the publisher.

Marshall Michel,*The Eleven Days of Christmas: America's Last Vietnam Battle.* New York: Encounter Books, 2001. Reprinted with permission of the publisher.

Karl J. Eschmann, *Linebacker: The Untold Story of the Air Raids Over North Vietnam.* New York: Ivy Books, 1989.

About the Editor

John Prados is a senior fellow and project director of the National Security Archive in Washington, D.C. He is the author of twenty published works on assorted aspects of national security, intelligence, military, or diplomatic history. Recent books include *Normandy Crucible* and *How the Cold War Ended*. His book *Vietnam: The History of an Unwinnable War* won the Henry Adams Prize in history. Prados's books *Unwinnable War*, *Combined Fleet Decoded*, and *Keepers of the Keys* were each nominated for the Pulitzer Prize. His articles, papers, and reviews have appeared widely. Prados is also the designer of award-winning boardgames. He holds a PhD in Political Science (International Relations) from Columbia University.